D1558874

Edith Wharton: Matters of Mind and Spirit considers Wharton as a novelist of morals rather than manners, a novelist who in the exercise of writing sought answers to profound spiritual and metaphysical questions. Carol Singley analyzes the short stories and seven novels in light of Wharton's religious and philosophical development and her attitudes toward Anglicanism, Calvinism, Transcendentalism, and Catholicism.

Singley situates Wharton in the context of turn-of-the-century science, historicism, and aestheticism, reading her religious and philosophical outlook as an evolving response to the cultural crisis of belief. She further invokes the dynamics of class and gender as central to Wharton's quest, describing the ways in which the author accepted and yet transformed both the classical and Christian traditions that she inherited. By locating Wharton in the library rather than the drawing room, *Matters of Mind and Spirit* gives this writer her literary and intellectual due, and offers fresh ways of interpreting her life and fiction.

Edith Wharton

CAMBRIDGE STUDIES IN AMERICAN LITERATURE AND CULTURE

Editor
Eric Sundquist, *University of California, Los Angeles*

Founding Editor
Albert Gelpi, *Stanford University*

Advisory Board
Nina Baym, *University of Illinois, Champaign-Urbana*
Sacvan Bercovitch, *Harvard University*
Albert Gelpi, *Stanford University*
Myra Jehlen, *Rutgers University*
Carolyn Porter, *University of California, Berkeley*
Robert Stepto, *Yale University*
Tony Tanner, *King's College, Cambridge University*

Continued on pages following the Index

Edith Wharton

Matters of Mind and Spirit

Carol J. Singley
Rutgers University, Camden

CAMBRIDGE
UNIVERSITY PRESS

Published by the Press Syndicate of the University of Cambridge
The Pitt Building, Trumpington Street, Cambridge CB2 1RP
40 West 20th Street, New York, NY 10011-4211, USA
10 Stamford Road, Oakleigh, Melbourne 3166, Australia

First published 1995

Printed in the United States of America

Library of Congress Cataloging-in-Publication Data
Singley, Carol J., 1951–
Edith Wharton : matters of mind and spirit / Carol J. Singley.
p. cm. – (Cambridge studies in American literature and
culture ; 92)
Includes bibliographical references (p.   ) and index.
ISBN 0-521-47235-0 (hardback)
1. Wharton, Edith, 1862–1937 – Criticism and interpretation.
I. Title. II. Series.
PS3545.H16Z878   1995
813'.52 – dc20   94-46344
                                                       CIP

A catalog record for this book is available from the British Library.

ISBN 0-521-47235-0 Hardback

For my husband, Gordon

Contents

vii

Preface

On se lasse de tout excepté de comprendre.
(One tires of everything except understanding.)
Edith Wharton, commonplace book

EDITH Wharton wrote a total of twenty-five novels and no-vellas, including the Pulitzer Prize–winning *The Age of Innocence;* eighty-six short stories; three books of poetry; an autobiography; a book on the theory of fiction; eleven books or pamphlets of nonfiction; and scores of articles, reviews, and translations. At one point, her earnings from her writing exceeded those of any other living American writer. She continued to write until her death in 1937, collecting her ghost fiction in a volume the year she died and leaving another novel unfinished.

By any measure Edith Wharton's career was successful and her life full and adventurous. Yet expressions of longing appear throughout her letters and memoirs. Especially in the early years of her career, Wharton yearned for recognition from the New York aristocracy she so incisively portrayed in her stories and novels. Except for one cousin, however, her family and society treated her as an aberration, completely ignoring her literary achievements. Although Wharton later cultivated enduring, rewarding friendships with like-minded artists and intellectuals, she still voiced discontent. Cynthia Griffin Wolff detects a persistent tone of desolation and loneliness in her letters, noting that their most frequent refrain is "I have no one to *talk* to" (*Feast* 24). Wharton also desired better communication with her readers, wishing them to find deeper meanings in her fiction. For example, in response to the charge that sentimentalists found her work "cynical & depressing," she hoped that "those who see the 'inherences' recognize my ability to see them too" (*Letters* 39). By the same token, the view of her as a Jamesian disciple and chronicler of narrow, upper-class interests caused no end of consternation: "The continued cry that I am an echo of Mr. James . . . & the assumption that the people I write about are not 'real' because they are not navvies & char-women, makes me feel rather hopeless," she confided to her publisher in 1904 (*Letters* 91).

Always in Edith Wharton's writing there is an undercurrent of dissatisfaction, a sense that the full value of her work was unappreciated and her life-long project incomplete. Writing to Margaret Chanler in 1925, Wharton voiced doubt about her place in American letters: "As my work reaches its close, I feel so sure that it is either nothing, or far more than they know. . . . And I wonder, a little desolately, which?" (*Letters* 483, original ellipsis). It is not unusual for writers to complain of slights or seek sympathy from their readers. Nathaniel Hawthorne, after all, had set the tone for novel-writing successors with his plea in "The Custom-House" for understanding by a loyal, select few (6). However, unlike Hawthorne, who struggled for years with barely a nod of recognition, or Herman Melville, who died believing that *Moby-Dick* had missed its mark, Edith Wharton enjoyed extensive popular and critical acclaim once she committed herself to the pen. Yet despite success, she always felt a lack of recognition and understanding from her readers.

Contributing to this misunderstanding is the early critical view of her as a novelist of manners, a view that persists despite fresh, insightful approaches by feminists, new historicists, and other critics who address the range and complexity of Wharton's themes and narrative techniques. Wharton, I argue, is also a novelist of morals: a writer not only of society but of spirit; a woman who, in life and in art, searched for religious, moral, and philosophical meaning. This search for fulfillment is evident in her comments about fiction. For example, she defends its power to transcend the mundane in an article on literary criticism, in which she argues that the "conclusions of the tale" "must be sought, not in the fate of the characters, and still less in their own comments on it, but in . . . the light it casts on questions beyond its borders" ("Criticism" 210). She similarly argues in another essay: "any serious portrayal of life must be judged not by the incidents it presents but by the author's sense of their significance" ("Vice" 519). Wharton's search for meaning is also abundantly clear in her numerous short stories and novels, as this book demonstrates.

How can we describe this kind of writer? Wharton is not didactic, insistent, or judgmental in her treatment of moral issues. On the contrary, she is circumspect to the point of appearing tentative; she strikes a note of inquiry rather than of declamation. Wharton's tireless and ultimately unfulfilled quest for spiritual and philosophical answers is best thought of as longing – a desire that cannot be satisfied, yet endures. The dimensions of her quest encompass several forms: Christianity, from Calvinism to Catholicism; classical thought and religion; and modern philosophy – all negotiated within complex and rapidly changing American social structures. Because Wharton depicted turn-of-the-century society with such accuracy and detail, it has been all too easy for critics to focus on her social themes and neglect her deeper insights into human nature. This approach not only ignores her lifetime interests in religious and philosophical issues, but it relegates her to the status of second-rate novelist. And it obscures Wharton's roles in the American literary traditions of Calvinism, transcendentalism, and modernism, as well as realism.

We have looked for Edith Wharton in the drawing room; we must also seek her in the library, voraciously consuming volumes of philosophy, history, art, science, and religion, as well as literature. Wharton was well read in philosophy; she pored over volumes of Greek religious history and Christian theology; and she was fully informed about nineteenth-century science. Readers know of Wharton's expertise in interior design, architecture, and gardening, but few realize how deeply she was drawn to metaphysical questions, and that her library contained more books on religion than on any other subject (Lewis 510).

This book is the first to explore the dimensions of Wharton's religious, spiritual, and philosophical search, and to place her life and writings in the context of American intellectual thought and religious history. It owes debts to the many recent feminist readings of Wharton, which have not only illuminated her struggles as a female novelist but have affirmed the extraordinary quality of her mind. It was originally inspired by R. W. B. Lewis's descriptions of Wharton's religious reading in his groundbreaking 1975 biography. It also attempts to correct Percy Lubbock's myopic observation that "the lively leap of her mind stopped dead when she was asked to think . . . about any theoretic enquiry" (44). Wharton's writing, I argue here, reflects both a mind and spirit intensely engaged in abstract questions; one can no more separate her religious and philosophical perspectives from her fiction than one can divorce T. S. Eliot's Christianity from his poetry.

This book also owes a debt to Marilyn Lyde's early analysis of the relationship between Wharton's faith and conventionality. Lyde astutely notes that Wharton's upper-class background and grande dame image are obstacles to understanding her moral concerns, but she still approaches Wharton's morality through social forms and manners, concluding that Wharton solves the problem of "Absolute Ethics" by finding a "necessary balance between individual morality and group convention" (45). In contrast, I argue that Wharton was a deeply religious person who never found completely satisfactory answers to metaphysical questions; social forms, although useful guides, always fell short of the ideals to which she aspired. I similarly resist the idea that for Wharton "morality is contextual" (White 80). Although circumstance and situation play major roles in Wharton's plots, she never abandoned the search for absolute standards that can unify and transcend experience.

One's thoughts and beliefs do not develop in a vacuum. I therefore consider Wharton's religious, spiritual, and philosophical concerns in relation to nineteenth-century discoveries in science, history, anthropology, and philosophy, explaining how these developments challenged traditional systems of belief and, in some cases, led to unbelief. In so doing, I read Edith Wharton as a preeminently American author, despite her long years of French expatriation. Finally, I consider Wharton's gender and class, tracing the meaning of faith and reason for an upper-class female writer of the Victorian and modern eras. Wharton, I argue, both reproduces and transforms the predominantly male, Christian and Neoplatonic traditions that she inherits.

Wharton's grasp of religious, spiritual, and philosophical matters was deep and broad, and, as an explorer of uncharted territory, I have necessarily drawn some boundaries. An introductory chapter situates Wharton's religious and spiritual development in the context of late nineteenth-century Christianity, evolution, aesthetics, philosophy, and feminism. Six chronologically arranged chapters address the relationship between Wharton's life and writing by focusing on the short fiction and seven representative novels: *The House of Mirth, Ethan Frome, The Reef, Summer, The Age of Innocence, Hudson River Bracketed,* and *The Gods Arrive.* These chapters explore in detail Wharton's intellectuality and interest in Darwinism (Chapter 1); her Episcopalian background and affinity for Calvinism (Chapter 2); her fascination with ancient goddesses and matriarchies (Chapter 3); her experimentation with aestheticism as a substitute for religion (Chapter 4); her construction of Platonic idealism (Chapter 5); and her near conversion to Catholicism (Chapter 6). Tracing the various intellectual and religious features of Wharton's fiction reveals how systematically she pursued difficult spiritual and philosophical questions. Although Edith Wharton never found completely satisfactory answers, she never gave up her search. This book is a tribute to that search and the longing that accompanied it.

Many teachers, colleagues, and friends have generously guided this project. I thank Barton St. Armand, whose extraordinary knowledge of and enthu-

siasm for nineteenth-century American literature helped me to place Edith
Wharton in a rich literary and intellectual tradition. I also thank David
Hirsch and Robert Scholes for their early readings of the manuscript
and valuable suggestions for its development. The Edith Wharton Society
provided welcome forums for presenting chapters-in-progress; I am grateful, in particular, to Kathy Fedorko, Susan Goodman, Katherine Joslin,
Helen Killoran, Scott Marshall, Kay Mussell, Alan Price, Abbe Werlock,
Cynthia Griffin Wolff, and Annette Zilversmit for their expert advice.
Edward Kessler, Walter Benn Michaels, Kevin Moore, Carmen Nocentelli,
and students from my seminars provided helpful comments on individual
chapters. Warm appreciation goes to Gordon Kinsey, Mariah Martin, Ro-
berta Rubenstein, and Susan Elizabeth Sweeney for their careful reading of
chapters and unfailing intellectual and emotional encouragement. I also
extend a warm thank you to Edith Wharton's godson, William Royall
Tyler, whose many conversations helped me keep le sacré feu for Edith
Wharton burning. Finally, a Research Council Grant from Rutgers University helped provide the necessary time and funds to bring this project to
completion.

   The cover photograph and quotations by Edith Wharton are reproduced
with permission of Scribner, an imprint of Simon & Schuster. Quotations
by Edith Wharton are also reprinted by permission of the author and the
Watkins/Loomis Agency. Letters to Lily Norton (bMS Am 1193 [337]–
[431]) and letters to Sara Norton (bMS Am 1088.1 [997], [1000]—[1017])
appear with permission of the Houghton Library, Harvard University.
Quotations from the Edith Wharton collection appear with permission of
the Yale Collection of American Literature, Beinecke Rare Book and
Manuscript Library, Yale University.

Edith Wharton

Introduction

> No story teller . . . can do great work unbased on some philosophy
> of life.
>
> Edith Wharton, "A Reconsideration of Proust"

IT is easy to overlook the religious and spiritual dimensions of
Edith Wharton's life and fiction if we view her primarily as a novelist of
manners. The label "aristocratic lady novelist" – a designation revealing the
biases of gender and class – also discounts her intellectual seriousness. In
fact, Wharton infuses even her most socially minded texts with religious,
moral, or philosophical reflection.[1] And although she resisted the more
vociferous forms of feminist activism at the turn of the century, her voice
is often clear and dissenting, calling for moral as well as social equality for
women. Concerns for ideals and for women's place in structures that often
exclude or marginalize them are consistent motifs in Wharton's life and
writing.[2]

Morals *and* Manners

Although Edith Wharton thought of herself as a novelist of manners, she might have chosen a different designation had she foreseen the
limitations of the term. To understand this category of realism, I take Lionel
Trilling's definition: a novelist of manners writes of society's conventions,
including not only etiquette and decorum but principles, rules, and laws
that are established by tacit assumption ("Manners" 200–1). However
useful the label "novelist of manners" may be, it exerts a subtle bias,
allowing critics to focus on the social features of a writer's portrayals at the

1

expense of her deeper levels of insight into human nature.³ In Wharton's case, it implies little or no development of moral problems except in terms of social convention. Thus, Louis Auchincloss writes that society is Wharton's "medium" (*Edith* 11), and Robert Spiller declares her commitment to it "in its narrowest sense" (1209). This label shortchanges works like *Ethan Frome* (1911) and *Summer* (1917), which do not depict wealthy New York society, and it opens Wharton to charges such as those made by Vernon Parrington when he dubbed her "our literary aristocrat": that her upper-class characters are unrepresentative and her poor, rural ones inauthentic.

One need not look far to find evidence of Wharton's religious, moral, and philosophical concerns, despite what others have suggested. A survey of her fictional titles, themes, and forms leaves no doubt that she was richly influenced by classical and Christian traditions and that she engaged these traditions to explore the contemporary crisis of faith brought on by Darwinism and industrial capitalism. Some of her titles suggest a philosophical or religious outlook. As Wharton notes, the title of her second short-story collection, *Crucial Instances* (1901), is a term drawn from philosophy that "keeps a sort of connection" with her first collection, *The Greater Inclination* (1899) (*Letters* 43). She borrows the title of her third volume of stories, *The Descent of Man* (1904), directly from Darwin. Titles of other fictions are explicitly religious, even when ironic: "The Twilight of the God," "The Duchess at Prayer," "The Angel at the Grave," "The Confessional," "Expiation," "The Seed of the Faith," and "The Confession." Wharton goes directly to the Bible for some appellations – *The Valley of Decision* (Joel 3.14), *The House of Mirth* (Ecclesiastes 7.4), *The Fruit of the Tree* (Genesis 3.3), and "That Good May Come" (Romans 3.8) – using it, as did many Victorians, not so much as sacred text but as mythology or ethical touchstone.

Wharton's interest in these issues goes deeper than her choice of titles. Even texts ostensibly concerned with material or social issues reveal a moral, spiritual, or religious sensibility. The name Lily in *The House of Mirth* (1905), for example, alludes not only to Matthew, as many have noted, but to the Song of Songs. When Songs is juxtaposed with Ecclesiastes, which gives the novel its title, the novel's contrasting themes of spiritual despair and ideal love become evident. In Wharton's satirical masterpiece, *The Age of Innocence* (1920), the New York elite, besieged by industrialists and the nouveau riche, hear a Thanksgiving Day sermon not of gratitude but of denunciation. By having the rector draw his text from the prophetic book of Jeremiah, Wharton delivers an ironic commentary on the collapse of a spiritually depleted society intent on worshiping false gods of taste rather than truth. And the butler in "The Lady's Maid's Bell" (1902) recites "dreadful texts full of brimstone" (*Stories* 1: 464) when his master enters the house. His diatribes – like those of Isaiah, whom he quotes – rail against moral bankruptcy and the servant class's destiny of suffering.

Much of Wharton's fiction abounds with characters facing moral choices or seeking nonmaterial values, but because she does not accentuate these difficulties, they are easily missed. The short stories "The Pretext," "The Verdict," "The Potboiler," and "The Best Man" – all published in *The Hermit and the Wild Woman* (1908) – turn on moral problems, as Cynthia Griffin Wolff notes (*Feast* 151). Odo Valsecca searches for God in Wharton's early novel, *The Valley of Decision* (1902); the speaker in the poem "Margaret of Cortona" (1901) appeals to Christ for help with grief; and Vance Weston is heartened by the words of St. Augustine in the late novel, *The Gods Arrive* (1932). Other characters struggle to find faith in a disillusioning age: Christian charity eludes Lily Bart in *The House of Mirth;* Mattie and Ethan suffer spiritual as well as physical deformity in *Ethan Frome;* Ann Eliza Bunner stops believing in a caring deity, although her sister converts to Catholicism ("Bunner Sisters" [1916]), as does Lizzie Hazeldean in *New Year's Day* (1924); and Grandma Scrimser pursues a vague transcendentalism in *Hudson River Bracketed* (1929).

Clerical figures and religious controversies also abound. In fact, the sheer range of religious references found in Wharton's narratives – to Catholic views on divorce, New England fundamentalism, Episcopalian governance and laxity, and spiritualism – shows how keenly she followed religious developments. A Catholic priest stands at the dock while the divorced Lydia Tillotson decides whether to leave her lover, a silent reminder of the sacrament she has broken ("Souls Belated" [1899]); a vain bishop manipulates the media for personal gain and lies about the identity of his church's benefactor ("Expiation" [1903]); and Charity Royall, pregnant out of wedlock, meets a raging fundamentalist preacher en route to the Mountain and her mother (*Summer*).

Wharton's fiction describes past as well as present religious controversies. Ecclesiastical intrigue plays a role in her ghost story "Kerfol" (1916), which is commonly read as a tale of tangled romance and vengeance. But as Helen Killoran points out, it also describes a historical Jesuit–Jansenist conflict ("kerfol" = foolish quarrel) over religious fidelity. Two stories, in particular, trace the effects of late nineteenth-century conflicts between science and religion. In "The Descent of Man" (1904), Professor Linyard sees his scientific research misappropriated by a populace eager for assurance that the old faith is still possible; "The Blond Beast" (1910) explores challenges to traditional faith posed by the higher criticism; and in "Xingu" (1911) "maturer-looking" volumes such as *The Confessions of Saint Augustine* compete with studies of genetics for a place in Mrs. Ballinger's drawing room (*Stories* 2: 214). Wharton also shows how comparative studies of religion cast new doubts on Christianity. In "The Seed of the Faith" (1919), a missionary in Africa witnesses his mentor's collapse and concludes that his life's work has been futile because the doctrines he preaches are true only in a relative, rather than absolute, sense. The missionaries have come to convert "the poor ignorant heathen — but were not they themselves equally ignorant in everything that concerned the heathen?" (2: 441).

Wharton suggests moral or spiritual concerns through her narrative forms as well as themes. Indeed, she constructs many fictions as allegories, parables, or fables — forms often used in religious or philosophical teachings.[4] The short story "The Fullness of Life" (1893), commonly read as a criticism of marriage, is a fable about the search for spiritual fulfillment on the earthly plane. And "After Holbein" (1928), as Lawrence Berkove points out, is a parable of Old Testament judgment against hardheartedness. To the extent that forays into the unknown express a desire to explain life's meanings and mysteries, Wharton's ghost stories, of which she wrote many, constitute moral or spiritual inquiries. We can also see the instructive dimensions of Wharton's longer narratives. *The House of Mirth* recounts the failure of Christian love, charity, and redemption in turn-of-the-century society. *Ethan Frome* is a modernist allegory of Calvinist sin and frozen human will; *The Reef* (1912), an attempt to reinstate the feminine divine through the character Sophy Viner, who alludes to the ancient Sophia; and *The Custom of the Country* (1913), a contemporary jeremiad that rails against reckless materialism. And in *The Age of Innocence,* Wharton uses Plato's allegory of the cave to represent Newland Archer's search for truth and love.

Wharton developed a fondness for the fable form early in her career, as "The Valley of Childish Things, and Other Emblems" (1896) demonstrates.[5] Focusing on the first of ten vignettes, critics tend to read the tales as lessons about love's disillusionment (Lewis 77) or as political or personal statements about female inequality (Ammons 4, 9; Wolff, *Feast* 228). However, these didactic stories, which Scribner's rejected for being "too esoteric" (Lewis 76), convey moral and spiritual messages. The first fable sympathizes with a woman who seeks higher goals but is told she "ought to have taken better care of [her] complexion" (*Stories* 1: 59); the second satirizes financial waste and lack of common sense; the third laments that marriage is the only future for intelligent women. Desire is the subject of the next three stories: a man regrets that he "never had enough happiness to make a sorrow out of" (1: 60); a couple achieves a mutual relationship despite society's crippling restrictions of women; and a soul is reminded that whoever tarries in "the land of Gratified Longings" rather than in "the desert of Unsatisfied Desires" grows blind. With this tale, Wharton emphasizes the value of the spiritual search, regardless of its outcome.

The seventh story, a forerunner of Wharton's third novel, *Sanctuary* (1903), introduces the theme of moral integrity: an architect guilty of poor workmanship is too proud to accept the "judgment angel's" proposal to rectify his flaws (1: 61). The eighth tale satirizes a man's desire for a wife who merely reflects his own ego. The ninth story cautions against moral detachment: a gentleman who "disliked to assume any responsibility" and prides himself on aloofness is visited by Death (1: 62). When he attempts to put Death off with the lie that he has invited friends to dinner, the devil carries him away. In the tenth and culminating tale, a man despairs because he sets out to build his god a temple like the Parthenon but can produce only a thatched, mud hut. A passerby explains two worse plights: "one is to have no god; the other is to build a mud hut and mistake it for the Parthenon" (1: 63). In this last fable, Wharton underscores what for her constitute basic truths: the need for goals beyond material ones, the importance of effort, and the awareness of human insufficiency. The last fable also bears Wharton's hallmark: a combination of Christian faith and classical reason.

Finally, Wharton's literary aspirations themselves take the form of spiritual quests. She believed that a moral, spiritual, or philosophical system was vital to the artistic imagination and documented that belief in her writing. Her theoretical book, *The Writing of Fiction* (1925), includes mandates such as: "a good subject . . . sheds a light on our moral experience" (28); art "must illustrate some general law, and turn on some deep movement of the soul" (146); and "in vain has it been attempted to set up a water-tight compartment between 'art' and 'morality' " (28). Two qualities distinguish great literature, Wharton elaborates in "Permanent Values in Fiction." One is the writer's ability to create living characters and the other to relate these characters "to whatever general law of human experience made the novelist choose to tell this tale rather than another" (604). An unpublished article, "Fiction and Criticism," provides the clearest statement of Wharton's moral theory. Drawing on Matthew Arnold's assertion that fiction is "a criticism of life," Wharton writes, "it does not follow that great fiction should not communicate a moral emotion." The aesthetic pleasure of the text is crucial; however, the writer's treatment of his subject – "his faculty for penetrating below the surface of his fable to the 'inherences' which relate it to life as a whole" – determines the success of the creative work (2).

Wharton further explains: "every serious picture of life contains a thesis.
. . . The novelist ceases to be an artist the moment he bends his characters
to the exigencies of a thesis; but he would equally cease to be one, should
he draw the acts he describes without regard to their moral significance"
(4–5).

From the beginning of her career, Wharton consciously followed her
own prescription that art have a moral dimension. She described her
narrative practice as one that keeps "in sight only the novelist's essential
sign-post; the inner significance of the 'case' selected" (*Backward* 115).
Despite its biblical title, she did not consider her first best seller a religious
novel,[6] but when Morgan Dix, rector of Trinity Church, commended her
on *The House of Mirth,* she enthusiastically wrote back, outlining her views:

> I could not do anything if I did not think seriously of my trade; & the
> more I have considered it, the more has it seemed to me valuable &
> interesting only in so far as it is "a criticism of life." – It almost seems
> to me that bad & good fiction (using the words in their ethical
> sense) might be defined as the kind which treats of life trivially &
> superficially, & that which probes deep enough to get at the relation
> with the eternal laws. . . . *No* novel worth anything can be anything
> but a novel "with a purpose," & if anyone who cared for the moral
> issues did not see in my work that *I* care for it, I should have no one
> to blame but myself – or at least my inadequate means of rendering
> my effects. (*Letters* 99, original emphases)

Wharton is adamant about the moral import of her writing: she stresses not
only fiction's "ethical sense," which refers to society's standards, but a
deeper "relation with the eternal laws," from which ethics are derived. The
tone of this passage is revealing: not only does she suspect that readers will
misunderstand her, she is willing – in a manner that suggests her insecurity
as a female author – to accept blame for their failure to grasp her purpose.
Wharton was no heavy-handed moralizer; in fact, she despised explicitly
didactic literature. However, she believed that "so much of one's own
soul" goes into the writing of fiction (*Backward* 212). Her keen sense of
social detail notwithstanding, Wharton incorporated "soul" in her fiction
and admired it in other writers such as George Eliot and Marcel Proust.

American Roots and Rootlessness

A study of Edith Wharton's religion and spirituality must place
Wharton in the context of late nineteenth- and early twentieth-century
American intellectual, social, and religious developments, expanding that

context as necessary to include Western traditions and values. Whereas the designation "novelist of manners" excludes Wharton from the mainstream traditions of American literature – "the fact is," Trilling asserts, "that American writers of genius have not turned their minds toward society" ("Manners" 206) – a contextualized approach acknowledges her American roots; develops her relationship to "moral" writers such as Nathaniel Hawthorne and New England local colorists and sentimentalists, with whom she also shares a Calvinist legacy; and establishes her as a realistic and modernist innovator in her own right.

Although she seemed to downplay her American connections once she settled in France, Wharton indicated that she wished to be considered in a native tradition when she borrowed the title for her memoir *A Backward Glance* from Walt Whitman's *A Backward Glance O'er Travel'd Roads* and thus positioned herself in an honored nineteenth-century tradition. Recent studies have explored her American connections beyond the Jamesian ones. Feminist scholars, in particular, have done much to rescue Wharton from the category "minor writer." However, despite attention to the myriad social, economic, and psychological factors that affected her authorship, Wharton is still inadequately situated in the history of ideas and beliefs. Considered too advanced for the Victorians and too old-fashioned for the modernists, she lacks an intellectual or philosophical "room of one's own."

Wharton's religious sensibilities developed as a result of widely different and rapidly changing factors in American society. When she was growing up in the 1870s and 1880s, religion still played an important role in everyday American life. Wharton recalls, for example, reading the Bible and notes her family's regular attendance at church services (*Backward* 70; "Little" 362). However, discoveries in science – especially of evolution – as well as new practices in historical biblical criticism, anthropology, and comparative religion rocked the cultural foundations of religious faith. Americans of the late nineteenth and early twentieth centuries radically questioned and eventually abandoned traditional notions of faith for more reasoned, secular, and individualized approaches – all made possible by adherence to rational thought and positivism. According to this new rationalism, as James Turner notes, knowledge developed historically and must be verified by experience; the scientific approach and experimentation were superior to feeling and intuition; and empirical truths superseded transcendental reality (133–35). These theories threatened traditional church teachings and made the sacredness of the Bible seem obsolete. It was an age, as Henry Adams wrote, when every individual had to invent a "formula of his own for his universe" because "the standard formulas failed" (*Education* 472).

The changes and controversies that swept American culture profoundly influenced Edith Wharton. She was especially affected by her position in society as an upper-class Victorian woman. With characteristic understatement, she attempted the unthinkable for a woman of her class and time: she strove to understand the underlying issues of the science–religion debate. This meant not only taking religious doctrines seriously but developing the intellectual capacity necessary to digest technical and scientific material. Although Wharton's background and training presented significant obstacles, development of her mind became a crucial first step on her spiritual path.

Wharton's privileged New York society faced the crisis of belief with casualness bordering on indifference, but she never shared its complacency. Unlike more introspective Protestants – evangelicals, who feared God's rejection, or moderates, who entertained nagging doubts about individual worthiness – aristocrats felt that material and social well-being also guaranteed them God's grace. They made a virtue of necessity, viewing God's increasing distance from everyday human endeavors as fortuitous, and – following Anglican rather than Calvinist models – deeming intense piety or introspection superfluous. They accepted scientific theories of evolution as popularly presented to them, especially those of Herbert Spencer, who preached moral and social progress; they did not inquire of science too deeply. Instead, they tended to adopt an evolutionary optimism, a secular form of Protestant liberalism, which permeated the upper tiers of society and, as Jackson Lears notes (21–23), had the practical effect of encouraging the status quo.

Wharton also inherited this benign faith through her gender as well as her class. Coming of age in the second half of the nineteenth century meant immersion in the ideologies of domestic and religious sentimentality and exposure to novels by Protestant women intent on recuperating religion in the age of Darwin. Such writers, as Barbara Welter notes (129), were read more widely at this time than were Emerson, Rauschenbusch, and William James. Although some novels – for example, Margaret Deland's John Ward, Preacher and Mary Wilkins Freeman's Pembroke – defended Calvinism or dealt anachronistically with the effects of twisted will, many more upheld sentimental creeds.[7] Sentimentality gave a new face to an old faith. As Ann Douglas explains, it constituted a shift from a harsh Calvinist doctrine in which God enacts his divine plan through Christ's death to one in which Christ becomes the sympathetic, vicarious sufferer for human sins. The focus moved from God to human as God's power was lessened – and his post-Darwinian absence explained – through human appropriation. In this optimistic theology, the notion of Atonement became a "fantasy . . .

of the weak that the strong will spontaneously give up the[ir] pre-eminence," a dream "honoring . . . enforced passivity" (151). Christ, the supreme example of selflessness, graciously succumbed so that others might model themselves on him. Women were the perfect candidates for this Christlike sacrifice: they willingly gave of themselves to compensate for their spiritually inferior male counterparts and to better the race as a whole. The sacrifice was made through the daily execution of domestic duties, but it was also accomplished, as was Christ's, through death. Harriet Beecher Stowe's Little Eva in *Uncle Tom's Cabin* and Mara Lincoln of *The Pearl of Orr's Island* exemplify the edifying effect of this ultimate display of female sacrifice. Wharton rejected this sentimental model, as she did the aristocratic one.

Wharton stands in uneasy relationship both to genteel Episcopalianism and popular sentimentality. First, she was too serious about religion to be fashionable. Although she obeyed her parents' mandate to keep religion a private affair and never impose her beliefs on others, her godson William Royall Tyler remembers her as a "devout person . . . always close to the metaphysical aspect of life, always" (Interview, 29 October). "She would broach the substance of religion without putting it on the table as a subject," Tyler recalls; she had "a deep religious sense" (Interviews, 12 April, 29 October). He cites as examples her well-used copy of the Apocrypha and her annotated, leather-bound *The Imitation of Christ,* which bears a Saint-Brice-sous-Forêt bookplate but is so worn that it must have been read over many years (Letter). These comments as well as compelling evidence in Wharton's writing demonstrate her difference from other members of her class, who weighed social lapses more heavily than spiritual ones.

Second, Wharton parted ways with social elites and sentimentalists because, by temperament, she was disinclined toward their facile accommodation of suffering and redemption. Although she favored a cultural ethos of compassion over competition, she rejected "separate sphere" ideologies that made spiritual salvation the sole province of women. She was equally unwilling to accept the relativism and materialism that newer empirical theories fostered. Although she applauded gains brought about by reason and technology, she feared that the emphasis on money and status that late nineteenth-century capitalism encouraged led to disintegration of crucial spiritual values. Third, Wharton enthusiastically followed current scientific developments and set out to master theories propounded by figures such as Darwin, Spencer, Huxley, and Haeckel. She strove for intellectual credentials that would distinguish her from nineteenth-century domestic writers – she wanted to be known for the sharpness of her mind as well as for the generosity of her heart. Unlike her leisured compatriots, Wharton took evolution seriously and abhorred its trivialization by dilettantes. She considered the Darwinian challenge to religious certainty one of the most important issues of her time.

As this overview suggests, Edith Wharton's theology evolved as a result of complex social and personal factors. Appreciating her keen intelligence and unwavering drive to develop her intellect is a crucial step toward understanding her religion and spirituality because at the turn of the nineteenth century, religion was severely undermined by secular theories. For the thinking person, simple, unproblematic belief was no longer possible. Chapter 1, "Priestess of Reason," traces Wharton's arduous journey toward intellectual autonomy, explaining the various religious and secular forces that helped to chart her path. Each of the subsequent chapters explores a different facet of Wharton's spiritual, religious, and philosophical development, with focused attention on its expression in seven of Wharton's novels, numerous short stories, and selected nonfiction.

Exploring the interplay of Wharton's scientific and spiritual concerns leads to consideration of her first best seller, *The House of Mirth* (1905). This novel, discussed in Chapter 2, "Spiritual Homelessness," represents with brilliant irony the dangerous relativism and feelings of rootlessness that followed from society's casual adherence to Darwinian principles and abandonment of spiritual values. Lily Bart's problem in this novel, spiritually speaking, is the same as the speaker's in Robert Frost's poem "The Oven Bird": "what to make of a diminished thing" (line 14). Wharton presents a post-Christian society in which "the word" – of God, faith, love, and redemption – is tragically lost. Her heroine, an ironic spiritual pilgrim adrift and alone, struggles futilely in a materially rich but spiritually destitute world. The ending of *The House of Mirth* – a scene of beautiful, feminine death – also vividly demonstrates Wharton's ironic stance toward sentimentality. Lily's death is preceded by a visit to Nettie Struthers's cozy kitchen, but no redemption follows: traditional forms of feminine acceptance, submission, and forgiveness have become impossible in the modern world. The novel's conclusion is troubling, not soothing; the reader is left with a terrible emptiness that Lily's death cannot alleviate.

That Wharton had reluctantly rejected a sentimental solution to the crisis of faith is apparent not only in *The House of Mirth* but in her next novel, *The Fruit of the Tree* (1907). The plot resembles that of Margaret Deland's "At the Stuffed-Animal House," in which a retarded girl, Annie, administers a fatal dose of chloroform to end her sister's suffering. In Deland's story, the minister – named Dr. Lavendar to suggest his sympathy with the sentimentalists – accepts Annie's decision as an act of feminine, natural wisdom over religious doctrine. No such approval greets Wharton's heroine: Justine Brent loses her husband and her happiness for her act of euthanasia. She is motivated by a phrase by Bacon that she finds in one of her husband's books: *"La vraie morale se moque de la morale"* (True morality mocks conventional morality) (429); in her world, however, conventions determine morality.

Many of Wharton's female protagonists share Lily's and Justine's fates. Again and again, generous natures are sacrificed to petty ones without apparent reward, and complacent or corrupt institutions contribute to the heroine's demise. As Amy Kaplan notes, Wharton's desire to become a professional writer was itself a repudiation of an earlier generation of female authors who often attributed their gifts to men or God (66–74).[8] Although Wharton longed for a return to nurturing feminine principles, she found sentimental notions of Christological redemption untenable in contemporary society.

The ending of *The House of Mirth* suggests what was to become a major theme in Wharton's fiction: apparently meaningless personal sacrifice. This bleak outlook may be traced not only to Wharton's readings in evolutionary science but to a distinctly American theological and cultural influence: Calvinism. In Chapter 3, "Calvinist Tortures," I discuss what Wharton herself referred to as an excruciating "God-intoxication." She, more perhaps than any other American realist, entertains a dark vision of necessity. The origins of this vision – early American Protestant doctrine as well as nineteenth-century Darwinism – are often overlooked. Thus William Shurr traces the formative influence of Calvinism on nineteenth- and twentieth-century American writers without mentioning Wharton at all, and Samuel Chase Coale omits her from his list of writers who fall "in Hawthorne's shadow." It has been standard practice in Wharton criticism to comment on her bleakness (Howe 17), the universality of her "spiritual conflicts" (Herrick 41), or her "Christianity of the Old Testament" (Hartwick 385), but not to elaborate on the nature or source of this outlook.[9]

Although raised a genteel Episcopalian, Wharton was drawn to more fundamentalist faiths. She engaged in voracious sermon-reading while an adolescent, becoming enthralled by a Protestantism resembling the early Puritans'. In keeping with the austere doctrines of Calvin, this creed included a harsh, judgmental deity who demanded payment for pleasure and rewarded suffering with more pain rather than forgiveness. Corresponding to Wharton's sense of a punishing God was an inability to accept the Christian doctrine of Atonement. This authoritarian God was not obliged to sacrifice a son for human offenses or to consider that sacrifice a guarantee of forgiveness. Wharton thus declined New Testament celebrations of God's mercy in favor of Old Testament interpretations of his anger and justice. Her God had little in common with the approving divinity popularized by her sentimental predecessors and pleasure-seeking contemporaries. It was, however, readily adaptable to Darwinian theories of competition, struggle, and natural selection. Although Darwinism and Calvinism flourished in vastly different contexts, both emphasized human powerlessness before overwhelming forces.

We can see this conflation of Calvinist past and Darwinian present in *Ethan Frome* (1911), discussed in Chapter 3. Reproducing an Old rather than New Testament sensibility, *Ethan Frome* reinterprets Calvinist notions of original sin and insufficiency for a disenchanted modern age. Like Nathaniel Hawthorne's *The Scarlet Letter, Ethan Frome* recounts an ill-fated love triangle, but unlike Hawthorne, Wharton allows no release for her characters through death, good works, or love. They endure a living hell without possibility of salvation. Wharton's sense of social desolation and dark moral necessity links her not only to Hawthorne but to other proto-modernist and modernist writers who also struggled with alienating natural and social forces.

Early on, Edith Wharton wrestled with an angry, indifferent God; later, however, she sought alternatives to what she came to think of as a crippling, Christian split between body and spirit. This search coincided with her own experience of passion in an extramarital affair with Morton Fullerton. Beginning around 1908, the year the affair began, Wharton began a period of astounding creativity matched by spiritual and religious experimentation, in which she not only criticized existing structures but imagined alternatives. Her experimentation took several forms: an embrace of ancient feminine principles; a consideration of art and culture as replacements for religion; and a pursuit of transcendental and Platonic ideals.

The Feminine Reclaimed

Edith Wharton's midlife explorations included a search both for positive female roles and for transcendant, self-affirming, non-Christian values. She was disappointed with Christianity's tendency to split women into a spiritualized, maternal Mary or sexualized, promiscuous Eve. She also understood that the Christian conception of God as male father meant diminishment of the feminine principle of divinity. Wharton's religious feminism is not readily apparent, however, when we compare her with other progressive women of her day. Turn-of-the-century feminist theological critics were busily addressing problems of patriarchal Christian religion and working to revise religious stereotypes that depicted them either as romanticized, spiritually superior beings or carnal sinners.[10] Many feminists also protested unsympathetic religious institutions. Anne Carr explains, for example, that Christian churches at the time played a major role in defeating the early women's movement, leading some women to break ties with the church completely, or – in the case of Anna Howard Shaw – to become outstanding preachers themselves (11). Douglas argues that besieged Protestant ministers struck an alliance with middle-class women, salvaging their own decreasing power by sentimentalizing feminine virtues.

Wharton did not openly sympathize with these activities. There is no evidence, for example, that she read Elizabeth Cady Stanton's *The Woman's Bible* (1895–98) or that she considered her or other feminists important to her own spiritual quest. She seems at first glance as aloof from feminist theological disputes as she was from the hotbed of female literary activity just neighborhoods away from her on the Left Bank of Paris. Yet a closer look shows Wharton quietly criticizing traditional religion's views of women. Such a critique is implicit in her range of sexually active yet morally responsible female characters, from Sophy Viner to Charity Royall and Ellen Olenska. And as early as 1894, Wharton was registering discontent with traditional biblical interpretations of women. In her story "That Good May Come" (1894), for example, a character muses that "there's something tremendously suggestive" in the notion "that tradition has misrepresented the real feelings of all the great heroes and heroines." It might just be possible, the story continues, that Esther, known for selfless sacrifice on behalf of the Jews, was really in love with Haman and "decoyed him to the banquet with Ahasuerus just for the sake of once having him near her and hearing him speak" (*Stories* 1: 21). That Wharton portrays Esther as capable of having and acting on her own desire while heroically serving her people demonstrates her interest in revising roles for women within the Judeo-Christian tradition.

Wharton was also critical of Pauline doctrine, which granted women's moral equality with men but prescribed their social subordination – a belief that reinforced the double standards of behavior for men and women. Elizabeth Cady Stanton strove to redress this imbalance in *The Woman's Bible,* deploring any religion that "teaches woman's subjection and man's right of domination" (1: 79). Wharton explores the same issue in her early short story "Souls Belated." Lydia Tillotson defies conventions by leaving her husband and living with her lover. Since they seem compatible, she assumes that they both equally question and reject society's view of marriage. As Lydia explains:

> We neither of us believe in the abstract "sacredness" of marriage; we
> both know that no ceremony is needed to consecrate our love for
> each other; what object can we have in marrying, except the secret
> fear of each that the other may escape, or the secret longing to work
> our way back gradually – oh, very gradually – into the esteem of
> people whose conventional morality we have always ridiculed and
> hated? (*Stories* 1: 110)

But Wharton makes it clear that Lydia struggles with society's limiting
moral values and practices much more than her lover does. In pondering
the renovation of the entire social fabric, she follows in the footsteps of
Hester Prynne in *The Scarlet Letter,* who contemplates the "dark question"
of the "whole race of womanhood" and realizes women's lot could never
be happy without tearing down "the whole system of society" (1: 165).
Lydia's problem, like Hester's, is that she thinks too much. When her lover
complains, "you judge things too theoretically . . . I didn't know we ran
away to found a new system of ethics" (1: 110), he indicates not only his
satisfaction with their loosely defined liaison but his vested interest in
preserving the status quo. Lydia faces a double bind: if she celebrates her
freedom from marriage, she is a promiscuous Eve; if she follows marital
conventions, she becomes a respectable Mary but must repress her own
desire. She is alienated both by existing structures *and* by a critical intelligence that questions those structures. Not surprisingly, she has "the exasperated sense of having walked into the trap of some stupid practical joke"
(1: 107).

Wharton's story demonstrates the problem that all serious, reflective
women face when they attempt to renegotiate alienating patriarchal systems
of thought and belief. Contemporary theorists such as Julia Kristeva, for
example, argue that ethics for women lies not in adherence to laws or
systems, but in disruption of existing systems: ethics can no longer be seen
as "ensuring the cohesiveness of a particular group" but must arise "wherever a code . . . must be shattered in order to give way to the free play
of negativity, need, desire, pleasure, and jouissance" ("Ethics" 23). The
protagonist in "Souls Belated" would like to establish a new ethical code,
but she lacks historical and theoretical bases from which to proceed. The
priest who stands silently nearby as Lydia decides whether to return to her
lover symbolizes her – and all women's – inscription in restrictive Judeo-
Christian traditions.

The problem that Wharton addresses in "Souls Belated" was not easily
solved in present society. Dissatisfaction with Christian representations led
her to search for alternatives, and especially to look backward to classical
and preclassical cultures in which women once played significant spiritual

roles. Wharton joined a number of nineteenth-century writers, from Margaret Fuller and Thomas Higginson to Charlotte Perkins Gilman, who attempted, in Sarah Sherman's words, to "resuscitate dead goddesses" (16). Visions of matriarchy flourished in the second half of the century, encouraged by recent studies in the classics, anthropology, and archaeology.[11] Sociologists, philosophers, and anthropologists such as J. J. Bachofen, Edward Westermarck, Robert Briffault, and Gilman debated the origins of the human race and, in particular, the relations between the sexes, finding in matriarchal societies the symbols of feminine strength and wisdom.

The recuperation of the Greek goddesses, with their vast powers, complex personalities, and active sexuality, provided welcome relief from nineteenth-century feminine stereotypes. Feminist theorists seized the opportunity of these discoveries to criticize Western religion as a whole. Matilda Joslyn Gage, for example, argued in *Woman, Church and State* (1893) that the demise of matriarchal societies led to legal subordination of women to men; she railed against Judaism, Christianity, and the "rule of men whose lives and religion were based upon passions of the grossest kind" (qtd. in Ruether and Keller 14). Gage was a forerunner of contemporary feminist theorists such as Mary Daly, Naomi Goldenberg, and Carol Christ, who wish to recast mythology and language to free women from Christianity's negative images, and who posit a female-centered spirituality focused on worship of the mother goddess, the individual's inner spiritual power, and sisterhood. The nineteenth-century revival did not always lead to gains for women, however. Bachofen, for example, stacked the deck against women in *Mother Right* by proposing a theory of cultural evolution in which patriarchy was the natural and preferable outcome, and Henry Adams maintained that "an American Virgin would never dare command; an American Venus would never dare exist" (*Education* 385). Still, despite opposition, many believed that through matriarchal societies one could recapture the essence of feminine spirituality that was so lacking in contemporary religion.

According to Rosemary Ruether and Rosemary Keller, the interest in matriarchy was a modern attempt to recapture and validate the sentimental and Victorian aspects of femininity (2), a connection Sherman also makes (21). But Joan Chamberlain Engelsman places the movement in the context of a broader cultural repression of the feminine in Christianity. She draws on Erich Neumann to show how Western patriarchal religion virtually eliminates the power of the mother by emphasizing father archetypes and consciousness. The worship of the mother goddess gave way to dependence on an all-powerful male God; previously distinctive male and female principles were subsumed by the Trinity of Father, Son, and Holy Spirit; and woman – supplementary, subordinate, or repressed – was charged with the original sin and weakness of the flesh. If ancient feminine power is evoked in Christianity, it is always in a dangerous or threatening form: as a wanton or bad goddess in contrast with the good God (35–36). Protestants hold most rigidly to this relationship with the male deity, whereas Catholics allow the disguised return of the Great Mother in the form of the Virgin Mary.

It is impossible to know whether Wharton would have agreed with Engelsman's interpretation. Her view was never overtly radical; she did not develop in coherent form what Elisabeth Fiorenza calls "a critical theology of liberation" (xxii). But Wharton did experiment with ancient models of feminine divinity, creativity, and power. She alludes to Greek myths and goddesses throughout her fiction, and she felt the lack of maternal spirit in religion in general, and in Calvinist-inspired Protestantism in particular. In *Ethan Frome,* Wharton's most Calvinist novel, for example, maternal energy is absent or malevolent. Indeed, in much of her fiction, as Wendy Gimbel notes, female characters are bereft of their mothers. Even potentially strong maternal figures, such as Kate Clephane in *The Mother's Recompense* (1925), are disempowered by social codes that forbid the coexistence of sexuality and motherhood. In *Hudson River Bracketed* and *The Gods Arrive,* Wharton venerates the Virgin Mary in her portrayal of a Madonna-like heroine, Halo Tarrant, but Halo is still secondary to Vance Weston, who is the novels' true artist and spiritual pilgrim.

By the time of the Greek pantheon, the ubiquitous power of the Great Mother – once consolidated, sacred, and potent – had been weakened and distributed among various goddesses, who represented only discreet aspects of the total feminine divine (Harrison 257–321). It is not surprising, then, that most Victorian seekers of lost matriarchies favored a docile, feminine ideal that mirrored the sentimental cult of domesticity. Thus it is that Persephone – the ambivalent, submissive maiden and deprived, perpetual daughter – emerges as a dominant figure in Wharton's writing.[12] But Wharton also evoked more active goddesses – Medusa, Artemis, Aphrodite, and Demeter – in her fiction. These references suggest a longing to see contemporary women in terms of their once powerful foremothers and to recuperate the vibrant strength of the feminine as well as its qualities of submission, stability, and nurturance.[13] Lily Bart and Charity Royall are such characters in embryonic form; Ellen Olenska is a more fully realized, sexually powerful woman who acts responsibly for herself and others. The remnants of a powerful matriarchal network are also found in Ellen's relatives, Mrs. Manson Mingott and Medora Mingott, whose eccentricities push the limits of the rule-bound world of *The Age of Innocence.* Yet even

Ellen is relegated to the background in much of *The Age of Innocence* and at the end of the novel disappears altogether – as if to suggest that such feminine power is too strong for representation. Wharton's longing for an integrated, vital feminine energy is most vivid in her haunting portrait of Sophy Viner in *The Reef* (1912), which I discuss in Chapter 4, "Fragile Freedoms." Sophy – a vibrant woman who disrupts social conventions and is rejected by the society she challenges – is an incarnation of the ancient Sophia, a female divinity who ruled with the authority of God until she was displaced by Hebrew and Christian monotheism. Through this allusion to Sophia, whose name means wisdom, Wharton expresses her quarrel with patriarchy and the need for greater acceptance of a full range of women's feelings and powers in contemporary society.

Transcending Boundaries

Wharton valued Christianity because it is a transcendent faith, promising the pious and worthy a permanent spiritual home in heaven. She never wavered in her pursuit of spiritual ideals. However, she struggled with the concepts of Atonement and forgiveness that would secure the soul's immortality, and she resisted Christian proscriptions against pleasures of the flesh. Thus, her outlook was idealistic without always being expressly Christian. In midlife, especially between 1908 and 1920, Edith Wharton explored other non-Christian, transcendental philosophies. She was, for example, briefly captivated by Friedrich Nietzsche's celebration of the irrational and his radical critique of Christianity. Although Wharton does not mention Nietzsche in her fiction, her letters reveal how important he was in helping her solve a spiritual crisis brought on by a passionate, extramarital love affair. Wharton also flirted with Emersonian transcendentalism as an antidote to the materialism of modern life. She does refer to Emerson – and to Emerson's poet Walt Whitman – in her fiction, especially in her novel *Summer,* which, as I discuss later, incorporates both romantic exuberance and hardheaded realism.

In 1908 or 1909, at the height of an adulterous affair with journalist Morton Fullerton, Edith Wharton was temporarily enthralled with the anti-Christian proclamations of Friedrich Nietzsche. Referring to his *Beyond Good and Evil,* she enthusiastically wrote to Sara Norton in 1908, "this is *great* fun – full of wit & originality & poetry. . . . He has no system, & not much logic, but wonderful flashes of insight, & a power of breaking through conventions that is most exhilarating, & clears the air." In the same letter, she also voiced her strongest disagreement with traditional faith: "there are times when I *hate* what Christianity has left in our blood – or rather, one might say, taken out of it – by its cursed assumption of the split between body & soul" (*Letters* 159, original emphasis).

Nietzsche argued against any celebration of the pure spirit at the expense of the body and attacked Christianity: "The Church combats passions by means of excision of all kinds: its practice . . . is *castration*. . . . The method of the Church is hostile to life" (*Twilight* 27, original emphasis). He also criticized Christianity because, by teaching perfection not in this world but the next, it encourages resignation to mediocrity. The will to otherworldliness, which is essential to Christianity, Nietzsche argues, is actually motivated by the will to power of the weak who have despaired of fulfillment in this life. Christianity, the revolt of the weak upon the strong, "has waged deadly war against this *higher* type of man" and "has corrupted even the reason of the strongest intellects by teaching that the highest values of intellectuality are sinful, misleading and full of temptations" (*Antichrist* 130, original emphasis). Nietzsche provided an antidote to Wharton's personal doctrine of payment for pleasure; he relieved her guilt over the illicit affair with Fullerton, and for a brief moment he unleashed the self-control that otherwise marked her habits of thought and action.

Nietzsche was also significant for Wharton because he rejected the downward cycle of evolution and the leveling effects of Darwinism. "The general condition of life," Nietzsche argued, is "not one of want or famine, but rather of riches . . . where there is a struggle, it is a struggle for power" (*Twilight* 71). In his view, all humans have a will to power, which is to perfect themselves, to become creators instead of the created. This ideal he called the "overman." Only when people fail in this endeavor do they seek crude power over others as a substitute. Nietzsche rejected evolution – whether biological or social – on the grounds that it leads not toward the overman but toward the "last man," an uncreative conformist and complacent hedonist. Too lazy to exert himself or even care, this last man epitomizes modern civilization. Nietzsche also rejected the notion of human progress. The image of eternity for him was a circle: all events recur eternally at gigantic intervals. The world is not governed by purpose but by endless play. The challenge to the overman was to make the best of this reality. Nietzsche applauded Goethe – whom Wharton also deeply admired – as a man of intelligence strong enough to claim his freedom: "such a spirit, *become free,* appears in the middle of the universe with a feeling of cheerful and confident fatalism. . . . *He no longer denies.*" He embodies the energy not of Apollo but of Dionysus (*Twilight* 110, original emphasis).

Nietzsche called forth in Wharton the Neoplatonic quality of will that seeks transcendence without limitation. Deeply involved in her first passionate relationship, Wharton yearned to seize the freedom that Nietzsche's theories promised, but, as R. W. B. Lewis notes, her "puritanical" sensibility interfered. She felt especially constrained by her gender. A letter to Fullerton written just days after her affair began shows Wharton desperate for life's pleasures but wracked by conflict:

> How strange to feel one's self all at once *"Jehnseits von Gut und Böse"* ["Beyond Good and Evil"] . . . It would hurt no one – and it would give me my first last draught of life . . . Why not? I have always laughed at the *"mala prohibita"* – "bugbears to frighten children." The anti-social act is the only one that is harmful "per se." And, as you told me the other day – *and as I needed no telling!* – what I have given you is far, far more . . . (qtd. in Lewis 221, original emphases and ellipses)

Wharton decided, of course, to take that "first last draught of life" and enjoyed with Fullerton a passion that her marriage did not provide. Ultimately, however, she was too conventional to exercise a truly Nietzschean freedom of will. In another letter to Fullerton in May 1910, after the romance had begun to cool, she writes of opportunity lost: "Nietzschean! There would have been a time for such a word – last autumn, when I held absolute freedom in my hand, & didn't take it because I saw that you thought I ought not to" (*Letters* 215). Both letters convey the dilemma that women face when they try to overcome the cultural restrictions of their passion. In 1908, Wharton was exhilarated by the possibilities of freedom; in 1910, however, she hesitated to claim her full measure of joy because of Fullerton – that is, her Nietzschean energy was checked because she thought and felt through her male lover. It is impossible to know whether Wharton ever acknowledged that Nietzsche designed his themes not for generic "man" but for men, but in *The Twilight of the Idols,* she would have encountered his antifeminism: "Man thinks woman profound – why? Because he can never fathom her depths. Woman is not even shallow" (5).

Closely connected to Nietzsche was Ralph Waldo Emerson, whose essays, Wharton maintained, were the chief influence on the German philosopher. Emerson, as well as Edgar Allan Poe and Walt Whitman, held a special attraction for Wharton; they spoke to her sense of romantic possibility, of personal power, originality, and fulfillment. Writing to Scribner's publisher William Brownell about Poe, Wharton said, "I should like to get in that Nicean bark with you – and in time gently steer it toward the 'far-sprinkled systems' that Walt sails among. Those two, with Emerson, are the best we have – in fact, the all we have." After rereading Emerson's poetry, she was "amazed at his facilities, and his clear cold

amenity, flushing now and then like some beautiful bit of pink crystal."
Just as she had praised Nietzsche's "power of breaking through the conventions," she detected a trace of Walt Whitman in Nietzschean phrases such
as "Man is a *sick animal*" (qtd. in Lewis 236, 230, original emphasis).
Emersonian transcendentalism – with its emphasis on intuitive truth, disregard of external authority, and communion with nature – offered Wharton
relief from society's pressures and from Calvinism's burdensome moral
audits.

Wharton reveals this search for transcendence in some of her fictional
depictions of nature. Her natural scenes are usually cultivated ones: they
often include gardens seen in relationship to houses or art (as in *Italian
Villas and Their Gardens,* and *The Decoration of Houses*); or vistas seen from
particular perspectives (such as the ones Lily Bart enjoys in *The House of
Mirth,* Grace Ansley and Alida Slade admire in "Roman Fever," or Wharton herself constructed at her Lenox, Massachusetts, home).[14] However,
she shows interest in the effects of uncultivated nature in her 1917 novel.
Summer celebrates the unrestricted fullness of the season named in its title
and constitutes, more than any other novel, Wharton's version of American
transcendentalism.

In *Summer,* which I discuss in Chapter 4, Wharton draws not only on
Emerson but on Whitman. Her favorite American bard, Whitman appealed
to what Wharton called "the accepting soul" (*Backward* 159). The power
of his poetry to heal divisions, celebrate passion, and see the connectedness
of all life countered the polarizing effects of modern life and called forth
erotic as well as creative impulses. *Summer* describes the flowering of a
woman's first romance in terms of Emerson's and Whitman's optimistic,
transcendent philosophies. However, the fact that the novel ends with
autumn's approach and is set in Calvinist New England, with an ominous
"Mountain" nearby, demonstrates that for Wharton, the search for a transcendent philosophy could only be partially fulfilled. Although *Summer* is
Wharton's most passionate, sympathetic novel, it bears the mark both of its
Calvinist setting and of Darwinian determinism. Charity Royall embraces
nature and her own desire only to find her self-expression stifled: transcendental ideals are mediated by biological and social realities, and individual
dreams are sacrificed to common interests. *Summer* represents Wharton's
search for non-Christian ideals – for guiltless personal freedom and a
spiritual home to which one may return for good – but this cosmic
optimism is tempered by the stronger sense of what is rather than what
might be.[15]

Aesthetic Salvation

Although instances of upper-class complacency rarely escaped Wharton's sharp eye and incisive satire, she, like many late nineteenth-century Americans, lamented the dissolution of cultural standards and traditions. "The value of duration" proved little match for "the welter of change" fostered by technology and burgeoning capitalism (*Backward* 5). For Wharton, the problem was spiritual as well as social; the solution, if one existed, lay in recovering hallowed traditions and practices of previous times.

Like Matthew Arnold, whom she admired, Wharton felt that modern life had destroyed an important historical continuity. For Arnold, "the time of harmony is always past" (J. H. Miller 215). For Wharton also, her disappearing New York society "was like an empty vessel into which no new wine would ever again be poured" (*Backward* 5). Both writers viewed contemporary social forms with alarm. Once reflecting the human relationship with God and divine truth, such social conventions were now hollow shells. In *Culture and Anarchy,* Arnold criticizes the chaos that permeated all classes of society as people pursued whatever pleased them rather than what they could justify through divine sources; similarly, in novels such as *The House of Mirth* and *The Custom of the Country,* Wharton documents how gross materialism and selfish desire replace traditional morality and even common decency. Like Arnold, Wharton sought unity and transcendence, once guaranteed through faith in God but now imperiled and perhaps lost forever. Like him, she rejected modern psychological theories that divided human nature. She shared Arnold's distrust of purely secular ethical codes and sought to elevate them through an identification with God or divinity. And just as Arnold ultimately resigned himself to God's absence and waited for some future but vaguely understood spiritual renewal, so Wharton, too, mixed her realistic skepticism with idealistic hope for a return to spiritual absolutes. In an age when faith no longer seemed viable, she attempted to reinvigorate the spiritual sense by locating it in art, history, and religions of past cultures.

Something akin to a "religion of culture" flourished among the upper and middle classes in both England and the United States at the turn of the century, with art museums and music halls replacing churches as the new temples. Aestheticism accompanied the general American preoccupation with high culture after the Civil War and the gradual movement away from Calvinism and toward more fashionable Congregationalist or Episcopal styles and rituals. Aestheticism adapted "nature" – for generations of Americans an emblem of possibility – to a changing industrial and urban setting. It was a timely solution for a culture in social, economic, and religious upheaval because it permitted a dissociation from issues and controversies while still meeting the need for spiritual renewal.

Artists and intellectuals such as Henry Adams turned to Europe and the Middle Ages as the highest expression not only of religion, but of art and culture. Victorians turned also to non-Western models. Wharton's friend, William Sturgis Bigelow, for example, was fascinated with Japanese art and Buddhism. Anthropologists visited primitive cultures in Africa and Asia, and classicists explored Western culture's roots by reviving the Greeks. In varying ways, the past helped late nineteenth- and early twentieth-century spiritual seekers like Edith Wharton cope with the present and hope for the future. American writers, of course, had long been nostalgic for the past they never had: in the early 1800s, Washington Irving wrote of wanting "to escape . . . from the commonplace realities of the present, and lose myself among the shadowy grandeurs of the past" (744). This yearning intensified in the wake of industrialization and Darwin. Medieval religion and art filled a spiritual gap created by science: even if faith were lost, the Virgin Mary might still be worshiped as she appeared in great works of art. Americans haunted Europe's holy places; Wharton's endless motor flights to cathedrals, monasteries, and convents place her firmly in this tradition of religious-seeking dilettantes.

Art, with its principles of order, balance, and beauty, offered an alternative to traditional faith; at the very least, it provided abstract values for a materialistic age. As Turner writes: "The best painting, poetry, and music drew out the best in human beings. . . . Immersed in art, one lost sight of the minuteness of individual limits in the lasting grandeur of the race. Reverencing art, one revered the spiritual in humankind" (252). In fiction as different as "The Daunt Diana" (1909) and *The Age of Innocence,* Wharton considers the possibilities and limitations of a theology based on art and culture.

The turn-of-the-century aesthetic movement struck a deep, responsive chord in Wharton. She enthusiastically describes her "keen interest in architecture, furniture and works of art in general" in her memoir (*Backward* 148). The aesthetic movement's roots were in Germany and in Kant, who proposed that pure aesthetic experience consists of a disinterested contemplation of an object without reference to external reality, utility, or morality. Priests of this culture were Arnold in England and Charles Eliot Norton in America, both of whom preached the moral usefulness of art; heretics included Walter Pater and to some extent Henry Adams, who inclined toward a purer aestheticism. Wharton also encountered aestheticism through Oscar Wilde and John Ruskin.[16] Earlier American nineteenth-century models included Washington Irving's stance as distanced observer; Hawthorne's artists, caught between the demands of beauty and human connection; and Poe's poetic principle, which severed art from intellect or conscience (Freedman 386).

Like many of her contemporaries, Wharton was most at home in Europe, which represented the epitome of aesthetic value. America paled in contrast: "What could New York offer to a child whose eyes had been filled with shapes of immortal beauty and immemorial significance? One of the most depressing impressions of my childhood is my recollection of [its] intolerable ugliness," Wharton writes in *A Backward Glance* (54). She was particularly offended by the "ugliness" of her aunt's New York home:

> The effect of terror produced by the house of Rhinecliff was no doubt partly due to what seemed to me its intolerable ugliness. . . . My photographic memory of rooms and houses . . . was from my earliest years a source of inarticulate misery, for I was always vaguely frightened of ugliness. (28)

However inclined Wharton was toward European traditions, she did not entirely reject native products, as she demonstrates in indigenous fiction such as "Bunner Sisters," *Ethan Frome,* and *Summer,* and in her glowing praise for Emerson and Whitman. She also combined her craving for beauty and order with a deep appreciation of the practical. In this respect, she joined a distinctly American tradition as well as a European one.

Wharton also followed cultural trends with her fictions about the supernatural, such as medieval fairy tales and ghost stories. In 1868, John Ruskin complained that modern nursery stories were too didactic, and that only a revival of the traditional fairy tale would restore freshness to the child's imagination (19: 233–39). Wharton makes a similar point when, in *A Backward Glance,* she deplores the didactic juvenilia of her youth and thanks her parents for saving her from such inferior literature. For many turn-of-the-century children – and adults – stories of ghosts, elves, legends, superstitions, and fantasies filled the need for the supernatural and connected one to primitive impulses. If science was prosaic, the reasoning went, then poetry could be poetic or even religious; and made-up characters could be much more interesting than real ones. Ghost and fairy tales permitted a suspension of rationality and allowed the imagination to participate in a process of picture making that scientific methods ignored. They also spoke to a childlike heart, in which authenticity is less important than what one *believed* to be true, and they provided therapeutic relief from the pressures of modern life (Lears 170–72).

The fairy-tale movement was championed by Charles Kingsley, a historian and Cambridge professor from 1860 to 1869, who believed that history taught moral lessons and that the wicked received their just punishment (Chadwick 190, 195). His fairy-tale heroes, often Greek characters, satisfied a religious need for transcendence as well as literary and historical needs. Fairy tales, with their requisite endings of triumph over adversity and justice over injustice, affirmed a morality and order missing from modern life. As such, Lears argues, both medieval revivalism and the taste for fairy tales constituted a resistance to modernity (170). Wharton does employ heroic imagery and fairy-tale motifs, but she does so ironically and thus aligns herself with the modernist rather than Victorian outlook. For example, in *Ethan Frome* Wharton uses heroic imagery ironically: the narrator imagines that Ethan once walked as "gallantly" as a Greek warrior, but now he is "a ruin of a man" (4, 3). Wharton also uses fairy-tale plots throughout her fiction, as Elizabeth Ammons notes, but she seldom writes happy endings. Lily, the Sleeping Beauty in *The House of Mirth,* never awakens; Zeena rules as the wicked witch in *Ethan Frome;* and Anna Leath is rudely awakened from her storybook dreams of love in *The Reef.* Wharton's fairy tales confirm injustice and moral chaos. More ironic – and modernist – than nostalgic, they reject simplistic solutions to difficult spiritual or moral problems.

Wharton's ghost stories are similarly complex. Ghostly tales of terror, after all, are but the other side of fantasies of delight. Like fairy tales, ghost stories may reinstate the mystery of the unknown, defend against a mechanistic age, and even replace the sense of the supernatural once provided by religious faith. Wharton fully understood the function of these stories, inquiring of her readers in her preface to *Ghosts* (1937): "Do you believe in ghosts?" In an age of toasters and telephones, the ghost story reaches to "the warm darkness of the pre-natal fluid far below our conscious reason"; it needs neither "sources" nor "evidence" (vii–viii). Wharton's ghost fiction – a secular substitute for religion – keeps alive the supernatural in an age of skepticism and rationality, but it never offers easy reassurance.

Wharton joined the aesthetic flight to medieval times in her short stories "Dieu D'Amour" and "The Hermit and the Wild Woman"; both, as Lewis notes, deal with the "conflict between sacred and profane love" (470). The former story was written after a 1926 Aegean cruise, which included a visit to the castle Dieu d'Amour, named by the Crusaders for the Greek god of love, Eros. In Wharton's tale, however, spiritual love triumphs over erotic passion. "The Hermit and the Wild Woman," published twenty years earlier, reflects the cultural enthusiasm for saints' lives and, as Lears notes, a longing for elements lost to late Victorians: communion with nature, simple faith, and sexual innocence (151),[17] but Wharton departs from the mainstream by giving the story a feminist twist.

In "The Hermit and the Wild Woman," an austere hermit who strives to live a pious life retreats from the perils of culture and isolates himself in a hillside cave. There he meets a "wild woman" who has run away from a nearby convent because its rules forbid her the one pleasure that her being craves: to bathe herself in fresh streams of water. Knowing the frequency with which "the demon . . . had taken the form of a woman" (*Stories* 1: 577), the hermit distrusts the wild woman, although he becomes increasingly convinced of her goodness when he witnesses her ministering to others and effecting miraculous cures. He exhorts her to heed God's will and resist the sin of bathing; when she promises to obey, the two live "side by side" (1: 585) in separate reclusiveness, until one day he discovers her drowned body in a nearby stream. Convinced of her evil, the hermit bewails his failure to dissuade her from sin. The reactions of visiting townspeople, however, help him to realize that he has witnessed not a sinner but "a dying saint" (1: 588–89).

The reader is initially led to think of the hermit, not the wild woman, as a candidate for sainthood. By the story's end, however, it is clear that this sensuous, natural creature of woods and streams – more a classical image of strength than a Christian example of virtue – is indeed the holy one; but Christianity has no place for such female qualities. The woman remains outside the pale – "wild."[18] In Christian tradition, woman is associated with corruption of the flesh, whereas man is capable of true spirituality. The hermit can only see the woman's bathing – which Wharton describes sensuously as "furtive touches," a clinging "embrace," and "kisses" (1: 581) – as corrupt. Wharton's cry against Christianity's split between the body and the flesh, a clear subtext of the story, qualifies her enthusiasm toward the Middle Ages as a time of lost ideals: such ideals and freedoms did not extend to women.

Many of Wharton's friends and peers were also attracted to aestheticism, both for its own sake and for spiritual uplift. Some proponents of aestheticism became agnostics, as did Charles Eliot Norton, but others saw in art a greater spiritual potential. That art might substitute for religion was the belief of Edith Wharton's close friend Bernard Berenson, who had been Norton's student at Harvard and whom Wharton praised as having superseded Pater, John Symonds, and Vernon Lee as the premier authority on art (Vita-Finzi 11). For Berenson, art not only supplanted religion; religion could become art: "Taken as objective reality it is the art of the unaesthetic; but taken consciously as subjective . . . [religion] is perhaps the highest form of beauty" (qtd. in Samuels 283). Turner notes that even clergymen participated in the replacement of religion with art by drawing analogies between God and poetry. Analyzing God in this way, they explained, brought God out of the transcendental sphere and into the human one (253).

Edith Wharton, however, never abandoned the goal that art serve a higher purpose than itself. When she described the architectural delights of French medieval cathedrals, for example, she affirmed that their "chief value, to this later age, is not so much aesthetic as moral" (*Motor* 9). Art, she argues in her book on the theory of fiction, should never lose touch with life: the ideal short story – "a shaft driven straight into the heart of human experience" – must illustrate a simple, compact moral situation (*Writing* 36, 42–43). The artist must present "crucial moments" of existence that reveal "some recognizable relation to a familiar social or moral standard" (*Writing* 13–14).

Wharton frequently couples art with moral ideas, suggesting the insufficiency of art alone. She reveals in her autobiographical fragment, "Life and I," that her "moral tortures" were alleviated aesthetically and intellectually: "Happily I had two means of escape from this chronic moral malady. One was provided by my love of pretty things – pretty clothes, pretty pictures, pretty sights – & the other by my learning to read" ("Life" 1072, 1074). Wharton's characters similarly find spiritual solace in beauty or books. For example, in *The House of Mirth,* Lily Bart instinctively seeks the most aesthetically pleasing setting for her naturally good looks, and this beauty suggests a moral sensibility superior to her companions'. In the story "The Quicksand" (1902), a mother and a girlfriend who are distressed by a man's ethics unexpectedly encounter each other at an art museum, where they "find pictures a great help" (*Stories* 1: 405). And in *The Age of Innocence,* Ellen Olenska and Newland Archer also select the haven of an art museum to decide whether their romance can survive the conventions of old New York. In other fiction, reading lifts the spirit and offers compensation for life's disappointments. Ethan Frome wistfully examines technical journals; Ralph Marvell retreats into books to escape Undine's relentless materialism; and Newland Archer feels that more real life goes on in his library than anywhere else. The contemplation of art soothes the spirit; conversely, an active intellect enhances art's salutary effect.

Although art is a vehicle for spiritual or religious uplift, it is often compromised and must compete with powerful social forces. Much of Wharton's fiction about aesthetics develops this theme of failed ideals. In her early story "The Portrait" (1899), for example, Wharton aligns art with truth, but it is a truth that the populace does not value. A famous artist's ability to capture his subjects' essence leads viewers to compare his portray-als with "the day of judgement." The premise of the story is that if there is no core – "no real person" – the true artist can paint "nothing" (*Stories* 1: 174); therefore, when the artist paints a spiritually empty tycoon's portrait, he makes him "more monstrous than ever, as an ugly image reflected in clear water is made uglier by the purity of the medium" (1: 179). More fashionable painters – "purveyor[s] of rose-water pastels" (1: 173) – criticize the artist's lack of idealism, oblivious to the fact that he upholds the very highest moral ideals.

In another early story, "The Fullness of Life" (1893) – a transparently autobiographical account of incompatible marriage – Wharton explores the conflict between social and personal expectations. She begins with a Dickinson-like description in which the female protagonist feels death overtake her as a thickening, drowning darkness. While her grieving hus-band walks dejectedly away, she enters a new reality and understands with gratitude and surprise that "death is not the end after all." Wharton ad-dresses the question of the soul's immortality in an age of scientific skepti-cism with the protagonist's comment, "I believed in Darwin, of course . . . but then Darwin himself said that he wasn't sure about the soul . . . and Wallace was a spiritualist." The protagonist then compares her new ethereal setting with the beauty of "Shelley's vaporous creations" or Leonardo's paintings (1: 13), linking the spiritual and the aesthetic. She next con-fronts the "Spirit of Life," to whom she divulges her deepest regret that she has yet to experience "the fullness of life" – a state inadequately conveyed by the words "love" and "sympathy" but exquisitely captured through rare, isolated experiences in nature or literature ("the perfume of a flower . . . a verse of Dante or of Shakespeare . . . a picture or a sunset") (1: 14–15). More rarely, the woman says, such a gift comes through conversation with another human being, although never her husband, whom she sums up as wearing creaking boots. It may also come through the church. The woman recalls one special moment in a cathedral in Florence, when the meaning and beauty of the ages converged in medieval splendor:

> I had never been in the church before. . . . The marble, worn and mellowed by the subtle hand of time, took on an unspeakable rosy hue, suggestive in some remote way of the honey-colored columns of the Parthenon, but more mystic, more complex . . . such a light as illumines the missals in the library of Siena, or burns like a hidden fire through the Madonna of Gian Bellini in the Church of the Re-deemer, at Venice; the light of the Middle Ages, richer, more solemn, more significant than the limpid sunshine of Greece. . . .

I felt myself borne onward along a mighty current, whose source
seemed to be in the very beginning of things. . . .
As I gazed . . . all the plastic terror and beauty born of man's hand
from the Ganges to the Baltic quivered and mingled in Orcagna's
apotheosis of Mary. And so the river bore me on, past the alien faces
of antique civilizations and the familiar wonders of Greece, till I swam
upon the fiercely rushing tide of the Middle Ages, with its swirling
eddies of passion, its heaven-reflecting pools of poetry and art. (1: 15–
16)

The Spirit tells the woman that all of these blessings of culture can be hers
for eternity; indeed, the woman's dreams are fulfilled when she meets her
soul mate, with whom she will share every experience. But when the
woman remembers the husband she left behind, she is overwhelmed by
guilt and decides to forgo her beautiful future to wait for him.

Critics commonly view the protagonist sympathetically, as a version of
Wharton trapped in an unsuitable marriage to Teddy Wharton. However,
the story is also an allegory about a misguided spiritual seeker. The protagonist is limited by conventionality and hubris. For example, although the
Spirit cautions, "do not be too sure," the woman is convinced that she is
indispensable to her husband: "he will never be happy without me" (1:
19). Her decision to wait for the "creaking of his boots" (1: 20) is as selfish
as it is selfless. Despite the Spirit's warning, the woman follows conventional thought by assuming that she alone can make her husband happy and
misses her own chance for spiritual uplift. In this story, the nineteenth-
century ideology of female domesticity works against aesthetic fulfillment.

Aestheticism's healing potential was also weakened by the present-day
emphasis on greed. It is all too easy, Wharton writes in her story "The
Verdict" (1908), to "transmute [money] into objects of art and luxury" (1:
656). The artist, of all people, must guard against opportunities to prostitute
art for wealth. Such is the theme of "The Potboiler" (1904), in which a
talented, struggling painter must cater to popular tastes in order to survive.
Fashionable society hires "the painter of the hour" to do sentimental,
unoriginal sculptures and portraits (the women wish "to be carved in sugar
candy, or painted in maple syrup") but avoids "the truth about itself or
about anything." A true artist cannot please two gods – the marketplace
and higher ideals. "Prophets," the artist ruefully comments, "have always
lived in a garret" (1: 670).

Another story, "In Trust" (1906), published two years after "The Potboiler," demonstrates how even the noblest intentions give way to material
and selfish interests. Paul Anson, like his New Testament namesake, has an
"apostolic" mission: he wishes to achieve "the ultimate aesthetic redemp-

tion of the whole human race, and provisionally restor[e] the sense of beauty to those unhappy millions . . . who . . . now live and die in surroundings of unperceived and unmitigated ugliness" (1: 616). He proposes to found an Academy of Arts, but he procrastinates and then dies before the project is begun. The task falls to his friend, who also delays because wife, children, new houses, and trips to Europe keep intervening. Paul's apostolic dream is never realized, and the "wider nature" loses the "war with the petty inherited instinct of greed" (1: 618).

A further problem with the aesthetic movement was that, despite its claim of timelessness, it was contextually situated. This fact had great impact on women, since aesthetic values ended up reinforcing gender and class biases. Although the turn-of-the-century arts and crafts movement opened up new possibilities for women as producers of art – china painting, for example, became very popular (R. Stein 31–32) – women's participation was still viewed as a temporary concession. Their rightful sphere remained hearth and home, where they became, as Thorstein Veblen notes, "conspicuous consumers" of male production. The aesthetic movement's praise of women was but a variation on the familiar "biology is destiny" argument, as William Henry Fry's comment indicates:

> The flowers of the field, the waving palm, the wondrous birds. . . .
> The expression, the charm, the molding of these by ideal conception
> comes intuitively to the American woman. The nature endowed
> aptitude of most women makes them the ready exponents of the
> creed-beautiful. . . . All that is beautiful, all that is true in art, appeals
> to her very nature. (qtd. in R. Stein 33–35)

Fry praises female art but calls it the result of "intuition" and natural fulfillment rather than of concerted effort, training, and dedication. He also ignores the fact that art is subject to the pressures of the market. Wharton, on the other hand, understood the myriad ways that women's natural beauty and talents were commodified and sold. In *The House of Mirth*, for example, she makes Lily Bart both a creature of nature ("lily") and of the market economy ("barter"). Although Lily has a naturally aesthetic sensibility and Lawrence Selden finds her an appealing candidate for the Republic of the Spirit, her artistic gifts are no help in the hatshop, where she is fired for slow production. Likewise, Lily's portrayal of Reynolds's Mrs. Lloyd in the tableau vivant at the Blys' ball – an inspired, creative imitation – stuns her audience, but it is no substitute for the economic and social independence that Lily fails to achieve in the novel.[19]

Another danger of worshiping art was that women themselves became the objects of worship. Wharton brilliantly examines this problem in "The

Muse's Tragedy" (1899), in which Silvia Anerton is described as "one of those old prints where the lines have the value of color" (*Stories* 1: 67). Had the great poet Rendle married her, "it would have been like 'restoring' a masterpiece" (1: 70). Nowhere is the aestheticization of women more prominent than in *The House of Mirth*, in which Lily is reduced to "a beautiful object" (Fetterley, "Temptation"). This novel reproduces not only fin-de-siècle attitudes toward women, but the entire tradition of Western art in which women are the observed, not the observers; the muses or consumers of art, not the producers. The relatively few female artists and many male artists in Wharton's fiction demonstrate how thoroughly she internalized this tradition. In all of her fiction, Wharton depicts only one successful female artist. Helen Dale, in "Copy" (first published as "Copy: A Dialogue" in 1900), writes best sellers and is called "the greatest novelist . . . of the age" (1: 276); yet her success is marred by an unhappy love affair, as if to suggest that female art comes at the cost of romantic fulfillment. Aestheticism reinscribed woman as an idealized or sexualized other rather than as agent in her own right and thus restricted female expression.

Philosophical Idealism

Although art and culture were important sources of spiritual consolation, they never completely answered Wharton's spiritual needs. In part, this was because, despite the most ardent intentions, moderns could not rekindle the religious fervor of the past. Wharton knew as much when she visited Chartres and observed the few worshipers who, like "stranded driftwood," were the only remains of the medieval multitudes:

> On the prayer-worn floor,
> By surging worshippers thick-thronged of yore,
> A few brown crones, familiars of the tomb,
> The stranded driftwood of Faith's ebbing sea –
> For these alone the finials fret the skies.
> ("Chartres" lines 6–10)

Some spiritual seekers – Charles Norton, for example, the friend and mentor who helped Wharton research *The Valley of Decision* – thrived by developing creeds of agnosticism; others continued to worship art instead of God. Edith Wharton, however, sought more.

It is therefore a mistake to claim, as Blake Nevius does in his study of Wharton's fiction, that Wharton's values were based exclusively or even primarily on aesthetics.[20] She sympathized with the kind of aestheticism that cultivates taste, observing that "in our hurried world too little value is attached to the part of the connoisseur and dilettante" (*Backward* 150), and she counted taste as one measure of morality; but the worship of form alone was dangerous and irresponsible. Wharton could never envision a completely successful retreat from life's issues and questions. This view is at the heart of her criticism of the insular, staid society in *The Age of Innocence*. It also explains her objection to decadence, the aestheticism espoused by Baudelaire and celebrated in the late Roman Empire and Byzantine Greece.

Decadence, with its artifice, opposition to nature, and general expressions of lassitude and satiety, was too attentive to form, led to an excess of detail, and inhibited spiritual advancement. In Wharton's fiction, decadence is portrayed as deviant or depraved. Male dilettantes in ghost stories such as "The Eyes" (1910) and "A Bottle of Perrier" (1926), for example, are sinister – even murderous – aesthetic connoisseurs. Wharton also associated decadence with homosexuality, which she ungenerously characterized as moral bankruptcy and a vampirish desire of older men for younger ones.[21] Wharton gravitated instead toward the philosophical idealism implicit in art and the classical traditions that had nurtured it. This interest in absolute values led in two directions: toward cultural idealism, such as that espoused by George Santayana, and toward a Platonic idealism, which transcended culture altogether. Both promised relief from the oppressive proscriptions against pleasure without sacrificing absolute standards.

In Wharton's time, George Santayana became an exemplar of aesthetic ideology, believing that although the opportunities for authentic experience had diminished, they were still possible through art. Santayana's ideas were particularly congenial to Wharton, who, although fluctuating between Christian orthodoxy and more rebellious stances, was enough of a conservative to think that spiritual renewal was possible by preserving the best features of Western civilization.[22] Skeptical of skepticism, Santayana worried in his 1900 essay, "The Poetry of Christian Dogma," that abandoning the Christian system of rewards and punishments undermined moral action: "The good souls that wish to fancy that everybody will be ultimately saved, subject a fable to standards appropriate to matters of fact, and thereby deprive the fable of that moral significance which is its excuse for being" (65). A philosophical materialist, Santayana espoused an anti-Calvinist *and* antitranscendentalist idealism, with which Wharton could sympathize. She also appreciated his understanding of the history of philosophy and his theoretical bent, which leaned heavily on the Greeks, especially Plato. Santayana brought together religion, art, and science; he directed attention away from literal religious interpretations that conflicted with science and toward religion that expressed true moral propositions in aesthetically pleasing ways.

In *The Winds of Doctrine* (1913), Santayana articulates the end of an entire civilization. There is a discrepancy, he argues in his famous essay, "The Genteel Tradition," between America grounded in particulars ("the one is all aggressive enterprise") and America absorbed by the abstract ("the other is all genteel tradition"). America was a country with two mentalities. In the realm of higher things of the mind – religion, literature, and morality – its hereditary spirit prevails, but in the practical matters of inventions, industry, and social organization, the new mentality has taken over (188). The term "genteel tradition" refers to this old mentality inherited from Europe, which, by the early twentieth century, people had abandoned in exchange for sheer vitality, movement, and change.

Santayana's and Wharton's perspectives are so similar on this point that one may speculate about which one influenced the other. In novels dating from *The Custom of the Country* (1913) to *The Gods Arrive* (1932), Wharton, like Santayana, criticizes the irresponsibility, contempt for reason, and unjustifiable hilarity that swept modern American culture. Santayana's description of American society in "Materialism and Idealism in American Life" (1920) is remarkably like Wharton's account in *The Custom of the Country* of social climber Undine Spragg and her entrepreneurial accomplice Elmer Moffat, both rootless midwestern arrivals with no regard for eastern traditions. Elmer and Undine are so self-centered and materialistic that the only "custom of the country" they respect is their own. Santayana describes them perfectly:

> Consider now the great emptiness of America: not merely the primitive physical emptiness . . . but also the moral emptiness of a settlement where men and even houses are easily moved about, and no one, almost, lives where he was born or believes what he has been taught. . . . Your detachable condition makes you lavish with money and cheerfully experimental; you lose little if you lose all, since you remain completely yourself. At the same time your absolute initiative gives you practice in coping with novel situations, and in being original; it teaches you shrewd management. . . . You will not understand why anybody should make those little sacrifices to instinct or custom which we call grace. (172–73)

Santayana further argues that turn-of-the-century America is a young society so occupied with practical conditions of life that anything without immediate or apparent usefulness is considered worthless. This new American credo translates into "the more existence the better." The emphasis on quantity is not simply childish greed, but a sincere belief that abundance

truly is a "form of the good" (181–82). This "material moralism" characterizes the American: "for in his dealings with material things he can hardly
stop to enjoy their sensible aspects, which are ideal, nor proceed at once to
their ultimate uses, which are ideal too" (185).

Two years after Santayana's essay appeared in *Character and Opinion in
the United States,* Wharton published her novel *Glimpses of the Moon* (1922),
a study of rich Americans abroad. Her main character, Susy Lansing, a cross
between Lily Bart and Undine Spragg, knows that money is a false god,
but she has difficulty resisting its powers. The "glimpses of the moon" that
Susy and Nick briefly enjoy after marrying are based on their ability to
succeed at something that Santayana observes is alien to the American
character: "to be poor in order to be simple" ("Materialism" 188). Wharton, like Santayana, exalts ideality, which does not so much exclude the
material as allow for a freedom beyond it. Wharton also shares Santayana's
understanding of the link between the aesthetic and the moral. In *The
Sense of Beauty* (1896), Santayana maintains that aesthetic judgments are
expressions of artistic taste and that "to make a judgment is virtually to
establish an ideal" (11). Wharton's attraction to aesthetics includes this
idealizing impulse.

Santayana's idealism was based in material culture. Wharton's aesthetic
impulse also led her toward a philosophical idealism that is immune – at
least theoretically – to such contemporary pressures. A visionary idealist as
well as a social realist, Wharton pursued the possibility of absolute perfection available not only through the blend of creative imagination and
culture but through contemplation alone. Platonic theory, in particular,
afforded her this kind of spiritual uplift. It also provided a way to unite
body and soul with principles of truth, and it offered women an escape
from Western proscriptions about their expression of eros. Platonic allusions appear early in Wharton's fiction, beginning with *Sanctuary* in 1903
and culminating in *The Age of Innocence* in 1920.

Wharton's Hellenism is evident in her admiration for Violet Paget, a
brilliant scholar and art historian who published numerous books and essays
(under the name of Vernon Lee), including the widely renowned *Studies of
the Eighteenth Century in Italy.* The two met in 1894 at Paget's villa in
Maiano, near Florence (Lewis 72), and maintained a lifelong friendship.
Wharton kept several of Paget's books in her library and even helped to
arrange an American speaking tour for her on the subject of aesthetics.[23]
Vernon Lee's 1913 introduction to aesthetics, *The Beautiful,* is based in
Platonic theory. She defines the beautiful not only in terms of pleasure or
satisfaction but as contemplative order, innately passive and distinguished
from a practical or scientific aesthetic. Therein lies its value: "The restor-

ative, the healing quality of aesthetic contemplation is due . . . to the fact that, in the perpetual flux of action and thought, it represents reiteration and therefore stability" (109–10). Lee explains that since Plato, the beautiful has been equated with purification and spirituality: "Such contemplation of beautiful shape lifts our perceptive and empathic activities, that is to say a large part of our intellectual and emotional life, on to a level which can only be spiritually, organically, and in so far, morally beneficial" (151–52). One seeks the aesthetic, she continues, for "spiritual refreshment" (155). Wharton not only read Lee, she immersed herself in Platonic theory, reading the *Republic,* the *Symposium,* and the *Phaedrus.* She found the latter texts, with their emphasis on kinds of love, "overpowering" (Lewis 159).

In her masterpiece, *The Age of Innocence* (1920), discussed in Chapter 5, Wharton considers Platonic idealism, contrasting it to the tradition-bound world of old New York. She develops an aesthetic *and* philosophical ideal of the sort fostered by Pater and rooted in Plato. She had experimented with Platonic ideals as an antidote to the materialism of modern life in *The House of Mirth.* However, Lawrence Selden's "Republic of the Spirit" is a poorly executed – and ironically presented – alternative to the mundane. In *The Age of Innocence,* Wharton associates Platonic ideals with truth, beauty, and love, and inscribes these qualities – without irony – in her heroine, Ellen Olenska. She also employs the Psyche figure, as does Plato, not just as illustration of love's illusions, as many have noted,[24] but as allegory of the progress of the soul guided by love. Ellen Olenska and Newland Archer's forbidden romance represents a conflict between passion and social duty that Wharton often developed in her fiction. But Ellen also serves as a beacon of light for Newland Archer, who is trapped in a closed, petty world. Wharton portrays Ellen as a puritan Hellenist, extraordinary in her combination of art, eros, and integrity, who attempts to lead Archer beyond the confines of narrow conventionality. Ultimately, however, Archer fails to don Psyche's wings, and Ellen cannot realize her true passionate nature. Although Ellen is Wharton's most fully realized heroine, her Puritan self-denial competes with her Platonic idealism, thus undercutting Wharton's vision of ideal love.

Roman Fever

Although Wharton's quarrel with Christianity was at times intense, she never completely broke with her original faith. She continued to seek new systems of belief that could unite the disparate elements of mind, body, and soul, but she came in later years to value the established over the new. By the end of World War I, the country, which had once believed in ethical values and steady progress, had become directionless. Religious fads and psychological trends attempted to fill the gap left by Christianity. Spiritualism, metaphysical science, theosophy, the I A M movement, and New Thought were some expressions of spiritual restlessness in these early decades. Wharton was as wary of these new fads as she was of nineteenth-century creeds of optimism.

New Thought, for example, was a doctrine of loose Christianity that saw itself gathering up the best of all religions. Its central message was the power of positive thinking and the identification of the Divine as immanent within each person. New Thought practitioners convinced themselves that by adopting a proper spirit, one could be free of all negativity, poor health, and bad fortune. Ella Wheeler Wilcox, New Thought's chief proponent, affirmed the New Testament as the true universal religion over the gloomy creed of orthodox Christianity, a "false, unholy and blasphemous 'religion' " which, by believing "that all men are vicious, selfish and immoral is *projecting pernicious mind stuff* into space" (qtd. in Ruether and Keller 39, original emphasis). Wharton ruthlessly criticizes the escapism of New Thought in her novel *Twilight Sleep* (1927). Pauline Manford is a self-centered, spiritual faddist caught up in quick metaphysical fixes. She ignores her family's problems to the point that her daughter Nona nearly dies from her and others' irresponsibility. Even then, Pauline is unrepentant. To counteract her recklessness, Wharton reinstates Calvinism, expressed through Nona, a "little Puritan," who assumes the family burdens and forgoes her own happiness.

In the last decades of her life, Edith Wharton found another answer, not in alternative visions, but in the oldest of all Christian faiths, Catholicism. That she should knock, finally, at the Roman Catholic door should not be surprising. Wharton was raised an Episcopalian, in the Protestant faith that most resembled Catholicism. The choice for the Church of Rome seemed particularly appropriate for her, an upper-class woman who never totally abandoned elite conservativism. While Wharton rejected genteel facades and decried the hypocrisy and collusion among secularized clergy and their wealthy parishioners, she remained a conservative person, drawn to tradition and its rituals. Catholicism, with its claim as the first and true church, seemed a purer form of Christianity. Catholicism also united the upper-class interests in aesthetics with traditional faith. As Lears notes, the Catholic movement at the turn of the century displayed "a Janus face": it both supported a taste for luxury, consumption, and decorative taste and reflected a cultural anxiety about those very developments by focusing on issues of personal moral responsibility (184). The medieval church, in particular, linked art with religion and history. Moreover, its ancient roots in Platonism connected Christianity with classicism, giving an idealizing touch to prosaic modern life; and its reverence for the Virgin Mary revived, at least to some extent, a sense of female power that was lost in the transition from matriarchy to patriarchy. Ever mindful of the split between flesh and spirit, the Catholic Church also eroticized statues and paintings, making manifest the same tension that Wharton herself experienced between passion's expression and prohibition.

Like many other early twentieth-century American intellectuals and writers, such as T. S. Eliot, Henry Adams, and Willa Cather, Wharton was drawn to Catholicism's history, mysticism, and stability. The Catholic Church represented permanence and continuity; when Wharton embraced it, she affirmed a creed that had survived centuries of turmoil. "America is not the country it was in my youth. All this aimless turbulence has . . . wrecked the old idealism," she confided to Elisina Tyler just weeks before she died. The two friends agreed during the same conversation that among religions, "the Catholic Church ranks highest, as a great social force for order, and for its finest ritual, its great traditions, its human understanding" (E. Tyler n.p.). Catholicism provided the cultural stability that World War I had destroyed. And its rituals and assurance of absolution in return for faithful practice granted peace unavailable through more austere forms of Protestantism.

Understanding Edith Wharton's Catholicism in terms of an entire social-cultural-philosophical outlook helps to see her similarity with a contemporary like T. S. Eliot. Like Eliot, Wharton lamented the disintegration of traditional values and the increasing materialism in modern society. Like him, she also turned to earlier periods and forms – in her case, classical, medieval, and neoclassical – to find the stability so lacking in modern life. Both Wharton and Eliot placed their faith in a Christian scheme at a time when it was unfashionable to do so. Both writers believed that the artist needed to be in contact with the living record of creative achievements of the past. Themes that Charles Berryman notes characterize Eliot's writing in the thirties – "the importance of tradition and the primacy of the supernatural" (189) – also apply to Wharton's novels of the twenties and thirties and to her collection of ghost fiction, compiled in 1937. In Wharton's case, however, tradition is not always distinguishable from convention; social concerns therefore seem to eclipse religious and philosophical ones. Wharton is also less overtly theoretical than Eliot, and her opinions, appearing in her later, less polished novels, reached a narrower audience. Yet, as Lewis notes in his biography, "maturity and the religious sensibility were becoming related in her mind" (510); these interests were similar to Eliot's. Although Wharton did not unequivocally reject the humanist tradition of individualism, she did abhor its legacy of crass, money-hungry ambition, and she wished to preserve the social moral fiber in the midst of deteriorating standards. For Wharton, Christianity – and Catholicism, in particular – provided a base from which one gained comfort for the "dark night of the soul."

Wharton did not convert or actively practice her faith,[25] although she spoke with increasing assurance of the presence of God and an afterlife, and of the importance of the contemplative life over the material one. Her godson, William Royall Tyler, recently found her 1898 edition of *The Imitation of Christ,* a fifteenth-century religious treatise that, except for the Bible, is said to have had more influence on Christianity than any other book. In it, Wharton marked numerous passages, recording her interest in the argument that God's work of salvation is a mystery that cannot be explained or defined, and that individual faith is strengthened through the example of Christ and participation in church liturgy, especially the Lord's Supper (Letter). Paradoxically, then, Wharton – who had always prided herself on rationality – valued religion at the end of her life because it embraced mystery. "It is not difficult to believe," Wharton affirmed, "and easiest to believe when inside a Church with its atmosphere, its glamour, its associations; easy enough then to fall into the spiritual attitude of belief – but not to try to explain or justify belief" (E. Tyler n.p.).

Catholicism was in many respects a logical culmination of Wharton's lifelong spiritual search, contrasting positively with her earlier quarrels with Protestantism and bringing full circle connections she found between Greek and Christian theology and philosophy and between art and ideals. But if this faith fulfilled Wharton's need for a creed that would order and celebrate life's mysteries, it also left a gap. The church demanded loyalty, a quality that Wharton honored in her associations, religious and otherwise, but which required her to compromise some of her deepest feminist principles. Wharton's Catholicism represented, at best, an uneasy alliance between mutually exclusive spiritual and feminist longings. In the end, Catholicism was no more the *right* faith for Wharton than any other, but it is fitting that she embraced it in her final years because it embodied so many of the tensions with which she had struggled throughout her life.

No doubt, Wharton, wishing not to denigrate but to validate the feminine, chose Catholicism as an appropriate venue. Whereas both Protestantism and Catholicism reinforced the social inferiority of women, Catholicism alone taught women's spiritual and moral superiority through its veneration of the Virgin. Wharton had been actively engaged in recuperating the feminine principle in much of her work, exploring matriarchies, Greek goddesses, and primordial maternal forces such as those found in

Goethe's *Faust*. These interests are evident in her last two completed novels, *Hudson River Bracketed* (1929) and *The Gods Arrive* (1932), which are discussed in Chapter 6, "Catholicism: Fulfillment or Concession?" The novels may be read both as *künstlerromane* and as veiled endorsements of Catholic traditions, rituals, and mysticism.

Vance Weston, a talented but restless young writer, sets out to build a career and found a new religion. After many missteps, he discovers the words of Augustine, which inspire him to return to the woman he loves and begin his life and work anew. This early church father and the tradition he represents offer Vance a blueprint for a productive, meaningful life. Wharton ends *The Gods Arrive* with Vance in the role of paterfamilias, ready to begin a successful career. For Halo Tarrant, however, the story is somewhat different. She must sacrifice her own intellectual and artistic ambitions in order to serve Vance's. Vance never loses sight of his "irreducible core of selfness" (*Hudson* 272) and pursues his quest with Halo's loyal support, even when he neglects her. While Wharton treats Vance with gentle satire, exposing his impulsivity and naiveté, she seems to take his quest seriously. She seems similarly sincere in her depiction of Halo, who is more a self-sacrificing wife or mother than a primordial goddess. When at the end of the novel, Vance returns to Halo's open arms, their relationship is a committed but unequal one. Although their tone is mixed, these novels embrace conservative, patriarchal ideas about women that in earlier fiction Wharton challenged or rejected.

Life Wonderer

Edith Wharton is both a product of her time and an exception to it. Because she was a private person – Marilyn Lyde speculates that religion "lay too close to her heart for casual discussion" (53) – it is difficult to assess precisely the intensity and direction of her faith. However, a certain pattern does emerge when Wharton's biography and writing are considered together. Like many late Victorians, Wharton wrestled with spiritual meaning in the context of scientific rationalism. These secular interests in science, as well as art, history, and anthropology, may easily be construed as signs of unbelief rather than as efforts to establish belief. However, although tensions and even paradoxes characterize Wharton's spiritual quest, to confuse religious and spiritual uncertainty with a lack of interest or commitment is seriously to misinterpret her life and fiction.

Wharton began as an elite Episcopalian but answered the call of native Calvinism. This is not to suggest that she was an evangelical. She was skeptical of the extreme emotions generated by revivalists and freely expressed disdain for them – in a letter to Morton Fullerton, for example, she explains that she encouraged a young man to abandon his book entitled "New Revelation" "because I told him it sounded like a Drummond title," and to write one instead "on the origin of life" (*Letters* 147–48).[26] Nevertheless, Wharton's Calvinism arose more from temperament than from choice. She was drawn to this austere creed to counter contemporary frivolity and irresponsibility. She also developed a personal affinity for the faith. However, Calvinism, a doctrine that held the believer in extreme states of hope or despair over the possibility of salvation, created parallel states of ambivalence in Wharton. While she welcomed its robust moral codes, she struggled against what she saw as its rigid proscriptions against human pleasure and creativity – especially women's.

Like many of her contemporaries facing science's challenge to religion, Wharton sought alternative sources of spiritual comfort in art, history, and philosophy. She was fascinated by discoveries that placed the primitive, classical, and Christian roots of Western culture in a comparative light. She looked for new as well as established foundations for faith in ancient goddesses, Greek myths, and medieval cathedrals. She also explored aesthetic and philosophical escapes from time altogether. Transcendental philosophies, as Fred Kaplan suggests, may be seen as equivalents to an obsolete cult of sentimentality: both defend "the vision of the ideal against the claim that the universe and human history are governed by mechanical, or rational, or deterministic, or pragmatic forces" (6). Wharton's Platonic idealism may thus be viewed as an antidote to sentimentality, which she found limiting.

Wharton also dared to explore religious and philosophical traditions from the perspective of a woman who was frequently excluded or restricted by those traditions. Although she was not explicitly feminist or revisionary in her treatment of Western religion, philosophy, and ethics, she was a "resisting reader." to borrow Judith Fetterley's term for a woman who needs to read against herself or adopt a male point of view from within patriarchy (*Resisting* xx). Wharton not only expresses dissatisfaction with existing structures; she poses alternatives, even if they appear unattainable.

Edith Wharton spent a lifetime exploring and questioning. From her early days of sermon reading in her father's and rector's libraries to her final days celebrating the Feast of the Virgin at St. Brice, she was in the best sense of the word, a religious, spiritual, and philosophical experimenter. Lyde suggests that Wharton's critical sensibility precluded her from accepting any one creed on the basis of faith alone (50); Wharton herself admitted that she was not one of "the happy few who have found a way of harmonizing the dissecting intellect with the accepting soul" (*Backward*

159). She embraced science and technology, but she never believed that science held all the answers to human mysteries. Unlike many Victorians, she foresaw neither smooth progress nor apocalyptic reform. Instead, she persisted in raising difficult moral and spiritual questions in an upper-class society that considered such inquiries a breach of good taste, and she sought to affirm individual moral responsibility amid widespread complacency.

Below Wharton's incisive, realistic descriptions and superb irony, then, we find a reflective spirit, an old-fashioned moralism, and an insistent idealism. Although her protagonists are grounded in social reality, they sometimes hazard a gaze upward at some transcendental value that will affirm rather than annihilate their sense of self. The fact that these characters fail to recognize or achieve their ideals in no way lessens the strength of their effort. "The world is a welter and has always been one," Wharton wrote in her memoir; "yet there are always . . . a thousand little daily wonders to marvel at and rejoice in" (*Backward* 379). Throughout her life, Wharton questioned religious and philosophical forms and ideas, struggled against an encroaching modernist sense of spiritual futility, and aspired to free herself and her characters from cultural restrictions of gender and class. As the following chapters explain, she sought to understand individuals, not just in relation to society, but in relation to themselves and their universe.

1

Priestess of Reason

I was a failure in Boston . . . because they thought I was too fashionable to be intelligent, and a failure in New York because they were
afraid I was too intelligent to be fashionable.

Edith Wharton, *A Backward Glance*

D ISCOVERIES in science, which played key roles in the late
Victorian struggle with faith, are crucial to understanding Edith Wharton's
religious choices. Especially important is her effort to develop her intelligence and claim a role for herself, as female, in the world of ideas and art.
Wharton's intellectualism, impressive by any measure, was astounding for a
nineteenth-century woman with no formal education. Wharton placed
great importance on learning and strove to develop her innate intelligence
through reading, writing, and conversation. Her keen rationality helped to
unlock doors to philosophy, theology, and metaphysics, thus deepening the
possibilities for her spiritual inquiry. At the same time, her intelligence also
competed at various points in her life with her ability to suspend judgment
and accept on the basis of faith alone.

Especially early in her life, Wharton resisted religious teachings because
they omitted the important faculty of reason. As the philosopher Vivaldi
explains in the novel *The Valley of Decision* (1902): "against reason the fabric
of theological doctrine cannot long hold out. . . . We have not joined the
great army of truth to waste our time in vain disputations over metaphysical
subtleties" (1: 154). Wharton's spiritual longings are usually guided by
rational inquiry, and – in some cases – by a desire to solve metaphysical and
supernatural questions through the exercise of mental muscle. " 'Origins' of

all sorts fascinate my imagination," she wrote to Bernard Berenson in 1910, alluding both to Genesis and Darwin (*Letters* 209). Because Wharton's intellectual development was inseparable from her spiritual development, it is useful to begin by considering the efforts she made to distinguish herself from the traditional, nineteenth-century stereotype of the feeling rather than thinking woman.

If reason is important to the development of Wharton's religious and spiritual outlook, so is the role of male influence in shaping that outlook. Expanding rational faculties meant breaking nineteenth-century codes of femininity that confined women to intuition and feeling. As Barbara Welter explains, women's very distance from reason became the measure of their femininity (78).[1] Because their natural, childlike state and simple piety would be compromised if taxed by mental labors, women were taught to refrain from critical speculation or analysis. They were barred from the institutions of learning where ideas are handed down from master to disciple, considered less female if they risked transgression into male territories, and expected to acknowledge male mentors if they did succeed – in a spirit of cooperation rather than competition. The so-called hard disciplines of theology, philosophy, and ethics remained the province of men; women were associated with passive or submissive piety. Many women who have become philosophers – for example, Héloïse or de Beauvoir – have done so through their love of a man, as Michèle Le Doeuff notes in her discussion of women and philosophy. Such an "erotico-theoretical transference" occurs because "it is only through the mediation of a man that women could gain access to theoretical discourse" (185). To some extent, the realm of art afforded women greater latitude – it was no coincidence that Wharton launched her career with books on interior design and landscape architecture[2] – but in general, women were associated with decorative arts while the fields of art history and philosophy remained a male domain. From the eighteenth century on, references to women's incapacity for theory proliferated, reaching full force in the nineteenth century – a reaction perhaps to the increased threat that progressive women seemed to pose. Hegel sums up the prevalent view in Wharton's time: "Women have culture, ideas, taste, and elegance but they cannot attain to the ideal" (qtd. in Le Doeuff 184).

Wharton's relationship to Victorian intellectual culture is thus complex – even somewhat paradoxical. As the epigraph suggests, she sought an intellectual and spiritual home somewhere between the world of fashion and the realm of ideas. Wharton was ahead of her time; at the turn of the century, women could only imagine such a place.

The Strain of Looking Up

Like many nineteenth-century girls, Edith Wharton never attended school. Her brothers, considerably older, were educated at home; the young Edith eavesdropped on the library steps, picking up what she could. However, Wharton's relatively poor education fails to account for her tremendous intellectual capacity and drive – just as her genteel background fails to explain her serious interests in religion. Indeed, Wharton's ambitions were so anomalous that a rumor circulated that she was the daughter not of George Jones, but of her brothers' tutor (Lewis 535–39). Wharton's parents, not totally remiss, did instill in her the importance of good English. Other learning came from governesses, family trips abroad, and reading. Travel expanded her horizons and perhaps for that reason figured prominently throughout her life and writing. Stays in Europe, including one lengthy one, contributed to Wharton's knowledge of history and art, and helped her to develop proficiency in French and German and familiarity with Italian, Greek, and Latin.

Wharton always possessed an insatiable appetite for books, but her childhood love of reading and writing alienated her from her mother, who, "herself so little of a reader," invoked the same reading rules that had applied in her own childhood, prohibiting *any* novel reading without parental permission (*Backward* 51, 65). Wharton's passion for literature drew her closer to her father, who, although he boasted few intellectual accomplishments, possessed enough poetic capacity to inspire and encourage her. His reading of sermons and travel literature also served as a model ("Life" 1083). In *A Backward Glance,* Wharton describes the pleasure of her father's library, that inner sanctum where she spent hours in "a secret ecstasy of communion" (69). The library contained seven or eight hundred "well-chosen" volumes of the sort found in affluent Victorian households: English, French, and German classics, as well as history, letters, journals, criticism, and philosophy (64–69). Although Wharton's father guided her early reading, she soon surpassed him, reading widely and deeply in a broad range of subjects that included not just literature and art, but science, philosophy, religion, and religious history. Her father died in 1882, before Wharton had time to establish herself as a writer. Her mother, true to her word, never acknowledged her daughter's literary achievements, and Wharton grew so distant from her that she did not even attend her funeral. Indeed, no relative save a cousin ever spoke to her about her writing.

Wharton experienced a division of loyalties common to gifted young women – a conflict between their so-called feminine and masculine halves. Margaret Fuller, the nineteenth-century female American writer whom

Wharton perhaps most resembles intellectually, wrestled with the same painful split. Fuller writes, for example, of her father's active role and her mother's passive one in her educational process, and she articulates in *Woman in the Nineteenth Century* the great dualism that is a woman's fate in American culture. Wharton demonstrates this same dualism when she writes in an autobiographical fragment "Life and I" that there were "two deep-seated instincts of my nature – the desire to love & to look pretty" (1071) – and then excitedly describes learning philosophy as the act that will save her from traditional femininity: "Now I was going to know all about life! Now I should never be that helpless blundering thing, a mere 'little girl,' again!" (1086). "Life and I" also describes a young woman living in "complete mental isolation" (1077), desperate for stimulation.[3] One need not search out unpublished documents for evidence of Wharton's struggle. In *A Backward Glance,* she considers whether there were any benefits to growing up "where the arts are simply nonexistent." She concludes, with a mixture of modesty and Puritan-like fortitude, that the answer is yes: she "escaped all premature flattery"; developed the ability to accept criticism without undue sensitivity (since her craft had been "held in such small account"); and learned to value kindred spirits all the more (121–22). These kindred spirits were slow to come, however; Wharton was nearly forty years old before she established a circle of friends whose interests in art and ideas matched her own.

Wharton continued to read voraciously as an adolescent, inspired by another male model, her parish rector, in whose library she and Dr. Washburn's daughter Emelyn spent many joyful hours. The habit of reading extended unabated into adulthood, as hundreds of references to books in Wharton's letters suggest. It was at this time that she read books on moral, philosophical, and religious subjects, acquiring tastes that would last her entire life. Kenneth Clark, to whom Wharton bequeathed her library, observed that she had more books on religious subjects than on any other (Lewis 510).[4] Reading about religion does not necessarily make one religious or spiritual; in Wharton's case, however, the intellectual and spiritual inquiries dovetail. In Wharton's driving need to penetrate the surface of life, science and philosophy often showed the way; at other times aesthetics took the lead; but always spiritual and metaphysical issues were paramount.

In addition to her father and rector, Wharton associates Egerton Winthrop, a friend of her family, with early, positive memories of learning. He acquainted her with important male thinkers and texts.[5] Wharton describes the thrill of gaining access to scientific knowledge, which by 1932, when she penned her autobiography, most could take for granted: it is "hopeless to convey to a younger generation the first overwhelming sense of cosmic vastness which such 'magic casements' let into our little geocentric universe" (*Backward* 94). In time, men such as Walter Berry – who provided "a fleeting hint of what the communion of kindred intelligences might be" (*Backward* 107) – Paul Bourget, Henry James, and Bernard Berenson also expanded Wharton's world.

Bohemians and Other Aberrations

Even after she became well known as a writer, society persisted in thinking of Edith Wharton's accomplishments as aberrant and embarrassing. In *A Backward Glance,* she reflects that she probably seemed to her small circle "more formidable and less 'smart' than before [she] . . . had appeared in print." She also tells a story about a fashionable hostess who apologized to friends for having invited "Bohemians" to her dinner party. Wharton, one of the invited guests, arrived to find that she and two other writers were these designated Bohemians (*Backward* 120). Wharton sums up the pleasure-seeking, anti-intellectual members of her society in her story "Souls Belated" (1899): "they had unlimited leisure and an accumulation of mental energy to devote to any subject," but "new topics were in fact at a premium" (*Stories* 1: 105).

Unfortunately, Wharton was similarly misunderstood and underrated by critics. Before feminist scholars focused attention on her issues of female authorship – exploring expressions of this anxiety in Wharton's narrative structures, images, and themes[6] – critics treated Wharton little better than society had. Unable to reconcile her femaleness and creativity, they undermined her work even while ostensibly praising it. Edmund Wilson, for example, in an essay ironically titled "Justice to Edith Wharton," describes her writing as "the desperate product of a pressure of maladjustments" and claims her best period – a full fifteen years from 1905 to 1920! – was brief because it was fueled by "emotional strain" rather than true intellectual drive (20, 27).[7] Even Henry James, that most perfect of friends, spoke of Wharton as being "almost too insistently Olympian" – that is, too self-consciously intellectual (qtd. in Edel 658).

Wharton's first biographer, Percy Lubbock, inflicted the most damage and set a critical tone by describing her as an insatiable mental predator:

> Like a hungry young hawk, her mind was somehow to be fed; and she clutched at any sustenance within reach, wherever it appeared, tearing her way through it all with the passion to know, to see, to judge, which was her particular and private possession, never to be

quenched or satisfied. An odd young thing, so rightly elegant, so acceptably attractive, so properly gay – and such a sharp beak of intelligence within. (12)

Lubbock has difficulty reconciling Wharton's thirst for learning with her traditionally feminine charms: her intellectual curiosity and "elegance" are therefore "odd" to him. Elsewhere in his book, he implies that Wharton was unable to discuss philosophy or metaphysics: "the lively leap of her mind stopped dead when she was asked to think, I don't say only about the meaning and the ends of life, but almost about any theoretic enquiry" (44). It does not occur to him that Wharton had views about these issues but simply preferred to remain silent about them. Lubbock also discusses Wharton in relation to James and other male intellectuals and artists, as if her accomplishments can only be explained by her proximity to a male intellect. When he does admit her intelligence, he describes it as masculine and insists that she liked the company of men because "she had a very feminine consciousness and a very masculine mind. . . . She liked to be talked to as a man" (54). Lubbock also circulated the rumor – which he declared "true and just" – that Wharton enjoyed being thought of as "a self-made man" (11).

Although she did not complain loudly, Wharton accepted and felt victimized by these late nineteenth-century and early twentieth-century judgments. She described herself as "a persistent prowler among books" (*Letters* 63), who studied and mastered sociology, science, history, philosophy, religion, and art. The very term Wharton chose – "prowler" – implies that she thought of herself as a thief, furtively robbing what properly belonged to men. An ambivalence toward literary achievement, which elsewhere Susan Elizabeth Sweeney and I have identified as "anxious power," prevented her from beginning a literary career until her thirties. Even then, she sent her first poems to publishers with her visiting card attached (*Backward* 109). Early letters repeatedly document Wharton's typically feminine misgivings about her literary ability. "I am not a good judge of what I write," she told her publisher Edward Burlingame in 1894. After he rejected a story that appeared six years later in *Youth's Companion,* Wharton begged for his advice, explaining, "I seem to have fallen into a period of groping. . . . I am very ambitious to do better. . . . I have lost confidence in myself at present." When Burlingame replied, Wharton thanked him for "giving so much time & thought to so trifling a subject" (*Letters* 31–33). She describes her amazement when editors actually began to seek her stories: "*I* had written short stories that were thought worthy of preservation! Was it the same insignificant *I* that I had always known?"

And she writes that she read early reviews with feelings "of mingled guilt and self-satisfaction" (*Backward* 113, original emphases). The sense of being out of place and of needing to conceal or apologize for the transgression of reading and writing is clearly evident in Wharton's notoriously circumspect autobiography. In *A Backward Glance,* she discusses writing in such oblique ways that her achievements appear to spring not from intelligence or creative effort, but from a complex network of social alliances. Barely a quarter of the memoir's 365 pages discuss Wharton's life as a writer; three-quarters comment instead on dinners, family friends, and social events of all sorts – including her coming-out party, arranged by her parents as a way to dissuade her from writing. Thus, *A Backward Glance* camouflages the pain of female authorship with charming reminiscences. As Carolyn Heilbrun notes about women's autobiography, "nostalgia has for so many years imprisoned women. . . . Nostalgia, particularly for child-hood, is likely to be a mask for unrecognized anger" (15). In Lacanian terms, Wharton had transgressed into the domain of the father to appro-priate the phallic word. In religious terms – her own – she yielded to temptation that leads to the "sin" of authorship. As she describes her "fall" into literature: "the call came regularly and imperiously; and though . . . I would struggle against it conscientiously . . . the struggle was always a losing one" (*Backward* 35). Wharton's use of religious language in her autobiography underlines her attempts at penance and expiation for the sin of writing at all.

Wharton's early fiction also demonstrates her awareness of barriers to women's intellectual growth. In *The Touchstone* (1900) – written when she was struggling to transform herself from aristocratic lady to serious writer – she notes the threat that intelligent women pose to men: "If man is at times indirectly flattered by the moral superiority of woman, her mental ascendancy is extenuated by no such oblique tribute to his powers. The attitude of looking up is a strain on the muscles" (54). Her well-known quip from this novel – "genius is of small use to the woman who does not know how to do her hair" (55) – expresses the dilemma of being both fashionable and intelligent.

The ambivalence resulting from the impossibility of pleasing both herself and her New York world is clearly discernible in "The Mission of Jane" (1902), an autobiographical story in which an upper-class couple adopts a child late in life – an allusion to the rumor that Wharton was the offspring of the tutor, not George Jones. Jane's parents, like Wharton's, are non-plussed by their daughter's precocious intelligence, and her mother is frustrated when Jane's erudition leads to her failure as a debutante. Express-ing misgivings about her own intellectual gifts, Wharton satirizes Jane as well as her mother, by creating a young girl with a head full of information but no true understanding: Jane "seemed extraordinarily intelligent," but her "ideas did not increase with her acquisitions. Her young mind remained a mere receptacle for facts: a kind of cold storage from which anything . . . could be taken out at a moment's notice, intact but congealed" (*Stories* 1: 372). Jane is Wharton as she knew herself: precocious but undirected, eager but insecure.[8]

Jane eventually attracts a pompous but doting husband – a character unmistakably like Teddy Wharton – and marries after obligatory displays of hysteria and reluctance. Relieved to have her safely off their hands, her parents resume their superficial social life. Wharton's story of young female intelligence unfortunately but predictably collapses into sentimentality, with Jane married and ostensibly subdued. At this point in her career, Wharton could envision no alternative. She figures Jane – and by association her own intelligence – as an unfathomable mystery or quirk. At no time does the reader learn what Jane thinks or feels; we see her only as an object of others' bemusement, an inexplicable aberration.

In other stories Wharton manages the question of intellectual and literary ambition either through satire, such as that found in "The Mission of Jane," or through the projection of female authorship onto a male character. When describing men, Wharton was better able to talk about ideas. "My best beloved companions had been books," Wharton confides in *A Backward Glance* (91), but her fiction often demonstrates this seductive power of learning in characters most unlike herself. In "The Descent of Man" (1904), when Professor Linyard, one of Wharton's few favorably drawn academics, encounters an idea, it is as if "an invisible traveler had in fact accompanied him, and if his heart beat high it was simply at the pitch of his adventure: for the Professor had eloped with an idea. . . . Professor Linyard would not have changed places with any hero of romance pledged to a flesh-and-blood abduction" (1: 347). In this story, ideas hold power and acquire the charm of friends – and even of lovers. Wharton also describes ideas in terms of Platonic idealism, as the true reality rather than its approximation. The realm of thought is an "enchanted region which, to those who have lingered there, comes to have so much more color and substance than the painted curtain hanging before it." Ideas are seen as creating the world and its meaning; Wharton writes approvingly of the professor as "one of the great army of weavers at work among the threads of that cosmic woof" (1: 348, 349).

The fact that Linyard in "The Descent of Man," like most artists in Wharton's fiction, is male demonstrates how difficult it was for Wharton – a nineteenth-century woman – to conceive of sustained female achievement outside the home. Wharton brilliantly exposes the cultural contradiction between womanhood and critical intelligence in her 1898 story "The Pelican," a satire which, as Amy Kaplan notes, sounds "a death knell for the domestic tradition" (72), and yet also expresses Wharton's hope that there might be room for bright, cultivated, talented women in modern culture. Mrs. Amyot begins lecturing on evolution in order to support herself and her young son. People attend in droves, the narrator tells us, mostly because she is a widowed mother and they feel sorry for her. In keeping with sentimental standards of feminine modesty and piety, Mrs. Amyot apologizes for taking on masculine, rational, and controversial subjects like science: "the growing demand for evolution was what most troubled her. Her grandfather had been a pillar of the Presbyterian ministry, and the idea of her lecturing on Darwin or Herbert Spencer was deeply shocking to her mother and aunts" (*Stories* 1: 95). The reader feels amused condescension for Mrs. Amyot when it is disclosed that she is still lecturing – and still using her son as an excuse – well after the boy has grown up.

But closer reading reveals that it is the male narrator who creates the impression that Mrs. Amyot is foolish – an impression that is based on the narrator's outmoded sentimental bias: "I don't think nature had meant her to be 'intellectual,' but what can a poor thing do, whose husband has died of drink when her baby is hardly six months old." The male narrator repeatedly comments on Mrs. Amyot's appearance – "she was very pretty" (1: 88) – and criticizes her lack of humor, Wharton's clues that he judges her more as an ornament than as a thinking human being. The only way of stopping her lectures, he suggests, is for someone to marry her.

In fact, Mrs. Amyot is a self-supporting woman whom the narrator neither understands nor respects. She not only earns her own way, she works with ideas, a male domain – but because of cultural restrictions, she finds it impossible to acknowledge her ambition and creativity openly. She is therefore forced into acting the part of the intellectual, even though, Wharton carefully tells us, the stance is not entirely feigned. Mrs. Amyot comes from a line of intelligent women: a celebrated poet-mother, an aunt who was dean of a "girls' college," and another aunt who translated Euripides (1: 88). The narrator, however, discounts all of these accomplishments as well as Mrs. Amyot's knowledge of diverse subjects such as Greek language and art, Shakespeare, Gothic architecture, and Schopenhauer. Wharton's sympathy with her character is apparent in her title, an allusion to Psalms 102, which is a cry of the afflicted: "I am like a pelican of the wilderness": "mine enemies reproach me all the day; and they that are mad against me are sworn against me" (6, 8).

"Radiant Reasonableness"

Over time, Edith Wharton became more assertive. She identified the 1899 publication of her collection of short stories *The Greater Inclination* as the event that "broke the chains which had held [her] so long in a kind of torpor." She stopped trying so hard to "adjust" to her married life with Teddy and instead sought out those who shared her interests. Again, male figures are prevalent. Two unnamed friends – presumably male – helped broaden her interests, although she adds that one of them could not understand her "longing to break away from the world of fashion and be with [her] own spiritual kin." She also names Paul Bourget as "one of the most stimulating and cultivated intelligences" she ever met and recalls his advice to give up her "life of wearisome frivolity" and enjoy the company of other creators and thinkers (*Backward* 122–23). One can only guess what Bourget finally thought of this ambitious, intelligent woman, but some early impressions are recorded in his 1893 book on the United States, *Outre-Mer*. His description is uncannily like Wharton's 1902 portrait of the protagonist in "The Mission of Jane"; his backhanded compliment may even have influenced her story:

> [She] has read everything, understood everything, not superficially, but really, with an energy of culture that could put to shame the whole Parisian fraternity of letters. . . . There is not a book of Darwin, Huxley, Spencer, Renan, Taine, which she has not studied, not a painter or sculptor of whose works she could not compile a catalogue, not a school of poetry or romance of which she does not know the principles. . . . Only she does not distinguish between them. She has not an idea that is not exact, yet she gives you a strange impression as if she had none. One would say that she has ordered her intellect somewhere, as we would order a piece of furniture, to measure, and with as many compartments as there are branches of human knowledge. She acquires them only that she may put them into these drawers. (qtd. in Auchincloss, *Woman* 53–55)

Wharton took Bourget's advice to spend more time in London, but her husband, bored whenever he was away from the sporting set, pressured her to curtail her visits. The couple struck a compromise when they decided to build a home in Lenox, Massachusetts, where Wharton spent six months of each year, from 1904–1911. Far removed from "watering-place trivialities" of Newport, the Mount gave Wharton her first real freedom to think and write (*Backward* 124). The marriage, however, was never satisfactory; Teddy could not understand his wife's love of learning and literature. When, well into their marriage, he criticized her for reading R. H. Lock's *Heredity and*

Variation by asking, "Does that sort of thing really amuse you?" Wharton cried out in exasperation, "Oh, Gods of derision! And you've given me twenty years of it! *Je n'en peux plus* [I've had enough]" (Lewis 228–29).

Until she built the Mount, Wharton walked a fine line between pleasing others and herself. She knew that she had to forge an identity of her own, but she lacked confidence to set her own intellectual or artistic course, and she was reluctant to blame masculine structures for her difficulties. For example, in her autobiography, she writes that early in life she found it easy to adapt herself to others for the simple reason that her "powers of enjoyment . . . [were] so varied." Wharton became convinced of her literary abilities only when popular and critical acclaim left no doubt of them: "It was only some years later, when I had written several books, that I finally rebelled, and pleaded for the right to something better," she writes in *A Backward Glance* (124). Even as late as 1912, however, after the warm reception of novels like *The House of Mirth* and *Ethan Frome,* Wharton still referred to herself as a "half-talent," lamenting that "if only my work were better it would be all I need" (*Letters* 285).

It is not surprising, given the pressures she faced, that when Wharton did achieve success, she permitted – even cultivated – an image of herself as a cold rationalist, perhaps to avoid giving the opposite impression of sentimentality. A certain coldness also appears in her characters: Lily Bart, for example, feels more deeply than anyone in *The House of Mirth* yet seems aloof. And Anna Leath in *The Reef* lacks a sensual expression that comes naturally to her rivals Kitty Mayne and Sophy Viner. Wharton realized that a creative woman who revealed the heart or exposed the soul risked being labeled "feminine" and therefore less serious. She thus erected a barrier – a cool, detached exterior that masked great feeling and drew attention away from her more visionary side. She also sometimes projected an air of imperiousness with publishers and associates, another overcompensation for being both assertive and female. Only close friends – a select society (like those chosen with great care by the speaker in Emily Dickinson's poem "The Soul selects her own Society") – glimpsed Wharton's true nature. This reserve was so refined that critics sometimes mistake it for Wharton's actual nature, and even Wharton seems surprised when her reason gives way to feeling. Writing to Margaret Chanler in 1925 about the disappointing critical response to *The Mother's Recompense* (1925), for example, she reflects, "you will wonder that the priestess of the Life of Reason shd take such things to heart; & I wonder too" (*Letters* 483).

In another letter – to her lover, Morton Fullerton – however, Wharton reveals her sensitivity to the intuitive *and* the rational. Both, she insists, must work harmoniously together. She credits Fullerton with " 'radiant reasonableness,' " a quality she also possesses: "you & I . . . are almost the only people I know who feel the 'natural magic,' au-delà, dream-side of things, & yet need the netteté, the line – in thinking, in conduct – yes! in feeling too!" She then defends reason as an essential rather than extraneous aspect of love and life: "I've always felt about that poor dear maligned Goddess of Reason as somebody in Comus does about Philosophy –" (*Letters* 151). This comment suggests not only that Wharton identified with reason but understood that, as a female figure, it is easily maligned. She hints that as the self-declared priestess of reason, she herself felt maligned.

Wharton worked throughout her life to maintain a balance between reason and emotion, intuition and empiricism, although at various times, one or the other predominated. In the years when she struggled to gain a foothold in the public realm of literature, reason was dominant, and she tended to criticize what could not be cognitively verified. In the early story "The Angel at the Grave" (1901), for example, she takes a dim view of nineteenth-century transcendentalism as compared with Darwinian science, and satirizes both the current pseudointellectualism and the nineteenth-century tradition of feminine service of masculine genius.

The story focuses on Pauline Anson, who devotes her life to preserving the memory of her deceased grandfather, Orestes Anson, a famous transcendentalist who unmistakably suggests Emerson. Wharton satirizes transcendentalism by referring to the nineteenth century as a time when "people were apt to base their literary judgments on their emotions, and when to affect plain food and despise England went a long way toward establishing a man's intellectual pre-eminence" (*Stories* 1: 246). Privileging feeling over reason, transcendentalism offers fuzzy subjectivity: Anson's "sonorous periods, his mystic vocabulary, his bold flights into the rarified air of the abstract, were thrilling to a fancy unhampered by the need of definitions" (1: 248). In this story, Wharton is decidedly unimpressed with what she calls "the cloudy heights of metaphysic," where "respiration was difficult" (1: 246). A year later, in 1902, she registered a similar objection in a letter to Sara Norton after reading Schopenhauer's *The World as Will and Idea:* "how strange it is rummaging in all that old metaphysical lumber! – As for the saintfood, I prefer it as I find it in Pascal & St Francis de Sales –" (*Letters* 56).[9] And yet, as both the story and comment on Schopenhauer suggest, Wharton manages to mock transcendental metaphysics while retaining the notion of ideality. In "The Angel at the Grave," Pauline Anson does well to serve a purpose larger than herself. Much later, the Catholic faith would offer Wharton a similar opportunity for reaching beyond one's own boundaries.

However, Pauline is disappointed to find the house and the papers she curates overrun by intellectual tourists and trendsetters – "historians who were 'getting up' the period [and] . . . ladies . . . beg[ging] for an interpretation of phrases which had 'influenced' them, but which they had not quite understood" (1: 248). Wharton satirizes an indiscriminate public, people who praise Anson more for what he might have eaten for breakfast than for what he said in his books, which they do not read. The great man's reputation passes "from the heights in which he had been grouped with the sages of his day to the lower level where he had come to be merely 'the friend of Emerson'; 'the correspondent of Hawthorne' " (1: 252). Pauline despairs of ever accomplishing a higher good, but her faithful worship at Anson's grave is rewarded when one day a visitor discovers that Anson has made a monumental contribution – not to transcendentalism but to the theory of evolution, which Wharton presents here as a superior alternative. Pauline's years of caretaking have not been in vain, although the ideas she thought she was defending are trivial. With this ending, Wharton hammers a nail in the coffin of transcendentalism, arguing that the search for higher truth only through science or reason is immortal. She only partially redeems female self-sacrifice, however; Anson's work was worth preserving, but it takes a male scholar to recognize the genius that Pauline mindlessly served.

"The Angel at the Grave" reflects Wharton's rationalism at its peak; the story also helps to explain her lukewarm response at this time to William James's pragmatism, which was influenced by Emerson's philosophy of intuition and was considered by some to be irrational, overly personal, and unnecessarily mysterious (May 7). James subordinated faith by showing that every belief system derives from the inner or personal rather than from the supernatural. He gave sentiment, or feeling, as well as reason and experience a decisive role in forming metaphysical and religious beliefs in *Principles of Psychology* (1890) and *The Will to Believe* (1897). By 1919, in *A Pluralistic Universe,* he defended a form of anti-intellectualism very close to that of Bergson and philosophical romanticism. Not unlike Edwards or Emerson, James posited that one *might* accept, on the basis of faith, a proposition for which there is no support of reason or experience. His theory, although not completely unattractive, struck Wharton as dangerously vague and imprecise. In 1906, she accused him of "psychological-pietistical juggling" (*Letters* 101–2).

Awakeners

Considering the priority that Wharton placed on rational faculties, it is not surprising that she noted as significant in her development figures who are closely associated with logic. She credits four men as having "ranked foremost among my Awakeners": Henry Coppée, William Hamilton, Blaise Pascal, and Charles Darwin (*Backward* 71–72). The first two were most likely found in textbooks used by Wharton's brothers (Lyde 28n.); the others would have appeared on her father's library shelves. Wharton read their difficult books before the age of seventeen. They made such an impression on her that she cites them years later as the foundation for the development of her mental faculties. Wharton's four "Awakeners" suggest, as Marilyn Lyde notes, "a mind at once strongly rational and objective, yet tinged with the metaphysical cast" (26). Coppée and Hamilton are philosophers; Pascal and Darwin are scientists whose writings have major philosophical and religious import.

One woman – George Eliot – might be added to this list, although Wharton does not mention her. Eliot served as both a literary and moral model; her proficiency in literature as well as in science and theology showed Wharton that novelists could draw on nonliterary fields to address moral issues. Because science added legitimacy to all the professions in the late nineteenth century and distinguished the specialist from the lay person (A. Kaplan 75), female writers who utilized scientific concepts and metaphors had a greater chance of escaping traditional categories of femininity. Thus it is no surprise that Wharton defends Eliot's fictional use of science and metaphysics in her 1902 review of Leslie Stephen's biography of Eliot, arguing that science has always inspired great writers, such as Milton and Goethe. Could it be, Wharton wonders, that "because these were men, while George Eliot was a woman, that she is reproved for venturing on ground they did not fear to tread?" (248).[10]

We can only speculate how each of Wharton's four "Awakeners" contributed to her intellectual and spiritual development. It is impossible to know which sections of Henry Coppée's slender, textlike volume, *The Elements of Logic,* Wharton valued the most: the treatment of formal aspects of logic – terms, propositions, syllogisms, and fallacies – or more descriptive chapters, such as "An Historical Sketch of Logic."[11] Whatever the case, her enthusiasm was great:

> It was Coppée who made the greatest difference to me! Here again – explain who will; I can only state the fact. I shall never forget the thrill with which my eye first lit on those arid pages. . . . I felt at last as if I had found the clue to life – as if nothing would ever be so dark & bewildering again! As I read, it seemed as if I had known it all before – my mind kept on saying "Of course, of course," as my fascinated eyes flew on from page to page. ("Life" 1086)

Henry Coppée (1821–95) satisfied Wharton's yearning for the traditionally masculine rigors of thought. As Wharton puts it, "this first introduction to the technique of thinking developed the bony structure about which my vague gelatinous musings could cling and take shape" (*Backward* 71–72). He also offered a thumbnail sketch of logic in the Western world and divided history into four sections: Aristotle; Christianity and logic; Bacon and the rise of inductive science; and the present perception of harmony between logic and faith. Edith Wharton was no doubt attracted to this seamless fit of reason and faith. Instead of seeing conflict between the two, Coppée writes that in the Christian age, logic "found not a rival, but a guide" (221). Christianity was a boon for reason: "this, then, was the crowning glory of Christianity, that it gave to man pure Truth, and furnished him with a world of new facts upon which to reason" (237). His views of revelation as a starting point for all knowledge reinforced both Wharton's sense of faith and her Platonic tendency to conceive of real existence apart from worldly approximations. Coppée also contrasts with Darwinians in that he finds a grounding for reason and faith, which they dismantled.[12]

In "Life and I," Wharton cites "Sir William Hamilton's *History of Philosophy* as her second formative work. She raves about him, "Oh, thrice-blest discovery! . . . The two little black cloth volumes, with their yellow paper & small black type, were more precious to me than anything I possessed . . ." (1086, original ellipses).[13] The ideas of William Hamilton (1788–1856) are so extensive that it is impossible to pinpoint which would have been of greatest use to Wharton; however, one idea colors the entire body of his work: that knowledge is only relative because human faculties are ultimately limited. Hamilton thus left ample room for a deity with omniscient power. His argument that inability to know the Creator was in no way a deterrent to belief that such a God exists provided a basis for Wharton's acceptance of religion without unnecessary metaphysical mus-ings. Hamilton also endorsed the classist view that the elite must provide guidance for the masses: "mankind in general . . . are wholly incapable of forming opinions for themselves on many of the most important objects of human consideration. . . . It is manifest that a heavier obligation is thereby laid on those who enjoy the advantages of intellectual cultivation" (37). From Hamilton, then, comes Wharton's conviction that customs have moral as well as social significance and that an upper-class status bears responsibility.

The ideas of Blaise Pascal (1623–52), Wharton's third "Awakener," modify Hamilton's. Wharton listed his *Pensées* on her list of favorite books in 1898 (Lewis 86). Pascal, like Hamilton, believed that simple reason is inadequate to apprehend the absolute because the senses distort and fragment truth. Pascal also believed in convention to order life and keep it from becoming pure chaos. To use Wharton's phrase – the title of her 1912 novel – there is only "the custom of the country" to govern us. But when society establishes custom as the equivalent of natural law, it makes a grave error, for human reason is too weak to create conventions founded on eternal truth. Custom, though necessary, is only the weak makeshift of humans. Pascal's importance to Wharton resides in his refusal to separate morality and spirituality. The ideal of spiritual perfection is inseparable from the Christian life; no salvation is possible apart from the heartfelt desire for truth, together with a love of God that works to destroy all self-love. Pascal thus displaced reason in order to establish it more firmly in its proper place. Valuing intuition without sacrificing reason, he allowed Wharton to shift authority from the outer world to the inner, even if that meant defying convention.

Charles Darwin (1809–82), Wharton's fourth "Awakener," is the figure most often associated with her, both because of the strong determinist strain in her fiction and because of the monumental position Darwin occupied in the nineteenth century. Wharton considered theories of evolution and the processes of reason that accompanied them of paramount importance, and she followed all the current scientific developments. A self-proclaimed student of "the wonder-world of nineteenth century science" (*Backward* 94), she listed in her commonplace book "definitions of a large array of sciences and scientific philosophies" (Lewis 108). She also chatted comfortably with Sara Norton about a "rather painful" book by Alphonse Aulard, which "demolishes Taine's methods as a scientific historian, & shows him to have been rather a brilliant fantaisiste, absolutely 'de bonne foi' but constitutionally incapable of objective representation of facts." Hippolyte Taine, Wharton continued, "was one of the formative influences of my youth – the greatest after Darwin, Spencer, and Lecky" (*Letters* 136).[14]

A letter that Wharton wrote to Morton Fullerton in 1908 brims over with scientific talk, although here one also detects Wharton's self-censorship – a desire to disguise the full extent of her learning with "feminine" cuteness:

> I've read Lock's "Heredity & Variation," & begun Dépéret's "Transformations du Monde Animal." . . . That reminds me – do you know "L'Hérédité" by Delage, which Kellogg constantly speaks of as the best on the subject? And if you do, could I understand it, even in

bits? I must confess to being always a little ahurie [bewildered] when I meet with biophors & determinants – although they seem like old friends after allelomorphs & heterozygotes in Lock's "simple" exposition of Mendelism. – My biological reading is always embarrassed by the fact that I can't help seeing all these funny creatures with faces & gestures – the biophors, for instance, small & anxious to please, the determinants loud & domineering. . . .

Oh, dear – what nonsense to send three thousand miles! (*Letters* 151)

This passage is coy and disarming. Wharton flatters her lover by asking whether he thinks she can understand such difficult material, even though there is no doubt that she comprehended complex, technical ideas and even enjoyed showing off her erudition.

Knowledge of Charles Darwin was inescapable for any thinking person at the turn of the century. Darwin's findings permanently destabilized systems of faith, providing Wharton and others with a basis for agnosticism. It would be a mistake, however, to think of Edith Wharton as an unquestioning follower of Darwin, or to label her fiction as unproblematically naturalistic.[15] Wharton was inclined to accept Darwin's rational conclusions, but she remained skeptical of easy Victorian assumptions about moral or social progress. In Darwin's universe, natural selection was due to chance only – mention of a Creator appears only on the last page of *The Origin of Species* (1859). Wharton's view more closely resembled that of Asa Gray, whose book, *How Plants Grow* (1858), was in her library when she died. Gray insisted that there was an order of faith as the basis of science, and thus a divine ordainer. Wharton preferred to base her standard in a system of absolute rather than relative value; she never completely relinquished this search for divine or ideal order. And she detested the heaviness of Darwin's prose. Nevertheless, of all the philosophers, theologians, and scientists whom Wharton encountered, Darwin was perhaps the most important – both because of the magnitude of theories and because of the range of others' interpretations of them. His discoveries disrupted the traditional relationship between humans and God and thus opened a world of questions and possibilities for Wharton.

Darwinian Descent and Dissent

Edith Wharton's careful following of Darwinian theory is evident in her fiction. Her approach to Darwin was by no means a simple one, however; and the commonplace interpretation of her as a literary naturalist must be predicated on understanding her relationship to Darwin, the social evolutionists who followed him, and the upper-class society that serves as a backdrop for much of her fiction.

Wharton subscribed to the Darwinian notion that all development proceeds, through competition, from the accumulation of useful qualities over time, and that a culture builds upon the foundations of its past. She also followed him in believing that intelligence is the bridge between social instincts and conscience. "A moral being," according to Darwin, "is one who is capable of comparing his past and future actions or motives, and of approving or disapproving them" (*Descent* 1: 127). This fact "affords the strongest argument for educating and stimulating in all possible ways the intellectual faculties of every human being" (*Descent* 3: 637). There is always a strong correlation between morality and intelligence in Wharton's characters, as Lyde notes (42–43). Wharton was skeptical, however, about whether society's judgment was always in the direction of the good. In this respect, she also followed Darwin, who expressed doubt about the social body: the community's judgment "will not rarely err from ignorance and from weak powers of reasoning. Hence the strangest customs and superstitions, in complete opposition to the true welfare and happiness of mankind, have become all-powerful throughout the world" (*Descent* 1: 137). Wharton's social satire, *The House of Mirth*, stems from this doubt about society's moral evolution.

Further, Wharton believed that intelligence might just as easily be used for deception as for truth, for greed as for charity. She rejected the relative standard that Herbert Spencer believed was the only outcome of the clash between society's and an individual's values.[16] Again Wharton followed Darwin, who, in addition to questioning the existence of a divine creator, raised critical questions about the evolution of morality. In *The Descent of Man* (1871), Darwin proposed that moral sense develops from the social instincts of the lower animals, by a process similar to the development of physical characteristics: natural selection. Morality was just a series of accidents that served a useful purpose and therefore were preserved. Some critics rejected Darwin's theory of morality because he could not prove the analogy between moral and biological development. But if one believed his hypothesis, it meant a fundamental shift in the focus from divine decree to social practicality – it meant that there was no longer an extrinsic, divinely established or eternal law of morality. Morality could therefore become merely relative, dependent upon one's particular environment. Practicality, or mere individual preference, might substitute for absolute values.

Although Darwin produced no evidence that organisms moved toward an ideal form – the connection between biological and moral development is only by analogy (Levine 117) – many social evolutionists seized upon his theories as justification for maintaining that morality had evolved and was still evolving. Herbert Spencer (1820–1903), one such Darwinian interpreter, developed theories that were broad enough to satisfy agnostics and theists alike. Spencer enjoyed unparalleled popularity in the history of philosophy and was highly influential in the United States. He won the support of respected intellectuals and writers such as Matthew Arnold, Leslie Stephen, George Eliot, Henry Lewes, Winwood Reade, Grant Allen, and Samuel Butler. Valuing the individual over society and science over religion, Spencer upheld the doctrine of laissez-faire and progress. His synthesis of scientific principles produced a sociology that was accessible, comprehensive, and reassuring; he became the great exponent of Victorian optimism – "the metaphysician of the homemade intellectual, and the prophet of the cracker-barrel agnostic" (Hofstadter 32). Spencer – and disciples such as John Fiske[17] – also placed unquestioned faith in the rightness of public opinion.

Spencer's very popularity and facile application of science to society made Wharton wary. For example, the protagonist in the story "The Pelican" appears ridiculous because of her effortless "reconciliation of science and religion" (*Stories* 1: 96). Wharton also attacks the doctrine of "New Ethics," as she calls it in her story "The Reckoning" (1902): it appeals to the "mentally unemployed – those who . . . like to have their brain food cut up for them" (1: 420). "The Descent of Man," the title story in a 1904 collection named for Darwin's book, expresses Wharton's strongest criticism of popularized science.

Professor Linyard, an early researcher of naturalist phenomena, finds his field overrun with amateurs. Initially, Linyard's audience comprised only those well-versed in science – both skeptics and believers, "as their habits of mind predetermined." Within a quarter of a century, however, "this little group had been swallowed up in a larger public. Everyone now read scientific books and expressed an opinion on them. The ladies and clergy had taken them up first; now they had passed into the schoolroom and the kindergarten." The narrator – who speaks for Wharton – sees science prostituted in the process:

> The very fact that scientific investigation still had, to some minds, the flavor of heterodoxy, gave it a perennial interest. The mob had broken down the walls of tradition to batten in the orchard of forbidden knowledge. The inaccessible goddess whom the Professor had served in his youth now offered her charms in the market place. And yet it was not the same goddess, after all, but a pseudo-science masquerading in the garb of the real divinity. (1: 349–50)

The "hazy transcendentalism" (1: 350) of this pseudoscience blurs morality's hard edges and fosters mental and spiritual laziness. When Linyard
decides to write a parody avenging false interpreters of naturalist phenomena – mixing science, theology, natural history, and "the all-for-the-best
element which is so popular now" (1: 357) – he is exasperated to find his
book lauded by an ignorant populace who thinks that his sentimental
exaggerations are sincere. Naive readers value the professor's presumed
"confession of faith" (1: 352) even more highly because it comes from a
scientist: "it is well . . . when from the dessicating atmosphere of the
laboratory there rises this glorious cry of faith and reconstruction" (1: 357).
Wharton's skepticism takes over by the end of the story: public opinion –
and the money it brings – seduces even the loyal Linyard. He begins
writing trendy "Scientific Sermons" and giving hundred-dollar interviews
on every subject while he deludes himself that he can lead "a double life"
of both popular philosophizing and scientific research (1: 360).

In his *Principles of Psychology* (1855, 1872), Spencer popularized the view
of the mind as simply the end product of an evolution of the animal
nervous system. Although his theory undermined literal interpretations of
the Bible, Spencer envisioned no decline of religion; wanting to have it
both ways, he argued the existence of a great "Unknowable." American
writers had already seized upon this concept: Emerson and Whitman
extolled its brighter aspects; Jonathan Edwards and Melville its darker ones.
Spencer further argued in *The Principles of Ethics* (1892–93) not only that
human morality evolved, but that it did so in accordance with the criterion
of pleasure. Darwin, on the other hand, had maintained social utility as a
test of morality rather than happiness, although he said that the two were
generally mutually inclusive (*Descent* 1: 136). Wharton is clearly more
aligned with the tempered Darwinian view than the optimistic Spencerian
one, more like Edwards than Emerson. The protagonist in "The Lamp of
Psyche" (1895), for example, speaks for Wharton: "people had a right to
be happy; but . . . it was a right seldom recognized by destiny" (*Stories* 1:
42). Happiness in Wharton's view is neither an entitlement nor a corollary
of moral evolution.[18] Nor does Wharton believe that evil and sin can be
eliminated by a simple refusal to acknowledge their existence. In "The
Descent of Man," exuberant reviewers misread and then praise Professor
Linyard's book on evolution, hailing the author's "faith in man's destiny
and the supremacy of good, which has too long been silenced by the
whining chorus of a 'decadent nihilism' " (1: 357); but Wharton suggests
that such "nilhilism" is not entirely unfounded.

Just as Edith Wharton expressed only qualified enthusiasm for Spencer,
she was equally wary of "agnosticism," a term derived from Conte and

coined by social evolutionist Thomas Huxley (1825–95), who claimed that
the basic unit of life was protoplasm and God was therefore superfluous in
biology. In the latter half of the nineteenth century, agnosticism became "a
self-sustaining phenomenon" and was eagerly taken up by a host of intellectuals (Turner 171), including Charles Eliot Norton, president of Harvard
University, editor of the *North American Review,* and friend and mentor of
Edith Wharton.[19] Norton spelled out his agnostic beliefs for himself and
many others:

> The relation between God and the soul is original for every man. His
> religion must be his own. No two men think of God alike. No man
> or men can tell me what I must think of him. If I am pure of heart, I
> see him, and know him; – & creeds are but fictions that have nothing
> to do with the truth. (qtd. in Turner 133)

Norton's ideas meant that society floated without spiritual grounding in
anything but its own practices. It thus made the best of moral relativity
introduced by social evolutionists. To Norton, agnosticism seemed the
only logical choice; to Wharton, who owned all ten volumes of Huxley's
writings (Maggs), it spelled danger.

Agnosticism's appeal is not difficult to understand. Technological advances as well as biological discoveries had made God seem superfluous. If
humans could explain and control the world, then why cling to the concept
of a divine creator? And for what purpose retain the old-fashioned belief in
human inadequacy and dependency? Since reason, not faith, was the new
measure, accepting life, death, or the afterlife on the basis of faith alone
seemed increasingly naive. As Turner notes, if belief in religion meant
"bowing to the yoke of authority . . . rather than investigating for oneself,"
then "infidelity [to Christianity] became a moral obligation as well as an
intellectual necessity" (159). Whereas the old Calvinist doctrine had bound
believers to God, the new doctrine gave individuals choice, releasing them
from God altogether. Calvinist predestination became "an odious and
unacceptable notion. . . . A sovereign God who would choose to elect
some, but not all, men was undemocratic in the extreme" (Fishburn 129).
Similarly repellent was a creed based on innate human fallibility and a God
who would allow suffering. Sin was whitewashed as simply an excess of
ego, an act not against God but against fellow humans.

The church's role also changed. Theologians who had struggled to meet
the demand for scientific verification and maintain confidence in the Bible
as God's infallible word resolved the issue by the end of the century with
an "intuitionist theory of inspiration" (Fishburn 130) and an assumption
that since reason had evolved, so must faith. The church's mission was now

to support culture and to preach ethics and morals in place of theology. Agnosticism allowed Norton to declare, in 1868, "But so far as the most intelligent portion of society is concerned, the Church in its actual constitution is an anachronism" and to praise "the loss of religious faith among the most civilized portion of the race as a step from childishness toward maturity" (qtd. in Turner 165, 174).

Late Victorians wrote of the relief that dissociation from belief and church gave them. Congregationalist minister Samuel Putnam, who later lost his faith in God, stated, "I never did like to ask anybody about the state of their soul. I was of the opinion that it was none of my business" (qtd. in Turner 209). Wharton criticizes this new ecclesiastical laxity in her many portraits of Episcopalian parishes. In her story "The Line of Least Resistance" (1900), for example, a wealthy Episcopalian feels about the clergy "much as he did about his library: he had never quite known what they were for" (*Stories* 1: 223). And in her memoir "A Further Glance," she describes the blurred distinction between the sacred and the secular: "the gilt chairs" for old New York's dances were hired from the Grace Church sexton, "who so oddly combined ecclesiastical and worldy duties" (13).

The Bible's role was also transformed, from God's word to a spiritual guide to life. The individual, not scripture, was the source of theology, and Christ became an exemplar of human behavior rather than a divine being. A letter to an 1878 Freethinkers Convention claimed that "the Christian virtues are the slave virtues: meekness, obedience, credulity, and mental non-resistance" (qtd. in Turner 210). In this new atmosphere, ethical rather theological studies flourished. Noteworthy were John Stuart Mill's *Utilitarianism* (1863), which Wharton owned (Maggs), and G. E. Moore's *Principia Ethica* (1903). Ernest Renan's *Vie de Jesus* (1863), also in Wharton's library in translation (Maggs), gave a historical account of Jesus as a model individual rather than divine savior and, despite clerical uproar, became immensely popular.

Edith Wharton did not rest easy in the comfort of these liberal interpretations. By temperament she remained committed to a more austere, old-fashioned version of faith, sin, and judgment. This Calvinist sensibility was incompatible with the more "enlightened," secular outlooks. Wharton also rejected social evolutionists' facile applications of scientific principles to all of society's problems. For her, absolute measures of value were preferable to relative ones, and the present state of society warranted skepticism, not blithe optimism, about the future. She also recognized the problems for women that the new creeds created. Although many women welcomed the break with traditional faith as a sign of freedom, in the end they achieved less equality than they desired. Ingrained gender biases persisted, as did sentimental codes. Moreover, in the push for rational thought and positivism, the intuitive, "female" aspect was lost along with the sense of the divine.

A considerable problem for women was that secularism itself was gendered. Science and the march of knowledge became equated with manliness, whereas belief was construed as a sign of weakness and submissiveness to authority. Looking back in old age, Charles Norton could write:

> One may sigh for all that one loses in giving up the old religion, as one sighs for the disappearance of any romantic sentiment that once held possession of the heart. But the new irreligion is the manlier, honester & simpler thing, and affords a better theory of life and a more solid basis for morality. (qtd. in Turner 244)

Religious belief, Norton argued, "enfeebled the spirit of manliness" (qtd. in Turner 235). What, then, was agnosticism's effect on women? Did it make women more manly as well? The equation of manliness with skepticism and rationality created a dilemma for women like Wharton, who embraced reason as the appropriate response to the world but who also wished to retain an identity as female. Wharton's mental toughness and self-sufficiency had already alienated her from sentimental religion. The business of doubting required a stoic firmness associated with a masculine rather than feminine personality – a stance not at all pleasing to men who expected softer sensibilities. A clever or intellectual woman was thus bereft of the traditional assurances of femininity but found little comfort in the new rationalism.

Wharton examines the new religion's inability to solve age-old problems of good, evil, and moral responsibility in her story "The Reckoning" (1902). In this tale of marriage and divorce, Julia Arment leaves her first husband when she grows tired of him and begins a relationship· with John Westall that results in an unconventional marriage. Their wedding ceremony – "an unimportant concession to social prejudice" (*Stories* 1: 427) – is predicated on the understanding that each party is free to leave whenever the attachment weakens. Convinced of "the immorality of marriage" in the present social system (1: 421), Julia adamantly defends this new "religion of personal independence" (1: 424), which is no more than an ego-centered relativism. Despite her pronouncement of radical theories, Julia gradually finds herself settling into more traditional patterns of thought and behavior. She is therefore devastated when, after ten years of marriage, Westall claims his freedom and leaves her for another woman.

The new dispensation, which has made possible both Julia's desertion of her first husband and John's abandonment of her, is *"Thou shalt not be unfaithful – to thyself"* (1: 420, original emphasis). Wharton distrusts this "new creed," and she demonstrates the danger of refashioning marriage laws in the same way that one who is "tired of the conventional color scheme in art and conduct" might paint "purple grass and a green sky" (1: 421). What Julia Westall finally learns is the true meaning of the Golden Rule. Harry Arment, the first husband, was "the victim of the code she had devised" (1: 432); now Julia herself is its victim. One evening, lost in a moral wilderness, Julia decides to make amends to her first husband. She visits his house and offers an apology that reflects her new understanding of the need to "recognize an inner law . . . the obligation that love creates" (1: 436, original ellipsis). Having achieved this small reparation, however, she finds herself still "outside in the darkness" (1: 437).

Limited Naturalism

Wharton's sense of the absolute and her conviction that individuals as well as society fail to meet moral responsibilities limit her as a literary naturalist and link her instead to Christian – or even Platonic – traditions. Because of Wharton's qualified acceptance of social Darwinism, the assumption that she is a naturalist merits reexamination. Naturalism transpires from two impulses: the loss of faith and the desire for reform – although the latter sentiment is often subsumed by the former. Naturalists reasoned that if evolution pointed to the animal nature of humans and the brain was little more than gray matter, then a spiritual life seemed impossible. Humans might not possess a soul to elevate them above the physical realm at all. Likewise, if natural selection were mere chance, then there could be no order to the universe. To the naturalists, then, evolution implied both a moral and a spiritual "descent of man."

Naturalists underplay individual choices and power; Wharton, however, although acknowledging limitations, gives her characters some measure of moral freedom. Naturalists logically hold that no one is to blame in a world subject to natural laws; Wharton makes her characters morally accountable, even if they are not morally aware.[20] She shared the naturalists' despair over the possibility of social reform, but she retained the hope of individual reform. She never entirely gave up the search for immanence through transcendence; therein lie the spiritual and moral dimensions of her work. Fundamentally, then, Wharton possessed a metaphysical sensibility rather than a mechanistic one.[21]

Naturalists also focused on common denominators of human experiences, often of the lower class. Although she sometimes portrayed the poor and disenfranchised, Wharton denounced fiction that depicted "the man with the dinner pail" (*Backward* 206), and she often adapted Darwinian principles to upper-class settings and customs. Wealth, privilege, and tradition became the external forces with which her characters – especially her women – contend. Even more fundamentally, however, naturalism was a revolt against what later came to be called the genteel tradition in society. To some extent, Wharton remained supportive of standards of "ideality" or "decency" that Malcolm Cowley reminds us were buzzwords of the genteel writers (116). In principle, Wharton's class exempted her from the category "naturalist"; in practice, however, she fell somewhere between the naturalist and genteel categories that Cowley describes:

> On one side was religion; on the other, business. On one side was the divine in human beings; on the other, everything animal. On one side was art; on the other, life. On one side were women, clergymen, and university professors, all guardians of Art and the Ideal; on the other side were men in general, immersed in their practical affairs. (117)

Rather than choosing sides, Wharton's fiction astutely criticizes both religion and business; art and life; the ideal and the practical.

Wharton differed from the naturalists in another important way. She never fully accepted their unified world view as an alternative to the Christian synthesis. Her struggle with issues of morality separated her from both the blithely optimistic Spencer and the scientific Huxley. Rather, Wharton might be compared with Ferdinand Brunetière (1849–1906), whose books, *Études critiques sur l'histoire de la littérature française* (1893) and *Honoré de Balzac* (1906), were in her library (Maggs). A controversial critic, Brunetière explored evolutionary science and comparative religion. He strongly criticized Zola and made critical studies of Pascal, Bossuet, and George Eliot, all figures whom Wharton admired (she presented her godson with a copy of Bossuet's *Sermons* just weeks before she died [W. Tyler, "Memories" 104]). An interview with Pope Leo XIII in 1894 decisively changed Brunetière's outlook, whereupon he became an apologist for Catholicism. His progression from skepticism to faith provides a better blueprint for Wharton's course than do those of the evolutionists or agnostics. In Wharton's case, Catholicism represents not just a discovery of faith, as it does for Brunetière, but a return – although in different form – to religious interests that had occupied her in adolescence.

Finally, it is tempting to think of Wharton's emphasis on human pain and suffering only in terms of scientific naturalism, but it is, in fact, a determinism born equally of a harsh theology as well as science. Upper-class Victorian culture, obsessed with material comfort, avoided pain and the nettling questions of individual moral responsibility as much as possible. Wharton, in contrast, adopts a more Calvinist creed. She lets her characters suffer and makes them individually accountable, even if they rarely have power to effect change in themselves or others. Even when she embraced Catholicism at the end of her life, Wharton retained her belief in human fallibility and suffering without redemption – remnants of her Calvinist sense of a punishing God. The frequent mention of fate and chance in her fiction refers not just to scientific determinism, but to this theology.

2

Spiritual Homelessness

You can make a religious woman believe almost anything: there's the habit of credulity to work on. But when a girl's faith in the Deluge has been shaken, it's very hard to inspire her with confidence.
Edith Wharton, "The Quicksand"

I wish you felt a little more kindly toward poor Lily!
Edith Wharton, *Letters*

D URING the first quarter-century of evolutionary science, theologians attempted to accommodate Darwin's theory. They envisioned an orderly, progressive development from inferior conditions and morals to superior ones, with no need to dispense with the First Cause; they still attributed Creation to divine intervention (Warren 69). But the truce between faith and science could not last; even the most resistant believers saw traditional faith undermined. If humans were mere matter, could a spiritual life be possible? Was there no foreordained design of the universe? Did evolution suggest a random play of forces rather than divine plan, or, worse, a God who still governed but refused to intervene directly in human affairs? Writers of all religious persuasions tried to answer these questions in their fiction. As Gillian Beer notes, Darwinian theories lent themselves to a variety of interpretations that nineteenth-century novelists both resisted and assimilated. Evolution influenced novels at levels of organization as well as theme, disrupting traditional notions of cause and effect and producing contradictory philosophies of progress or degeneration (8–9).

Edith Wharton grappled with the conflict between religion and science in her first best seller, *The House of Mirth* (1905). Her use of Darwinian theory has led critics to note the novel's economic, aesthetic, or social

67

determinism. However, *The House of Mirth* is more than a tragedy of "waste" (Nevius, *Wharton* 55–56; Fetterley, "Temptation" 200). It also describes, as Elizabeth Monroe suggests, "the spiritual impoverishment that comes from devoting all of one's vitality to pleasure" (117). Wharton accepted Darwinian principles of natural selection, competition, and survival of the fittest, and she exploited the notion of chance occurrence in her fiction, as many have noted.[1] However, she trained herself to read technical as well as popular treatments of evolution: she was, therefore, less dependent on secondhand interpretations of Darwin than were less rigorous readers.

As popularly understood, evolution had either ominous or reassuring repercussions depending on one's social position. Financially and socially comfortable Victorians adopted the optimistic Spencerian view that evolution unequivocally meant social or moral progress. This perspective, predicated on the moral sentiment of each individual, reinforced the status quo. Wharton differed from her elite group in her rejection of this upper-class, secular, self-justifying view of progress, as her accounts of the poor in *Ethan Frome* and "Bunner Sisters" suggest: she understood that laissez-faire economics conveniently ignored vast numbers of individuals for whom "progress" did not mean improvement. She also duly noted, as we shall see in her portrait of Lily Bart, that although privilege did not protect one from social or economic onslaughts, some qualities were capable of transcending circumstances of birth or breeding.

Wharton also differed from champions of the poor such as Stephen Crane and Frank Norris, who believed that humans, subject to biological and environmental forces, were in a losing battle for survival. Although Wharton's characters may fail just as miserably as any naturalists', her fiction never loses its spiritual or moral dimensions. For Edith Wharton, material and social considerations do not outweigh moral or spiritual ones. It became fashionable among the upper classes to dispense cheerfully with God altogether and among the lower to curse his absence, but Wharton's response was somewhere between these two extremes. She criticized the privileged – who were capable of acting responsibly – for using their advantage indiscriminately and selfishly, and she sympathized with the weak, who by all measures deserved better than they received.

The influence of Darwinian theory – the notions of competition over cooperation, of the strong over the weak, and of events connected by chance rather than divine order – is unmistakable in *The House of Mirth*. Lily Bart, beautiful and single at age twenty-nine, must outdo other contenders and strengthen her position in fashionable New York by finding a wealthy husband. However, she seems ill-suited for this kind of life, and a run of bad luck keeps her from realizing the future she seems destined for. In keeping with Darwinian theory, the seeds of Lily's conflict are planted long ago, first by a managerial mother and then by peers who have trained her to be both "ornamental" (480) and calculating.

Wharton constructs her novel in such a way that it is possible – indeed, deceptively easy – to read Lily's story as a failure of means rather than ends; as an inability, as Adeline Tintner writes, "to do the right thing at the right time" (n.p.). But Wharton is interested in more than chance or expediency. Lily dies not only because she fails to escape her fate or vanquish her competition but because she rejects – sometimes inadvertently, sometimes deliberately – the shallow, materialistic values of her society. *The House of Mirth* thus combines a purely deterministic outlook with a more idealistic one. This idealism, as we shall see, derives from the Christian doctrines that are under assault by science.

Within the narrative structure that traces Lily's fall from social prominence to poverty and death, Wharton embeds three ironic allegories about the fragility of spiritual values in a materialistic culture. Each of these allegories draws upon the referent system "Christianity," and all three work together to express Wharton's concern over the loss of religious certainty in the twentieth century.

First, Wharton addresses the aimless motion and social mobility that characterize turn-of-the-century upper-class life by treating Lily's homelessness and eighteen-month wanderings as an inverted spiritual pilgrimage, such as that taken by Christian believers. Second, she ironically describes Lily's search for a rich husband not only in terms of sentimental romance but as an idealized quest for perfect love, such as that found in the biblical text, Song of Songs. Song of Songs serves the novel through its juxtaposition with another biblical text, Ecclesiastes, which is about resignation and despair. A spiritualized as well as erotic love poem in which two lovers joyously unite and celebrate their love, the Song of Songs provides ironic contrast to Lily and Selden's abortive attempts at romance. Finally, Wharton allegorizes Lily's decision to destroy evidence that will secure her social and material power by evoking the story of Christ's sacrifice. Again, Wharton undercuts the message of redemption that Christ's death holds for believers, for at her death Lily is more a faded flower than an emblem of resurrection. These allegorical structures reveal the novel's religious as well as Darwinian subtexts. Wharton does not write a religious novel per se – such an act would have violated her own aesthetic principles. She does, however, use allegory to demonstrate modern materialism's threat to traditional religious values.

The House of Mirth disseminates meaning through contrasts – between the future that the reader expects Lily to have and that which occurs; between her society's material abundance and its spiritual depletion; between ostensible gentility and the actual viciousness with which individuals manipulate events and each other. Wharton contrasts Darwinian theories of chance, change without growth, and relativity with the Christian belief in a divine pattern of existence leading to salvation by God. These material and secular discourses compete for voice and position in the text and ultimately overwhelm the discourses of the spirit. Wharton is thus skeptical, and ruthlessly ironic, about the viability of spiritual values in turn-of-the-century society. The novel fails to affirm the redemption that is so painfully needed and concludes not in marriage but in pointless death in a dilapidated rooming house, a conclusion that, while showing Lily's failure to transcend her society, still demonstrates the need for such transcendence.

Prosaic and Ideal in *The House of Mirth*

Wharton expresses the tension between the real and the ideal throughout the novel, from her choice of a title to her imagery and characterization. She selected a biblical title, from Ecclesiastes 7.4 – "The heart of the wise is in the house of mourning; but the heart of fools is in the house of mirth" – after rejecting two other titles.[2] Ecclesiastes, a skeptical, pessimistic text, has special relevance for a society engaged in material and spiritual debate at the turn of the century. The speaker does not actually deny God, but he finds attempts to penetrate the secrets of life and divinity useless. The result of all human endeavor, he claims, is vanity and foolishness. To the assertion that God punishes the wicked and rewards the good, the speaker points to evil, not justice, in the world; to the belief that God tests humans through suffering, he answers that death is the great leveler of all. With its emphasis on human futility and folly, then, Ecclesiastes parallels the Darwinian view that human beings are essentially helpless before the forces of environment. Its world-weary philosophy leaves little room for individual achievement or transcendence. However, Ecclesiastes is also a sacred text. Its ultimate goal is to express the value of human life and to affirm the existence of a divine plan hidden from human eyes. Thus, despite its blatant despair and obscured faith, Ecclesiastes is a reminder that although worldly pleasures are legitimate, indulgence without acknowledging the Creator who made all possible is mere vanity. Wharton's use of this biblical text emphasizes the tragedy of the novel: the human failure to distinguish the authentic from the inauthentic.

Wharton's interest in the religion–science controversy is evident in the novel's imagery as well as its title. Consider the much-quoted description of Lily as "a water-plant in the flux of the tides" (84) and "an organism as helpless out of its narrow range as the sea-anemone torn from the rock" (486). Here Wharton clearly uses the language of science. But we miss the novel's spiritual dimension if we do not also realize the sea anemone's biblical significance. A marine animal with expanded disks and tentacles and a blossomlike appearance, the anemone is named for the flower that scholars believe is the lily mentioned in Matthew 6.28 (Myers 657–58). This double meaning of anemone would be lost on most readers, but Wharton, whose knowledge of biblical and horticultural literature was extensive, exploited it to explain the conflict between religion and science. The text of Matthew is a parable addressed to people without faith, exhorting them not to worry about material well-being but to trust in God's care ("why take ye thought for raiment? Consider the lilies of the field, how they grow; they toil not"). The example of the sea anemone, on the other hand, demonstrates that survival depends not on God, but on successful negotiation of external factors. These two diametrically opposed views remain in tension throughout *The House of Mirth* and describe Lily's dilemma as she struggles to answer the competing calls of Christian surrender and Darwinian survival.

Lily's character also embodies the conflict between religion and science. Despite Lawrence Selden's judgment that she is "a victim of the civilization which had produced her" (10), Wharton shows her heroine to be more than the sum total of her biology and environment. Although Lily shares their background, she does not grow up to be like others in her circle. She is not a Bertha Dorset, who stops at nothing to achieve her goals, or a Judy Trenor, who "knew no more personal emotion than that of hatred" for women who gave bigger parties than she (64). Neither does Lily inherit unbridled, maternal greed: "she was secretly ashamed of her mother's crude passion for money" (55). In a society of takers, Lily has a sense of reciprocity. "Long enough in bondage to other people's pleasure," she is "considerate of those who depended on hers" (43). She maintains a friendship with her impoverished cousin Gerty Farish, gives to charity, and even muses about sharing her winnings with others: "Isn't it possible that, if I had the opportunities of these people, I might make a better use of them?" (113), she asks.

Although Lily is accused of being mercenary and superficial, other characters in the novel are more deserving of these labels. Gus Trenor attempts rape as repayment for his loan to Lily; Julia Peniston disowns her simply because of rumors; and Lawrence Selden abandons her when she most needs a friend. They, not Lily, place primary importance on appear-

ances. Lily is so unfamiliar with bachelor flats like Selden's that she does
not realize the risk she takes when she visits one. Although she claims to
enjoy money and power, she relinquishes them at every turn. Despite
Simon Rosedale's importance, for example, Lily snubs him because she
despises social climbing. And when at the end of the novel her aunt's
legacy saves her from financial ruin, she promptly writes a check, not to
order dresses but to settle old debts. In short, Lily has ideas of her own: she
wants financial stability *and* a clear conscience; she expects money *and* love.
Within the world of the novel, however, such a combination is impossible
because Lily's moral principles – even when most flexible – are not relativistic enough.[3] She adheres to standards that others ignore and thus finds
herself on the outside of a group that by conditioning, intelligence, and
beauty she should handily dominate.

Wharton also lends an "idealizing touch" and "vein of sentiment" to
her heroine's "most prosaic purposes" (54). The emblem on Lily's personal
stationery – a flying ship and the word *"Beyond!"* (249, original emphasis) –
suggests her longing for a realm beyond the material one. Lily herself takes
exception to the view that she is a pawn in a deterministic world: she "had
never been able to understand the laws of a universe which was so ready to
leave her out of its calculations" (42). Wharton even calls her an "idealist
subdued to vulgar necessities" (407), whose extensive reading of sentimental fiction and attraction to "lost causes" (55) reveal a romantic rather than
material nature. Although critics fault Lily for moral inconstancy (Lewis
154) and a childlike narcissism that precludes tragic heroism (Lidoff 538),
it is clear that Wharton did intend her novel to have tragic dimensions. As
she writes in *A Backward Glance:*

> In what aspect could a society of irresponsible pleasure-seekers be said
> to have, on the "old woe of the world," any deeper bearing than the
> people composing such a society could guess? The answer was that a
> frivolous society can acquire dramatic significance only through what
> its frivolity destroys.

The "tragic implication" of such a story, Wharton concludes, "lies in its
power of debasing people and *ideals*. The answer, in short, was my heroine,
Lily Bart" (*Backward* 207, my emphasis).

Although Lily falls short of tragic heroism, she aspires toward higher
values than those in the world around her.[4] Wharton suggests as much by
describing her beauty, grace, good taste, and aversion to dinginess. Elsewhere in her writing, Wharton associates an aesthetic sensibility with a
superior moral capacity. In *A Backward Glance,* for example, she contrasts
"the intolerable ugliness" of New York with the "immortal beauty and

immemorial significance" of Europe (54). Her autobiographical fragment, "Life and I," similarly equates moral and aesthetic ugliness, describing the "moral tortures" and "suffering" experienced from "certain images – impressions of scenery and more sharply-drawn visions of rooms" – that she encountered during a childhood stay in Europe (1073). In *The House of Mirth*, then, words like "dingy" and "dreary" refer not only to superficial material conditions but to an entire quality of life. Dinginess, "a quality which assumes all manner of disguises," is "as latent in the expensive routine of her aunt's life as in the makeshift existence of a continental pension" (57). In contrast, Lily possesses finer aesthetic and moral sensibilities – however embryonic.

Lily joins a long line of naysayers, from Anne Hutchinson and Emily Dickinson to Herman Melville's Bartleby, who say "I prefer not to" to the world. She alone repudiates the values of her society, sometimes unconsciously, when she squanders opportunities to snare Percy Gryce, and sometimes consciously, when she drops Selden's and Bertha's love letters into the fire. Her death thus represents more than the ruin of the weak by the strong. As Carry Fisher explains, Lily refuses to be false to herself: "sometimes I think [she fails] because, at heart, she despises the things she's trying for" (303).

Lily Bart is caught at a cultural intersection of the secular and the sacred. Her hesitation at Grand Central Station in the opening scene – she has missed one train and waits for another – emblematizes her choices throughout the novel between gross materialism and abstract moral values. Wharton's allegorical structures show that Lily is a dislocated spiritual pilgrim, futilely making her way when such pilgrimages are becoming obsolete. She would like a marriage based on love and trust rather than greed, but society discourages such marriages; and even Lawrence Selden, her would-be lover and mate, betrays her at critical moments. Unfit for a society that requires her to manipulate others through power, or money, or looks, Lily has no alternative but to die. Her death, however, while evoking the nineteenth-century tradition of sentimental sacrifice, results not in redemption but in continued alienation. Through each of three Christian allegories embedded in her novel, Wharton expresses modernist disillusionment resulting from the clash of the material and the spiritual.

Railroads and Pilgrims

Paul Pickrel has noted the satiric similarities between Wharton's *The House of Mirth* and Thackeray's *Vanity Fair,* which was itself a parody of John Bunyan's *Pilgrim's Progress.* Wharton's novel also evokes another adaptation of Bunyan's work, Nathaniel Hawthorne's "The Celestial Rail-road" (1843). The railroad, a popular metaphor in nineteenth-century prose and verse, often represented Christian pilgrims engaged in spiritual voyages (St. Armand 221). Wharton, whose adolescent reading familiarized her with sermons of all kinds (Lewis 25), would surely have known of this convention. And she certainly read Nathaniel Hawthorne, who plays a larger part in her fiction than her disparaging comments about him lead us to believe.[5]

The similarities between "The Celestial Rail-road" and *The House of Mirth* are striking. Both emphasize modern conveyances and selfish plea-sures, and both draw on Ecclesiastes to depict vanity and materialism. In Hawthorne's text, a narrator crosses a bridge of "elegant" but "slight" construction over the "Slough of Despond" containing discarded books on morality, philosophy, and religion (10: 186–87). Arriving at a train station, he encounters "parties of the first gentry," including women, "those flow-ers of fashionable society . . . so well fitted to adorn the most elevated circles" (10: 188), who patronize the railroad in search of amusement. A few pilgrims still labor in the old-fashioned way, by foot and with burdens on their backs, "excit[ing] great mirth among our wiser brotherhood," who ride nonchalantly in comfort, *their* burdens stowed neatly in the baggage car and "religion . . . thrown tastefully into the back-ground" (10: 191, 188–89). Bound for the Celestial City, these "comfortably seated" passengers set forth "as cheerfully as if the pilgrimage were merely a summer tour" (10: 191, 188). They seek pleasure and profit at various stops, in particular at Vanity Fair, which is "at the height of prosperity, and exhibits an epitome of whatever is brilliant, gay, and fascinating, beneath the sun." The narrator observes that "such are the charms of the place, that people often affirm it to be the true and only heaven" (10: 197). Travelers on this railroad never reach their actual celestial destination, however: after succumbing to "a singular drowsiness" (10: 204), they board a bellowing steam ferry that they realize too late is bound for hell, not heaven.

Wharton's *The House of Mirth* depicts the same frivolous society and in the same terms. Her allusion to Hawthorne allows her to criticize a vain, materialistic world *and* emphasize her heroine's resistance to such a world. Following Hawthorne's structure, we see Lily as one of the complacent travelers, a "flower[ ] of fashionable society," "comfortably seated," riding from one pleasure spot to another. However, Lily both craves luxury and relishes breaks from her busy social calendar and pleasure-seeking friends. Significantly, Wharton uses imagery of transportation to describe Lily's expected course and its alternative. She establishes these metaphors from the very beginning of the novel. Lily compares her life to "a long white road without dip or turning" and rejoices that "she was to roll over it in a carriage instead of trudging it on foot" (88). Yet when we first meet her, she has missed her train to Bellomont and a weekend of amusement.[6] She stands "apart from the crowd" at Grand Central Station (3); asks, "Why not sit out a train?" (4); and walks to Selden's apartment instead of riding in a cab. Admittedly, Lily has many moments of weakness. For example, at Bellomont, although "she wanted to get away from herself" (26), she rejects "self-communion" (38), gambles extravagantly, sees her friends as "lords of the only world she cared for" (79), and allows the Trenor mansion to gratify "her craving for the external finish of life" (38). Yet as the novel progresses, Lily rides less and walks more.

Wharton uses Hawthorne's contrasting structures of riding and walking to comment on Lily's role as a spiritual pilgrim. Throughout the novel, her self-centered impulsivity is checked by momentary introspection. Despite her taste for luxury, the narrator informs us that she "knew very little of the value of money" (49). Lily also has "fits of angry rebellion against fate, when she longed to drop out of the race and make an independent life for herself" (61). And to her credit, while she hopes to avoid the trials of an arduous path, she knows that the easy route is a misguided one. Increasingly, then, Lily resembles Hawthorne's weary toilers rather than his complacent passengers. At Bellomont, the equivalent of Hawthorne's "Slough of Despond," with its library that was "never used for reading" (94), Lily misses the omnibus to church and the chance to impress Gryce with her piety. Instead she walks, taking a path that leads, not to the wealthy, dull bachelor who might "do her the honour of boring her for life" (39), but to Selden and his antimaterialist "Republic of the Spirit."

Lily's distance from her pleasure-seeking friends widens. Aboard a yacht, poignantly named the *Sabrina* to evoke Bertha Dorset's social cut, Lily is publically humiliated. The glamorous *Sabrina* – Wharton's version of the belching steamer that ferries its passengers to hell – contrasts with the dejected stroll that Lily next takes with Lawrence Selden. Not long after, when Lily joins the Gormers for a weekend party at the Van Alstyne estate, she is repelled by the garish, "social Coney Island" atmosphere and has "the odd sense of having been caught up into the crowd as carelessly as a passenger is gathered in by an express train" (374, 375). A walk exploring the site of the Gormers' new mansion just before Mrs. Gormer snubs her to gain Bertha Dorset's favor affords Lily "a welcome escape from empty noises of her life" and a momentary release from "being swept passively along a current of pleasure and business in which she had no share" (389). Quiet moments such as this one bring opportunities for reflection and distinguish Lily from others, including her materialistic mother, who after the family is bankrupt, sits "with the provisional air of a traveller who waits for a belated train to start" (51).

Wharton continues to emphasize Lily's pedestrian activities, coupling them with her decreasing social and economic position. Some fourteen months after the visit to the Gormers' property, a fatigued Lily walks in the chill November air and rejects Rosedale's offer of marriage in exchange for using Selden and Bertha's love letters for blackmail. She walks from the milliners to Gerty Farish's apartment after being fired for failing to trim hats. She again walks with Rosedale, reiterating that she can not accept the conditions of his offer of a loan; and finally, she walks to Selden's apartment where she burns the love letters and, with them, all possibility of regaining her social power. By the end of the novel, Lily's walks signify a separation from her old way of life and its values. In keeping with the spiritual allegory that gives the novel its structure, they also suggest her pursuit of a moral path.

Obviously, *The House of Mirth* is not the uncomplicated spiritual narrative that its predecessors are – and Lily is no pure, dedicated spiritual pilgrim. Wharton uses Hawthorne's model disjunctively. The reader, in turn, is invited to view Lily ironically. We wonder, for example, whether she is aware of the spiritual dimensions of her choice when she takes the footpath instead of the train. And as twentieth-century skeptics, we doubt that her spiritual travels do more than retrace well-worn circuits. Moreover, the reader seldom has insight into Lily's consciousness. She is presented either through an ironic and somewhat unsympathetic narrator, or through Lawrence Selden, who sees only an amusing, beautiful object or a shrewd husband-hunter. This narrative distance emphasizes not only Lily's alienation from others, but the disconnection between self and spirit that characterizes her world.

The conventions of gender also contribute to her difficulty. Lily's spiritual journey is socially determined in a way that Hawthorne's travelers' is not: when she leaves Selden's apartment alone, she is seen not as a toiling pilgrim, but as a promiscuous woman. The lie she impulsively tells Rosedale about having been at her dressmaker's ironically makes her more vulnerable to the very group she has escaped by walking. In the street, Lily is subject to a speculative society in ways that men are not. Her frustrated complaint when she surveys Selden's comfortable rooms – "What a miserable thing it is to be a woman" (9) – expresses the despair of this "highly specialized" product (6) who is unsuited for any but the most decorative function. For a woman in her society to be seen walking in the street alone – even if it is the way to a life of simplicity – is a breach of good manners and morals that carries the risk of being considered a streetwalker.[7] Her development is also constrained by the romance genre which, competing with the spiritual allegory, requires that her journey end in marriage or death.[8] According to the conventions of this female genre, *The House of Mirth* is a failed romance; because Lily does not marry, she must die and thereby fail.

In sum, then, Wharton draws on the elements of spiritual allegory to criticize Lily, her vain society, and popular views of social and moral evolution. The goal of a Christian spiritual narrative is to chart the pilgrim's "progress" toward moral perfection, achievable finally only in heaven. Optimistic Victorians strove for such progress, but by applying evolutionary concepts to the social order as a whole and viewing the world as imminently perfectible. Edith Wharton rejected this Spencerian notion of social evolution and adhered instead to Darwin, who wrote, "I believe . . . in no law of necessary development" (351). In *The House of Mirth*, organisms – demonstrating a capacity to adapt – become more complex and specialized biologically and socially, but they do not progress morally. The most highly evolved upper-class characters – Judy and Gus Trenor, Bertha and George Dorset, even Lawrence Selden – are the weakest morally. Only when the highly fashioned, highly adapted Lily Bart *devolves* socially and economically into a common hat-maker can she rise morally.[9] Wharton also understood Darwin's principle that perfection through natural selection is such only in a relative sense: natural selection "tends only to make each organic being as perfect as, or slightly more perfect than, the other inhabitants. . . . [It] will not produce absolute perfection" (Darwin, *Origin* 201–2). Spiritual allegory implies absolute values, but "the fluctuating ethical estimates" (417) that regulate Lily's relativistic society make the use of such allegorical structures disjunctive and ironic.

Lilies of Love

Although critics frequently assume that Lily's name ironically alludes to Matthew 6.28 – "consider the lilies of the field, how they grow; they toil not" – Wharton may have had another biblical text in mind when creating her heroine. Lilies are also prominent in the Song of Songs, a series of lyrical poems, which Wharton studied (*Backward* 70) and which biblical scholars consider to be a countertext to Ecclesiastes.[10] Songs, an erotic book of heterosexual love and joyful anticipation, contrasts with the despair and resignation of Ecclesiastes. In the Christian tradition, Songs is also an allegory of spiritual union both between Christ and his church or God, and between the human soul and Christ or God. Whereas Ecclesiastes mocks Lily's toils, claiming no meaning beyond the worldly one, the Song of Songs elevates them to an idealized – although ironic – quest.

In the Song of Songs, lilies connote pure love. They adorn committed lovers and serve as metaphors for them. This biblical book's five alternating movements of longing and fulfillment begin with the female lover, who describes herself as "the rose of Sharon, and the lily of the valleys," and her love as a rarity, a "lily among thorns" (2.1–2). She is answered by her beloved, who calls her "a lily growing in the midst of brambles" and "beloved among women." A chorus of women attend her, asking: "Whither is thy beloved gone . . . that we may seek him with thee" (6.1). The bride responds that he has gone to feed in the garden and "to gather lilies," for "I am my beloved's and he is mine: he feedeth among the lilies" (6.2–3). As feminist theologians note, the Song of Songs is unusual because it does not denigrate or dismiss woman's sexuality. The woman's physical traits inspire her mate's celebration, as do his inspire hers. Songs describes a love relationship in which there is no tension or stereotyping of either sex (Trible 965), and in which equality replaces the traditional patriarchal biases established in Genesis 3.16 (Laffey 203). Moreover, unlike the lilies found in Matthew – which grow in passive expectation of God's grace – the lily in the Song of Songs actively pursues her desire.

Just as Wharton employs the structure and imagery of spiritual pilgrimage as a metaphor for life, she engages the allegory of Songs to comment on Lily's search for love and marriage. Wharton's allusion to Songs, however – like her allusion to "The Celestial Rail-road" – is disjunctive when applied to the narrative structure of The House of Mirth. The alternating patterns of union and separation in the Song of Songs are replicated wherever Lily and Selden meet – Grand Central, Selden's apartment, Bellomont, the Stepney–Van Osburgh wedding, the Sabrina, Lily's hotel, and Selden's apartment. However, Lily and Selden's relationship never progresses, and their meetings lead not to marriage but to separation.

Like the woman in Songs, Wharton's Lily is a beauty among thorns who sees herself as different from others and who longs for an ideal mate. But whereas in Songs the female confidently describes herself, in The House of Mirth, the reader's first knowledge of Lily comes from Selden, whose phrase, "there was nothing new about Lily Bart" (3), echoes the cynical narrator of Ecclesiastes: "there is no new thing under the sun" (1.9). Women gather to adorn and celebrate the speaker in Songs as she prepares for her mate, but no one in Wharton's novel helps Lily. Judy Trenor, Mattie Gormer, and Norma Hatch need her to write invitations or grace dinner parties; Bertha Dorset uses her to cover up her affairs. Even well-meaning women offer minimal help: Gertie Farish is herself in love with Selden, and Carry Fisher offers only social advice. The only wedding in the novel is the ostentatious Stepney–Van Osburgh union, which Lily attends as "merely a casual spectator" rather than a participant (140). The soft, amorous imagery of the Song of Songs is degraded into lust, violence, and selfishness, as Gus Trenor tries to collect for his "loan" and Simon Rosedale barters marriage for social standing. The Song of Songs ends with the lover rejoicing over having found his beloved, but in *The House of Mirth,* Selden gathers only Lily's dead body when he arrives, too late, with his avowal of love.

Wharton's use of Songs also allows her to comment on contemporary society as well as on Lily's failed romance. In the Old Testament books of Hosiah, Isaiah, Jeremiah, and especially Song of Songs, nuptial imagery typically signifies God's union with his people. In a fin-de-siècle society disillusioned by Darwin, however, estrangement from God rather than reunion is the norm. Wharton's allusion to Songs also comments on women's position in a patriarchal Christian tradition at the turn of the century. The celebratory portrayal of female autonomy in Song of Songs leads Phyllis Trible to argue that it and other Old Testament texts constituted a "counterculture" to patriarchy (965); however, Judith Ochshorn questions whether such representations signaled any real change in patriarchal power during the exilic and postexilic periods, or whether Songs' nonhierarchical depictions of love corresponded to any legal, social, or cultural practices affecting women (210–17). *The House of Mirth* affirms the more negative outlook. Lily defies her society by wanting to marry for love instead of money, but her search for a husband who is also an equal has no impact on social norms. Wharton implies that patriarchal double standards and materialistic interests existed long before Lily Bart and will endure long after her.

Once we see how the narrative structure of *The House of Mirth* alludes to the allegory of idealized love in Song of Songs, we can better understand how much Lily's lover falls short. If Lily is the seeker of ideal love, then Lawrence Selden would appear to be her ideal partner; however, he is not. Despite his claim – "the only way I can help you is by loving you" (222) – Selden fails Lily at every critical point. He assumes she is having an affair when he sees her leave the Trenor house late at night; he fails to head off Bertha's attack aboard the *Sabrina* or intervene with the reporter afterward;[11] and when Lily falls from social grace, he turns away from her hotel because she is registered with people he deems disreputable.

And what of Selden's Republic of the Spirit? Although evocative of Plato, Selden's republic is based on material rather than spiritual principles.

Although claiming a freedom "from money, from poverty, from ease and anxiety, from all the material accidents" (108), Selden betrays a reliance on appearances and things, not ideas. "What I want is a friend" who won't "use me or abuse me," Lily says (12). She "longed to be to him something more than a piece of sentient prettiness, a passing diversion to his eye and brain" (152). However, Selden views Lily in the very terms that his republic rejects: she is "exquisite," expensive, and amusing – made from fine material "that circumstance had fashioned . . . into a futile shape" (7). The pivotal conversation between the two at Bellomont, designed to let Lily see "the poverty of [her friends'] achievement" (88), actually reveals the impoverishment of Selden's own.

In contrast to the lover of Song of Songs, Selden views Lily as a creature designed for his detached aesthetic enjoyment, whom he smugly judges as unqualified for the Republic of the Spirit. Lily, in contrast, probes the nature of this republic. Although he is himself materially secure, Selden cites scripture to assert that rich men cannot enter the kingdom of heaven, a judgment that Lily counters with her observation that at least for a woman, "the only way not to think about money is to have a great deal of it" (110). (Ironically, it is a penniless Lily who later proves herself the more qualified candidate for the heavenly realm Selden mentions.)[12]

Selden also uses the language of science rather than religion to communicate his views. Lily observes that Selden spends a lot of time in the kind of society he criticizes. He responds that he is an "amphibious" creature, that is, a highly adapted member of society who not only accepts his role in a competitive universe but intends to survive in it at all costs: "If we're all the raw stuff of the cosmic effects, one would rather be the fire that tempers a sword than the fish that dyes a purple cloak." He is outraged that "a society like ours wastes such good material in producing its little patch of purple! Look at a boy like Ned Silverton –" (111–12). The shame, in Selden's opinion, is that people are used in one way and not another; he never questions that, like commodities, they are to be used.[13] To Lily's question, "Why do you make the things I have chosen seem hateful to me, if you have nothing to give me instead?" Selden replies that it is "natural" to belittle what he cannot offer; that is, he follows Darwinian rather than spiritual laws. Lily vainly pleads for him to acknowledge her personhood, her essence – "But you belittle *me*, don't you . . . in being so sure [money and appearances] are the only things I care for?" (115, original emphasis).

In fact, Lily cares far more than Selden imagines. Because she cares, she becomes the fish used to produce the patch of purple in Selden's example: she refuses to sell his and Bertha's love letters and is herself sacrificed. However, Selden overlooks this sacrifice, as Lily suggests when she uses scientific terms to accuse him of being "so sure of me that you can amuse yourself with experiments" (116). Here Darwinian imagery prevails over the religious imagery found in Song of Songs. Selden, Wharton once asserted, is "her negative hero" (qtd. in Lewis 155). His name suggests that he will "sell" Lily out and that he and his Republic are "seldom" adequate. As Selden himself admits, he has "nothing to give" (115).

One might argue that Lily is also poorly equipped to be the kind of lover suggested by the Song of Songs. However, despite her social constraints, she is a successful lover in one instance. Although her appearance as Reynolds's Mrs. Lloyd in the tableau vivant has been regarded as the novel's most egregious example of female artificiality and display (Wolff, *Feast* 125–27), it is also notable as the one occasion – except for her death – when Lily briefly transcends the petty world in which she lives. It is a secular transcendence, to be sure, but a transcendence nonetheless.

The tableaux are theatrical masquerades designed for the amusement of an idle, bored crowd. But Lily's performance as a married woman lovingly engraving her husband's initials on a tree – as a lover enacting the Song of Songs – surpasses all expectations and transforms pageantry into something rare and inspired. This idealized scene is a triumphant moment when Lily's true essence is revealed, not because Lily transfixes the gaze of her observers, but because in selecting her subject, she forgoes the "advantages of a more sumptuous setting" and overcomes the fear "that she was risking too much in dispensing with" such supports (219). Lily appears simply as she is: the portrayal is "simply and undisguisedly the portrait of Miss Bart" (216). Her sense of power comes from no other tableau having been "received with the precise note of approval: it had obviously been called forth *by herself*, and not by the picture she impersonated" (219, my emphasis). For an instant, Lily escapes appropriation by the greedy eyes of her beholders and triumphs as exemplar of beauty and love. As she reflects just before she dies, holding the dress that she wore in the tableau, in this scene she briefly "disowned her fate" (513) and instead envisioned herself as the cherished lover of Song of Songs.[14]

Salvific Death

In the final chapters of the novel, Wharton contextualizes Lily's outcast position in society by evoking the Christian story of betrayal, sacrifice, and resurrection. Whereas earlier she contrasted Lily with the Old Testament "beloved," here she evokes her as a New Testament savior. Lily becomes a Christ figure destined to die for principles that her self-absorbed, ignorant "well-wishers" fail to recognize or honor. Lily is explicitly connected with Christ in Selden's mind, repeatedly declines offers for wealth and power, and refuses to seek retribution against those who malign her. However, unlike Christ's crucifixion, Lily's death redeems no one. With this allusion, then, Wharton demonstrates the unbridgeable gap between the Christian message of salvific sacrifice and modern-day materialism.

Lily's Christlike qualities are evident first in her self-restraint and silent endurance of others' injustices. She does not protest when her aunt unfairly cuts her from her will, or when her wealthy cousin Grace Stepney affects moral indignation before refusing her a simple loan. Instead, she turns the other cheek and – much to some readers' vexation – repeatedly fails to save herself when she has the means. She exemplifies the spirit of Christ's Sermon on the Mount, which not coincidentally occurs to Selden when he thinks of her: *"Blessed are the pure in heart, for they shall see God"* (247, original emphasis).

Imitating Christ's refusal of Satan's power and riches, Lily also several times rejects "the terrible force of the temptation" (394) that would allow her to vanquish those who shun her. After Selden has abandoned her, she thanks him for having loved her once. Although her "tired mind was fascinated" by the possibility of evening the score (417), she refuses to use his and Bertha's love letters for personal gain. She similarly rejects "the great golden vistas of peace and safety" (394) implied by George Dorset's suggestion that she testify against Bertha in a divorce suit. When a scheme to marry Freddy Van Osburgh to Norma Hatch presents itself, Lily with-draws from the transaction "in time to save her self-respect but too late for public vindication." The scandal is once again wrongly "ascribed to Miss Bart's connivance" (457–58); Lily herself is blameless. She rejects Rose-dale's suggestion that she marry in exchange for status and money and tells him only the barest facts about Trenor's attempt to extort sex for loans, circumspectly calling it "business" (472).[15]

Just as Christ was deserted by most of his supporters at the time of his death, so Lily is betrayed by apparent friends, including Selden, who takes "the conventional view" of her, finding "it was much simpler for him to judge Miss Bart by her habitual conduct than by the rare deviations from it" (438). Carry Fisher, after dutifully placing Lily at the milliners, rushes to the safety of less controversial figures. Simon Rosedale, although sympa-thetic to Lily's plight because of his own marginality, still sees her actions only as enhancing her "external rarity" (484). Even Gerty Farish, Lily's most loyal friend, has an ulterior motive: the "dream of her friend's renova-tion through adversity." Gerty wants to remake Lily – "piteously in want of aid" (423) – according to her own philanthropic plan.

Before she dies, Lily spends a few minutes in the comfort of Nettie Struthers's kitchen. This sentimental departure from realism – a mix of genre that marks the text as modernist – represents Wharton's ironic treatment of the Christian message. In this vignette, Wharton appears to revive the ethos of benevolent Christianity extolled by Stowe, Alcott, Fern, and other nineteenth-century female writers whose influence she explicitly disavowed,[16] to present a feminized Christianity in which woman is both savior and saved. Nettie Struthers was once rescued from poverty and despair by Lily's charitable gift and now seems to offer Lily similar relief. In Nettie's kitchen, which has the "frail audacious permanence of a bird's nest built on the edge of a cliff," Lily finds a welcome escape from houses that are not home: Nettie seems to Lily "to have reached the central truth of existence" (517). This religion of domesticity translates Christian doctrine for a sentimental age, offering what Jane Tompkins describes as "an extraordinary combination of sensual pleasures, emotional fulfillment, spiritual aspirations, and satisfaction in work accomplished" (166–67). The Struthers home is a haven from the world; their marriage an ideal union inspired not by Ecclesiastes but by Song of Songs.

Yet this sentimental ending is also presented ironically. Domestic shelters such as Nettie Struthers's are nonexistent in Lily's world, which is given over to competition and materialistic greed. Further, Wharton implies a critique of the nineteenth-century ideology itself. If sentimentality gave women "a principle of reversal" whereby feminine qualities were elevated above masculine ones (Tompkins 162), it also functioned as an opiate for oppressed women, doing "the dirty work" of teaching them submission (Douglas 11). We remember that Nettie, like Lily, was once victimized by a "gentleman" she trusted; unlike her, she found a caring mate. But Nettie's happiness, Wharton tells us, is still dependent: George's "faith in her had made her renewal possible" (517). Displaying the virtues of lovers as companions, Nettie also demonstrates the insufficiency of a woman alone. "I'd never have had the heart to go on working just for myself" (508), she tells Lily, who *must* go on alone and homeless. Myra Jehlen describes the problem of the "female tradition" that Wharton inherits from her nineteenth-century predecessors: what is depicted is "not actual independence but action despite dependence. . . . No woman can assume herself because she has yet to create herself, and this the sentimentalists, acceding to their society's definition [of women], did not do" (58, 593).[17] Lily's dying image of a home and a baby, then, is pure fantasy. She suffers not only domestic dislocation, but a pervasive and pernicious "spiritual homelessness" that Jackson Lears notes afflicted many turn-of-the-century Americans (42).

Wharton thus rejects the religious as well as domestic aspects of senti-mentality by problematizing Lily's death. As Sandra Gilbert and Susan Gubar note, the idea of a female Christ fascinated Protestant mystics at the turn of the nineteenth century, and advocates for women's rights enlisted this image of female martyrdom to depict antagonism between the sexes. Not all women, however, believed that sacrifice led to redemption (68). And it is with Lily as this Christlike sufferer, rather than savior, that we are left at the novel's end. Having detached herself from life's baser possibilities, she finds "that nothing now remained to her but the emptiness of renuncia-tion" (518).

In keeping with the Christlike imagery, the morning after Lily's death evokes Easter Sunday – not only because it is a Sunday in April that "rose mild and bright, with a promise of summer," but because it brings with it Selden's renewed faith. He hastens to Lily's house, having "found the word he meant to say to her" (523–24). However, the fact that this word – suggestive of God, faith, or love – is unspecified underscores the spiritual disconnection in the novel. Further, what Selden finds is a mere "sem-blance of Lily Bart," more a ghostly presence than a resurrected spirit. Yet he convinces himself that "the real Lily was still there, close to him, yet invisible and inaccessible." In a moment, "a light broke" and Selden receives a spiritual gift: "he saw deep into the hidden things of love" (526–28).

The moment is gone, however, when Selden's attention turns to the "outward things" in Lily's room. Familiar patterns of distrust surface as he fights the "temptation" to open the envelope addressed to Gus Trenor; the letter "made a mock of the word he had come to speak" (529). Although Selden resists reading the letter, he looks through Lily's desk, finding the note he once wrote to her and, with it, visible proof of her love. He realizes now "the cowardice which had driven him from her. For had not all his old doubts started to life again at the mere sight of Trenor's name?" (530). Selden then discovers the checkbook stubs that once and for all vindicate Lily. The "mystery" (531) solved is not the Christian mystery, however, only the simple matter of accounting for funds.

Having found proof of Lily's integrity – mere belief in her love has not been enough for him – Selden reverts to his deterministic outlook on life. Inverting the Christian confession, he draws from Lily's death the "courage not to accuse himself for having failed to reach the height of his opportu-nity"; and at the same time, he relies on a self-justifying perspective based on chance: "he saw that all the conditions of life had conspired to keep them apart. . . . And if the moment had been fated to pass from them before they could seize it, he saw now that, for both, it had been saved whole out of the ruin of their lives." A reconciled Selden now believes that their love, a "fleeting victory" over their situation, "had kept them from atrophy and extinction . . . and in him, had kept alive the faith that now drew him penitent and reconciled to her side" (532).

Love, of course, has not kept Lily from extinction. She has been the sacrificial vehicle for Selden's epiphany, but what is the quality of his realization? Wharton develops the theme of missed opportunity, as does Henry James in "The Beast in the Jungle"; but she gives the screw another turn, as she similarly does with Hawthorne. For while James's John Marcher ends by knowing that self-absorption has cost him the love of May Bartram – who, James writes, "might have been a lily, too" (17: 98) – Selden has no sense of what he has lost. An anguished Marcher realizes that he "had been the man . . . to whom nothing on earth was to have happened" (17: 125), but Selden discovers only the "courage" to exonerate himself.[18]

It is true, as Nancy Bazin notes, that Lily can no more live in a Christian context than she can in an economic and social one, but the sentimental ending is not, as she suggests, a "defect in Wharton's vision" (97, 105). Robin Beaty similarly blames Wharton for blending irony and sentimentality at the end of the novel (264), but such a disjunction may well exemplify what Alan Wilde calls "postsatiric" or "absolute" irony, in which modernist literature fails "to fuse its contradictory elements" even though its ending is formally closed (29, 37). Lily's meticulous care with her finances suggests her craving for ideal order, but her inability to accomplish anything more than mere orderliness, a quality that Wilde also notes, indicates modernist despair (27–28).[19] Wharton's narrative and thematic strategy at the end of *The House of Mirth* expresses both the modern crisis of belief *and* women's vulnerability in such crisis. Women cannot save men both because the notion of salvation is itself in question and because women are unfairly asked to assume the burden of this sacrifice. In the final silence, "there passed between [Lily and Selden] the word which made all clear" (533). With this allusion to the Christian peace "which passeth all understanding" (Phil. 4.7), Wharton pushes the sentimental notion of salvation as far as it can go.[20]

The Heart of Wisdom

Wharton uses three different religious subtexts – spiritual pilgrimage, reciprocal love between God and his people, and Christ's sacrifice – to underscore the extent to which Christian models no longer work in a Darwinian age. Each allegorical narrative works through its structure and imagery to help us read *The House of Mirth* as a chronicle of spiritual alienation. Lily's gestures toward moral significance are overpowered by external factors. She owes no debt "to a social order which had condemned and banished her without trial," yet she has "neither the aptitude nor the moral constancy to remake her life on new lines" (485, 486). Critics who discuss Lily's desire for transcendence read it as an aesthetic craving to escape a suffocating or objectifying sense of self (Tyson; Wolff, *Feast* 127). However, it is important to note that for Wharton, an aesthetic ideal devoid of spiritual or moral meaning is not enough. Lily herself is confused about the difference when she poses in the tableau vivant scene, as Cynthia Griffin Wolff points out (*Feast* 125–27), although, to her credit, she makes good use of the materials available to her. Selden always mistakes the aesthetic for the spiritual; thus his Republic of the Spirit preaches nonmateriality but nothing more, and his penitent posture over Lily's dead body suggests fetishism rather than worship. Even though she fails to attain her goal, Lily Bart is the only character who reaches beyond the material *and* the aesthetic.

Hawthorne could write satirically but unambiguously about moral choice, depicting a narrator who, although initially reluctant to abandon his "plan of gliding along easily and commodiously," becomes convinced of luxury's "miserable delusion" (10: 202) and wakes to find his experience a dream. By the turn of the century, however, no such dream is possible. Lily toils like Hawthorne's pilgrims, who are "persecuted with taunts and gibes" (10: 205); and she is helped only by a few well-meaning souls like Carry Fisher, whose sympathies are always with "the unlucky, the unpopular, the unsuccessful, with all her hungry fellow toilers" (402).[21] Unlike the pilgrims, however, Lily is applauded at her journey's end by no "multitude of Shining Ones" (10: 205). Instead, she sinks like the complacent travelers into a sleepy death. Likewise, her quest for ideal love, allegorized in Song of Songs, ends not in union with her beloved but in abandonment and isolation.

Lily's death is loss without visible gain; even its circumstances – the ambiguous suicide – place Christian redemption in question. Her death thus echoes the meaninglessness of her life. In this respect, *The House of Mirth* differs greatly from another narrative of spiritual quest, Kate Chopin's *The Awakening* (1899), in which the heroine's death is a personal, spiritual triumph. Edna Pontellier overcomes social alienation through a mystical union with self and nature. In her analysis of *The Awakening* and other novels about female spiritual quests, Carol Christ notes a pattern of "experience of nothingness" followed by "mystical awakenings" and "new naming of self and world" (119–20). But Lily's death sequence is arrested at the stage of nothingness. She fades away, slipping into an oblivion, which Freud called the "oceanic feeling" (64–65) and which Lears notes characterized spiritual confusion in the late nineteenth century (175). Lily's manic drive for power and money on one hand, and her passivity on the other, reflect a longing to lose the self in the face of increasing commodification. Such a yearning for dependence was once satisfied by a belief in God; but by the turn of the century, when belief was no longer possible, it was experienced, as Wharton writes, as "the feeling of being something rootless and ephemeral . . . without anything to which the poor little tentacles of self could cling before the awful flood submerged them" (515–16).

Finding nothing in the novel but waste and missed opportunity, we can read the ending as an exercise in futility, as if it does no more than fulfill the expectations of the titular allusion to Ecclesiastes. We can also read the novel as a failure of the spiritual ideals celebrated in Song of Songs. But Wharton offers a third option – that provided by the Book of Proverbs. Although she does not refer to this book as explicitly as she refers to Song of Songs and Ecclesiastes, she most certainly knew that the texts comprised a unified whole. All three are ascribed to Solomon and together express the optimism of youth, the acquisition of wisdom in middle years, and the ultimate despair of old age. Indeed, Proverbs, the missing text, points a way toward bridging the distance between Ecclesiastes and Song of Songs – between disillusionment and hope for love and redemption.

In Proverbs, which is ostensibly missing from *The House of Mirth,* wisdom is incarnate as a woman. *The House of Mirth* rejects the New Testament message of Christological redemption, but it does not exclude the Old Testament message of understanding and wisdom. Proverbs exhorts readers toward wisdom, which is defined as knowledge of, and obedience toward, God's will. Its speaker preaches the courage of nonconformity – "walk not thou in the way with [the sinners and fools]" (1.15) – and the rightfulness of prudence – "discretion shall preserve thee, understanding shall keep thee" (2.11). The wise, like Lily, welcome rebukes; the foolish, like the "society of irresponsible pleasure-seekers" (*Backward* 207), delight in their own simplicity. Lily may represent, then, the woman of valor or virtue found in the last chapter of Proverbs – "Who can find a virtuous woman? for her price is far above rubies" – although ironically, Lily, unlike the woman of Proverbs, has no "husband [who] doth safely trust in her" (31.10–11). Still, Proverbs promises a reward for virtue: "Strength and honour are her clothing; and she shall rejoice in time to come" (31.25).

In a cultural atmosphere of doubt, Edith Wharton turns to biblical books about spiritual depletion and renewal – Proverbs, Ecclesiastes, and Song of Songs. These books of "wisdom," as they are collectively called, make

Lily's experience both specific to her gender and class, and universal. Leaving the superficial values of her society behind, Lily does indeed follow Ecclesiastes' pronouncement that "the heart of the wise is in the house of mourning; but the heart of fools is in the house of mirth" (7.4). And ultimately, embodying wisdom through experience, she becomes the vehicle by which readers reach their own wisdom about Wharton's text. For the reader, the price of wisdom is the sacrifice of comfortable reading habits that threaten to inscribe us in the very "house of mirth" we pride ourselves on escaping.[22] Wharton's extraordinary genius in *The House of Mirth* is that she gives us the finish of life with such skill and precision that we glide along its surface commodiously, like complacent travelers. But if we labor diligently, she also rewards us with the "deeper bearing" that her novel has on the "old woe of the world" (*Backward* 207).

3

Calvinist Tortures

That Calvinist sense of Innate Depravity and Original Sin, from whose visitations, in some shape or other, no deeply thinking mind is always and wholly free.

    Herman Melville, *Hawthorne and His Mosses*

That heart of New England which makes so pretty a phrase for print and so stern a fact, as yet, for feeling.

    Henry James, *The American Scene*

Life is the saddest thing there is.

    Edith Wharton, *A Backward Glance*

EDITH Wharton's elite social background places her in the tradition of genteel Protestantism. Yet a closer look reveals another sensibility that can only be characterized as evangelical – the spirituality commonly associated with Calvinism.[1] Wharton's relationship to Calvinism is complex and even paradoxical, not only because Calvinism contrasted sharply with her upbringing, but because she resisted, on intellectual and aesthetic grounds, the austere doctrines to which she felt spiritually drawn. Her life and fiction reflect these ambiguities: deep moral belief tempered by rational skepticism, love of life's pleasures restrained by fear of their cost. Throughout Wharton's writing we can see this battle between conscience and convenience. In her New England fiction, particularly in *Ethan Frome,* Wharton gives full rein to her Calvinist impulses. She rejects the sunny interpretations of Darwinian theory that dispensed with God, sin, and punishment; she returns instead to the austerity of Calvinism, using it as a trope for the modernist condition of uncertainty and alienation.

Out of Religious Fashion

One of Edith Newbold Jones's earliest religious memories is at-
tending Episcopal services with her family at Calvary Church, also the
girlhood parish of her mother, Lucretia Jones. She writes of returning to
the Renwick-designed Gothic Revival structure for evening services and
of disliking the church architecture. Her comment that "even in that day
of hideous religious edifices, few less aesthetically pleasing could have been
found" ("Little" 362) reflects the upper-class tendency to privilege the
aesthetic – and principles of taste and tradition – over the religious.[2] Indeed, as Wharton explains, in her society displays of upper-class fashion followed close on the heels of piety: "On Sundays after church the fashionable
of various denominations paraded [on Fifth Avenue] on foot, in gathered
satin bonnets and tall hats" (*Backward* 2). She underlines this point in her
short story "That Good May Come" (1894), in which the most significant
aspect of Lent is the requisite sacrifice of society balls (*Stories* 1: 26).

Many of the families who composed Wharton's closed world could trace
their American ancestry back three hundred years, as could the Puritans,
but in her autobiography *A Backward Glance,* Wharton emphasizes differences between the two groups. Although some of her forebears went first
to Massachusetts, their descendants, "not being of the stripe of religious
fanatic or political reformer . . . transferred their activities to the easier-
going New York, where people seem from the outset to have been more
interested in making money and acquiring property than in Predestination
and witch-burning" (9). Wharton attributed her ancestors' relaxed religious
and moral temperament to Anglican rather than Calvinist influences. Although she wrote appreciatively of this legacy, she was also ambivalent
about it. The culture she had inherited offered distinct social advantages,
but overall, Wharton faulted its willingness to compromise moral principles
and to embrace ideals that privileged form over substance.

In her society's favor was a "greater suavity and tolerance" than that
found among her Puritan counterparts. Equally valuable was her ancestors'
respect for ritual. To the "distinctively Episcopalian" New York of her
youth, Wharton writes that she owes "my early saturation with the noble
cadences of the Book of Common Prayer, and my reverence for an ordered
ritual in which the officiant's personality is strictly subordinated to the rite
he performs." She considers her ancestors fortunate to have escaped the
soul-wrenching introspection of Calvinism:

> May not the matchless beauty of an ancient rite have protected our
> ancestors from what Huxley called the "fissiparous tendency of the

Protestant sects," sparing them sanguinary wrangles over uncomprehended points of doctrine, and all those extravagances of self-constituted prophets and evangelists which rent and harrowed New England? Milder manners, a greater love of ease, and a franker interest in money-making and good food, certainly distinguished the colonial New Yorkers from the conscience-searching children of the "Mayflower." (*Backward* 9–10)

Genteel New York Episcopalians took salvation for granted and thus minimized their need for onerous religious doctrine. Confident of God's grace, they experienced the world without guilt and accepted the self without shame. For them, all aspects of culture – reason and emotion, individual distinction and social cooperation, science and intuition – operated together in a harmonious whole; ease, not struggle, characterized their material and nonmaterial life. Furthermore, unlike evangelicals, who developed social gospels but still stressed individual conscience, Episcopalians stressed group rights and duties. Wharton's *The Age of Innocence* (1920) brilliantly analyzes these social and moral loyalties. In fact, most of Wharton's major fiction, published between 1905 and 1920, records in one way or another a dying culture's emphasis on good English, old wine, dinner parties, opera, gardening, decorating, and travel – in sum, a life which was "mild and leisurely" but which "timorously avoided" serious treatments of art, music, and literature (*Backward* 61). Although religious doctrines were relaxed, specific rules of behavior preserved the integrity of the group, insulating it from outsiders. For example, one was taught never "to talk about money, and think about it as little as possible"; and to be "polite, considerate of others, [and] careful of the accepted formulas, because such were the principles of the well-bred" (*Backward* 57, 52). In her autobiographical fragment "Life and I," Wharton elaborates upon the secular rather than religious nature of her parents' moral code:

> The Christian sense of an abstract law of conduct, of any religious counsel of perfection, was completely absent from their talk, & probably from their consciousness. My mother's rule of behaviour was that we should be "polite" – my father's that one should be kind. Illbreeding – any departure from the social rules of conduct – was the only form of wrong-doing I can remember hearing condemned. (1073)

Wharton's forebears were originally merchants, bankers, and lawyers; by the time Wharton memorialized them in her fiction, their material security had increased to the point that retailers and other financial dealers were excluded from their set "as a matter of course" (*Backward* 11). Over time, these enterprising bourgeois colonials and their republican descendants transformed themselves into a social aristocracy – financially comfortable, insular, and static. However, the world of New York brownstones into which Wharton was born had radically changed by the end of the century. The first wave of upheaval came in the 1880s, with new wealth from the West, followed by industrial barons like the Carnegies, Rockefellers, and Vanderbilts – people whose "dearest ambition . . . was to assimilate existing traditions" (*Backward* 6). Next came the crass money-makers and spenders who cared nothing for the past.

The New York of Wharton's childhood refused to acknowledge the commercialization that steadily and rapidly transformed American life. Her circle remained blindly committed to an old order, placing their faith in the universality of moral values and the slow march of progress; in Thomas Bender's terms, they "worshipped at the altar of the ideal" (207). By World War I, however, the changes were so profound and the old society's extinction so "sudden and total" that Wharton's use of an archaeological metaphor is apt: "The compact world of my youth . . . can only be dug up in bits by the assiduous relic-hunter"; "my great-grandfather . . . was no more than a museum-piece to me" (*Backward* 7, 9). Indeed, more changes occurred in the generations separating Wharton's parents from postwar Americans than in the previous four generations.

To some extent, Wharton lamented the passing of her society's traditions and the disintegration of its values. She would continue to measure life in terms of these old standards, and modern life would always fall short. In her later novels, in particular, the taste and order of this bygone age constitute an almost mythic ideal against which materialism and moral misdirection are criticized. Wharton looked ruefully at the now moribund, moral contributions of "nearly three hundred years of social observance: the concerted living up to long-established standards of honour and conduct, of education and manners." She even used quasi-religious language to convey her guilt over not appreciating this culture enough: her closed world was like "an empty vessel into which no new wine would ever again be poured," and she "should like to atone for [her] unappreciativeness by trying to revive that faint fragrance" (*Backward* 5).

But Wharton also knew that while her elite group nurtured a refined sense of history, it offered little to the future. Old New York had failed to grapple with the modern realities of science and industry. In particular, Wharton criticized her culture's insularity and lack of adventuresome spirit, suggesting that prosperity had bred complacency. She also found her society's "blind dread of innovation, an instinctive shrinking from responsibility" inimical to creative expression: "My little-girl life, safe, guarded, monotonous, was cradled in the only world about which, according to Goethe, it is impossible to write poetry. The small society into which I was born was 'good' in the most prosaic sense of the term" (*Backward* 22, 7). Wharton also evoked the settlers of New England when she speculated on the difference between her own society and that of the past: "What had become of the spirit of the pioneers and the revolutionaries? Perhaps the very violence of their effort had caused it to exhaust itself in the next generation, or the too great prosperity . . . had produced, if not inertia, at least indifference in all matters except business or family affairs" (*Backward* 57). Old New York had achieved harmony, but it had sacrificed the tension out of which all great thought, faith, and art grow. It was, spiritually – and therefore artistically – empty.

Most important, Edith Wharton rejected her culture's easy equation of proper conduct and moral righteousness. Confident, prosperous Victorians handily conflated the "covenant of good works" and the "covenant of grace," believing that through the simple fulfillment of moral obligations they themselves imposed, they were assured God's favor. As Max Weber argues in his study of American Protestantism and capitalism, material well-being served as a sign of election. Increasingly, the Episcopal Church, like the opera, was a place to see and be seen, with ministers as well as parishioners courting social display and material consumption. The concern for appearances was part of a larger trend that Jackson Lears notes began in the 1830s, when the Episcopal Church began adapting medieval art and Catholic ritual to liturgical purposes (198). By the end of the century, it had become blatant materialism. The rector of St. Mark's Church in Philadelphia, for example, complained about the "cheapness" of his church's decoration and scolded his flock that medieval congregations, unlike them, eagerly filled their churches with costly treasures. Liberal Protestant ministers modified religious practices to cater to their affluent congregations; Henry Ward Beecher discouraged fasting except for health reasons and referred to Lent as a "social vacation" for overly busy ladies (qtd. in Lears 199, 24). Episcopal church membership, swelling with the rise in population, became more and more unified and exclusive, giving rise to the cliché, "Episcopal equals elite." Unlike their more reformist Protestant counterparts, Episcopalians felt little responsibility toward the poor, even imagining themselves the underclass when they felt threatened by nouveau-riche invaders or immigrants.

Wharton satirizes this fashionable, turn-of-the-century religion in much of her fiction. In her story "Souls Belated" (1899) Lydia Tillotson's stifling New York life includes "having a front pew in church and a parterre box at the opera" and listening as a matter of course "every Sunday to a

fashionable Presbyterian divine the inevitable atonement for having
thought oneself bored on the other six days of the week" (*Stories* 1: 106).
In "The Line of Least Resistance" (1900), Wharton similarly describes a
parishoner who "owned a pew that was almost as expensive as his opera
box" (1: 223) and an Episcopal priest who felt that "a man who had
accepted the Thirty-nine Articles was justified in accepting anything else
that he chose. . . . He listened affirmatively, as it were" (1: 225). In this
story, the rector joins family and friends in suggesting that a man ignore his
wife's love affair in order to keep up appearances; that is, he encourages
"the line of least resistance." Wharton also expresses disenchantment with
dissolute, ineffective, or fastidious clergymen in her portrayals of Reverend
Lynde in *The Fruit of the Tree* (1907), Lizzie Hazeldean's father in *New
Year's Day* (1924), and Dr. Arklow in *The Mother's Recompense* (1925). She
shows hypocrisy at its height in *The Custom of the Country* (1913), when the
rector of a wealthy parish, who receives money for a chantry from Elmer
Moffat, confidently declares that the new benefactor "was not wholly a
materialist" (296). Wharton also satirizes the parishioners of those clergy.
In *The House of Mirth* (1905), Percy Gryce's mother presents a special
edition of the Sarum Rule[3] to every clergyman in the diocese and then
displays their letters of thanks in a gilt album that "formed the chief
ornament of her drawing-room table" (34). In this same novel, Wharton
writes that Mr. and Mrs. Wetherall's "circle was so large that God was
included in their visiting-list. They appeared [at church], therefore, punc-
tual and resigned, with the air of people bound for a dull 'At-Home.' "

   While Wharton was biting in her criticism of self-serving faith, relativism, and greed, she also understood the fin-de-siècle difficulty of establishing absolute moral values. In the story "That Good May Come," for
example, a poet unable to sell his work sells his soul instead and publishes
an exposé of a socialite's extramarital affair. He uses the money for a good
cause – to buy his impoverished niece a confirmation dress – but repents of
his act until he discovers that the woman he exposed has no moral scruples
and even flaunts her infidelity at church. A sympathetic friend tells him
that the biblical axiom, that no good can come from evil (Rom. 3.8), does
not apply today: "no generalization of that sort is final. . . . One ill act may
become the strongest rampart one can build against further ill-doing"
(*Stories* 1: 40). The artist cannot accept his friend's rationalization, but
neither can he find support for his own absolute values in current religion.

   Wharton often portrays women as special victims of the church's dis-
honesty and spiritual emptiness. In her story "Expiation" (1903), for example, she brilliantly exposes both church corruption and the loss of female
power. When Paula Fetherel's new novel fails to sell, she reluctantly gives

up her theory that "every book must stand or fall on its own merits" (1: 450) and allows her uncle, an Episcopal bishop, to denounce it. As expected, the press reviews the book and sales immediately soar. With her earnings, Mrs. Fetherel anonymously purchases a chantry window that the bishop has long coveted. In his address to the congregation, however, the bishop only obliquely credits Mrs. Fetherel as the benefactor and claims that *his* book was responsible for her conversion. In this story, a woman's art and intentions are appropriated by a male religious authority. Mrs. Fetherel, a writer who resembles Wharton herself at the early stages of her career, believes that "it was her duty [in her writing] to lay bare the secret plague spots of society" (1: 453). However, except for an astute friend who calls the bishop a "prehistoric ass" (1: 451), people misunderstand her work because they rely on the church and press to assign it meaning. In "Expiation," Wharton associates writing – and female writing, in particular – with moral purpose but implies that it can only survive outside male structures. In the end, Wharton, like Mrs. Fetherel, found Episcopalianism, however refined and aesthetic, too worldly and complacent. She needed a spiritual path that valued substance over style. An alternative was the unadorned doctrine of Calvinism, the very creed her forbears had so assiduously avoided.

"God-Intoxication"

Nothing in Wharton's society or family background accounts for her "Puritan" predilection. It is clear from her memoir *A Backward Glance,* however, that Puritanism is a favorite subject. Over the span of several pages, for example, Wharton contrasts New England ancestors with members of her own society. In one instance, she reveals her concern, not only with Puritan culture in general, but with woman's place in particular, making a wry comment about a romantic scandal involving a male cousin and "some woman." Predictably, she tells us in this anecdote, society blamed the woman, not the man: "to her respectable sisters her culpability was as certain in advance as Predestination to the Calvinist" (24).

Calvinism could also be found close to home, in the Episcopal service book that Wharton read each week in church. At the end of the Book of Common Prayer are Calvin's "Thirty-nine Articles of Religion," a reminder that this genteel faith finds its origins in a harsher one. Although most frequently associated with the Church of England, the Episcopal Church shares roots with Calvinism as well (Tyree 34). These thirty-nine articles, as Perry Westbrook notes, provide the tenets of Calvinism "in greatly abridged but unmistakable terms" (8). Here Wharton would have read that humans are born in a fallen state, sinful and unregenerate (Article 9). Although a person may exercise limited free will, the will is imperfectly constructed so that it may accomplish only evil, not good, leaving one totally dependent upon God's grace and redemption (Article 10). God, all-knowing and all-powerful, predestines all things, according to which some are chosen to become members of the Elect, but others are not (Article 17). Although one can do nothing to ensure election or God's grace, one still must live a righteous life, ever hopeful yet undeserving of salvation (Article 12). Whether Wharton familiarized herself with these principles while she sat in the family pew is impossible to say, although in her autobiography, A Backward Glance, she describes reading the Book of Common Prayer as a child (10), and she even cites it – albeit incorrectly – in her depiction of the marriage service in the first printing of The Age of Innocence (Lamar 38).

Edith Wharton developed a religious enthusiasm that far surpassed that of her family. When she was thirteen, she struck up a friendship with Emelyn Washburn, the daughter of her parish rector. She visited Emelyn often at the rectory, where they trimmed hats, typed out archaic languages – Old Norse, Icelandic, Old German – on Dr. Washburn's typewriter, and read books in the library. In warm weather they climbed outside Emelyn's bedroom window and read Dante together. Wharton was so close to Emelyn that she shared her first novel, a melodrama called Fast and Loose, only with her; Emelyn, in turn, was "passionately, morbidly attached" to Edith. As intimate as the two girls were, however, Emelyn had a rival for Edith's attention: her father, the rector Dr. Washburn. As Wharton explains:

> I fell in love with our clergyman. . . . He was a scholar & a linguist, & had a beautiful voice. . . . It was ecstasy to me to sit in the dusky shadowy church, & hear him roll out: "What though I have fought with the beasts at Ephesus?" or "Canst thou loose the sweet influences of the Pleiades?" I was about thirteen when this consuming passion fell upon me, & it raged for three or four years to the exclusion of every other affection. ("Life" 1085)

This adolescent infatuation is notable for its intensity and duration, and – more important – for its impact on Wharton's fictional imagination. Early in her life, Wharton associated the religious with the erotic, something she does in stories such as "The Duchess at Prayer" (1900) and "The Hermit and the Wild Woman" (1906). She also began developing the plot of an intelligent woman unable to win or keep the devotion of an inaccessible man – for the clergyman remained unavailable, even to a bright young girl

willing to learn odd languages in "the hope that Dr. Washburn might fall
in love with me" ("Life" 1085). The fact that the object of desire was a
friend's father – and therefore a father figure to Wharton – may also help
explain the incest themes that she explores in her "Beatrice Palmato"
fragment and fiction such as *Summer* (1917) and *The Children* (1928).
Wharton connects erotically charged parental authority with erotically
charged religious authority. Finally, Washburn's inaccessibility and position
as a clergyman highlighted a conflict inherent in Christianity: female sexual
desire, although natural and fundamental, conflicted with the church's
insistence on viewing women as either chaste Marys or lustful Eves. Wharton's adolescent infatuation with her minister passed, but its key aspects
remained important to her writing.

Wharton's explicit interest in Calvinism began about this time, when, as
R. W. B. Lewis notes, she "began to read widely and indiscriminately in
religious literature, particularly sermons of every kind of doctrinal persua-
sion" (25). Wharton notes in "Life and I" that as a young girl she first
wrote sentimental poems and stories "but soon passed on to blank verse
tragedies – & sermons!" The punctuation reveals her surprise that what
started as intellectual and literary interests evolved into religious ones. She
continues, "I loved writing sermons, & I really think I should have been an
ornament to the pulpit" (1090). Specifically, Wharton developed a sense of
God as authoritarian, judgmental, and unforgiving. Like the early Puritans,
she was also plagued by self-doubt, struggled to discipline her will, and held
herself to impossibly high standards of conduct. She describes her driving
need for spiritual answers:

> Meanwhile my religious preoccupations were increasing, probably
> because of my absorbing passion for our venerable Rector; & I read,
> à tort et à travers [at random], every "religious" work I could lay
> hands on, from the sermons of Frederick Robertson to those of Revd
> Dr Cumming, who belonged to some dissenting sect in England, &
> devoted floods of fiery eloquence to expounding – literally – the
> number of the Beast and other Cryptic allusions of the Apocalypse.
> ("Life" 1090–91)

The Anglican sermons of the influential Frederick W. Robertson (1816–
53) were collected in several volumes that Wharton probably read at the
Washburn home. Robertson, who brilliantly analyzed human motives and
behavior, may have contributed to the keen sense of character in Wharton's
fiction. Other material that Wharton read reinforced her affinity for a
severe form of Protestantism. Of particular interest is her mention of the
Reverend John C. Cumming, who was part of a second wave of apocalyp-

tic exegetes writing in the 1840s. His views, Wharton realized later, repre-sented "the rankest heresy" to members of the Episcopal Church ("Life" 1091). Cumming's group of Victorian scholars and clergymen approached the apocalypse of St. John as a mirror of "continuous history" of the world from the beginning of the Christian era to the end of time. As Wharton's brief description suggests, enthusiasts made elaborate studies and calcula-tions to explain every historical event in terms of Apocalyptic and prophetic philosophies; they looked forward to the fulfillment of the third and last septenary of the Apocalypse, which would herald the approach of the Second Coming, and would occur, some believed, before the turn of the century. Cumming's lectures borrowed freely from, but simplified and condensed, the massive commentaries of Edward Bishop Elliott. His popu-lar writings had provoked a response from George Eliot, whom Wharton regarded as an important literary predecessor.[4] Eliot was critical of millenar-ian enthusiasts like Cumming, castigating him in an essay for giving a "charter to hatred" by politicizing "the visible advent of Christ in 1864" rather than in the "kingdom [of God] within" (qtd. in Carpenter 62, 20).

Wharton was not so influenced by Cumming's apocalyptic reading as Eliot had been; nevertheless, her reference to Cumming is interesting in light of her later attraction to Catholicism. The Protestant school of "con-tinuous historical" apocalyptics describes history as divided between a Ro-man and a Protestant era, a division analogous to the distinctions between the classical and Christian traditions. Cumming was vehemently Protestant, attacking the Tractarian assertion that the Catholic Church before the Reformation was the true Church (Carpenter 19). Whereas Cumming polarized the two Christian denominations, Wharton accommodated them, both in her life and fiction. Her interests in religion were more broad-based than his and her tolerance for competing or contradictory doctrines greater.

Wharton reveals her Calvinist tendencies most profoundly in "Life and I," an autobiographical fragment that she never published. This fifty-page handwritten memoir – which might be termed her spiritual autobiogra-phy – relates a particular childhood experience that profoundly affected her outlook on life, instilling pain and deep moral responsibility quite at odds with a genteel culture that rejected an ethos of suffering. Wharton begins by describing childhood years spent pleasantly in Europe, but she interrupts the account to observe that she also experienced "the most excruciating moral tortures" and "suffering from ugliness." The source of the problem was exposure to certain rooms and scenes that offended her aesthetic sensibility. Here Wharton not only reveals her sensitivity to art and beauty, she gives that sensitivity a moral value – creating connections that she would later develop in her fiction.

Wharton goes on, however, to focus not on aesthetics but on morals, recounting a traumatizing experience, at the age of six or seven, at a dancing class run by Mlle Michelet.

> Mlle Michelet . . . had a small shrivelled bearded mother whom I could not look at without disgust. This disgust I confidentially revealed to the little boy I was in love with at the time (I was always in love with some little boy, & he was generally in love with another little girl.) I described Mme Michelet as looking like "une vieille chèvre [an old goat]," & the description was greeted with such approval that, if I had been a normal child, I should have been delighted with the success of my witticism. Instead of this, however, I was seized with immediate horror at my guilt; for I had said something *about* Mlle Michelet's mother which I would not have said *to her,* & which it was consequently "naughty" to say, or even to think. (1072, original emphases)

As Wharton herself notes, the transgression was trivial, but her remorse and guilt were great. Even more striking, she continues, is the "curious fact that my compunction was entirely self-evolved": "I had been brought up in an atmosphere of truthfulness, & of moral fierté [pride], but I had never been subjected to any severe moral discipline, or even to the religious instruction which develops self-scrutiny in many children." This disclosure separates Wharton from her genteel society. She can trace her sharp pangs of moral conscience to no known influence – neither to her "easy-going affectionate nurse"; nor "a succession of gentle young nursery-governesses, who never preached or scolded, or evoked moral bogeys"; nor her parents, who were "profoundly indifferent to the subtler problems of the conscience" (1073).

Wharton had independently designed a strict, unforgiving code that was harsher than any that parents or church could have prescribed and from which she was powerless to deviate. Her conscience left her few options. Having "worked out of my inner mind a rigid rule of absolute, unmitigated truth-telling, the least imperceptible deviation from which would inevitably be punished by the dark Power I knew as 'God,' " Wharton did the only thing she could do – she confessed, with unfortunate results:

> I had further evolved the principle that it was "naughty" to say, or to think, anything about any one that one could not, without offense, avow to the person in question; with the grim deduction that this very act of avowal would, in such cases, be the only adequate expiation of one's offense. I therefore nerved myself – with what anguish, I still recall! – to the act of publicly confessing to Mlle Michelet, before the assembled dancing-class, that I had called her mother an old goat: & I perfectly remember . . . a distinct sense of disappointment when,

instead of recognizing & commending the heroism of my conduct, she gave me a furious scolding for my impertinence. (1073)

It is hard to say which disturbed young Edith more: the guilt that led to her confession, or the shock of hearing its disapproval. She had searched her soul and risen to her own high standard of truthfulness. She was devastated when the outer world honored no such standard. The message was clear: truth was unacceptable in society; lying for appearance's sake was. The disillusioned young girl suffered her "first sense of moral bewilderment – of the seeming impossibility of reconciling an ideal of conduct with the unexpectedness of human experience" (1073–74). And the artist-to-be, confronted with an unresolvable conflict between individual and society, acquired valuable materials for future novels.

Specifically, the incident established a basis for Wharton's obsession with integrity. Because readers tend to focus on her social themes – marriage, especially – they overlook the fact that moral truth is a concern in most of her fiction, beginning with her earliest novels. For example, in *The Touchstone* (1900), a lover breaks his promise and sells a dead woman's love letters for financial gain. In *The Valley of Decision* (1902), betrayals of all kinds plague individuals, politics, and the church. And in *Sanctuary* (1903), deceit passes from father to son when a young architect attempts to pass off another's work as his own. In fiction as diverse as *The House of Mirth* (1905), *The Reef* (1912), *Twilight Sleep* (1927), and *The Gods Arrive* (1932), plots turn on basic failures to tell the truth. Wharton's more admirable characters struggle, often unsuccessfully, to salvage their integrity despite hostile social conventions. Indeed, Wharton seems almost instinctively to construct her plots around the hypocrisies that such conventions foster. Many years after Mlle Michelet's dancing lessons, for example, Ellen Olenska voices Wharton's concern about incompatible moral and social codes when she asks Newland Archer, "Does no one want to know the truth here?" (78).

The dancing-school incident also illuminates Wharton's view of moral differences between men and women. Although she discusses the episode in her published autobiography *A Backward Glance,* she gives it full treatment only in "Life and I," which she suppressed. Both autobiographies begin with descriptions of a little girl dressed in her very best on a walk with her father. However, in the unpublished account the girl meets a male cousin, whose kiss produces an "extremely pleasant sensation," and declares that her "first conscious sensations were produced by the two deepest-seated instincts of my nature – the desire to love & to look pretty" (1071). This passage quickly gives way to less traditionally feminine concerns – the accounts of aesthetic ugliness, impulsive self-expression, and the "excruciat-ing moral tortures" centered around Mlle Michelet's studio. As "Life and I" demonstrates, the little boy's kiss and the "moral tortures" are related. Wharton expresses her opinion of Mlle Michelet's mother to a boy with whom she professes to be in love and whom she wishes to please. How-ever, the boy, although impressed by her wit, neither understands nor shares her moral "pangs." He is, moreover, "generally in love with another little girl" – one, we might infer, who is less scrupulous. Wharton thus learns that moral integrity is incompatible with romantic success; on the contrary, it often leads to spiritual and social isolation. In novels as diverse as *The House of Mirth, The Fruit of the Tree, The Reef, Summer,* and *The Age of Innocence,* she develops this insight, portraying morally responsible women vainly trying to win the affection and understanding of less respon-sible men. These heroines risk and often endure social exile when they act on their moral beliefs.

Finally, the experience in Mlle Michelet's dancing class sheds light on Wharton's troubled relationship with her mother and her fictional portraits of deficient mothering. Wharton's distress after the incident "was increased by the conviction that my mother would have disapproved of the whole thing – & of the act more than the thought leading up to it." As she explains, her parents "were profoundly indifferent to the subtler problems of the conscience. My mother's rule of behaviour was that we should be 'polite' " ("Life" 1073). Cynthia Griffin Wolff describes Wharton's relationship with Lucretia Jones, a cold and disapproving woman whose rigid views inhibited her sensitive and gifted child, as nothing less than domination (*Feast* 9–48). When her mother learned of her daughter's transgression and responded with reproach rather than understanding, Wharton felt bewildered and betrayed. She compared her mother's judg-ment to that of an enigmatic male God who exercised arbitrary, absolute power:

> For years afterward I was never free from the oppressive sense that I had two absolutely inscrutable beings to please – God & my mother – who, while ostensibly upholding the same principles of behaviour, differed totally as to their application. And my mother was the most inscrutable of the two. ("Life" 1074)

Mother and God were equally powerful. Unlike God, however, Lucretia judged on the basis of appearance only; she objected to breaches in form, not substance. Because of her mother's rigid and shallow response on this and other occasions, Wharton felt estranged from her throughout her life. This filial distance expressed itself in Wharton's writing. Her many fictions about orphans may be read in terms of the pain she felt over her mother's failure to understand her innermost struggles. Especially in *The House of Mirth, Ethan Frome, Summer,* and *Twilight Sleep,* mothers are distant or controlling, abandoning their children at times of moral crisis. In *Ethan Frome,* in particular – Wharton's most "Puritan" novel – Zeena, a mother figure disguised as disapproving, angry wife, assumes the punitive powers that Wharton ascribes to her own "inscrutable" God-mother.[5]

The "darkness of horror" that followed Wharton's rejected confession recalls not the sunny Episcopalianism of old New York but a gloomy Calvinism of the Puritans. Wharton describes her spiritual despair:

> Nothing I have suffered since has equalled the darkness of horror that weighed on my childhood in respect to this vexed problem of truth-telling, & the impossibility of reconciling "Gods" [*sic*] standard of truthfulness with the conventional obligation to be "polite" & not hurt any one's feelings. Between these conflicting rules of conduct I suffered an untold anguish of perplexity, & suffered alone, as imaginative children generally do, without daring to tell any one of my trouble, because I vaguely felt that I *ought* to know what was right, & that it was probably "naughty" not to. It is difficult to imagine how the sternest Presbyterian training could have produced different or more depressing results. I was indeed "God-intoxicated," in the medical sense of the word. ("Life" 1074, original emphasis)

Wharton's "God-intoxication" intensified to the point that her spiritual crisis manifested itself in physical illness. When she was nine years old, she fell critically ill of typhoid fever and "lay for weeks at the point of death." She explains that "this illness formed the dividing line between my little childhood, & the next stage. It obliterated – as far as I can recall – the torturing moral scruples which had darkened my life hitherto, but left me the prey to an intense & unreasoning physical timidity." During her convalescence Wharton's "one prayer was to be allowed to read," but a "robber-story" brought on a serious relapse and left her in a "world haunted by formless horrors." This Calvinist-like experience of possession and haunting – "like some undefinable menace, forever dogging my steps, lurking, & threatening" – lasted a full seven or eight years. Wharton writes, "I had been naturally a fearless child; now I lived in a state of chronic fear" ("Life" 1079–80).

Despite this fear – or perhaps because of it – Wharton continued in the role of dutiful daughter, obeying her mother's social rules and avoiding her sanctions as best she could. Compliance, however, resulted in a disastrous marriage to Edward Wharton, whose Brahmin background and sociability suited everyone's tastes but Wharton's. Only years later – with homes of her own in Massachusetts and France, an awakening to sexual fulfillment with Morton Fullerton, a divorce from Teddy, and an increasingly bright literary future – could Edith Wharton release herself from childhood fears. The developing writer eventually found a way to turn Calvinist "moral tortures" into art. Wharton, who writes in "Life and I" that "til I was twenty-seven or eight, I could not sleep in the room with a book containing a ghost-story" ("Life" 1080), wrote over a dozen ghost stories and thrillers.

Wharton continued to invest her fictional characters with the kinds of morally difficult choices that had confronted her in the dancing class. Just as she subjected herself to the unforgiving authority of Mlle Michelet, her mother, and God, so, too, characters like Lily Bart, Ethan Frome, Ann Eliza and Evelina Bunner, Newland Archer, and Charity Royall succumb to overpowering, arbitrary forces. In Wharton's childhood, mother and society wielded God-like power that threatened her very existence. In her fiction, characters wage similarly intense moral battles with society, the equivalent of this "inscrutable," arbitrary God. This transference of God's dark power to society accounts, as much as Darwinism, for the strong deterministic strain in Wharton's fiction.

Unavailing Atonement

Wharton's sense of God as a "dark power" resulted in moral codes of payment for pleasure and renunciation without reward. Not surprisingly, then, she focused on aspects of Christianity that brought not solace, but guilt and despair. In particular, she was unable to accept the doctrine of the Atonement. The beauty of the church attracted her, but the Crucifixion both appalled and repelled. In "A Little Girl's New York," another autobiographical fragment published, like "Life and I," after her death, Wharton describes an Episcopal service: "The service was 'low,' the music indifferent, and the fuliginous chancel window of the Crucifixion a horror to alienate any imaginative mind from all Episcopal forms of ritual" (362).

Whereas the story of Christ's birth, death, and resurrection offered the believer redemption through God's grace, Wharton emphasized suffering, submission, and alienation. She did not share in the Christian faith that redirects pain into hope. Furthermore, she questioned the purpose of sacrifice altogether. In "Life and I," still casting her mother as God, she explains her bewilderment:

> But passionately as I was interested in Christianity, I was always
> horrified by the sanguinary conception of the Atonement. I remem-

ber saying to myself again & again, in moments of deep perplexity:
"But if the servants did anything to annoy Mamma, it would be no
satisfaction to her to kill Harry or me." ("Life" 1091)

For Wharton, punishment was unjustly related to the offense; and God was
not a benevolent caretaker, but a "dreadful Being" – "one of the dark
fatalities . . . [who] seemed to weigh on the lives of mortals" (1091).[6]
     In general, then, Wharton possessed an Old rather than a New Testa-
ment sensibility. She describes delightful hours spent in her father's library
reading Isaiah, Solomon, and Esther (Backward 70), and she drew from the
Old Testament for fictional titles.[7] Wharton especially admired these
books' literary sophistication and stylistic beauty.[8] She also appreciated their
sense of religious history and their focus on interpreting God's divine plan.
Wisdom literature appealed to her because it maintained a reverence for
God while entertaining claims by rival theological systems; the prophetic
books presented useful models for present-day society. The Old Testament
prophets, empowered to convey God's will to the people, warned and
chastised against moral misdirection. Their message of spiritual and social
crisis resonated for late nineteenth-century readers who were embroiled in
controversies over scientific and religious authority: traditional faith did
not bow to science without issuing its own impassioned warnings about
worshiping false gods. The prophets spoke about disintegrating social structures, the need to guard against complacency, and God's judgment and
punishment before eventually restoring his people; Wharton enlisted them
to comment on her own smug, sheltered society's loss of hegemony in
changing times. The jeremiad at the Thanksgiving Day service in The Age
of Innocence, for example, ironically compares old New York, threatened by
moneyed newcomers, to God's chosen people.
     Wharton's Old Testament sensibility persisted in her choice of decora-
tive and literary forms. When she constructed her home in Lenox, Massachusetts, in 1904, she selected for the fireback in the drawing room – the
most elaborate room in the house – a representation of Abraham's sacrifice
of Isaac. For her own boudoir, she chose a vivid depiction of a shepherd
futilely attempting to save his sheep from large birds of prey. In this
fireback, which combines Christian and mythological imagery, Christ, the
symbol of universal life and renewal, fails to save his flock.[9]
     Wharton's writing also expresses the bitterness of loss and the horror of
death without salvation. Her bleak sensibility is evident in "Bunner Sisters,"
written in 1892, in which a dejected Ann Eliza "faced the awful problem
of the inutility of self-sacrifice. . . . She felt she could no longer trust in the
goodness of God, and that if he was not good he was not God, and there

was only a black abyss above the roof of Bunner Sisters" (420–21). The short story "The Bolted Door" (1909) gives this theme an ironic twist by juxtaposing scientific empiricism with old-fashioned principles of right and wrong. A fashionable New Yorker commits the perfect murder. When his conscience bothers him, he tries to confess, but because no evidence links him to the crime, no one – not even the authorities – believes him. He suffers from his guilt until he finally goes mad. The story demonstrates that the paths to confession and expiation are obstructed in modern society: the guilty penitent seeks release but finds only "the bolted door." Wharton turns from religious to classical themes in the poem "Pomegranate Seed" (1912), but she still depicts death as extinction, with the ruling powers indifferent to human pain. And as late as 1926, in the poem "The First Year [All Souls' Day]," she describes life's joys as an illusion ending in "black earth" and "leaden loam in [the] eyes."

When Wharton uses New Testament imagery or themes of redemption through sacrifice, she often does so ironically, emphasizing the futility of selflessness in the modern world. Thus Lily Bart's generous decision not to use illicit love letters for blackmail is incomprehensible to her peers and even to some readers. Two stories in Wharton's first collection, *The Greater Inclination* (1899), also on this topic, may be called predecessors of *The House of Mirth*. In "A Coward," a man spends his life atoning for letting a friend die in an earthquake and commits himself to repaying money stolen by a dead brother. Society, however, is insensible to his sacrifice because "what is the use of doing something difficult in a way that makes it look perfectly easy?" (*Stories* 1: 130).

In the second story, "A Cup of Cold Water," Woburn speculates in the stock market with embezzled money in order to court a wealthy woman. In an ironic contrast to Hawthorne, Wharton makes poverty – not the violation of the human heart – the "unpardonable" sin (1: 152). Woburn leaves a glittering ball on the evening before his theft will be discovered, noticing the "spectral tracery of trees" against the "fretted mass" of St. Luke's Cathedral (1: 151), and he sees the society he desperately longed to join in a new light: "Was it to live among such puppets that he had sold his soul?" (1: 156). He wryly reflects that had his investment paid off, he would have been welcomed with open arms; even now were he to go off and make his fortune (similarly, in Lily's case, were she to marry someone rich), he could come back without impunity:

> They would all deny that anything had been proved against him.. . .
> Well – why not? Was not all morality based on a convention? What
> was the stanchest code of ethics but a trunk with a series of false

bottoms? Now and then one had the illusion of getting down to absolute right or wrong, but it was only a false bottom – a removable hypothesis – with another false bottom underneath. (1: 157–58)

Woburn plans an escape to Halifax, but he first meets and decides to help an outcast, suicidal young woman. Her story, although more sentimental, is like his own: she has acted foolishly over love, leaving her husband for a lover who abandoned her. Her mother-in-law, supported by the Baptist minister, forbids her husband to forgive her or take her back. Woburn gives the woman his remaining money so that she can return home and appeal to her husband, who presumably still loves her. The story ends with Woburn deciding to face his own accusers, but expecting no reprieve like the one he has extended.

Wharton also develops the theme of useless sacrifice in her war novel, *A Son at the Front* (1922). George Campton is an artist – a creator – caught in a cruel game of destruction. His willingness to sacrifice himself in battle contrasts sharply with the self-serving interests of his parents and other protectionists at the beginning of World War I. With George's death, Wharton comments on the meaning of Christ's death for the modern world: selfless sacrifice serves little purpose because individuals no longer believe. War means destruction without regeneration. Wharton ironically inverts Christian meaning by giving the savior's initials to the father, John Campton, rather than the son; and by depicting a mother who, unlike Christ's mother, fails to love her son enough. If there is anything positive to be derived from George's death, John Campton must discover it himself: by "being able to do things for people" (421), keeping George alive in his consciousness, and returning to his art.

Similarly, in *Twilight Sleep,* a novel Wharton published five years after *A Son at the Front,* Nona Manford selflessly helps her family through one mishap after another, while her frivolous mother, a devotee of every spiritual faddist and transcendental guru who comes her way, insists that one should eliminate pain by simply refusing to think about it. Her mother announces cheerily, "being prepared to suffer is really the way to create suffering. And creating suffering is creating sin, because sin and suffering are really one." When she tells Nona that "we ought to refuse ourselves to pain. All the great Healers have taught us that," Nona quietly asks, "Did Christ?" (324–25). Her disquieting question is ignored, and later, when one of her pleasure-seeking relatives accidentally shoots her, Nona reenacts Christ's suffering and sacrifice. Her wound is more than physical; it is, as Allen Stein writes, "the destruction of her moral vision" (251). Wharton questions Christian redemption in this novel by having Nona, whom she calls "the little Puritan," endure pain without deliverance. When her mother suggests that she cheer up and get married, Nona replies that she would prefer to enter a convent – "a convent where nobody believes in anything" (373). In these and other texts, Wharton reveals modernist skepticism about New Testament messages of hope and redemption. Although she adheres to absolute systems that privilege truth and sacrifice, she sees little chance of these values' surviving in a materialistic and relativistic age.

Defeated Lives in *Ethan Frome*

Puritanism lingered in American literary forms and themes throughout the modern period, as Edmund Morgan, Perry Miller, Sacvan Bercovitch, and Henry May have demonstrated. One need only think of the Hemingway hero's code of payment for pleasure, or Addie Bundren's struggle against an avenging God in Faulkner's *As I Lay Dying,* to appreciate Calvinism's residual effect. Calvinism and modernism share the same sense of human limitation, understood as original sin in the former case and as natural or social restriction in the latter. Although modern secularism substituted "reason" or "nature" for God, it still found human suffering inevitable. With the disappearance of religious certainties, a sense of life's ambiguities heightened, as did the irony with which they were depicted. The devil, not God, might be turning the wheel of fortune; faith in reform became a pipe dream; and the individual felt powerless to halt the increasing machinery of life (Schneider 7–9). Wharton's novel *Ethan Frome* (1911), which led Blake Nevius to declare that Puritanism is the source of all of her ethical judgments (*Wharton* 122), is a modernist allegory about despair and irretrievably lost faith – in God, community, and self.[10] Despite secular progress, the novel suggests that life is still inscrutable and often insufferable. Wharton's most Calvinist novel, *Ethan Frome,* posits an unredeemed and unredeemable universe.

Ethan Frome is also the product of complex personal and literary forces that affected Edith Wharton throughout her life. The traumatic incident in Mlle Michelet's dancing class, as well as her adolescent sermon-reading, led Wharton to construct moral codes that resembled those of austere Calvinists. As an adult, she nurtured her affinity for the Puritan past with frequent visits to New England and residence there from 1904 to 1911. During these years, she struggled with her feelings about Calvinism and the New England landscape, resisting the area's harshness even while being drawn to it. Wharton's Calvinist sensibilities were heightened when she began an adulterous affair with *London Times* journalist Morton Fullerton in 1907.

The affair triggered the same moral terrors that had dogged her in dancing class – issues of deception, guilt, and moral responsibility. *Ethan Frome,* composed during a time of conflict between duty and passion, is thus a thinly disguised account of Wharton's struggle with divided loyalties to her husband Teddy and lover Fullerton.[11] The unending bleakness of all three main characters' lives reflects Wharton's sense that she would never extricate herself from this romantic triangle.

If *Ethan Frome* provided an occasion for Wharton to expose the Calvinist demons that had haunted her since childhood, it also gave her an opportunity to transcend that pain. On completing *Ethan Frome,* she reported a sense of satisfaction unlike any she had experienced with previous novels. Although she still entertained misgivings about her creative capabilities, *Ethan Frome* produced in her a "state of fatuous satisfaction" (qtd. in Lewis 297). She was especially pleased with the novel's narrative frame; years later, she stated that she was "sure that its structure is not its weak point" (*Backward* 209). Indeed, *Ethan Frome* is a technically sophisticated novel in which Wharton revisits Calvinism – as Nathaniel Hawthorne did a half century earlier in *The Scarlet Letter.* Wharton goes beyond Hawthorne, however, by engaging the Puritan tradition as a literary as well as moral aesthetic. *Ethan Frome* is neither wholly romantic nor realistic in its treatment of Calvinism. Rather, Wharton evokes Calvinist doctrine as many modernists evoked the past – as a mythic framework that allows her to comment poignantly and ironically on a contemporary spiritual malaise.

Calvinism was well suited to Wharton's contemporary situation. Although by the early twentieth century, fundamentalist religion seemed obsolete, especially in the context of sentimentality and rationalism, Calvinist sensibilities corresponded with modern uncertainty and alienation. Wharton's conceptualization of a fierce God who was more aligned with the Old Testament than the New was readily adaptable to late nineteenth- and early twentieth-century Darwinian models of competition and struggle for survival: although constructed in vastly different contexts, both Darwinism and Calvinism emphasized human powerlessness before inscrutable and overwhelming forces. *Ethan Frome*'s grimness, then, may be traced to the pessimistic determinism born both of Calvin and Darwin. Wharton was selective in her use of Calvinism, emphasizing only gloomy aspects that seemed to her to describe the modern spiritual crisis: ineffectuality of human will; pain without profit; and suffering without redemption. Like many modernists, she engaged the past, not to recover a lost religious or mythic order, but to criticize and resist it, and to reveal her own twentieth-century skepticism.

The austerity of Calvinism also offered Wharton a ready aesthetic for modern times. The novel's stark beauty and economical expression represent a technical accomplishment. Completed at the dawn of a new literary movement, it was, in fact, a bold, modernist literary innovation. In keeping with many modernist writers, Wharton emphasizes the psychological rather than the social dimensions of pain; she renders her story in spare language suitable to a machine age; and she allows Ethan Frome's tale to emerge as a subjective experience pieced together from fragments of conversation and observation. *Ethan Frome,* then, marked an important milestone for Wharton. It allowed her to reinterpret Calvinism for her own spiritual purposes, to comment on the contemporary crisis of belief, and to experiment with new literary style and form.

New England Revisited

Once we acknowledge the complex interplay of personal and literary forces that led to *Ethan Frome*'s creation, we can better understand the novel's anomalous position in Wharton's oeuvre and in American literature in general. We can also appreciate how Wharton continues the literary traditions of writers such as Jonathan Edwards and Nathaniel Hawthorne while adding her own modernist perspective. Wharton began the novel in France in 1906 or 1907 – before she began seeing Fullerton – as an exercise in her new language.[12] She returned to the novel after the affair waned and finished it in 1911. Although she had achieved critical and popular acclaim with *The House of Mirth* in 1905, her next novel, *The Fruit of the Tree* (1907), lacked dramatic focus and force. *Ethan Frome,* an acknowledged success, established Wharton's reputation as an important American author.

Ethan Frome is distinctly American, although critics often debate its literary classification, suggesting either that it is realistic (because it focuses on external and restrictive circumstances) or romantic (because it demonstrates extremism and irreconcilability that Richard Chase finds typical of American romance).[13] Yet the novel is an anomalous romance, standing in similar relation to the American canon as Emily Brontë's *Wuthering Heights* does to the British.[14] In particular, it is a romance of failure. In *Ethan Frome,* nature offers no escape, as does Cooper's forest, Thoreau's pond, Melville's Pacific, or Hemingway's Africa; rather, it is hostile and entrapping. Wharton describes a Poe-like surrender of self and a mystifying loss of free will rather than an Emersonian celebration of self-reliance.[15] She writes of love lost, not fulfilled. Trapped with a bitter spouse he cannot escape and a crippled lover who resembles this complaining wife more each day, Ethan Frome lives a dream turned nightmare.

The novel fares no better as realism. Its intensity and gloom have led some critics to complain that a New York aristocrat such as Edith Wharton could never understand New England people and customs (Hamblen; Kazin 81; Sergeant), or that her portrayals suffered from mistakes in characterization (Ransom) and general "psychological insufficiency" (De Voto xvi). Wharton, however, vehemently defended her literary rights to the region. She staked her claim to New England in the opening sentence of *Ethan Frome*'s preface: "I had known something of New England village life long before I made my home in the same county as my imaginary Starkfield" (v). She also defended herself in her autobiography: " 'Ethan Frome' was written after I had spent ten years in the hill-region where the scene is laid, during which years I had come to know well the aspect, dialect, and mental and moral attitude of the hill-people" (*Backward* 296).

Wharton had a complicated relationship with New England. She both reveled in its natural splendor and decried its austerity; this ambivalence helps to explain how she could produce a novel of such technical beauty and thematic gloom. Wharton visited New England frequently from 1899 to 1908, becoming so attached to the area that she built a palatial home in Lenox, Massachusetts, in 1904. The Mount, a classically inspired house with exquisite gardens and views, was Wharton's "first real home" (*Backward* 125), where she spent portions of the next seven years in refuge from stifling New York society. Such a luxurious mansion seems to have little in common with the Starkfield farmhouse that Wharton describes in *Ethan Frome*. Nevertheless, Wharton came to associate the Mount with the same deprivation that she attributes to Ethan's home: in 1911 – the year she published the novel – financial and marital pressures forced her to sell the house. *Ethan Frome*'s bleakness derives in part from this painful loss.

While Wharton lamented the loss of her beloved Mount, she was openly critical of New England itself. She visited the region only in spring or summer and always in comfort.[16] She frequently voiced disapproval of its austerity, especially to her Boston friends Sara and Lily Norton. In a 1911 letter to Sara, Wharton commented on the cold weather's effect on her garden, mentioning a plant that may have inspired the half-dead vine on the Frome's porch: "no lovely flowering shrubs or creepers 'do' here. Even the clematis paniculata I had established so carefully is dead, & as for the other, big-flowered ones – j'en fais mon deuil! [I am mourning them!]" (Letters, 3 July). Wharton also disapproved of the New England way of life, which she believed interfered with enjoyment. Urging Sara to join her on a trip to Rome, she wrote, "now, don't raise all sorts of conscientious New England objections, but try to be a pagan, & see how nice this would be" (*Letters* 73).[17] Hearing that Charles Eliot Norton was corresponding with novelist Mrs. Gaskell, Wharton wrote to Lily, "What courage & vitality Mrs. Gaskell must have had to resist the combined depressing influence of Mr. Gaskell, and Manchester, & Unitarianism!" (Letters, n.d.). In 1928, Wharton also wrote to Lily, "I am glad you recognize that Sybarites are more intelligent than Puritans! It doesn't place them so *very* high. . ." (Letters, 22 February, original emphasis and ellipsis). And a year later, comparing her own lively activities with the dreariness she associates with Lily's Boston routine, Wharton lamented, "I am afraid your summer has been less happy than mine. Have you actually been spending it with that poor Grace Sedgwick? It sounds heroic – but was it of any use?" (Letters, 8 September).

Wharton particularly rejected the restriction of women's desire that she saw as part of the New England inheritance. Although Calvinist doctrine considered women the spiritual equals of men, it upheld a strict social hierarchy in which man ruled over woman, as God ruled over man. This doctrine also associated female sexuality with human fallibility and temptation. Wharton's difficulty in accepting the Calvinist view of women is apparent in *French Ways and Their Meaning* (1919), in which she complains, "the long hypocrisy which Puritan England handed on to Americans concerning the danger of frank and free social relations between men and women has done more than anything else to retard real civilisation in America" (112–13). She also criticizes Calvinism in "The Pretext" (1908), a story in which the New England town of Wentworth is one of those "little expiring centers of prejudice and precedent" that "sits in judgment not only on its own townsmen but on the rest of the world" (*Stories* 1: 636). The protagonist, Margaret Ransom, whose face "had grown middle-aged while it waited for the joys of youth" (1: 632), hesitates even to apply makeup or curl her hair. She misses life's pleasures because of overly fine moral distinctions: "was it right to try to make one's hair look thicker and wavier than it really was?. . . The specter of her rigid New England ancestry rose reprovingly before her" (1: 633).

Wharton was certainly not the first American writer to find the stony soil of New England fertile ground for the imagination. Henry James had encouraged Wharton to write of native subjects (Lewis 125); his own book about New England, *The American Scene,* published in 1907, even may have inspired her to write *Ethan Frome.* However, whereas James shied away from New England's more severe aspects, commenting, "You wouldn't . . . go back in winter on any account whatever" (*American* 39), Wharton seemed to enjoy writing about the region's natural and moral harshness. As her preface to *Ethan Frome* explains:

I had had an uneasy sense that the New England of fiction bore little
. . . resemblance to the harsh and beautiful land as I had seen it. Even
the abundant enumeration of sweet-fern, asters and mountain-laurel,
and the conscientious reproduction of the vernacular, left me with
the feeling that the outcropping granite had in both cases been
overlooked. I give the impression merely as a personal one; it accounts for "Ethan Frome," and may, to some readers, in a measure
justify it. (v)

In this passage, Wharton describes the duality of the New England
landscape. She distinguishes between its visible, natural beauty and its
underlying "granite outcropping"; she also indicates that she is most interested in the "granite," that is, in New England's Calvinist roots. In *Ethan
Frome,* then, Wharton resembles her Calvinist predecessor Jonathan Edwards more than fellow realist Henry James.[18] Like Edwards, she explores
the connection between natural and moral necessity, showing how Ethan
Frome's spiritual alienation is mirrored in his remote, isolated setting. Like
Edwards, she also presents nature as type; but it holds no delight for her as
it does for him because Wharton, a child of Darwin, questions divine order
and redemption.

But the writer Wharton most vividly evokes in *Ethan Frome* is Nathaniel
Hawthorne. She herself invited comparison of her writing with his. Responding to criticism about her other New England novel, *Summer* (1917),
Wharton railed against readers who "sought the reflection of local life in
the 'rose-and-lavender' pages of their favourite authoresses – and had
forgotten to look into Hawthorne's" (*Backward* 294). Like Hawthorne,
Wharton was drawn to New England's extremes; she keenly felt the lack
of sympathy and connection that results from polarizing private passion and
social duty. Both writers saw in the New England landscape a fundamental
and irreconcilable duality, a Manichaean opposition between good and
evil, spirit and flesh, that is indigenous to American Calvinism.[19] As early
as 1925, critics noted similarities between the two writers – "not since
Hawthorne has a novelist laid in New England . . . any tragedy of such
power and elevation as this" (Van Doren and Van Doren 67) – although
few have explored in any depth the dark vision of necessity that unites
them. Most critics cite *The Blithedale Romance* or "Ethan Brand" as touchstones for *Ethan Frome,* but these connections are tenuous. Zeena does not
drown herself in romantic despair as Zenobia does in *The Blithedale Romance;* Ethan Frome does not alienate himself from the human race because
of an exaggerated ego as Ethan Brand does.[20] *Ethan Frome* revises another
Hawthornian text: *The Scarlet Letter.*

Both *Ethan Frome* and *The Scarlet Letter* explore illict passion and the consequences of breaking moral and social law. Wharton's narrative, like Hawthorne's, "runs directly counter to the 'American Dream,' being neither romantic nor libertarian, but distinctly authoritarian and conservative" (Baym 214). The novels are also similar in technique, theme, and tone. Like *The Scarlet Letter, Ethan Frome* subordinates action to the effects of action; includes narrators who reconstruct a tale of adultery and failed escape from evocative details (a letter sewn on a scrap of cloth; a stride broken by a limp); and demonstrates how sexual transgression – which William Shurr terms the "one real evil" in the American psyche (123) – incurs repression.

Wharton's characters also parallel those in *The Scarlet Letter*. In her original version of *Ethan Frome*, Wharton called Ethan "Hart" rather than "Frome"; like Hester, he represents the "heart" in his capacity for feeling: "It's always Ethan done the caring," Harmon Gow tells the narrator (5). Rejected by indifferent spouses and drawn into adultery, both Hester and Ethan are destined to love and suffer. Eventually, their quiet endurance wins the sympathy of their townspeople, although Ethan remains more isolated than Hester. Zeena, like Chillingworth, is a wronged mate and gifted healer who is obsessed with illness rather than health. Both become cruel avengers of wrongs, inverting the Puritan notion of marriage as companionate union and, in the process, reducing themselves to shells of human beings. And Mattie – young, susceptible, and weak – loves Ethan just as Dimmesdale loves Hester. Like him, she has neither the courage nor means to flee with her lover and so chooses death rather than risk public disapproval.

If *The Scarlet Letter*, as Margaret Thickstun notes, argues against the conflation of female sexuality and spiritual inadequacy inherent in Puritan texts (132–34), then *Ethan Frome* extends Hawthorne's critique. For Wharton, Pauline doctrine offers no opportunity for feminine sexual expression or spiritual uplift. Whereas at the end of *The Scarlet Letter* Hester's sexual vitality is converted into an abiding, selfless maternity, and Dimmesdale and Chillingworth are released from earthly torment to face whatever afterlife each deserves, Wharton creates a bleaker, modernist ending, allowing her characters to suffer in "the most enduring triangle that fiction has recorded" (Ransom 273).[21] Mattie and Ethan are physically and spiritually crippled for their passion and attempted suicide; and Zeena, the loveless but legally empowered spouse, triumphs, a relentless reminder of their failures. Finally, whereas the meaning of Hester's "A" gradually encompasses "able" and even "angel," Ethan's "red gash" (3) – his badge of ignominy – remains an ugly scar, a perpetual mark of transgression and punishment.

Like *The Scarlet Letter, Ethan Frome* abounds with light and dark imagery. However, Wharton is more Manichaean – and modernist – than Hawthorne; she binds her characters, body and soul, to a dark world. Thus, Mattie Silver, whose name signifies light, only briefly brightens Ethan's life, and Ethan himself is repeatedly associated with darkness. He waits in the dark outside the church, "hugging the shadow" and keeping "out of range of the revealing rays" until Mattie leaves the gaily lit dance (15). He and Mattie meet afterward "in the black shade of the Varnum spruces" and stand "together in the gloom." Here the darkness of sin and the brightness of passion are held in momentary balance, with Ethan wanting to rub his cheek against Mattie's red scarf and "stand there with her all night in the blackness" (23), but they soon resume the dark path toward the Frome farm. Wharton also foreshadows the lovers' dark end when their conversation turns to sledding. They walk home "through the blackness of the hemlock-shaded lane," passing first farmhouses as "mute and cold as a grave-stone," and then the "shaded knoll" of the cemetery, which affords Ethan strange comfort:

> Now all desire for change had vanished, and the little enclosure gave him a warm sense of continuance and stability.
> "I guess we'll never let you go, Matt," he whispered, as though even the dead, lovers once, must conspire with him to keep her; and brushing by the graves, he thought, "We'll always go on living here, together, and some day she'll lie there beside me." (25–26)

Wharton's characters – "half-emerged from the soil and scarcely more articulate" (v) – are barely distinguishable from the gravestones themselves.

Although Wharton never acknowledged her debt to Hawthorne, she did comment on his elevated place in American literature; she even may have intended for her own New England tale of woe to rival his. In a 1908 letter to publisher William Brownell about his article on Hawthorne, Wharton commented that she "especially enjoyed your bringing out his lack of poetry and his lukewarmness.... My only two quarrels with you are for calling the Scarlet L. 'our one prose masterpiece' – I'd so much rather we had more than that one" (qtd. in Lewis 237). As Lewis notes, Wharton's "grudging reading of Hawthorne, whose impact on *Ethan Frome* a few years later would be unmistakable," conveys a younger writer's need to denigrate a predecessor in order to promote herself (237). But Wharton transforms rather than imitates Hawthornian romance. As Elissa Greenwald points out, extreme romanticism, with its subversion of certainties and subjective points of view, is a precursor of modernism (158). Wharton's "prose masterpiece" reinterprets the romantic world of *The Scarlet Letter* for a disenchanted age by refusing tragic heroism or mediating circumstances.

Lost Eden

Edith Wharton's sense of Calvinist extremes is evident in her description of nature and community, which she also presents in a modernist way. The Calvinist view of nature is immediately apparent in Wharton's setting and, in particular, in the name of Ethan Frome's town. Starkfield is a "stark field," a postlapsarian Eden where "starved apple-trees writh[e] over a hillside" and Ethan struggles for dignity and survival. While life in Starkfield is generally difficult for its inhabitants, Ethan is especially afflicted. His barren fields and "lonely" New England farmhouse, with a funereal "black wraith of deciduous creeper flapp[ing] from the porch," only "make the landscape lonelier" (11). Material prosperity, a sign to early New Englanders that they were members of the Elect, eludes Ethan. He toils constantly but has no heart for, and takes no profit from, his work. With his "saw-mill and the arid acres of his farm yield[ing] scarcely enough to keep his household through the winter" and more than his share of "sickness and trouble" (8), Ethan has missed his calling, a conception valued by early Puritans. His house, stripped of the structural "L" that connects it to the barn, is a "forlorn" "image of his own shrunken body" (11–12).

Seasonal imagery also conveys Ethan's isolation. Winter was commonly used in sermons of Puritan preachers to signify periods of doubt, divine trials, and perseverance. The clergy spoke of lapses in faith arising not from a deficit of grace but from the believer's human inadequacies: "so is it with the graces of God in mans soule, they have their spring and summer seasons, they have also their winter, wherein they seeme cleane blasted and decayed, as if there were no seeds of grace in their hearts." The faithful, believing that the season of winter is temporary, actively work to eradicate doubt from their psyches. In one minister's words, "it is not the office of faith to cherish and maintaine such feares and doubts, but to resist them, to fight against them, and so much as is possible to expell them, and driue them out" (qtd. in P. Miller, *New England* 54). In Ethan Frome's case, however, winter is a sure victor: the narrator notes "the vitality of the climate and the deadness of the community" (5). The "storms of February" and "wild cavalry of March winds" (6) vanquish human effort and deny – like T. S. Eliot's cruel month of April – any promise of spring and rebirth. Ethan succumbs to this winter of the soul so totally that he seems virtually "a part of the mute melancholy landscape, an incarnation of its frozen woe" (8).

Wharton further expresses human alienation from nature in her ending. In the actual 1904 mishap that inspired the climactic suicide attempt, a group of Lenox sledders collided with a lamppost; one girl was killed, one made lame for life, and one badly scarred. In Wharton's version, a "warm stillness" (75) like the "warm sense of continuance and stability" (26) that Ethan feels in the graveyard gently seduces the couple toward death – but not toward salvation. They clash with a symbol of nature, an elm tree, rather than one of society, a lamppost. Wharton's version is modernist in its depiction of the human spirit in battle with itself and its suggestion of psychological conflict and denial of will: although the lovers choose death rather than separation, they end up together and maimed, unable to control their destinies.

In addition to representing fallen nature, Wharton enlists the Calvinist notion of election to underscore Ethan's isolation. Puritans, hoping eventually to join God's saints in heaven, sought to replicate that community in human relations. As Miller and Johnson note, "it was not possible to segregate a man's spiritual life from his communal life" (181). The more confidence an individual experienced about his own salvation, the more positively he embraced the society in which he lived. Ethan Frome enjoys none of this community. Indeed, only he, Mattie, and Zeena seem singled out for their cruel fate. Other characters find some measure of happiness; in Puritan terms, they experience relief from universal sinfulness because they believe they are Elect. For example, Ruth Varnum is a healer like Zeena but is not blighted by moral tragedy; she is healthy – "hale" – as her married name implies. Ruth and Ned Hale marry and have children, unlike Mattie and Ethan, and their house – "at one end of the main street . . . looking down . . . to the slim white steeple of the Congregational Church" (6) – forms a social and spiritual center for the town. Mrs. Hale's knowledge of the Frome tragedy, an event that in Puritan times might precipitate a crisis conversion, accounts for the "insurmountable reticence" and "depths of sad initiation" in her voice when she speaks of the crash (6–7). Intuitively, neighbors keep their distance from Ethan: "his taciturnity was respected and it was only on rare occasions that one of the older men of the place detained him for a word" (4). Ethan's estrangement from community – like Young Goodman Brown's in Hawthorne's story – signifies his spiritual alienation.[22]

Wharton's modernist message in *Ethan Frome* is that paradise lost cannot be regained – in this life or the next. The ideal Puritan renounced worldy pleasure in anticipation of eternal joy in the hereafter, but Wharton, a modern skeptic, no longer trusts in God or the afterlife. Mattie and Ethan, guilty of sexual transgression born of original sin, merit no forgiveness. Wharton takes to a bitter, logical conclusion the Calvinist belief that human will can effect only evil, not good. It is not, then, as Edmund Wilson argues, that Ethan "lack[s] the force or the courage either to impose himself or to get away" (26–27), but that human efforts are already doomed. The self not only fails to assert itself in such a world but is reduced, as Mattie Silver's pained, mouselike *"cheep"* suggests (84, original emphasis), to the lower order of animals. No less etherized than Eliot's Prufrock, Ethan elicits pity because he cannot act; his will is as frozen as the landscape he inhabits. Wharton's version of the New England "errand into the wilderness" is, indeed, an errand gone awry.

Turn-of-the-century liberal theology and positivistic science had blurred the hard edges of old-fashioned religion to the point that *Scribner's* could mourn "The Passing of the Devil" in 1899, and a writer for the *Atlantic Monthly* could complain that "conscience has lost its strong and on-pressing energy." The agony of awaiting the conversion experience gave way to balmy notions like "the Safety and Helpfulness of Faith"; and hell, as clergyman William Gladstone noted, was "relegated . . . to the far-off corners of the Christian mind" (qtd. in Lears 46, 44). Followers of Darwin dispensed with God by turning him into a secular concept molded by human will. When Wharton resurrects the God force in *Ethan Frome,* she reinstates an element missing from secularized bourgeois culture: punishment for sin and the reality of hell. Wharton's view of Calvinism in *Ethan Frome* resembles Max Weber's: a doctrine dedicated to "the destruction of spontaneous, impulsive enjoyment" (119). She demonstrates that Calvinist doctrines were not dead at the turn of the century, only dormant.

Wharton's modernism is evident in her use of history as well as religion. Modernist writers broke with the immediate past and turned to pastoral or classical ideals, mixing earlier chapters of history in richly allusive, jarring ways. "Instead of narrative method, we may now use the mythical method," writes T. S. Eliot (178). Like other modernists, Wharton draws on classical and folk forms, but she criticizes rather than reinstates them. The chapter of history that Wharton most strongly evokes and rejects in *Ethan Frome* is Calvinist, as we have seen, but she also alludes to classical tragedy and European fairy tales. For example, the image of Ethan's "lean brown head, with its shock of light hair" that once sat "gallantly" "on his strong shoulders before they were bent out of shape" (4), suggests a Greek hero – but a defeated one. And, as in Greek tragedy, we learn the story of Ethan Frome – a "ruin of a man" (3) – from the choral laments of Harmon Gow and Mrs. Hale. Wharton also transforms the traditional form of the fairy tale, which, as Jackson Lears explains, allowed Victorian readers to escape reality and lose themselves in a primitive or mythic past. The fairy-tale movement provided a substitute for lost religious certainty and thereby represented an antimodern impulse (168–73). However, in *Ethan Frome,* Wharton employs this motif ironically – that is, modernistically – to convey religious skepticism. The wicked witch Zeena is not destroyed, and young innocents Ethan and Mattie do not live happily ever after. By distorting the fairy tale, Wharton subverts Victorian optimism and makes her tale "new" in the sense that Ezra Pound exhorted writers to invent new forms.

Inscrutable Powers

If *Ethan Frome* served as a cultural critique of Calvinism, it also permitted Wharton to explore the deep personal meanings that this bleak doctrine held for her. Although raised Episcopalian, at an early age she had developed a Calvinist sensibility that included a harsh, judgmental God who ruled through fear rather than love; who enacted strict payment for pleasure; and who was not obliged to redeem humankind through the sacrifice of his son. Wharton once again found herself wrestling with Calvinism when, in 1908, she began an adulterous affair with Morton Fullerton. This affair – and the lies it necessitated – reactivated the "moral tortures" that had obsessed her as a child in Mlle Michelet's dancing class. Wharton herself discounted this association, perhaps because it was so personal and potent. She claims instead that "a distant glimpse of Bear Mountain brought Ethan back to my memory, and the following winter in Paris I wrote the tale as it now stands" (*Backward* 295–96). However, Wharton was not in New England in 1909 or 1910 (Lewis 300); therefore a recent visit could not account for her renewed fascination with the area and its culture. Rather, her statement that "Ethan's history stirred again in my memory" must refer to her more general sense of the New England past, as well as her childhood experiences with Calvinist "moral tortures." Ethan Frome's drama of defeat reproduces Wharton's belief that she was waging a losing battle with Calvinist principles. In romantic despair and judging herself guilty of the same sins as Ethan and Mattie, she created a fictional world in which adulterous love means dependence and disfigurement.[23]

Wharton's personal life is discernible in all three of her main characters. She aligns herself with her protagonist through a similarity of names: Edith Jones and Ethan Frome. Ethan suffers when his mother becomes ill and strangely silent. After she dies, he marries her nurse, Zeena, in order to escape his terrible loneliness, but Zeena, too, turns sickly and querulous. Likewise, Edith Jones suffered from her mother's silence: Lucretia Jones disapproved so vehemently of her daughter's writing that she never spoke to her about it. Wharton also married a man of whom her mother approved – just as Ethan marries the woman closest to his mother. After years of incompatibility, she experienced, like Ethan, the thrill of an illicit passion; and she struggled, like him, with conflicts between romantic desire and marital commitment.

If Ethan suggests Wharton's thwarted passion, then Mattie represents the expression of that passion. Mattie is both Morton Fullerton, a charming, carefree lover, and Wharton herself as she encountered – at middle age and for the first time – the kind of romance usually reserved for youth. Mattie's feelings for Ethan are as unmindful of consequences as Wharton's for Fullerton initially must have been. By the same token, however, Mattie's devastating immobilization at the end of the novel emblematizes Wharton's fear that loving Fullerton might end in her own emotional crippling.

Wharton reserves her most complicated portrayal for Zeena. Zeena is like Teddy Wharton, a wronged spouse, who becomes vengeful rather than forgiving. She is also like Lucretia Jones, a deficient nurturer with all the fearsome, God-like powers that Wharton associated with her mother during the dancing-class incident. Much of Wharton's adult energy was spent freeing herself from maternal domination in order to achieve the writer's life she felt called to live. An icily intolerant woman, Lucretia Jones demanded social conformity and discouraged literary expression, at one point even denying her daughter writing paper – Wharton says that she "was driven to begging for the wrappings of the parcels delivered at the house" (*Backward* 73). Moreover, Lucretia Jones's rigid sense of propriety precluded meaningful communication between mother and daughter. Wharton's mother refused to tell her even the basic facts of life, so that when Wharton married Teddy in 1885, she was hopelessly ignorant about sexuality. In "Life and I," she details how her mother stifled her natural curiosities:

> And all the while Life, real Life, was ringing in my ears, humming in my blood, flushing my cheeks & waving in my hair – sending me messages & signals from every beautiful face & musical voice, & running over me in vague tremors when I rode my poney [*sic*], or swam through the short bright ripples of the bay, or raced & danced & tumbled with "the boys." And I didn't know – & if, by any chance, I came across the shadow of a reality, & asked my mother "What does it mean?" I was always told "You're too little to understand," or else "It's not nice to ask about such things." (1086–87)

Wharton's relationship with her mother – one of longing, disappointment, and fear – finds fictional expression in Zeena, a woman who punishes but does not love.

Wharton suggests Zeena's parental role in a number of ways. Although only seven years his senior, she seems old enough to be Ethan's mother; she "was already an old woman" (32). After Ethan's mother dies, he clings to her out of gratitude and need, as a child does to a parent: he had a "magnified . . . sense of what he owed her" and a "dread of being left alone" (35). But Zeena is no nurturer. She takes the dead mother's place by emulating her "silent," self-absorbed, and sickly behavior (36). Ethan and Mattie, in contrast, are portrayed as helpless children. They return home from a dance to find that a dispproving Zeena has locked the door. When she later decides, without consulting either of them, to evict Mattie and hire a new servant, neither can muster objection. And just as Lucretia Jones restricted her daughter's knowledge of the facts of life, Zeena guards the gates of passion. She keeps her red pickle dish, a wedding present and phallic symbol of desire, high on a shelf, just as Lucretia kept sexual knowledge out of her daughter's reach. As Elizabeth Ammons argues, Zeena is not only the wicked witch (63), but the "mother-antithesis" (200n.).

When Zeena leaves town overnight to see a doctor, Ethan fantasizes about an evening alone with Mattie. Wharton may have drawn on her experience with Fullerton for this scene: they spent one exquisite night together in June 1909, which she celebrated in a passionate poem (Lewis 258–59; Wolff, *Feast* 197–98). However, her fictional offspring are denied even this simple pleasure. First, Ethan's fantasy of "what it would be like that evening, when he and Mattie were there after supper" is marred by the pang he feels when he sees Ned and Ruth kissing openly at the place where he and Mattie once stood in secrecy. Unlike Ethan and Mattie, they "need not hide their happiness" (39). Second, he has a sense of foreboding when he passes the graveyard where his forebears Ethan Frome and Endurance are buried and realizes "the same epitaph would be written over him and Zeena" (40). And when Mattie and Ethan dare to use the red pickle dish – that is, to explore and express their desire – the cat, Zeena's occult emissary, jumps onto the chair, shatters the dish, and ends the romantic interlude. Ethan feels a thrill of phallic "mastery" – like "steering a big log down the mountain to his mill" (43) – when he imagines that he will be able to repair the dish, but Zeena later vanquishes him in an equally phallic allusion that associates masculinity with pickles and disease. She hands him a medicine bottle, commenting, "It'll do for pickles" (33).

By investing Zeena with enigmatic and absolute powers, Wharton extends her role from spouse to parent to deity – in the same way that in childhood she aligned her mother with the "inscrutable" God ("Life" 1074). An unforgiving scorekeeper whose "fault-finding was of the silent kind, but not the less penetrating for that," Zeena inflicts a double cruelty. She is an ironic inversion of the nurturing mother, and – through Wharton's childlike association – the exacting Calvinist God bent on condemnation and retribution. Mute and threatening, Zeena evokes "vague dread." Although Ethan tries to "imagine that peace reigned in his house," he can only "postpone certainty" that it does not (30–31). "Nobody can tell with Zeena," Mattie says (47). Having vowed vengeance, Zeena, a wrathful deity, "never changed her mind" (60).

Just as the Calvinist believer longed for happiness but was racked by guilt and unworthiness, Ethan alternates wildly between ecstasy and dejection: "now he thought [Mattie] understood him, and feared; now he was sure she did not, and despaired" (24). The end of the novel reinforces his powerlessness. Reviewing the opportunities that life with Zeena caused him to miss, Ethan cries out with the futility of Job, "And what good had come of it? She was a hundred times bitterer and more discontented than when he had married her; the one pleasure left her was to inflict pain on him" (64). His spirit rises up against such waste, but he can take no action.

Ethan's and Mattie's failed suicide also underlines their lack of control over their destinies. The lovers drive past "Shadow Pond," where Mattie once made them coffee "over a gipsy fire" (75), outside the reach of Christian law. At Corbury Road, they stand "between the indistinct white glimmer of the church and the black curtain of the Varnum spruces" (79), caught between God and nature. Then, with helpless abandon and "stricken faces," clinging to one another like children, they imagine they "can fetch it" (83) and start down the hill. Zeena – "no longer the listless creature who had lived at [Ethan's] side in a state of sullen self-absorption, but a mysterious alien presence, an evil energy secreted from the long years of silent brooding" (58) – again intervenes. As he points the sled toward the elm, Ethan suddenly sees Zeena's face, "with twisted monstrous lineaments, thrust itself between him and his goal" (83). Her image, like that of a wrathful God, causes the sled to veer from its course, and the lovers' hopes – and bodies – are dashed. In Hawthorne's novel of thwarted passion, Chillingworth's power over Dimmesdale and Hester dissolves with Dimmesdale's confession and death, but in *Ethan Frome,* even Ethan's and Mattie's attempted suicide is under Zeena's God-like control. They find themselves, to paraphrase Jonathan Edwards, sinners in the hands of an angry Zeena.[24]

Mattie and Ethan's plight, which Bernard De Voto complains lacks "correspondence with the reality of human life" (x), reproduces the Calvinist and Darwinian senses of forces beyond one's comprehension or control. In this regard, Wharton is not, as Lionel Trilling argues, a writer whose "limitation of heart" expresses itself "as a literary and moral deficiency." Nor is it true that *Ethan Frome* "presents no moral issue at all" ("Morality" 138–39). On the contrary, in this novel Wharton is obsessively, pessimistically, moral. She leaves no doubt about Ethan's condition; as the narrator exclaims, "he looks as if he was dead and in hell now!" (4).

A Usable Past

Ethan Frome conveys Wharton's experience of Calvinism as both a personal and cultural defeat. However, the novel's narrative structure suggests that she also envisioned escape from such restriction. *Ethan Frome* is the only one of Wharton's novels that makes use of a narrative frame. As Wharton notes in her preface, the unnamed narrator acts "as the sympathizing intermediary between his rudimentary characters and the more complicated minds to whom he is trying to present them" (vi). He also provides distance between the story and its telling. He is an outsider with limited perceptions, whose account is necessarily selective and speculative. Through him, Wharton permits a subjective rather than objective interpretation of Ethan's story.

This unreliable narration – a modernist technique – invites both the narrator's and the reader's participation. The narrator constructs the tale from his observations and neighbors' accounts, deciding on the meaning of what he has learned. The reader, provided with the same information as the narrator, similarly engages in acts of meaning-making. Frequent ellipses – for example, before and after the narrator's reconstruction of Ethan's story; when Ethan and Mattie imagine a life together, race downhill toward the tree, and awaken after the crash; and when Ethan introduces the narrator to Zeena and Mattie – also ask the reader to fill in "the gaps" in Ethan's story (5).[25] Expecting realism, critics look for verisimilitude in *Ethan Frome*, faulting minor inaccuracies such as Zeena's false teeth or Ethan's morning shave. In *Ethan Frome,* however, one's *response* to events is more important than the events themselves. Alfred Kazin correctly labels the novel "abstract," arguing that to fault Wharton because she "never knew how the poor lived in Paris or London" and "even less of how they lived in the New England villages" is to miss her characters' inner struggles (81). As early as 1915, Elizabeth Shepley Sergeant also perceived the novel's subjectivity: "it was just Mrs. Wharton's *own sense* of the blankness and emptiness . . . in Starkfield lives, that made her construct that tremendous fourth act for her lovers and condemn them to its gruesome, long-drawn epilogue" (20, my emphasis). A realistic novel might end with the lovers' resigned parting; however, Wharton's choice – to leave all three characters suspended in pain without resolution – conveys her modernist sense of uncertainty and indeterminacy.

Focusing on the narrator's perceptions of the story he tells also allows Wharton to present two sides of a conflict that warred within her: the Calvinist defeat represented by Ethan, and the rejection of that fate represented by a modern scientist and skeptic. The narrator, a sophisticated urban engineer, comes to the remote town of Starkfield to oversee the expansion of an electric power plant. There he encounters his dark double, Ethan Frome, a man who has forfeited dreams of technical achievement and romance, whose only future is to join his ancestors in the family graveyard. The engineer is associated with technology, education, choice, and worldly accomplishment; Ethan, with unyielding nature, lapsed potential, restriction, and suffering. Wharton herself held these two world views in tension, not only during the period that she wrote *Ethan Frome,* but during much of her life. On the one hand, she feared that determining forces would inhibit her growth as a writer; on the other, she hoped to shake off these restrictions and shape her own destiny.

The narrator expects to mold events to his own plan, but he encounters the same obstacles that hinder Ethan. For example, he must rely on an earlier mode of transport, horse and buggy, to travel to the plant site because the railroad does not fully serve the remote region. Nature has its way when Denis Eady's horses fall ill, and the narrator turns to Ethan for transportation. Snow then blankets the town, requiring a detour to Ethan's farmhouse and the figurative journey backward in time, when natural and moral necessity seem to predate and defeat reason. The narrator, an accomplished technologist, represents the post-Darwinian conviction that, as chemist John William Draper says, "there was no limit to understanding the world in natural rather than supernatural terms" (qtd. in Turner 200).[26] Ethan Frome, however, a failed engineer, evokes an earlier chapter in American moral history that focused on human limitation rather than potential. The narrator intuitively understands the effect of this Calvinist past when he takes Ethan for "an old man," even though he is "not more than fifty-two" (3).

The narrator tries to discover the cause of Ethan Frome's misfortune, but he can only speculate that it was "something in his past history, or in his present way of living" (10). He finds the answer in a look on Ethan's face "which . . . neither poverty nor physical suffering could have put there" (7). The narrator senses rather than deduces a "depth of moral isolation too remote for casual access" (8). Thus Wharton suggests that despite reason, science, and technology, the world is still unknowable and beyond human control. In the end, the narrator can only muse over the ruin of a man whose interest in science and books has not saved him. The search for meaning is as frustrated for us as it is for the narrator: we find within the text no rational explanation for Ethan's fate and means of altering it.

If the meaning of Ethan's story is indeterminate for both narrator and reader, it was not so for Edith Wharton. The very act of composing the novel released her from her Calvinist "moral tortures." Wharton clearly aligns herself with both Ethan and the narrator. Like Ethan, she is a sensitive yet discouraged aspirer who has "been in Starkfield too many winters" and cannot "get away" (5, 6); like the narrator, she is a designer with creative capabilities who does get away. Ultimately, however, one sensibility prevails: Wharton, writer and creator, identifies with the narrator rather than the mute and powerless Ethan Frome. Whereas Ethan laments, "Oh, what good'll writing do?" (78), Wharton seized the pen and imparted her story to others.[27]

The narrator gains power over the narrative in yet another way. Initially curious about and sympathetic toward Ethan's plight, he becomes more detached by the end of the story. His narrative ends when he meets Mattie and Zeena; we learn nothing of his reaction to their suffering. We can only imagine his relief at being able to escape the conditions that keep Starkfield under "siege like a starved garrison capitulating without quarter" (6). Furthermore, the narrator's position is not entirely neutral. If the characters' wracked, ailing bodies bear the marks of punishment by an avenging God who belongs to an outmoded faith, then the narrator's gaze serves to reinforce that punishment. In Foucauldian terms, his surveillance – a play of asymmetrical glances that the objectified individuals internalize – asserts his power over the scene. The novel opens, after all, with the narrator's gaze fixed on Ethan Frome as he pulls his horses to a stop and limps awkwardly to the post office. It ends with his invasive scrutiny of the Frome household – a visit that no Starkfield resident has ever made. Can Ethan Frome feel anything but humiliation and defeat when – already "a prisoner for life," with reality "closed in on him like prison-warders hand-cuffing a convict" (66) – he is further punished by the narrator's penetrating gaze?

Through the narrative frame in *Ethan Frome,* then, Edith Wharton allowed herself to survey and emerge victorious over the crippling effects of Calvinism. In writing the novel, as Debra Goodman notes, she created a scapegoat to bear her guilt and thereby "exorcized her own demons" (qtd. in Murad 103n.). Her affair with Fullerton had reactivated her Calvinist morality – what she once called a "cursed" "split between body & soul" (*Letters* 159) – but *Ethan Frome* healed the split.

Despite critical acclaim, Wharton never considered *Ethan Frome* her literary masterpiece. Some twenty years later, she wrote that, "far from thinking 'Ethan Frome' my best novel," she was "bored and even exasperated when I am told that it is" (*Backward* 209). Her godson, William Royall Tyler, corroborates: "She was always impatient about *Ethan Frome*. She wished that people wouldn't always talk to her about it. She didn't think of *Ethan Frome* as being her highest achievement or anything like it" (Interview, 25 April). Yet Wharton understood that the novel was a technical tour de force that enabled her to experience "the artisan's full control of his implements" (*Backward* 209). She also knew that it helped her lift a heavy personal burden. As she writes in the preface, the subject of Ethan Frome was the first "I had ever approached with full confidence in its value, *for my own purpose* (vi, my emphasis). Even if the novel's significance was private, it was still a source of power. As Wharton remarked about readers' responses to the novel: "They don't know *why* it's good, but they are right: it *is*" (*Letters* 261, original emphases).

Calvinism provided Wharton with a usable past that she could transform into modernist art. Like other female American writers such as Anne Bradstreet, Emily Dickinson, and Harriet Beecher Stowe, she found the patriarchal, Calvinist God oppressive, but in *Ethan Frome* she turns an austere theology into an austere aesthetic. She gives her narrator modern values and plain, economical speech. His efficient expression – a language *démeublé*, as Willa Cather puts it – heightens the novel's emotional impact: we feel the characters' suffering all the more because so much of their inner lives is left to be imagined. As Cecilia Tichi notes, a decade before Ernest Hemingway published his first major work, Wharton had mastered "the power of the machine-age plain style" – an "engineering aesthetic" (219, 217). Modernist writers often achieved a hard-edged quality with images of metals, especially steel; in *Ethan Frome,* Wharton accomplishes the same goal with New England granite. Commenting on her artistic method, she explains that in the "construction" of her novel, she resisted the "added ornament, or a trick of drapery or lighting" (vii) that is associated with Victorian realism. It is true that Wharton remained aloof from the Left Bank modernists just blocks away in Paris,[28] and she rejected some twentieth-century literary developments – for example, she called Joyce's *Ulysses* "a welter of pornography . . . unformed and unimportant drivel" and complained that Eliot's *The Waste Land* lacked the warmth of Whitman's poetry (Lewis 442). Nevertheless, *Ethan Frome,* although an American story, was drafted in France, amid the ferment of a new international literary movement. We can consider Wharton a modernist innovator whose *Ethan Frome* helped shape a movement and whose minimalist style influenced Sherwood Anderson, Gertrude Stein, and Ernest Hemingway.

Wharton continued to write about New England, but she never wrote another novel as bleak as *Ethan Frome.* No other fiction is so desolate in setting, theme, and tone, because at no other time did she wrestle so intensely with dark Calvinist issues. Wharton's childlike guilt and self-effacement before an exacting mother who resembled a fierce and judgmental God combined in *Ethan Frome* with the adult's determination to leave that past behind. Although themes of payment for pleasure and sacrifice without reward persist in her fiction, *Ethan Frome* was a gateway through which Wharton could explore other moral and spiritual paths. These included, as we shall see, qualities of feminine wisdom and power associated with the ancient divinity Sophia in *The Reef,* Emersonian transcendentalism in *Summer,* Platonic idealism in *The Age of Innocence,* and Catholicism in *Hudson River Bracketed* and *The Gods Arrive.*

4

Fragile Freedoms

Where [Edith Wharton] has made her mark here is in the creation of
that vivid young creature Sophy Viner. Sophy is real; she lays hold of
that in you which makes yourself real.
      H. I. Brock, review of *The Reef*

To name God in oneself, or to speak the word "Goddess" again after
many centuries of silence is to reverse age-old patterns of thinking in
which male power and female subordination are viewed as the norm.
      Carol Christ, *Diving Deep and Surfacing*

[*Summer*] is known to its author & her familiars as the Hot Ethan.. . .
I don't know how on earth the thing got itself written.. . . Anyhow,
the setting will amuse you.
      Edith Wharton, Letter to Gaillard Lapsley

"IF I ever have children," Edith Wharton wrote in her autobiography "Life and I," "I shall deprive them of *every pleasure,* in order to
prepare them for the inevitable unhappiness of life" (1091, original emphasis). Ethan Frome and Mattie Silver are, figuratively, two such children.
However, Wharton had others less afflicted. She followed the compressed
bleakness of *Ethan Frome* with a prodigious outpouring of fiction and
nonfiction, including *The Reef* (1912), *The Custom of the Country* (1913),
Xingu (1916), *Summer* (1917), *French Ways and Their Meaning* (1919), *In
Morocco* (1920), and *The Age of Innocence* (1920). Although these writings
are varied, many demonstrate a conscious search for alternatives to the
American status quo. Some of these texts indicate that, for Wharton, the
time was right for considered optimism – for casting off the burdens
of Calvinist fathers (and mothers) and enjoying freedom from Christian

127

proscriptions. After *Ethan Frome*, Wharton began a period of joyful rebellion. This chapter examines two of her fictional orphans, Sophy Viner and Charity Royall, who also make courageous bids for independence and romantic freedom.

Seeking Sophia in *The Reef*

In 1912, Edith Wharton wrote to Bernard Berenson that she was hard at work on *The Reef*, which she called "Ethan's successor" (*Letters* 266). *The Reef* continues the emotional drama of *Ethan Frome,* with its real-life parallel in Wharton's affair with Morton Fullerton.[1] Both novels are tangled tales of infidelity about two women's relationship to each other and to the same man. Overall, however, their differences outweigh their similarities. Whereas *Ethan Frome* employs a frame narrative to mediate the unarticulated passion of her characters, *The Reef* renders the tale directly through George Darrow's and Anna Leath's perspectives. Wharton's most Jamesian novel – which James himself praised for its "Racinian unity, intensity and gracility" (Powers 239) – *The Reef* is more analytical than *Ethan Frome,* reflecting *upon,* as well as reflecting, conflicting feelings of desire, guilt, and loss. The later novel explicitly confronts issues of intimacy, truth, and betrayal in relationships, whereas *Ethan Frome* leaves them to the reader's imagination.[2] In *The Reef,* one learns not just what goes wrong in a love affair, but how and why.

Changes in Wharton's relationship with Morton Fullerton, which began in 1908 and ended sometime in 1910, in part account for this shift in emphasis from *Ethan Frome* to *The Reef.* When *The Reef* was completed in August 1912, their affair was, practically speaking, over. Wharton's overwhelming guilt, which had found expression in *Ethan Frome,* gave way to different concerns about the nature of love, passion, and trust. Wharton now had time and perspective from which to review the relationship with her charming but inconstant lover. Unlike Wharton, for whom loyalty was inviolable, Fullerton moved casually in and out of emotional entanglements. He not only had previous lovers, both male and female, but he was secretly engaged to his cousin Katherine Fullerton while involved with Wharton. Time had shown Fullerton to be untrustworthy; his initial outpourings of devotion were followed by periods of indifference and neglect. Having survived the tumult of the first two years of the affair, a disappointed Edith Wharton wrote to Fullerton in 1910, "My life was better before I knew you. That is, for me, the sad conclusion of this sad year. And it is a bitter thing to say to the one being one has ever loved d'amour" (*Letters* 208).

The Reef provides insight about how and why Wharton reached this "sad conclusion." It is an incisive portrait of a conventional woman who struggles, as Wharton did, to open herself to passion only to face disillusionment. *The Reef* is a novel of sexual awakening, as Cynthia Griffin Wolff notes (*Feast* 208–9), but it is more than a study of passion. It criticizes the social and moral conditions of love between the sexes and exposes hypocrisy in early twentieth-century class and gender relations. Wharton voices frustration with a social system that accepts men's unfaithfulness but holds women accountable to arbitrary standards of "good" and "bad" behavior. She shows how this patriarchal, double standard diminishes the feminine spirit and enslaves women.

Ethan Frome and *The Reef* are predicated upon different spiritual and social world views. In *The Reef*, Wharton abandons Calvinism and the passive model of female behavior that it encourages. She rejects the dominant Western view of male superiority and instead turns to a prepatriarchal, feminine model. By denying traditional representations of the divine as exclusively male, Wharton goes "beyond God the Father," to use Mary Daly's phrase, to affirm the sacred feminine and, with it, principles of honesty and courage. She does so through her heroine, Sophy Viner. Sophy's name alludes to Sophia, the ancient embodiment of feminine wisdom and creativity. Through her, Wharton imagines a society restructured according to more feminine values. Her vision remains just that, however – a vision. By the end of the novel, Sophy is driven away, as was her namesake long ago, and both pairs of lovers forfeit happiness because they are afraid to challenge social conventions.[3] Thus, at the same time that Wharton criticizes society's conventions, she reveals her dependence on them. *The Reef* faults the present system, imagines alternatives and suggests directions for change, but ultimately falls short of realizing a brighter future for men's and women's relationships.[4]

The Oedipal plot of *The Reef* involves not three characters, but four. George Darrow plans to marry an old flame, Anna Leath; but on his way to visit her, he has a brief affair with a younger woman named Sophy Viner. Later, Anna unknowingly hires Sophy as her daughter's governess. The triangle is squared when Anna's stepson, Owen Leath, falls in love with Sophy and plans to marry her. The novel focuses, first, on Anna's pledge to convince Owen's aristocratic grandmother to approve of his marriage to someone below his class and, second, on Anna's efforts to cope with her discovery of Darrow's betrayal. What begins for Anna as a simple, motherly intervention becomes a monumental moral struggle. In the end, accommodation proves impossible. Sophy and Owen break their engagement, and Anna and Darrow's relationship is irreparably damaged.

In the relatively little critical commentary that *The Reef* has received,

Sophy and Anna are often seen as contrasting, even competing, figures.[5] However, Sophy is the novel's moral center, a measuring rod against which we assess both Darrow's and Anna's characters. Sophy, like the ancient Sophia, acts as a moral touchstone and catalyst for change. She brings false values to light and challenges the characters' – and even the reader's – comfortable assumptions about propriety, gender, and class. As Carol Wershoven notes, Darrow and Anna "live by the same safe attitudes"; Sophy Viner is the intruder who destroys their complacency (*Female* 97–98). Her poverty and youthful, free spirit contrast sharply with their affluence and gentility. More important, she violates the sexual and social standards that each uphold.

Although very little of the novel is devoted exclusively to Sophy, she is the most important character; as Wolff puts it, "what matters, always, is Sophy Viner" (*Feast* 210). Wolff faults Wharton for failing to present Sophy's character directly, but her vagueness may be deliberate. By presenting her as an elusive character, Wharton shows that frank, lively, and creative feminine qualities *are* elusive in twentieth-century culture. Sophy Viner – whose name alludes not only to the specific figure of Sophia, but to an entire tradition of feminine power and spirituality – represents the repressed feminine in Western culture. We are driven, as Wolff notes, "to define her, capture her essence, place her, somehow, in the larger categories of our lives" (*Feast* 210). When attempting to decipher Sophy's character, we also participate in this recuperation of the feminine. Just as we know little about Sophy's past, present, or future, few records of matriarchal culture and the age of reigning goddesses exist, and efforts to research them are often unsuccessful. Sophy holds our attention without being fully presented; we create her identity from fragments in the same way that we piece together the history of women's once powerful spiritual reign.

The figure Sophia, whose name means "wisdom," is important in the Hellenistic, Hebrew, and Christian traditions. She is related to the ancient goddesses, in particular to the great mother figures of Isis and Demeter, whose powers she rivaled (Engelsman 92–93). In Judaic and Christian cultures, she was originally a hypostasis of God and God's wisdom, but she fell victim to doctrines of patriarchal control and supremacy. Although there are more pages devoted to Sophia in the Old Testament than to almost any other figure – only God, Moses, Job, and David are treated in more depth (Cady et al. 16) – most modern readers know her only as an obscure, minor figure; even fewer understand the magnitude of her powers. She appears explicitly in Hebrew scriptures, especially Proverbs, Ecclesiasticus (or Ben Sirach), Baruch, and the Wisdom of Solomon, and indirectly in Christian gospels and epistles, but she is recognizable in biblical traditions by her quality, "wisdom," rather than her name, "Sophia."

Sophia's diminution began with the Jewish philosopher and writer Philo, who substituted the masculine Logos (meaning "word") for the feminine Sophia. Although the terms were once equated, Logos replaced Sophia and assumed her divine roles, including that of the firstborn image of God and the principle of order. Restricted to heaven, Sophia became limited to "Maiden, daughter of God" and "firstborn Mother." Logos, in contrast, became identified with the male authority (Engelsman 95–106; Cady et al. 11). The Bible continued this process of repression, replacing Sophia with Christ as personifed Wisdom. Parallels between Christ in the Gospels and Sophia in Proverbs, Wisdom, and Ecclesiasticus abound: in John, Christ even speaks words attributed to Sophia: "I am the true vine" (15.1); "I am the vine, ye are the branches . . . without me ye can do nothing" (15.5). Sophia's final repression came in the third and fourth centuries when the early church not only assigned her qualities to Christ, but further limited her role as equal to God by insisting on monotheism. Displaced by the male Jesus and subordinated to the male deity, Sophia effectively disappeared from the Christian tradition. Elaine Pagels notes that some of Sophia's female aspects were reflected in the figure of the Holy Spirit, but this role also marginalized and repressed her femininity (111–13). Catholics diminish Sophia's role by interpreting her as a prefigure of Mary, and Protestants tend to focus on the later chapters of Proverbs rather than the early chapters that she dominates.

Feminist scholars interpret Sophia's evolution and repression variously, but all agree on her importance in Judaic and Christian traditions and her role in modern contemporary religious consciousness. Feminist theologians, in particular, focus on Sophia's ability to integrate divisions propounded by patriarchy and at the same time to bear witness to the suppression of feminine power in religious history (Cady et al. 14–15). Elisabeth Schüssler Fiorenza argues that Sophia is the God of Israel expressed in the language and imagery of the goddess; in wisdom theology, unlike classical theology, Sophia is characterized by her inspiration rather than her fearsomeness. Fiorenza speculates that early Christians used wisdom theology to understand Christ as Sophia's messenger, prophet, or child, and that this practice, which amounted to a political proclamation of equality for women and other downtrodden people, resulted in a backlash and Jesus' crucifixion (133–35).

Although the Sophia tradition was historically repressed, it was nevertheless accessible at the turn of the century. Edith Wharton would have found mention of Sophia in her extensive reading of Greek religion and history. She also writes in *A Backward Glance* that she read wisdom literature in the King James version of the Bible (70); and a copy of the Apocrypha – including the Roman Catholic books of Ecclesiasticus and Baruch, in which much of the Sophia material appears – was in Wharton's library.[6]

Sophia was dismissed by the church fathers because she did not fit their rigid categories of human behavior; in particular, she was "too ambiguous and pliable to fit neatly into the discussion of humanity versus divinity" (Cady et al. 16). Wharton captures this elusive, richly ambiguous female quality – both repressed and resistant to repression – in her depiction of Sophy Viner. Despite male domination, Sophy remains resourceful and independent. Like her namesake, she also embraces contrarieties: although poor, she depends on no one but herself; although thoroughly acquainted with "the real business of living," she is "free without hardness and self-assured without assertiveness"; her "light-hearted philosophy" remains uncorrupted (26, 25). Sophy fits none of the ready-made categories for women. As Darrow admits, "she might be any one of a dozen definable types, or she might – more disconcertingly to her companion and more perilously to herself – be a shifting and uncrystallized mixture of them all" (60).

The ancient Sophia's central roles were those of sister, lover, teacher, and creator or life-giving force (Fiorenza 133; Cady et al. 18–29). Wharton draws upon all of these qualities in her portrayal of Sophy Viner. First, Sophy is the sister of Laura McTarvie-Birch, who functions as her dark double. Second, Sophy is the one character whom all the other characters love. As well as being George Darrow's and Owen Leath's lover, she is worshiped by her charge, Effie, and when the novel opens she is admired by Anna Leath, who already has begun to consider her a daughter-in-law. Third, Sophy, like her namesake, calls people not just to learn from her but to learn through her. Sophia may be thought of not only as knowledge to be possessed, but as "the learning process itself" (Cady et al. 26); becoming her pupil means an ongoing commitment to understanding the world in which one lives. Sophy Viner is this kind of powerful teacher: early in the novel, she looks for Effie's lost schoolbook, concerned about the girl's Latin lesson; later, she profoundly alters the course of Anna's, Darrow's, and Owen's lives. As Jean Gooder notes, both Anna and Darrow "watch Sophy to learn, not about her, but about themselves" (50). Sophy's affair with George Darrow provides opportunities for all the characters to change fundamental perceptions and actions.

Finally, Sophy's creative powers are suggested by her last name, Viner, an allusion to Wisdom's self-description in Ecclesiasticus 24.17 – "As the vine brought I forth pleasant savor" – and to Jesus' words in John 15.1, "I am the true vine," which scholars maintain were originally spoken by Sophia (Engelsman 114; R. Brown 671–72). As creative force, Sophy generates new relationships among the characters. Only Adelaide Painter, who believes that feelings and spirit should prevail over empty convention, approaches Sophy's creative vision: Painter, as her name suggests, is also an artist who attempts to "paint" a new picture for her friend Madame de Chantelle by persuading her to approve Owen's marriage to Sophy. (In contrast, Madame de Chantelle's name – Mary Lucretia – demonstrates patriarchy's division of women's powers: Mary is the chaste virgin, Lucretia the fallen woman.)

Sophy also plays another creative role in the novel: she is an aspiring actress yearning for a life in the theater. Wharton suggests not that drama is artifice but that life is drama; she arranges *The Reef* in five well-structured books or acts, with characters who mechanically follow social scripts until Sophy introduces them to new ones. Only Sophy has the gift of original and creative expression, as she demonstrates when Darrow brings her to see two plays, *La Vertige* and *Oedipe*. Both describe familiar occurrences in traditional society: thwarted romance and father–son competition. However, Sophy's "responsive . . . temperament" (50) helps even Darrow take a fresh view of *Oedipus:* for the first time he broke through "all the artificial accretions with which his theories of art and the conventions of the stage had clothed it, and saw it as he had never seen it: as life" (59). Darrow and Anna recite rehearsed lines – his voice is "like an amateur actor's in a 'light' part" (147) – and hers falters or falls silent without familiar cues. Neither character is able to create new lines or roles without Sophy's prompting.

Wharton's narrative structure also expresses her classical subtext. Like her namesake Sophia, Sophy rarely speaks for herself; when she does, her meaning is ambiguous and fails to capture her essence. Sophy's history – summed up in the statement that "everybody had been too busy to look after her" (22) – also describes Sophia's exclusion from Western culture. Wharton briefly relates Sophy's history at the beginning of the novel, but she chooses to start the narrative action at the point in her heroine's story when she, like Sophia, is already marginalized. Despite losing her powers during the transition from matriarchy to patriarchy, however, Sophia's spirit lives on. Sophy Viner is similarly disempowered – she has no money, family, or position – yet she survives, spirit intact. Orphaned, Sophy is first adopted by a traditional, patriarchal couple (the man is consumed by banking; his wife by health and religion). She then falls victim to double sexual standards when an employer's valet makes a pass and she is blamed for lacking "refinement and self-respect." Her next position as a lady's companion ends when her patroness marries. She finds friends in the "impecunious" Farlows but, in order not to be a financial burden, she takes a position with the wealthier Murretts (23). When the novel opens, Sophy is between positions and down on her luck. With typical spontaneity, she accepts Darrow's offer of a "holiday," a decision that confirms both her freedom of spirit and the costs of such freedom, for by the end of the novel, Sophy is again displaced and – like Sophia – destined to be both homeless and wandering.

Delicate Deceptions

Sophy's role, in accordance with her namesake, is to challenge other characters' conventional values. However, her edifying effect is difficult to discern because Wharton narrates the story through Darrow's and Anna's points of view. In book 1, in particular, Darrow's point of view is privileged over both women's – just as it is in society. Throughout the novel, Darrow tries to represent himself as honorable – or at least as sympathically fallible – but Sophy reveals his shallowness and duplicity.

On his way to Givré, where he hopes to ask Anna Leath to marry him, Darrow receives a blunt telegram delaying his visit. Even though he understands that Anna's cryptic phrase, "unexpected obstacle" (7), refers to family obligations, he is irritated by her lack of explanation and remonstrates her. She should have sent the telegram to his home instead of catching him in transit – "he had given her chance enough to learn where he lived" (9) – and, anyway, she should not have placed her family above him. The idea that Anna's needs are as important as Darrow's is inconceivable: her " 'reason,' whatever it was, could, in this case, be nothing but a pretext." Darrow also objects to Anna's disregard for his social importance: "she flung back the fortnight on his hands as if he had been an idler indifferent to dates, instead of an active young diplomatist who, to respond to her call, had had to hew his way through a very jungle of engagements!" (8). Thus, an ego-bruised Darrow constructs a case in his own defense even before he lays eyes on Sophy Viner and drifts into a ten-day affair with her.

Darrow is no stranger to romantic interludes, a fact the reader learns from Sophy, who in this instance and others conveys the truth, no matter how uncomplimentary. Sophy recalls that she and Darrow first met at Mrs. Murrett's, where Darrow was involved in a "headlong pursuit of Lady Ulrica Crispin" (14). Years earlier, while courting Anna, he also flirted with Kitty Mayne. Darrow is annoyed at Sophy's mention of the Crispin affair because he does not like "to be reminded that naturalness is not always consonant with taste" (16). Darrow's irritation is the first indication of his sexist conventionality. For him, women are either "ladies" or not; "he had instinctively kept the two groups apart in his mind." He permits no exceptions: his experience with the "Bohemian" or "third type" of women "left him with a contemptuous distaste for the woman who uses the privileges of one class to shelter the customs of another" (25). The rules of gender and class have always worked neatly to ensure Darrow's privilege and pleasure. That harmony is disrupted, however, not just when Sophy Viner reminds him of past flirtations but when, after their affair is over, she surfaces in a respectable position as governess to his fiancée's daughter and as his potential daughter-in-law.

Sophy and Darrow's encounter also reveals his self-centeredness. When he first sees her, she has just ruined her only umbrella, but Darrow contrasts her mishap with his own rejected plight, exclaiming, "It was food for the moralist that, side by side, with such catastrophes as his, human nature was still agitating itself over its microscopic woes!" (11). When Anna's second, explanatory note fails to arrive when he expects it, Darrow deals with his disappointment and powerlessness by exerting power over someone weaker, that is, by seducing Sophy. Overcome with "boyish misery" and the "blind desire to punish some one else for the pain it caused him," he twice "forgets" to mail Sophy's letter to the Farlows, preventing her from joining her friends (54). He imposes his will over hers, convincing himself that she has no will of her own: "It was easy enough to give her a few more hours of pleasure. And did she not perhaps secretly expect it of him?" (55).

Darrow's seduction of Sophy requires a fantasy of complicity: Sophy must be made to fit his category of the "bad girl" who invites her own ruin. Darrow therefore blames Sophy for not contacting the Farlows sooner, silently accusing her of gaining time with him through so "artless a device" (55) – even though he senses the truth: that she cannot afford to send a telegram. Later, ostensibly "ashamed of trying to better his case by an appeal to her pity" (68), Darrow uses his confession about the unmailed letter to gain Sophy's sympathy, persuading her to stay on with him for a holiday that "one friend may accept . . . from another without looking too far ahead or weighing too many chances" (70).

Darrow can hardly be thought of as Sophy's friend. He conducts his relationship with her as if she were a prostitute, twice offering her money to assuage his guilt and end responsibility for their liaison. As he later admits, the affair means nothing to him; its "essential cheapness . . . came home to him with humiliating distinctness. He would have liked to be able to feel that, at the time at least, he had staked something more on it, and had somehow, in the sequel, had a more palpable loss to show. But the plain fact was he hadn't spent a penny on it" (168). Sophy refuses Darrow's help or money, thus disrupting the terms of exchange that he proposes; she accepts assistance only if it is based on truth and friendship.

Darrow continues to show that he is not a friend by putting his own interests first when he discovers Sophy employed at Givré. He knows that he "must hold himself passive" in order to give her every chance to succeed as Effie's governess and Owen's fiancée (146), but he cannot stand to be ignored and contrives to be alone with Sophy on three different occasions. At their first meeting, Darrow lies about having waited for her to ask for help with her career on the stage. Sophy, however, states the truth: "You can help me to stay here" (150). Instead, Darrow rekindles his romantic feeling for her, thereby arousing Owen's and Anna's suspicions. The second time he speaks to her, his initial resolve "to do all he could for the girl" (167) collapses under the weight of class and gender prejudice. When Anna asks for assurance of Sophy's character, he hesitates, vowing instead "to find some way of securing [her] future without leaving her installed at Givré" (168). He also changes his mind about Sophy's acting career. In Paris, Darrow thought that acting was scandalous; now it is an attractive way to remove her from Givré. In the third conversation, Darrow reveals his jealousy of Owen. Sophy is relegated to the medium of exchange that Gayle Rubin explains takes place between men as they negotiate their power over women. Darrow charges that Sophy's engagement to Owen is not fair; the irony that he is himself engaged to Owen's stepmother escapes him. He again imagines that he is attracted to Sophy and tries to persuade her that marrying Owen is ill-advised: "He's too young and inexperienced to give you the kind of support you need. . . . He's a boy . . . with no more notion than a boy how to deal with the inevitable daily problems [of life]" (203).

Readers sympathetic to Darrow will point out that he is understandably distraught by discovering Sophy not only in Anna's employ, but nearly engaged to her stepson. Yet Wharton goes to great lengths to document his evasions and falsehoods. She also reveals his character by showing his closeness to Madame de Chantelle, Anna's snobbish mother-in-law. The marquise considers Darrow a kindred spirit indebted to the same "principles"; she "instinctively felt their unanimity of sentiment." In Madame de Chantelle's narrow view, Anna is "modern," and Owen "revolutionary" because he seeks to "apply his ideas" rather than, like his father, merely collect them (189). When she dismisses Sophy because she is poor with the classic prejudice: "I *liked* the girl. . . . But what's that got to do with it? I don't want her to marry my grandson" (190, original emphasis), she gives expression to Darrow's own doubt about "the disinterestedness of the woman who tries to rise above her past" (187). When Darrow is called upon to help Anna advocate for the engagement, he tells Madame de Chantelle that he cannot interfere. His evasive comment, "If there were anything I could possibly say I should want it to be in Miss Viner's favour" (215), wrongly implies a defect in Sophy's character.

Although Darrow admits to having "fallen below his own standard of sentimental loyalty" with Sophy (152), had she not appeared at Givré, he would not have given their affair a second thought. Sophy – "free from formality" and charming "to a young man accustomed to more traditional views" (14, 25) – was simply a diversion. For Darrow, the affair's "complex horror" (146) remains an offense against taste and discretion, not morality. Because his remorse is superficial, his solution is an expedient one. To "the ceaseless trip-hammer beat of the question, 'What in God's name shall I do?' . . ." (145, original ellipsis), Darrow replies pragmatically: hurt as few people as possible. He subscribes to the same practical ethics that Reverend Sewell espouses in William Dean Howells's *The Rise of Silas Lapham* when asked to remedy the romantic entanglement of the Lapham daughters. If Darrow must sacrifice Sophy and Owen for his own happiness, then the misery of two people is preferable to the misery of four.[7]

Perilously Aground

Sophy precipitates an unwelcome conflict in Darrow, but her effect on Anna is more subtle and profound, leading to a crisis of identity and morality as well as of form. However, since we first receive the story through Darrow's point of view, we are slow to appreciate the enormity of her struggle. As James Gargano notes, we are initially encouraged "to entertain an image of [Anna] that exaggerates her limitations" (42). Only in subsequent sections are the full dimensions of her dilemma clear.

As Moira Maynard points out, using Carol Gilligan's theory of moral development, Anna is interested in a complex "web" of relationship, whereas Darrow remains "remarkably indifferent to the emotional turmoil of souls he himself has wounded" (290). Accordingly, once Darrow acknowledges his mistake – "I see, a little more clearly, the extent, and the limits, of my wrong" (316) – he is ready to move on to marriage with Anna Leath. Anna, on the other hand, has internalized Victorian definitions of femininity, which lead her to believe that her loyalties will be reciprocated. When Darrow proves unworthy of her trust, she is devastated. Moreover, Anna's genteel society condones Darrow's actions so long as they are discreet, but it gives her no such latitude. Anna is thus forced to make a difficult choice between her passion for Darrow and her moral principles. Her situation is especially awkward since her actions serve as an example for her daughter Effie.

But if Darrow's response is problematic, so is Anna's. She builds a temple to her pain – no "discipline of piety could have been more torturing . . . its very cruelty attracted her" (305) – but it is a pain without profit. She assumes the sentimental role of exemplary feminine sufferer, but her moral uprightness saves no one: Sophy loses the chance to marry Owen, and Anna's relationship with Darrow is debased. Anna wants to believe that her problems will end with marriage to Darrow, but Wharton makes it clear that Darrow represents not freedom but continued imprisonment. Thus, rather than commending Anna's behavior and condemning Darrow's, Wharton undercuts both characters. They are, after all, two sides of a coin stamped by the same cultural press. Wharton criticizes Darrow's hypocritical, "modern" endorsement of relative moral standards *and* the nineteenth-century feminine cult of sentimentality that shapes Anna's behavior.

Darrow's egotism and need for mastery find their match in Anna's helpless dependence and romantic fantasies. Although Anna wishes differently, the categories of "good" and "bad" women dominate her outlook just as they do Darrow's. Ultimately, Anna proves to be too conventional to challenge the system that defines women's roles. The "truth" that Sophy Viner reveals to Anna is her own hopeless reliance on these conventional values.

Anna's dependent nature is most visible in her attitudes toward love. As Elizabeth Ammons notes, she lives in a fairy-tale fantasy, passively waiting for a shining knight to unlock her secret passions (80). She needs a man to animate the still life of her existence: "love, she told herself, would one day release her from this spell of unreality" (86). Because Anna is committed to a romantic ideal, she cannot achieve her own happiness. She is reserved and dependent to the point of being afraid of life itself. Using the language of theater and art, Wharton shows how, in contrast to Sophy, Anna fails to create her own life:

> a veil . . . had always hung between herself and life. It had been like the stage gauze which gives an illusive air of reality to the painted scene behind it, yet proves it, after all, to be no more than a painted scene.
>   . . . she learned to regard the substance of life as a mere canvas for the embroideries of poet and painter, and its little swept and fenced and tended surface as its actual substance. It was in the visioned region of action and emotion that her fullest hours were spent; but it hardly

occurred to her that they might be translated into experience. (84–85)

Anna's greatest problem is that, even after her failed marriage, she still believes not only that romantic dreams are attainable, but that she is exceptional – she will find "the magic bridge" between her present existence and "life" even though other women have failed (86–87). She once pinned her hopes on her husband, Fraser Leath; now she turns to George Darrow.

Unfortunately, there is little difference between the two men. Leath promised freedom from stifling social restrictions without sacrificing the status quo. But he turned out to be neither daring nor passionate: he "collected his social instances with the same seriousness and patience as his snuff-boxes"; he "exacted a rigid conformity to his rules of non-conformity" (92); and he bestow[ed] kisses that dropped on Anna "like a cold smooth pebble" (91). Anna learned that she had married not a prince but a man for whom "life . . . was like a walk through a carefully classified museum." Gradually and "insensibly she began to live his life" (94).

Darrow is similarly disappointing. Although he arouses Anna's passion in a way that Leath did not, he is not the devoted lover that her romantic creed requires. She imagines him as passionate, but he sees her as cool, serene, and refined, especially compared to red-blooded Sophy Viner or Kitty Mayne. Leath and Darrow hold the same view of women. They both wish to marry ladies but amuse themselves with women who are not ladies: Darrow once flirted with the "silly" Kitty (88); Leath once teased Anna's mother that this same rival should be invited to dinner. And after Anna discovers Darrow's affair with Sophy, she finds herself wondering whether her husband also had affairs. With Darrow settled at Givré, Anna is faced – as she was with her husband – of adjusting her life to his.

Hope for Anna resides not in marrying the "right" man – who does not exist – but in rejecting the conventions that make her dependent on such marriages. In one early scene, Wharton hints of Anna's potential for freedom by associating her with her stepson, Owen Leath, whose youthful "gambols . . . were the voice of her own secret rebellions"; Owen "had the courage she lacked" (96). "Seized by the whim to overtake" Owen (99), she runs like a young girl down the lawn of Givré, where in the freedom of nature they share hopes for their upcoming marriages. However, while Owen talks gleefully of the future, Anna feels the pull of the old house "send her back the mute appeal of something doomed" (105). This sense of doom is portentous, for Anna is too attached to Givré and its conventions to achieve freedom. Just before joining Owen outside, Anna recalls her predecessor, whose portrait hangs in "shrouded solitude" at Givré. She intuitively understands from the "stone-dead eyes" that Leath's first wife died of loneliness "long before they buried her" (97, 98). Anna is destined for the same fate.

Anna never overcomes her dependence on male approval and assistance. When, during their first courtship, Darrow's attentions wandered, Anna looked to him for reassurance, but he only tormented her by calling Kitty Mayne "good fun" (89). Much later, sensing discord at Givré, Anna again relies on Darrow to supply truth, but he lies or evades her questions. "I want our life to be like a house with all the windows lit: I'd like to string lanterns from the roof and chimneys!" she exclaims (120). She cannot understand the reason for their recent separation or earlier rift: "It's curious," she gropes, "how . . . something that I didn't understand came between us" – but Darrow blames their discord on their youthful impetuosity rather than his philandering. Sensing the falseness of his explanation, Anna presses, "it couldn't even then, have been as true of you as of me," but Darrow insists that only the present matters. With the "interrogative light" of Psyche (110–11), Anna asks why Darrow ignored her second letter – the letter he threw unread in the fireplace, but Darrow evades her question.[8] Soon afterward, he baldly lies, saying that he saw Sophy two or three times in London "several years ago," uttering the lie "deliberately" and amplifying it: " 'Know' is rather exaggerated; we used to pass each other on the stairs" (142–43).

Romantic dependence is not Anna's only problem. She fails to set a successful course for her life or meet Sophy's challenge because she is ultimately as patronizing and evasive as Darrow. Although Anna promises to help Owen, she postpones speaking to her mother-in-law about his engagement because she worries that Sophy is not a good enough match. When she asks Darrow about Sophy's character, she readily interprets his hesitation as proof of Sophy's unacceptability. Like Madame de Chantelle, Anna distrusts Sophy because she is an outsider and is quick to think the worst rather than best of her. When Sophy powders her face to hide tears that Darrow causes, Anna, like him, judges her use of a cosmetic as a sign of promiscuity. She also assumes, like her mother-in-law, that Sophy is a social climber who, once sure of her place in the family, "celebrat[es] her independence" by presenting "to the world a bedizened countenance" (236).

Anna is comfortable playing two roles with Sophy: those of mother and benefactor. Both give her a measure of control over the younger woman, whom she cannot accept as an equal. So long as Anna can conceive of Sophy as a sexually naive woman who needs charitable or maternal intervention, she can promote her cause. But after hearing that Sophy was Darrow's lover, Anna is consumed by envy and self-doubt, seeing Sophy as an "obscurely menacing" version of her rival Kitty Mayne (237). A part of Anna holds Sophy in high regard – she "had always felt a romantic and almost humble admiration for those members of her own sex who . . . had plunged into the conflict from which fate had so persistently excluded her" (236) – but she is also jealous of women for whom feelings come so easily. She hides her insecurity with displays of social and moral superiority, using her authority at Givré to disempower Sophy. "You'd no right to let Owen love you" (309), she charges, thus reinforcing society's judgments of women as either "good" or "bad." Sophy accepts her misjudgment, hoping that Anna will still be Owen's advocate: "you must know better; you feel things in a finer way. Only you'll have to help him if I can't," she acquiesces (310). But in these appeals, which require Anna to change her values, Sophy fails.

As the narrative progresses, Anna becomes more like Darrow, not less, developing his propensity for lying and self-interest. Ironically, in spite of her statements about the importance of truth, she conspires to keep the affair a secret from Owen, rationalizing that "she owed herself first to him – she was bound to protect him" (278). Even Madame de Chantelle is more candid than Anna about her objections to the marriage. Anna also pretends to Owen that she and Darrow have had no falling out, lying about Darrow's absence from Givré: "the words seemed to have uttered themselves without her will, yet she felt a great sense of freedom as she spoke them" (318). Sophy, in contrast, wants Owen "to know exactly what happened" (307). Since the sexual-social world in which Anna lives *is* a lie, she feels oddly secure with this dissimulation: "it was as though a star she had been used to follow had shed its familiar ray on ways unknown to her." As she admits, her stepson is a "pretext," not a "cause," for staying with Darrow, who has become "that which was most precious to her" (320).

Finally, Anna, no less than Darrow, becomes convinced that Sophy must leave Givré. In one painful conversation, Sophy says that in Anna's place she would have guessed that the affair with Darrow had taken place. Her frank disclosure alarms Anna because it so powerfully contrasts with her own genteel timidity. Anna uses the power of her class to pressure Sophy to leave Givré, disguising that power as concern, just as Darrow had earlier: "You make me feel too horribly: as if I were driving you away . . ." Anna falters. In this passage, Wharton's ellipses, always deliberate and often representing forbidden or censored emotion,[9] communicate Anna's hidden agenda – to make Sophy leave without Anna having to feel responsible for her going. Anna delicately continues, "Later on . . . after a while, when all this is over . . . if there's no reason why you shouldn't marry Owen −"; "I shouldn't want you to think I stood between you . . ." (285, original ellipses). Anna's words belie her true intention that Sophy never return.

Charting New Courses

Sophy complies with Anna's wish and leaves Givré, but not before telling Darrow that she loves him. Readers puzzle over her declaration of love for Darrow, since it contradicts her independence and is clearly an emotion that he neither deserves nor returns. Maynard, for example, charges Sophy with a "blind ignoring of reality and the choosing of an unusable past over a viable, if unromantic future" (289). But are we really expected to believe that Sophy loves Darrow? If so, Wharton succeeds only in demonstrating that women are indeed drawn to men who are bad for them. Sophy's outburst is better assessed in terms of its effect − as a strategy to reveal truth.[10]

Sophy's profession of love and her later defense of that love to Anna permit Wharton to demonstrate qualities in Sophy that other characters lack: passionate expression and honesty. As Sophy vehemently tells Anna in words that reject staid morality for individually designed freedom:

> I shock you, I offend you: you think me a creature without shame. So I am − but not in the sense you think! I'm not ashamed of having loved him; no; and I'm not ashamed of telling you so. It's that that justifies me − and him too . . . (309, original ellipsis)

Sophy challenges Anna to see her in more than one light and to accept passionate and honest expressions of love that fall outside conventional boundaries. An incarnation of Sophia-like wisdom and truth, Sophy also holds Anna and Darrow accountable for their actions. Her declaration of love for Darrow leaves him no easy "out"; she makes it impossible for him to trivialize or deny their affair. There is no evidence that Sophy still loves Darrow when she agrees to marry Owen; even if she does, she willingly puts the affair in the past. *Darrow* rekindles feelings between them; Sophy simply follows his lead. By playing the role of the emotionally helpless woman that Darrow's chauvinistic creed requires, she exposes his prevarications and insincerity: he never intended to marry her instead of Anna.

Sophy's admission of love for Darrow forces Anna to see the affair in terms of her own experience. Both women, after all, have made the mistake of trusting the same charming man. It also highlights Anna's dilemma: if she dismisses the affair and the feelings that it has engendered, then her distress over Darrow's behavior with women like Kitty or Sophy is an overreaction. If she considers the incident significant, then she must judge Darrow by Sophy's standards and find him deficient in loyalty and honesty. In either case, Anna must abandon romantic ideals. She first tries to shift this responsibility onto Sophy. If Anna can think of her as promiscuous, then she can find a reason to forgive Darrow. But as Anna must admit, Sophy is neither an "adventuress" nor a New Woman acting on "theories" (293). Although Anna would like to think of the affair as a sordid, "debasing familiarity" from which her thoughts "would never again be pure" (294), she must admit her resemblance to the woman she seeks to discredit.

Although Anna still clings to the belief that she will be love's exception – that "there *was* such love as she had dreamed, and she meant to go on believing in it" (304, original emphasis) – she briefly sets aside her fantasy to feel "the undercurrent of an absolute trust in Sophy" and their "kindred impulses" (320). When Anna admits her jealousy and her desire to feel the passion that Sophy has known, she accepts Sophy as her teacher. However, Sophy's lesson is not what Anna expects. By encouraging Anna to marry Darrow while she herself gives Owen up, Sophy begins to teach Anna how unworthy Darrow is. Anna at first resolves to follow Sophy's example and breaks with Darrow. She learns, in turn, that loss is gain: "Sophy Viner had chosen the better part . . . renunciations might enrich where possession would have left a desert" (334). Anna realizes that the "high things she had lived by" are a lie (304); the truth lies somewhere below the surface of genteel conventions. But when she weakens and returns to Darrow, she forfeits this truth and her freedom.

Thus Sophy leads Anna to the most painful truth of all – her own weakness and repression in the social order. All her life Anna has wanted love, but she has not understood that true intimacy follows only from trust and equality, which her society's values preclude. The novel's title reinforces this theme: a reef is hidden, dangerous; only if one knows it exists can it be safely navigated. Anna has sailed along the surface of life with only society's compass to guide her, unable to see that the Darrow she "worshipped was inseparable from the Darrow she abhorred" (302). Through Sophy, however, Anna sees more clearly: "the truth had come to light by the force of its irresistible pressure; and the perception gave her a startled sense of hidden powers, of a chaos of attractions and repulsions far beneath the ordered surfaces of intercourse" (353). Darrow, in contrast, remains superficial: "It seemed such a slight thing – all on the surface – and I've gone aground on it because it *was* on the surface" (316, original emphasis).

Sophy offers a new perspective through which Anna can reevaluate Darrow and understand that there are "obligations not to be tested by [his] standard" (360). Anna finally views Darrow critically – from her position as a mother, questioning whether he is an appropriate model for her daughter Effie,[11] and from her perspective as an adult woman. She has a dim understanding that the cost of choosing Darrow has been losing Owen, her youthful friend and potential embodiment of change, as well as Sophy, her sister spirit. Yet Anna's collision with the hidden truth so damages her fragile vessel of dreams that it sends her racing for the safe harbor of conventionality. Sophy charts a new course for Anna, but in the end Anna cannot follow it.

Rather than break with Darrow, Anna panics and strengthens their tie, with predictably negative results. She becomes more insecure, entrapped, and confused: she "could not speak; she no longer even knew what she had meant to say" (329). Passion is now "richer, deeper," but also "more enslaving" (319). Anna involuntarily compares her situation to the ancient Roman custom whereby "slaves were not allowed to wear a distinctive dress lest they should recognize each other and learn their numbers and their power" (316). She is so dependent on Darrow that losing sight of him even for a moment evokes "morbid terror" (344). Believing "that only his presence could restore her to a normal view of things," she longs "to return to her old state of fearless ignorance" (322–23). Even now, however, she still learns from Sophy's example. When she becomes jealous that her pleasures with Darrow are those that Sophy knew, she also must acknowledge that someday Darrow may treat her with the same indifference.

In despair, Anna seeks help for her "deadness of soul" from the one figure who can "save her": Sophy Viner (300, 361). But it is too late. Sophy has "kept her word" (345) and made a clean break from Owen, Darrow, and Anna. Her disappearance – more than a "sacrifice[ ] . . . to the exigencies of the plot" (Auchincloss, Introd. xiv) – represents, as it does for the adult Pearl in *The Scarlet Letter* and Ellen Olenska in *The Age of Innocence,* an escape from debilitating social conventions, a reaching out for spiritual and social values unattainable in the present culture. Although Anna has "so distinct a vision of what she meant to say to Sophy Viner that the girl seemed already to be before her" (362), when she arrives at her hotel, Sophy is gone. In her place is Sophy's brash sister, Laura McTarvie-Birch – actress, paramour, and ironic inversion of Sophy's true role as creator and lover.

In this final scene, Anna loses her remaining romantic illusions. Waiting in a smoky anteroom, scrutinized by male visitors, she has "the sense of being minutely catalogued and valued" (363). Her refusal of a cigarette – in her polite world, a sign for gentlemen to abstain also – is ignored. Laura, recumbent and imperious on her pink plush bed, shocks Anna, reinforcing her dread of life's sordidness and her original judgments about lower-class promiscuity. Laura delivers the final offending stroke when she loudly summons her lover, Jimmy Brance, and instructs Anna to order him to call the elevator. Repelled, Anna flees, driven back to the only world she knows: that of Darrow and Givré.

The meaning of this peculiar vignette, which readers frequently criticize as unrelated to the rest of the text,[12] is not entirely clear; but the passage relates to Wharton's feminist theme. Through her depictions of both Sophy and Laura, Wharton criticizes Western culture's repression of women and shows the need to integrate the multiplicity of feminine energies that were once associated with Sophia.[13]

Wharton presents Laura as a parody of conventional femininity. A performer, she paints and pretties herself for a paying audience. Her ostentation offends Anna, but, in fact, Laura's loud style and manners do no more than exaggerate, or mimic, the sexual dynamics of female desirability in Anna's world. More important, Wharton's allusion to Sophia shows that women possess – and should claim – a full range of feelings and powers. Sophia's distinguishing quality is that no one definition encompasses her; she is simultaneously nurturing and demanding, calm and angry, warm and harsh. Sophy embodies these qualities: she accepts Darrow's advances, but she greets his failure to mail her letter to the Farlows with wrath, and his argument that she leave Givré with bitter disdain. However, Western culture represses women's powers by dividing them into mutually exclusive categories of good and bad. In the biblical book of Proverbs, for example, Wisdom is exalted as a proper wife while her rival, Folly, is reviled as a loud, self-centered hussy. It is not surprising, then, that Anna – a woman who exemplifies one aspect of womanhood – seeks Sophy but finds Laura, her dark double in the Judeo-Christian tradition: "a woman with the attire of an harlot, and subtil of heart. She is loud and stubborn; her feet abide not in her house" (Prov. 7.10–11). A product of her culture, Anna cannot integrate these disparate feminine aspects. She therefore sees Laura as vulgar – as "what Sophy Viner might . . . become" (365). Bewildered by a system she thought would sustain her if she followed its rules, Anna is stranded in patriarchy, like a boat on a reef.

Because patriarchy rejected the feminine, the ancient Sophia was displaced. She remains rooted in consciousness, however, like a tree or vine; but she is destined to wander the face of the earth, waiting for the day when she will once again be welcomed, when she can regain her true home in heaven, alongside God or a pantheon of archetypal goddesses such as Isis and Demeter. Enoch 42.1–2 explains her rich multiplicity:

Wisdom found no place where she might dwell;
Then a dwelling-place was assigned her in the heavens.
Wisdom went forth to make her dwelling among the children of
    men,
And found no dwelling-place:
Wisdom returned to her place,
And took her seat among the angels.

(qtd. in Engelsman 81)

Sophy, like her namesake Sophia, is a wanderer, at home wherever she happens to be: Paris, Givré, or – at the novel's end – India with the Murretts. Anna, on the other hand, is bound to the small world of Givré and conventionality.

Edith Wharton worked hard to escape the society that impedes Anna, moving from New York to Europe to join communities of like-minded artists and intellectuals. Perhaps she, like Anna, also felt stranded after her affair with Morton Fullerton ended. Yet even if she initially identified with Anna, she later shifted her allegiance to Sophy, as she does to other independent, self-aware female characters, such as Ellen Olenska. Indeed, during the year that she wrote *The Reef*, Wharton was constantly traveling and visiting friends (Lewis 318–19), living a life that more resembled Sophy's peripatetic life-style than Anna's sedentary, staid one. Six years after writing the novel – reflecting on her distance from her heroine Anna Leath – Wharton told Bernard Berenson to "remember, it's not *me*, though I thought it was when I was writing it" (*Letters* 284, original emphasis).

Wharton's allusion to Sophia conveys her critique of contemporary culture. Sophia's spirit and power are elusive not only to Anna, but to much of modern society, which has lost touch with true feminine power and constructs false categories of women as a substitute. As Wershoven notes, "the misery in which the novel ends can be seen as a result of . . . the artificial and simplistic categories that Darrow and Anna use to define women" (*Female* 107). Thus, Wharton's allusion to the Sophia tradition establishes *The Reef*'s larger theme: the lack of a religious or spiritual system to accommodate female power and desire.

The writer and creator that Anna can never be, Wharton reaches into her imagination and evokes a female tradition to rival the existing one. She shows that wealth and privilege do not give women more freedom, and she criticizes a society that uses romance and genteel glamour to disguise women's subservience. Yet Wharton also expresses her own ambivalence toward women's roles – a hesitation born of the conservative background that she still shared with Anna. As Blake Nevius explains, Wharton "is able to preserve her detachment only so long as [her characters'] actions in no way threaten the values, standards, manners that she cherishes. From the moment they present themselves to her imagination in a subversive guise, they can expect no sympathy" (*Wharton* 138). Although Nevius may overstate the case, Sophy and her sister Laura remain outsiders. Wharton has difficulty envisioning an alternative to Anna's stifling, narrow world even as she longs for it; Sophy's perspective, after all, is never presented. The Apocryphal book of Ecclesiasticus compares the process of knowing Sophia to bearing shackles or a yoke, which, although holding promise of great reward, requires great effort:

> And put thy feet into her fetters, and thy neck into her chain. Bow down thy shoulder, and bear her, and be not grieved with her bonds. Come unto her with all thy whole heart, and keep her ways with all thy power. Search, and seek, and she shall be made known unto thee: and when thou hast got hold of her, let her not go. For at the last thou shalt find her rest, and that shall be turned to thy joy. (6.24–28)

At the end of *The Reef,* Wharton and the reader are left bearing the yoke of Sophia; that is, we seek possibilities for feminine self-expression without guilt, recrimination, or slavish dependence on patriarchal standards, but we realize that the fulfillment of that search is yet to come (again).

Whitman's Song in *Summer*

The Reef was a bold yet veiled experiment, evoking non-Christian symbology that did not discredit or trivialize women. In subsequent fiction, Wharton continued to analyze Western culture's impact on women. Her ruthlessly satiric portrayal of Undine Spragg in her next novel, *The Custom of the Country,* demonstrates the pernicious effects of twentieth-century materialism. Undine is all substance and no spirit, and the world she creates is destructive and hollow. Wharton also continued to explore alternatives to patriarchy, capitalism, and Judeo-Christian values. Her search for non-Christian options, which coincided with her liberating love affair with Morton Fullerton, included infatuations with Friedrich Nietzsche, Ralph Waldo Emerson, and Walt Whitman. Wharton admired Emerson's poetry, which she compared with Whitman's. Emerson and Whitman, as well as Poe, "are the best we have – in fact, the all we have," she wrote to William Brownell (qtd. in Lewis 236). She also admired Emerson's essays, which she maintained were the chief influence on Nietzsche, whom she appreciated for validating her own instinctive and erotic impulses. She praised Nietzsche's "power of breaking through the conventions" and detected a trace of Whitman in Nietzschean phrases such as "Man is a *sick animal*" (qtd. in Lewis 230, original emphasis). Whitman, in particular, held in perfect tension the values of the past and the energies of the present and future; Wharton saw in his poetry both a reverence for continuity and the courage to move forward. His poetic rhythms and themes played a key role in the construction of her 1917 novel *Summer.*

Nineteenth-century philosophers and writers had maintained a close relationship between nature and spirit: in the heyday of Emersonian transcendentalism, nature itself was imbued with the divine spirit of the Creator. But even in Emerson's time, the salutary effect of privileging individual will over culturally constructed values was challenged by the growing demands of the market. Toward the end of the century, and certainly by the end of World War I, economic and moral perspectives resembled a secular Calvinism: one needed to accept the whimsy of external forces – not of God within nature, but of nature without God. One could no longer talk with confidence about the good; one could only acknowledge the arbitrary interplay of natural, social, and economic pressures.

Some Victorians revived Emersonian theories as "intuitionist arguments for God" (Turner 187), finding in this last great advocate of humanitarian individualism a way to counter Darwinian determinism. Emerson claimed unity with universal principles, embraced both nature and technology, and held that the individual was the seat of spiritual value. His philosophy – radical, exploratory, optimistic, and predicated not only on the power of humans to enact change but on the goodness of change itself – added a welcome idealism in an age of skeptical materialism. Whereas earlier Wharton had held transcendentalism up to the light of reason and judged it lacking, she now embraced it as a vehicle for self-realization. She explores this Emersonian impulse toward autonomy and renewal in *Summer,* as we shall see.

Wharton's interest in transcendentalism is documented in notes she made in 1908 for an essay on Walt Whitman. She never wrote the essay, but her eleven pages of handwritten notes indicate that she planned an enthusiastic tribute to the poet, the man, and the ideas that inspired his verse. It may seem incongruous that refined, orderly, and class-conscious Edith Wharton should have high esteem for the unstructured, expansive verse of Walt Whitman, but there is no question that he was near and dear to her heart.

Wharton's love of Whitman is evident in her letters, notes, and published writings. In 1898, he appeared on her list of "favorite books" (Lewis 86). Nearly twenty years later, in 1917, she was reading the third volume of Horace Traubel's *With Walt Whitman in Camden* (*Letters* 391). Wharton alludes to Whitman in the title of her autobiography, *A Backward Glance* –

drawn from his "A Backward Glance O'er Travel'd Roads" – and in the plot of her ironic novella *The Spark* (1924), in which a wealthy New Yorker remembers being nursed by Whitman during the Civil War but fails to appreciate his poetic genius. In *The Custom of the Country,* Ralph Marvell does realize Whitman's greatness and tries to write a critical piece about him, as Wharton did herself. Active in World War I relief efforts, Wharton no doubt felt a special kinship with Whitman – another artist who put writing aside to serve during wartime. R. W. B. Lewis tells us that when Wharton met George Cabot Lodge through her friend Walter Berry in 1898, she and Lodge discussed their shared "reverential love for the poetry of Walt Whitman" (80–81). And in the fall of 1904, during Henry James's visit to Wharton's summer home in Lenox, James read aloud from *Leaves of Grass,* the two friends agreeing that Walt Whitman was the greatest of American poets (140). Wharton describes a similar ocassion with James in *A Backward Glance* (186). After Theodore Roosevelt died, she wrote a note of sympathy to his sister, Corrine Roosevelt, lamenting that "there is no Whitman singing in this generation" (*Letters* 466).

Walt Whitman's name was enough to raise eyebrows among the staid New Yorkers of Wharton's youth. Wharton was forbidden to read his free, expressive verse when she was child; *Leaves of Grass* was "kept under lock and key, & brought out, like tobacco, only in the absence of 'the ladies' " ("Further" 21). It is not surprising, then, that Wharton turned to Whitman when she was deeply involved in an affair with Morton Fullerton in 1908. She found her own passionate expression reflected and validated in Whitman's amorous lines.[14] Years later, when she composed her most passionate novel, *Summer,* she returned to Whitman, incorporating elements of his style and philosophy in her prose. In the eleven pages of notes for her essay, Wharton quoted words and phrases from Whitman's poems, briefly analyzed his verse, and made appreciative remarks about the power and beauty of his language. Among the notes is a topical outline, dividing the planned essay into five parts: an introduction, two sections that analyze Whitman's language – especially his "adjectives," "melody," and "rhythms" – and two sections that explore Whitman's ideas.

The first of the two sections on ideas concerns Whitman's cosmic vision – what Wharton described as "philosophy of life; Emersonian influences; evolution–influences; sense of continuity, rhythm & oneness, of the absolute beyond the relative." This section contains four subheadings: "Individualism," "Sympathy," "View of Death," and "Official pose as the Poet of Democracy." The second item, "Sympathy," is followed by a bracketed notation – three words joined by dashes, as if to suggest a progression. These worlds are "lover – love – asexual." In the second section on Whitman's ideas, Wharton planned to summarize her praise of Whitman, noting individual poems that best exemplified "nature," "human sympathy," and "cosmic philosophy."

The notes tell us which features of Whitman's poetry Wharton found most worthy of appreciation, and they serve as a guide for understanding *Summer,* which, unlike the planned Whitman essay, was completed in 1917, near the end of World War I. Wharton stressed the qualities of "nature," "human sympathy," and "cosmic philosophy" in her outline; these qualities also appear in *Summer,* her most expressive, romantic, and transcendental novel. Written as an escape from the pressures of the war, the novel is a tribute to individual will and freedom in nature. It is the most frankly passionate of all Wharton's novels, written, as she tells us in *A Backward Glance,* "at a high pitch of creative joy" (356).[15]

But *Summer* is not light romance. Wharton's enthusiasm for Emerson and Whitman is tempered – as it was earlier when she drew back from Nietzschean surrender. *Summer's* freedom is checked by a sense of inevitability that impedes choice; of determinism that contends with transcendence. The result is a novel that conflates comic romance with tragic loss, affirming transcendental ideals but resigning its heroine to social and environmental limitations. Its New England setting connects it to *Ethan Frome* and provides the first clue that the world of the novel is burdened by moral and sexual guilt – it is a world touched by Darwin and Calvin as well as Emerson, by Hawthorne as well as Whitman. A savage and ominous Mountain hovers over the town of North Dormer, and Charity Royall ends her romantic adventure with young Lucius Harney by marrying her guardian father, Lawyer Royall. The heroine's joyous adventure toward self-discovery and love is at best a compromise with, and at worst a capitulation to, social and biological forces beyond her control.

Critical readings of *Summer* have not reconciled the novel's disparate elements.[16] Such a synthesis is difficult because *Summer* incorporates the late nineteenth- and early twentieth-century debate that emerged over social evolution. One view insisted on the importance of a hostile environment as a selective factor in eliminating the weak, accepting the struggle for existence in the most literal sense. The other avoided these harsh conclusions and attempted to fuse individualism and natural rights with Darwinism's more progressive implications. Whereas the first view was bleak and mechanistic, the second was hopeful and organic. Emerson, aligned with the more optimistic creed, fought to keep the individual as the source of spiritual values worthy of preservation, but no amount of romantic enthusiasm could fully overcome the sense of resignation that followed from social Darwinism – which, in Wharton's case, was also associated with Calvinism.

Throughout her life, Wharton struggled – as do many of her characters – to reach this Emersonian ideal and to shake off Calvinist influences.) Although we seldom think of her in connection with American romanticism or transcendentalism, she was intrigued by the possibilities that these traditions offered to free the body and spirit from the prohibitions inherent in Christianity. Indeed, her use of Whitman's title "A Backward Glance O'er Travel'd Roads" for her own autobiography clearly aligns her with nineteenth-century romanticism. Wharton's argument with Christian, and particularly Calvinist, doctrine reached its peak at midlife, when she lamented its "split between body & soul" (*Letters* 159). The seeds of her discontent were sown even earlier, as early as 1898, when she copied the following lines from Whitman's "Song of Myself" into her commonplace book:

> I think I could turn and live with animals, they are so placid and self-contain'd,
> I stand and look at them long and long.
>
> They do not sweat and whine about their condition,
> They do not lie awake in the dark and weep for their sins,
> They do not make me sick discussing their duty to God,
> Not one is dissatisfied, not one is demented with the mania of owning things,
> Not one kneels to another, not to his kind that lived thousands of years ago,
> Not one is respectable or unhappy over the whole earth.
>   (684–91; qtd. in Wolff, *Feast* 90)[17]

The romantic poet Whitman also offered Wharton sexual and moral liberation. As Wharton's contemporary D. H. Lawrence wrote, Whitman provides "a doctrine of life. A new great morality. A morality of actual living, not of [Christian ascetic] salvation" (256). In his frank, unashamed celebration of sex, Whitman rejected Puritan notions of guilt and repression and proposed salvation through the flesh. Rejecting the woeful consequences of original sin, he celebrates these Adamic children in poems such as "From Pent-Up Aching Rivers": "Singing the song of procreation, / Singing the need of superb children and therein superb grown people" (lines 5–6). For a woman living, like Wharton, in an age of Victorian restraint and double standards, the sexual license that the speaker claims in "I Sing the Body Electric" was exhilarating:

This is the female form,
A divine nimbus exhales from it head to foot,

Be not ashamed women, your privilege encloses the rest, and is the
    exit of the rest,
You are the gates of the body, and you are the gates of the soul.
                                        (*Leaves,* lines 52–53, 66–67)

Edith Wharton's praise for Whitman's poetry and philosophy was nothing less than a celebration of her own sensuality, her own "animal" nature. Whitman granted permission to engage, guilt-free, in the pulsating rhythms of life and feel oneself immersed and reflected in nature. It is no accident, then, that "Terminus," Wharton's long and passionate love poem penned after a rendezvous with Fullerton in 1909, is written in Whitman-like lines with Whitman's sense of joyful, mobile, and struggling humanity. In "Terminus," Wharton gives desire a transcendent, almost religious meaning and identifies herself as one of the vast numbers of human beings who share in this common experience. This same passionate acceptance and abandonment fuels Charity and Lucius's innocent romance.

Wharton's heroine Charity Royall embodies the connection to nature that Whitman celebrates in his poetry. Margaret McDowell calls her a "child of nature" who prefers the company of birds and flowers to that of humans (71). Indeed, Wharton tells us that Charity is most at home in communion with nature: "She was blind and insensible to many things, and dimly knew it; but to all that was light and air, perfume and colour, every drop of blood in her responded." Wharton also describes Charity's joy in nature in a Whitman-like series of rhythmical descriptions that would resemble poetry if written in verse rather than prose:

She loved the roughness of the dry mountain grass under her palms,
The smell of the thyme into which she crushed her face,
The fingering of the wind in her hair and through her cotton blouse,
And the creak of the larches as they swayed to it.

                                                            (21)

In another passage, Wharton evokes the sensuous fullness of the spring vegetation, of the odors that "were merged in a moist earth-smell that was like the breath of some huge sun-warmed animal." Charity lies on the hill like the "placid and self-contain'd" animals in Whitman's "Song of Myself" (line 684), a transcendental fusion of all beings and nature.

A true romantic, Charity also eschews books and intellectual traditions for direct experience, wondering as she enters the library where she works whether old Honorius Hatchard, for whom the building is named, "felt any deader in his grave than she did in his library" (13). She sets her hat over the bust of Minerva – a classical symbol of wisdom – and looks not at books, but at a swallow's nest outside the window. An only child erratically indulged by an adoptive father, Charity is raised more in accordance with the rules of nature than of society, much like Pearl Prynne in *The Scarlet Letter* and Nan Prince in Sarah Orne Jewett's *The Country Doctor*. She declines a formal education and grows semiwild near the confines of her house, like the Crimson Rambler that Lawyer Royall buys her when she decides not to go away to school. When the novel opens, Charity is dreaming of how she can "get away" (32) from the sleepy town of North Dormer. She is stifled by its petty bourgeois conventions and longs for adventure. "It's no use trying to be anything in this place," she mutters (39). "How I hate everything!" she twice exclaims (9, 12).

Charity's roots in the Mountain society that overlooks North Dormer also associate her with a romantic and quintessentially American quest for freedom. As Lucius tells her, the Mountain people are outcasts who originally went to this remote area for freedom. They are a "queer colony . . . sort of outlaws, a little independent kingdom," who have nothing to do with people in the valley and even scorn them. These "rough customers," who "must have a good deal of character," retell America's story of settlement. Like the pioneers before them, these "first colonists" were men who went into the wilderness, followed by women and children, all of whom fall "outside the jurisdiction of the valleys" (65–66). Their mountaintop is a version of John Winthrop's "Citty upon a Hill" (295) – insular and fiercely independent. Charity is a rebel like them; she knows instinctively that "the Mountain people would never hurt her" (55–56); and when Lucius describes their independence, they seem to contain "the clue to her own revolts and defiances" (65). Charity's later journey back to the Mountain and her mother is an attempt to recapture this freedom.

Both Lucius Harney and Lawyer Royall keep Charity from realizing her goals. Lucius – sophisticated, handsome, and urbane – is, as his name suggests, the "devil" of society who keeps Charity tied to conventions – both socially and romantically. He is curious about Charity's wild origins, but his interest is superficial and fleeting. When his architectural study is finished, he returns to a bustling commercial center; both Charity and her region remain objects of study rather than opportunities for his own communion with nature. Lucius is literary twin of the young ornithologist in Jewett's "A White Heron," who wishes to find the rare heron so that he can take it back to the city for study and display.

Wharton writes sympathetically of Lucius and Charity's trysts in the abandoned summer cottage, a symbol of culture poised on the outskirts of nature. But the cottage offers only a brief escape, as does Hawthorne's sunlit forest glade where Hester and Dimmesdale meet to express their love. Charity and Lucius's meetings there also resemble those of the passionate lovers in Whitman's "Children of Adam" poems.[18] However, while the lovers celebrate themselves and each other, they can neither separate totally from society nor integrate with it. Ultimately, natural romanticism is no rival for urban, modern capitalism. Engaged to a woman of his own class, Lucius leaves Charity, unaware that she is pregnant. Just as Wharton and Fullerton never managed to get away to the "little inn in the country in the depths of a green wood" that she wistfully describes in her love diary (qtd. in Wolff, *Feast* 197), Charity and Lucius cannot find permanent refuge in their summer house. Summer wanes, Royall discovers the love nest, and Charity is left alone and pregnant. Their affair – Wharton's brief "Song of Myself" – is a fleeting lyrical moment, like the New England summer itself.

Lucius's abandonment of Charity and her inability to send the letter telling him of their coming child underline the inequality of their relationship. From the moment he first sees her – as "part of the furniture" (15) – until his appearance at the Old Home Week celebration with his fiancée, Lucius never sees Charity as an equal. She, in turn, believes she is socially inferior: the sight of Lucius coming down the main street of North Dormer makes her feel "ashamed of her old sun-hat, and sick of North Dormer, and jealously aware of Annabel Balch of Springfield" (12). The need to keep their affair secret also causes her the same kind of shame that she associates with her Mountain origins: "whenever she was with Lucius Harney she would have liked some impenetrable mountain mist to hide her" (126). Even the Fourth of July fireworks, an extravagant display that celebrates independence and represents the freedom of Charity's own sexual expression, is ruined by Royall's accusation, "you damn – bareheaded whore" (151). Social conventions and market forces also inhibit her. Charity is not free either to have her child out of wedlock (she will be ostracized by the town) or to choose an abortion (she lacks money to pay the abortionist). When early in the novel she lies in a field of grass and flowers, admonishing the Mountain boy, Liff Hyatt, for stepping on the blossoms with an irritated, "Don't you *see* anything?" (55, original emphasis), she foretells her own process of discovery – not only of nature, or the Whitman-like concepts of human sympathy, mutuality, and the diversity of love, but of restrictions in nature *and* society.

Wharton conveys the fragility and temporality of Charity's freedom throughout the novel by counterpointing exuberance with regret, dream with reality, youth with age, and innocence with experience. Charity finds a romantic lover, but she marries her guardian, a man old enough to be her father – indeed, a man who has been her father. Alone in her bedroom, she fancies herself Lucius's virgin bride; Royall tries to invade this space with drunken sexual propositions. The Fourth of July adventure is ruined not only by Royall's drunken outburst but by Charity's friend Julia Hawes, who represents the fallen woman Charity will become. And the idyllic setting of the lovers' summer cottage contrasts with both the forbidding, lawless Mountain and the narrow social order of North Dormer. New England nature itself is erratically benevolent and ominous, more Darwinian than Emersonian.

Returning Home for "Good"

Lawyer Royall is a more complex character than his rival, Lucius Harney, and Wharton's portrayal of him more ambiguous. As his name, Royall, and profession, lawyer, suggest, he is an elitist – more Tory than colonist, aligned with the established order rather than with rebellion; however, he barely functions in his professional role and is more likely to be found relaxing than practicing law. Although he is unlike them, Royall sympathizes with the Mountain people when he helps Charity's convict father by rescuing her, and he continues to look out for Charity's welfare. By the same token, however, he also vaguely threatens to make her "pay" for pleasures that exclude him (62). The fact that he marries his adopted daughter opens him to the charge of incest. Yet Wharton clearly had high regard for her character, writing to Berenson, "I'm so particularly glad you like the old man Royall. Of course, *he's* the book!" (*Letters* 398, original emphasis).

It may be difficult for readers to imagine how Wharton could applaud such a man, but when we recall the Oedipal plots in her other fiction – in *The Reef; The Children;* and the unpublished "Beatrice Palmato" incest fragment, in which father–daughter sexuality is portrayed as pleasurable – we understand the theme's powerful resonance for her. Even in her nonfiction, Wharton equates the father with sensual pleasure: she describes the secret ecstasy of entering her father's library, which held numerous volumes forbidden by her mother, and she writes of walking happily with her father beyond the threshold of the family home (*Backward* 1–2; "Life" 1071).[19]

One way to reconcile the disparate forces in Royall's personality is to view him in terms of Whitman's poetic philosophy. The Whitman persona itself provides a useful touchstone for understanding Royall. Whitman espouses an incorporation and acceptance of diversity, as well as the unjudgmental belief that what *is* is ultimately good. This is perhaps what Wharton meant when she wrote in her notes for the Whitman essay: "sense of continuity, rhythm & oneness, of the absolute beyond the relative." A Whitman-like reading of *Summer* invites us to accept life *as it is,* to imagine a cosmic significance beyond the immediate, mundane one. Although *Summer* focuses on Charity Royall's development, it is also about Lawyer Royall and, through him, about the relative and absolute qualities of "the good."[20] Wharton's comment to Berenson suggests that the fully human Royall, with all his failures, is the moral center of the novel. Certainly, he is the hub to and from which all social groups in *Summer* emanate. Like the free hero of Whitman's verse, he is complex and paradoxical: father and lover, rule breaker and interpreter, model of civic virtue and reprobate. Encompassing both the admirable and the reproachable – in effect, good and evil – Royall represents a perfectly *imperfect* human being, the same type of individual whom Whitman celebrates in his poetry. In this sense, also, Charity and Royall's developing relationship broadly parallels Whitman's quest for ideal truth or wisdom and for some communal, democratic ideal.

A key event revealing Royall's character is his spirited speech during Old Home Week. Royall plays a major role at this celebration, just as he later plays a role in Charity's personal homecoming. He uses "Old Home Week" – a patriotic occasion – not to advertise his superiority over the townspeople, but to claim equality with them and to emphasize – almost confess – his imperfections. Until this point in the novel, Royall's and Charity's privileged positions in the town have been unspoken licenses that each has used to "rule." In his speech, however, Royall places himself on par with the townspeople, humbling himself and identifying with them. We hear the words of Royall's speech only once, when Charity finds herself "arrested" by their powerful rhythms (192). We are all here for better or for worse, Royall tells his audience. "With pauses that seemed to invite his hearers to silent participation in his thought" and with "inflections [that] were richer and graver than [Charity] had ever known them," he makes his plea for accepting one's self and one's town, for returning to roots after following the call of ambition – even after failing:

> Most of you who have returned here today . . . have come only on a pious pilgrimage, and will go back presently to busy cities and lives full of larger duties. But that is not the only way of coming back to North Dormer. . . . [Some] have come back in another way – come back for good. . . . Come back to our native town because we'd failed to get on elsewhere. . . . What we'd dreamed of hadn't come true. (193–94)

Under these circumstances, Royall explains, one can return to North
Dormer "for *good* . . . and not for bad . . . or just for indifference": "the
fact that we had failed is no reason why we should fail here." Coming back
home can also make a difference in the place that one lives: returning to
"the old homes" can be worthwhile "for their good" (194, 195, original
emphasis and ellipsis).

Royall assumes the persona of the speaker in Whitman's "Crossing
Brooklyn Ferry," sharing his sufferings and self-doubts and imparting wisdom harvested from years of experience. Whitman's lines can easily stand
for Royall's as he addresses the crowd:

> It is not upon you alone that dark patches fall,
> The dark threw its patches down upon me also,
> The best I had done seem'd to me bland and suspicious,
> My great thoughts as I supposed them, were they not in reality
>   meagre?
>
> (*Leaves*, lines 65–68)

Royall's address is a kind of spiritual cleansing, an open declaration of his
strengths and weaknesses. He has failed by external standards, but he has
made peace with his failure. His statements foreshadow Charity's marriage
and return to North Dormer: "Even if you come back against your will
. . . you must try to make the best of it, and to make the best of your old
town; and after a while . . . I believe you'll be able to say, as I can say
today: 'I'm glad I'm here' " (195).

The oration lacks the exuberant optimism of Whitman's songs of American expansion and progress: the words are scaled down to suit the reality of
impoverished and depopulated late nineteenth-century New England
towns. Yet Royall's speech conveys confidence in the inherent goodness
of one's situation, no matter how diminished. And in a Whitman-like way,
Royall's words touch his audience. "That was a *man* talking –" the minister
tells a listener next to him (195, original emphasis), the phrase echoing the
famous line from Whitman's "So Long!": "Who touches this touches a
man" (*Leaves*, line 54).[21] The meaning of the speech is not lost on Charity.
Until this moment, Royall has been a parental inconvenience and impedi-
ment to her youthful longings. She has not acknowledged him as a source
of comfort or as a human being in his own right. However, at the
conclusion of the speech, when she sees Lucius with Annabel Balch,
Charity realizes the ephemerality of her summer romance. Overcome with
"terror of the unknown" and her "powerlessness" over Lucius, Charity
faints "at Mr. Royall's feet," beginning the homecoming that she will later
make (198, 199).[22]

Wharton's allusion to Whitman in her portrayal of Lawyer Royall, however positive, is not unproblematically sunny. Her title *Summer*, which refers to the season of fulfillment that Northrup Frye identifies with dramatic comedy, does not sufficiently describe the novel. *Summer* combines the comic *and* the tragic. All seasons of life – and cycles of birth, death, and rebirth – are important to Wharton's creative vision. They were also important to Whitman's. The "delicious word death," Whitman writes in "Out of the Cradle Endlessly Rocking" (*Leaves*, line 168). In "Song of Myself," he declares, "the smallest sprout shows there is really no death"; "it is just as lucky to die" (*Leaves*, lines 126, 132). In *Summer*, Royall's initial rescue gives Charity a second chance for life; the end of her affair with Lucius signals a new relationship with Royall; and Charity has new life within her when she visits the ramshackled Mountain house and lies on her mother's deathbed.

Wharton integrates the light and dark elements of the novel in minor as well as major ways. Mr. Miles, the North Dormer minister, visits the Mountain on occasions of birth and death; Wharton hints that Liff Hyatt, "a sort of link between the mountain and civilized folk" (55), who drives Miles and Charity to her mother, might be related to Charity; and the description of the Hyatt children as "sleepy puppies" "herded together in a sort of passive promiscuity in which their common misery was the strongest link" (258, 259) alludes to Darwinian survival of the fittest as well as to Whitman-like transcendence. Traditional religion becomes irrelevant: Charity tries to relate her Mountain experience "to the designs of a just but merciful God; but it was impossible to imagine any link between them" (259). The Mountain outcasts represent the "animal" nature in everyone; they are also the dregs of society that Whitman welcomes and includes in his verses, and they, too, must be incorporated into the vast oneness that is human nature.

The disparate qualities of human experience are nowhere so strongly brought together as in Charity and Royall's relationship. Struggle and rebellion at first characterize their interactions. Charity "rule[s] in lawyer Royall's house" (23) and makes him pay for his drunken transgression by ensuring her appointment as town librarian (even though she is unqualified for the post), and by hiring a domestic helper she does not need. Royall, in turn, also rules over Charity; she fears that if he finds out that she is pregnant and abandoned by Lucius that he will "make her 'pay for it' " (62). But Royall does not make her pay – at least not within the boundaries of the plot. In the warmth of Mrs. Hobart's kitchen, for example, Charity receives North Dormer's hospitality and learns that everything there need

not be hateful. And on her wedding night, Royall sleeps in a chair while
Charity slumbers undisturbed.

Charity at first interprets Royall's interventions in her romance as inter-
ference, but he maintains that he acts out of a sense of justice and concern.
He tells her at the summer house:

> You're always telling me I've got no rights over you. There might be
> two ways of looking at that – but I ain't going to argue it. All I know
> is I raised you as good as I could, and meant fairly by you always –
> except once, for a bad half-hour. There's no justice in weighing that
> half-hour against the rest, and you know it. If you hadn't, you
> wouldn't have gone on living under my roof. Seems to me the fact of
> your doing that gives me some sort of a right; the right to try and
> keep you out of trouble. I'm not asking you to consider any other.
> (205)

By the time Royall finds her on the Mountain road, Charity responds to
him with "relief of feeling that someone was near her in the awful emptiness" (265). Recognizing the effort and sacrifice that he has made to find
her, she feels "a softness at her heart which no act of his had ever produced
since he had brought the Crimson Rambler because she had given up
boarding-school to stay with him" (266). Charity struggles with her feelings: "I know I ain't been fair to you always; but I want to be now. . . . I
want you to know . . . I want . . ." (270, original ellipses). Royall, his tone
"strong and resolute," interrupts: "What's all this about wanting? . . . All *I*
want is to know if you'll marry me. If there was anything else, I'd tell you
so. . . . Come to my age, a man knows the things that matter and the things
that don't; that's about the only good turn life does us." At these words,
Charity feels her "resistance melting, her strength slipping away" (271),
and Royall turns the carriage toward Creston. Royall emerges as the only
solid, clear part of her troubled thoughts:

> As everything else in her consciousness grew more and more confused
> and immaterial . . . like the universal shimmer that dissolves the world
> to failing eyes, Mr. Royall's presence began to detach itself with rocky
> firmness from this elusive background. She had always thought of
> him – when she thought of him at all – as of someone hateful and
> obstructive, but whom she could outwit and dominate when she
> chose to make the effort. Only once, on the day of the Old Home
> Week celebration, while the stray fragments of his address drifted
> across her troubled mind, had she caught a glimpse of another being,
> a being so different from the dull-witted enemy with whom she
> had supposed herself to be living that even through the burning

mist of her own dreams he had stood out with startling distinctness.
(275)

When Charity wakes the day after her wedding, she realizes "that she is
safe with him." She feels "ineffable relief" and "a stir of something deeper
than she had ever felt in thinking of him" (284).

Wharton seems to lay the groundwork for a positive, loving relationship
between Charity and Royall. Admittedly, it is not a youthful, exuberant
romance. However, middle-aged herself at the time she wrote *Summer* and
having witnessed the death and grief of war, Wharton had come to value
aspects of life that mellow and ripen rather than blaze with romantic fervor.
Whitman also wrote in his notes for the "Children of Adam" poems about
the middle-aged lover who could rival his youthful counterpart:

> Adam, as a central figure and type. One piece presenting a vivid
> picture (in connection with the spirit) of a fully complete, well-
> developed man, eld, bearded, swart, fiery, – as a more than rival of
> the youthful type-hero of novels and love poems. (*Leaves* 90n.)

For Wharton, as for Whitman, the ideal hero is not a young innocent, but
an experienced postlapsarian figure with a fully developed, passionate but
seasoned nature – in short, the idealized father figure. Seen in the light of
Whitman's poetry, marrying one's "father" may not entirely rule out
passion.[23] Whitman's democratic and "cosmic philosophy" – to use the
phrase from Wharton's notes for her essay – includes all types of human
behaviors and all types of people: prostitutes, felons, drunkards, and repro-
bates.[24] It may well encompass Royall's incestuous union with Charity, for
it is precisely the animality of the sexual drive, with its urgent need for
contact with the other, that Whitman celebrates. In this case, Royall is not
reprehensible because he desires Charity; he is only the perfectly imperfect
man of Whitman's poems. Whitman's vision is an acceptance of what *is*,
without judgment.

The relationship may be seen positively from another perspective, as
Wharton's notes on Whitman also indicate. In the bracketed notation
following her entry, "Sympathy," she recorded "lover – love – asexual."
Applied to *Summer*, the words suggest a Platonic progression for both
Charity and Royall – a movement from a passionate fixation to an understanding of love beyond the sexual. This is Charity's experience as she
moves from heartache over Lucius to a "safe" relationship with Royall in
which they will raise her child together. And it may also be Royall's
experience as he attempts to be both husband and father.

Whitman notwithstanding, however, the fact of Charity's and Royall's disparate ages and father–daughter relationship remains. Regardless of whatever philosophy informs the novel, there is the reality of an imbalance of power between them. Royall's marriage proposal, even if well intentioned, represents male authority over a younger, vulnerable woman. If Royall offers Charity protection and stability, he also, as Wolff notes, "stands like some prophet of the Old Testament . . . a giver of laws" (*Feast* 282). Royall's absolute control over Charity – at the beginning of life and now – recalls the omnipotent patriarch of Calvinism, and Charity's child-like dependence on him recalls the helpless plight of the sinner facing God's judgment. Her helplessness resembles Ethan and Mattie's plight in *Ethan Frome*. All three characters face an indomitable parental authority with arbitrary powers that mirror the myriad material and social forces restricting free choice.

Appropriately, then, Charity appears lifeless and insensible when Royall takes her to Creston for the wedding ceremony. She experiences the same detached feeling that characterized turn-of-the-century spiritual uncertainty: "She had only a confused sensation of slipping down a smooth irresistible current; and she abandoned herself to the feeling as a refuge from the torment of thought" (273). Her feelings of summer romance fade completely – "she could no longer believe that she was the being who had lived them" – and she follows Royall "as passively as a tired child" (274). In the final scene of the novel, it is clear that Royall has "elected" Charity, just as God elects his saints, but it is less clear whether Charity has chosen him, or whether she even has the will to make such a choice. The father's return means a forfeit of the daughter's autonomy. Charity is safe in her hotel bed only because of *Royall's* decision. He sets the terms of their relationship here as he has previously with his judgment, "You're a good girl, Charity." Charity can only uncertainly repeat his words, "I guess you're good, too" (290–91). In the final analysis, Wharton evokes the Emerson not of "Nature" or "Self-Reliance," but of "Fate" – and aligns herself with Darwin rather than Whitman.

Both *The Reef* and *Summer* express Wharton's desire to find a religious or philosophical system that transcends traditional Christianity. But in both novels, however, independently minded, strong women are still inscribed within rigid Christian codes that even the most radical forms of rebellion cannot overcome. The allusion to Sophia in *The Reef* demonstrates that feminine qualities of wisdom, creativity, and passion, such as those that Sophy Viner possesses, are subsumed by biblical depictions of women either as subservient wives or brazen harlots. Similarly, Charity, whose name alludes to the New Testament qualities of love, benevolence, and vulnerability, is overpowered by her Old Testament counterpart, the patriarchal Lawyer Royall. In both novels, efforts to challenge the effects of rigid Christian doctrines fail. In her next major novel, *The Age of Innocence,* Wharton turns away from the Christian and toward the Hellenic, seeking Platonic models for women's freedom. However, these efforts, too, are only partially successful, as we shall see.

5

Platonic Idealism

The world is a welter and has always been one; but though all the
cranks and the theorists cannot master the old floundering monster,
or force it for long into any of their neat plans of readjustment, here
and there a saint or a genius suddenly sends a little ray through the
fog, and helps humanity to stumble on, and perhaps up.

Edith Wharton, *A Backward Glance*

Adopting the Platonic dialogue, with all its archaeological formulae,
seems to me enough to petrify or ossify any drop of new blood or
morsel of live flesh & bone.

Edith Wharton, Letter to Margaret Chanler

EDITH Wharton continued her search for spiritual meaning in
the post–World War I years. In previous novels, she wrestled with questions of spiritual meaning and sought alternatives to the Christian mind–
body split and prohibitions on the flesh. Old Testament teachings and
Calvinist doctrines influence *The House of Mirth* and *Ethan Frome;* the
wisdom and creativity of the ancient deity Sophia echo in *The Reef;* and
Emerson's and Whitman's transcendentalism provide the inspiration for
Summer. In *The Age of Innocence,* Platonic philosophy offers Wharton another base from which to explore familiar and haunting questions about
love, duty, and spiritual values.

Although the heroine of *Summer* cannot realize the full potential afforded by Emersonian transcendentalism, Wharton herself continued to
privilege Emerson's ideals, focusing, in particular, on the Platonic philosophy that informed his and other romantic theories of the nineteenth century. At the same time, she continued to develop an aesthetics of taste,
culture, and morality. Art had always offered welcome relief from worldly

pressures and materialism, as well as spiritual edification. Increasingly, Wharton came to value art not just for its principles of order and balance ("Order the beauty even of Beauty is," by Thomas Traherne, is the epigraph to *The Writing of Fiction*), but for the philosophical issues that it addressed. She believed that if science brought humans closer to matter, then art might bring the soul closer to the ideal.

In *The Writing of Fiction* (1925), Wharton explains that "the creative imagination is . . . two-sided, and combines with the power of penetrating into other minds that of standing far enough aloof from them to see beyond. . . . Such an all-round view can be obtained only by mounting to a height." She goes on to explain that literature is more than realistic reportage: the writer gives vision as well as form to matters of everyday life: "the attempt to give back any fragment of life . . . presupposes transposition. . . . If it did not, the writing of fiction could never be classed among works of art" (15–17). Art also offered a sense of permanence in the midst of social change. As Vernon Lee wrote in her 1913 book *The Beautiful,* "the healing quality of aesthetic contemplation is due, in large part, to the fact that, in the perpetual flux of action and thought, it represents reiteration and therefore stability" (109–10). Wharton shared Lee's view, especially in an atmosphere of religious doubt. A philosophy of aesthetics offered freedom from materiality and potential for limitless individual growth without imposing or burdensome religious doctrine.

Art did not inspire such noble possibilities in every situation, however. Emersonian and Platonic theories called individuals actively to seek and create, but for some, art generated instead a cult of taste and ritual without this dynamic element of self-improvement. Such a static adherence to form, traceable not only to convention but to a rigid, Puritan-like insistence on surrender to higher authority, characterizes the restrained world of *The Age of Innocence* (1920). Wharton's novel concerns not just cultural stability but spiritual stagnation and injustice that results from "a blind dread of innovation" (*Backward* 22). Her response to this stagnation is a Platonic idealism in which individuals – and women, in particular – might rise beyond the mundane to a higher level of reality. But such ascent is checked by an equally strong Puritanism.

Puritan Hellenism in *The Age of Innocence*

Edith Wharton wrote *The Age of Innocence* from 1919 to 1920, while recuperating from the shattering effects of World War I and the death of friends Henry James, Egerton Winthrop, and Howard Sturgis. As she writes in *A Backward Glance,* she "found a momentary escape in going back to my childish memories of a long-vanished America, and wrote 'The Age of Innocence' " (369). She describes the novel as a reminiscence; some critics even find it sentimental or conciliatory.[1] It would be a mistake, however, to think of *The Age of Innocence* as unproblematically nostalgic. Granted, at the end of the novel Archer assesses his life – his love and renunciation of Ellen Olenska, his subsequent devotion to his children and wife May Welland – and concludes that "after all, there was good in the old ways" (347). But not many pages later, he also concludes that "his life had been too starved" (357). What are we to make of these contradictory evaluations?

The Age of Innocence invites conflicting interpretations because it simultaneously develops two world views, one centered in the staid traditions of old New York, and the other in the dynamic life of Ellen Olenska. New York follows a predictable path in which traditional forms have become synonymous with ideas, and new ideas are as unwelcome as a December draft. Even art – creative expression that promises freshness and spiritual uplift – has been reduced to and is regulated by matters of taste. Newland Archer, a genteel New Yorker by birth and training, is nonetheless drawn to Ellen's free spirit and falls in love with her. After excruciating indecision, he chooses May and New York. It is a choice that he must make, given his background and circumstances, yet he spends half a lifetime regretting his lost opportunity.

Like many of Wharton's novels, *The Age of Innocence* develops the theme of conflict between the individual and society – between the urge for personal fulfillment and the need for group stability. It also criticizes old New York's worship of a Puritan aesthetic. The plot follows a protagonist who renounces desire in order to fulfill social duty. The genteel members of Wharton's childhood society had originally made their money through a Puritan work ethic and, indeed, took satisfaction from the belief that their success was evidence of God's favor. But when they became rich, they were torn between the Calvinist proscription against ostentation and the equally unattractive option of parting with the luxury and privilege that their wealth had conferred. They compromised by retaining piety without falling prey to gross materialism. They enjoyed their wealth while appearing to give it no importance – "Never talk about money, and think about it as little as possible" (*Backward* 57), Wharton's mother often told her – and they guarded their status as members of the "elect" with desperate vigilance. The Thanksgiving Day sermon in *The Age of Innocence* is thus drawn from Jeremiah, which pessimistically predicts siege, exile, and death while holding out the small hope of a restored covenant with God.

But Wharton does more than expose attenuated Puritan values in this novel. She draws on anthropology and philosophy to interrogate the entire moral structure of Ellen's and Archer's worlds.[2] Wharton was searching when she wrote *The Age of Innocence* for an order irrevocably lost by World War I. It was natural that she turned to the security of her childhood at such a time, but it was also inevitable, given her keen intelligence and experiences beyond New York, that she saw the limitations of such a society. Indeed, as her own description of the novel suggests, she had come to view old New York as "childish." It conferred assurances but was fundamentally immature, unwilling to look beyond its own narrow interests and unable to accommodate passion or change. Wharton demonstrates that Newland Archer's well-regulated New York is a society of the second order. Ellen Olenska, in contrast – a supremely confident outsider to that society – embodies levels of truth and reality beyond those possible within the confines of genteel culture. But even Ellen's powerful combination of reason and passion cannot withstand the self-denying Puritanism at the heart of New York society. Puritanism resides in the character of Ellen Olenska, Wharton's most courageous and independent heroine, because it is also within Wharton herself.

The novel is set in the 1870s, when the New York society that had evolved slowly over two centuries was under siege by newly moneyed classes. The response to this crisis was to draw the circle tighter, becoming more exclusive and ritualized. Wharton's description of old New Yorkers as a threatened tribe is apt. At the time she wrote the novel, Americans and Europeans were pursuing an unprecedented interest in primitive cultures, and anthropology was rapidly developing as a discipline. Wharton herself visited Morocco in 1917, recording her impressions of this exotic, uncharted land in *In Morocco,* which appeared in the same year as *The Age of Innocence.* Jackson Lears interprets the fascination with primitive cultures as an antimodernist impulse, arising from a crisis of cultural authority and backlash against logical order. The primal past reinstated sacred mysteries long since demolished by Darwinism and provided escape from the hectic and seemingly directionless pace of early twentieth-century life (142–43). Indeed, Wharton uses tribal language to suggest that instinct, not reason, rules old New York; and she writes *The Age of Innocence* – just as she writes *In Morocco* – as a guidebook to that primitive culture.

To understand the pressure of old New York's values on Newland Archer – and, in particular, the group's decision to marshal forces and send Ellen Olenska back to Europe – I turn to René Girard's analysis of sacrificial practices. Girard theorizes that the ancient ritual of sacrifice is the means by which a group controls and contains the disruption that threatens it from within: "the purpose of the sacrifice is to restore harmony to the community, to reinforce the social fabric" (8). These communal, ritual practices constitute a religion that helps the society come to terms with its own inadequacies; in more modern societies the same function is served by a system of justice. Wharton reflects both operations in describing New York society as a tribe and the decision making of the leading family, the van der Luydens, as a tribunal.

As Girard notes, the victims of such sacrifice are not chosen randomly. Rather, they are "exterior or marginal individuals, incapable of establishing or sharing the social bonds that link the rest of the inhabitants. Their status as foreigners . . . prevents these future victims from fully integrating themselves into the community" (12). Certain rules govern sacrifice: the victim cannot be in the position to avenge the violence done to her by the community, and the more critical the social crisis, the more "precious" the victim must be (18). Ellen Olenska, May Welland's cousin and the respected Mrs. Manson Mingott's niece, is an ideal victim. She returns home from Europe at a time when the clan needs to shore up its boundaries. She is also faintly exotic – her life on the continent, her notorious marriage and scandalous departure from it, her Sunday soirees with people whom her family and friends mistrust, even the unorthodox cut of her gown set her apart from others. Archer's attraction to Ellen further jeopardizes group unity, since New York regulates romance and passion as strictly as it does dinner parties. In a series of well-orchestrated but unacknowledged maneuvers, Ellen is expelled from the community. She becomes the means by which old New York reaffirms its traditions and seals cracks in its social fortress. Her removal from society becomes not only desirable but necessary for group survival. Revenge, Girard tells us, often passes for justice (24); thus New York thinks itself justified in expelling Ellen.

Ellen represents more than a social or romantic threat: she also challenges New York's ethical code. By the tribe's standards, Archer lives an exemplary life and Ellen a suspect one. Through the contrast of the two worlds, however, Wharton asks exactly what constitutes a good life. Old New York is a reactive, instinctual society whose ritualistic acts bring about concrete results – Girard notes the "strongly functional nature of the scapegoat operation" in such societies (276). But Wharton is concerned with quality as well as function. Throughout the novel, Ellen is committed to reasoned truth, not instinct. She bravely follows her conscience without regard for personal or material outcome. This commitment to her own path suggests a self-conscious philosophy rather than the blind following of ritual or convention. Specifically, Ellen represents three qualities simultaneously: Platonic idealism; a metaphysical quest for love and truth, which also embraces passion; and, to some extent, beauty and truth itself.

Higher Reality

Wharton had a lifetime interest in classical forms and ideas. She comments in *A Backward Glance* that the adult stories of Olympus held far more power for her than children's fairy tales and writes appreciatively of Henry Bedlow, the family friend who introduced her to Greek mythology (32–33). She compared the leisured class at play in Newport to the pantheon: "those archery meetings greatly heightened my infantile desire to 'tell a story,' and the young gods and goddesses I used to watch strolling across the Edgerston lawn were the prototypes of my first novels" (47). Her novels often allude to Greek myth and literature, and her plots exhibit the symmetry of classical drama. Even Wharton's architectural and decorative tastes favored the balanced lines of classicism, as evidenced by the clean, proportioned design of the Mount, her summer home in Lenox, Massachusetts. Wharton was also an avid reader of classical texts. Her personal library contained not only classical poetry and plays but books about Greek religion and philosophy, including J. P. Mahaffy's *Greek Life and Thought*, G. Murray's *Four Stages of Greek Religion*, E. Westermarck's *The Origin and Development of the Moral Ideas*, and G. L. Dickinson's *The Greek View of Life* (Maggs). In a letter to Sara Norton in 1905, Wharton writes of being "in the mood for the Hellenic," and of having read Plato's dialogues, Samuel Henry Butcher's *Some Aspects of Greek Genius*, and Walter Pater's *Plato and Platonism* (*Letters* 100). Her library contained a five-volume 1875 edition of Plato's dialogues (Maggs).

Plato appealed to Wharton because he emphasized the spiritual ideal, blended reason with mysticism, and promoted egalitarianism. He also attracted her – as he did other turn-of-the-century women struggling for liberation – because he posited ideal as well as erotic love. Plato opened the door for women's participation in government and philosophy with his statement in the *Republic* that "there is no occupation . . . which belongs either to woman or to man, as such" (153). Since the guardians of the state must be true philosophers, women might conceivably achieve this status.

Not surprisingly, nineteenth-century scholars, influenced by the ideology of separate spheres, disliked Plato's proposal for female guardians in the *Republic*. The English philosopher Bernard Bosanquet, for example, speaks of "the violent revolution" that Plato advocated (qtd. in Bluestone 58). Traditionalists seized upon Plato's further comment that "every occupation is open to both [sexes], so far as their natures are concerned" (153) and interpreted it as meaning that women were "naturally" suited to bear and raise children rather than reign as philosopher-queens. Some commentators, including John Stuart Mill, ignored Plato's program for the equality of women altogether while discussing other elements at length, such as the abolition of property and the family (Bluestone 71). Pater opposed Plato's notion of equality of the sexes, arguing that changing women's motherly roles would "deprive mothers of that privacy of affection, regarding which the wisdom of Solomon beamed forth." He relied more on Christianity than on Platonism in reaching his conclusion that Plato's is a "strange forbidding experiment" when one takes into account "laws now irrevocably fixed on these subjects by the judgment of the Christian Church" (257–58). Despite her generation's biases, Wharton joined a cadre of women who took Plato's commendation of women's qualities seriously. The first use of the term "philosopher-queen," according to Natalie Bluestone (71–72), is in Adela Adam's 1913 book on Plato. Adam writes that Plato was "undaunted by any national prejudice" and "artificial barriers"; his "images of philosopher-kings . . . represent also philosopher-queens" (126). In *The Age of Innocence,* Wharton portrays Ellen Olenska as just such a philosopher-queen. Ellen is a woman with profound integrity, who is neither wife nor mother and yet serves, through her patient, probing questions, as Newland Archer's spiritual guide.

Other classical influences on *The Age of Innocence,* which Wharton read in December 1905, are Plato's *Symposium* and *Phaedrus.* She found these works so overwhelming that she transcribed a long passage from the *Symposium* into her commonplace book, writing, "love will make men desire to die for their beloved . . . a woman as well as men" (qtd. in Lewis 159). In August of the next year, still intrigued by Plato, Wharton wrote her friend Sara Norton that she "finished off the evening by reading the Symposium" (*Letters* 106). Nowhere in *The Age of Innocence* does Wharton name the *Symposium* or the *Phaedrus,* yet these texts – as well as Plato's *Republic* – give the novel its shape and significance.

In the *Symposium* – the banquet is ironically transformed in *The Age of Innocence* into May's farewell dinner for Ellen – Socrates and others debate, in ways both earthy and sublime, the nature of love. Eros, which seeks possession of the love object, is praised by Alcibiades, who is infatuated with Socrates; but after Socrates' gentle questioning, eros is set aside in favor of a more spiritual craving for eternal beauty and truth. In *The Age of Innocence,* Ellen plays the role of Socrates, leading Archer to understand love that includes but also goes beyond the senses. The *Phaedrus* complements the *Symposium.* Its immediate subject is rhetoric, but Plato unites this discussion with one about the psychology of love and the immortality of the soul. He argues that the preexisting soul is restricted at birth to the bodily realm of the senses. To fall in love is to come under the influence of beauty and to awaken to possibilities normally ignored on the human plane. Through love, the soul grows wings and, as Psyche, ascends to its original high estate, which is Reality. The soul that has seen the most Reality becomes a "seeker for wisdom or beauty, a follower of the Muses or a lover" (31); this description resembles Wharton's portrait of Ellen.

The third text important to *The Age of Innocence,* the *Republic,* deals with humans not only as social creatures but as participants in eternity. Book 7, which includes the allegory of the cave, expresses Plato's belief in a reality beyond the perceptions of the senses, one intelligible only to the purified soul. Plato explains that what is commonly called "real" is, in fact, only an imitation of or incomplete substitute for the truly real, which is forms and ideas. His cave dwellers see mere reflections on the cave walls and believe them to be real; only a rare and intrepid seeker of truth ventures outside the cave to apprehend true forms, not shadows of images. The attainment of this metaphysical vision of reality is not only the philosopher's special purpose but the greatest human happiness.

Wharton's attraction to Platonic theory is consistent with her belief in the soul's immortality, and with her distinction in *The Age of Innocence* and elsewhere between the ideal and real. Although stressing life's compromises, she suggests heights to which one might aspire – whether through love, art, friendship, solitude, or nature. Equally important, Plato offers an alternative to the model of romantic love that pervades Western thinking and which, to a great extent, defines women's participation in culture. Christian doctrines associate women's sexuality with sin. But Platonic love accommodates erotic desire; moreover, Plato assures us that love's finest form is so far beyond the personal that we will gladly fall out of love with those whom we have held dear. Although romantic love is a theme in *The Age of Innocence,* it does not in and of itself represent fulfillment. Wharton asks whether there is a higher order of love beyond the senses – one that includes art, music, and good conversation. When she recorded her impressions of the *Symposium* in her notebook, Wharton was responding to the idea of a love that encompasses all desire, including the desire to find where one's true well-being lies. Plato argues that true love and rationality are one and the same. Rather than lead to a surrender to pleasure and passion, love is synonomous with self-control; its object "is in all truth beautiful and delicate and perfect and worthy." True love leads to happiness; false love does not (83–84).

Plato also appealed to Wharton's intelligence by acknowledging the possibility of female philosophers – like Ellen Olenska. Wharton's structure in *The Age of Innocence* parallels Plato's in the *Symposium.* When Socrates discusses and defines love, he draws on what he has learned from the wise woman Diotima; he recounts his dialogues with her for Agathon's edification. Similarly, in *The Age of Innocence,* Ellen – Wharton's wise woman – helps to lead Archer toward philosophical truth. Finally, Wharton engages Plato to suggest an overall approach to life. Plato's dialogues emphasize the need to live an examined life, providing an alternative to New York's smug complacency.

Wharton contrasts Plato's probing questions with the aristocracy's rigid rules; his inexhaustible search for higher meaning with an effete society's fearful dedication to self-preservation. Old New York refuses to examine – let alone change – its principles. Ellen's reflective and questioning spirit challenges that resistance. Her involvement with Archer provides both the occasion for a deep, romantic attachment *and* the opportunity to transform that love into enlightened search for ideal truth – while her Platonic stance also preserves the ethos of Christian community that she challenges.

When *The Age of Innocence* opens, Newland Archer is not so much a questioner or explorer as a blind follower. Indistinguishable in dress, action, and opinion from the rest of his circle, he arrives late at the opera because it is unfashionable to arrive early, and he grants convention complete authority: "What was or was not 'the thing' played a part as important in Newland Archer's New York as the inscrutable totem terrors that had ruled the destinies of his forefathers thousands of years ago" (4). Because Archer's opinions are already formed, he is "content to hold his view without analyzing it" (7–8). With perfect confidence, he thinks of himself as superior to others who lack his experience with books, travel, and love. Thus, when Larry Lefferts takes the lead in finding Ellen Olenska's appearance at the opera scandalous, he follows suit, convinced that the idea is his own: "Few things seemed to Newland Archer more awful than an offense against 'Taste,' that far-off divinity of whom 'Form' was the mere visible representative and viceregent. . . . The way her dress (which had no tucker) sloped away from her thin shoulders shocked and troubled him" (15).

Wharton writes that Archer conforms to New York's "doctrine on all the issues called moral" (8), but her phrasing casts doubt on his definition of morality.[3] Because he is "at heart a dilettante" rather than a philosopher (4), Archer confuses higher truth with mere taste. For example, although already attracted to Ellen, he enjoins May to announce their engagement early "because it's right." May, he is sure, "was always going to say the right thing." He does wish that the "necessity" of announcing their engagement early "had been represented by some ideal reason, and not simply by poor Ellen Olenska" (24), but he fails to notice that Ellen represents this "ideal reason." And he automatically joins the tribe in their self-protective maneuvers to condemn Ellen despite the fact that he is moved by her originality, beauty, and honesty. He will grow from an unquestioning acceptance of Taste as arbiter of right and wrong to a more reasoned understanding of Truth as the final measure of value – but only to a point.

Archer's dilemma is dramatized through Wharton's contrasting depictions of the two women in his life. May is the fair American girl whose lean, athletic body suggests the physical but not the sensual. Ellen, on the other hand, is the dark, passionate beauty touched with the mystery and experience of Europe. May represents the safe, secure world of New York gentility; Ellen the exotic, the original, and the unknown. Wharton's classical allusions sharpen this contrast.

May, whose face suggests "a type rather than person" (188), is associated with Artemis, the Greek goddess of the hunt. Her role as Artemis suggests her power over her husband: she is master of the hunt and thus of "Archery." According to Ovid's *Metamorphoses,* the virgin Diana (the Roman equivalent of the Greek Artemis) seeks vengeance against Acteon for watching her bathe naked in a sparkling fountain – that is, for seeing her true nature. Diana turns him into a stag who is then attacked by his own hounds. Archer is a modern-day Acteon who finally sees May as she is: a conventional woman with no imagination or capacity for change. Wharton somewhat satirically refers to Archer as her victim when May marshals the forces of his own "hounds" – his family – to send Ellen back to Europe. May is also a model of "Civic Virtue" and notable for her unchanging, pristine quality; but her virtue is "only primitive and pure" (189), like the savage society she upholds. Ellen, on the other hand, represents the qualities of virtue found in Plato's philosophy. She upholds truth at any cost; May dissembles, announcing an unconfirmed pregnancy in order to ensure Archer's faithfulness. Archer eventually discovers that May's "frankness and innocence were only an artificial product" (46); even her premarital offer to give Archer up is a calculated gesture based on her guess that his affair is already over (she suspects another woman, not Ellen). May is generous because she believes she has nothing to lose.[4]

Wharton associates Ellen with the Greek goddess Aphrodite, who reigns over all aspects of sexual love and beauty. In the Greek pantheon, Aphrodite was a divine force who humanized but also transcended sexuality. She stirred both mortals and immortals with desire, and she combined high emotion with sophistication and intelligence. Aphrodite is a liminal figure who easily crosses the boundaries of existing structures: Paul Friedrich notes her ability to "bridge[ ] physical reality and metaphysical belief" (134). Aphrodite's complexity is evident in Ellen Olenska's dual role as lover and philosopher in *The Age of Innocence.* Both Ellen and Aphrodite are of ambiguous origins, both make marriages with unlikely men, and both are identified with roses. Archer sends Ellen yellow roses after visiting her. Crimson and amber are the colors Ellen wears at the van der Luyden's party and at her farewell dinner – symbols of passion and decadence by Victorian standards, but also the colors most often associated with Aphrodite (Friedrich 75, 78–79). Significantly, Aphrodite, the model of womanly strength and power who gives birth to Eros or Cupid, is the goddess discussed in the *Symposium*. As Aphrodite, Ellen incorporates both erotic *and* higher conceptions of love.

Archer is irresistibly drawn to Ellen not only because of her physical beauty and originality but because of her commitment to levels of truth that he cannot find in May or her world. In contrast to May, who represents the status quo, Ellen is dynamic: she both sparks his romantic desire and initiates his spiritual education. In this respect, she resembles Socrates in the *Symposium*. Socrates is the object of Alcibiades' passionate infatuation as well as a philosopher-teacher. He calls for a life lived according to reason and encourages ascent from the love of a single individual to the love of beauty and goodness as values in and of themselves. Ellen embodies romantic, Hellenic desire – her name, after all, is (H)ellen – but she is also capable of leading Archer into rational reflection about the higher meaning of love.

Truth or Taste?

Ellen's technique is that of Socrates. She claims ignorance about the subject she wishes to teach and asks Archer for guidance instead of offering judgments or answers. "You'll tell me all I ought to know," she says when he first visits her. Ellen seems to accept New York at face value, calling it "heaven" and praising it for what it is not: "How I like it for just *that* – the straight-up-and-downness, and the big honest labels on everything!" However, her naive comments and transparent assessments are actually skillful challenges that require Archer to take a stand – to oppose or defend New York's ways. She encourages him – "I may simplify too much – but you'll warn me if I do" – and she puts action behind her words by agreeing to accept his advice about seeking her divorce (76–78, original emphasis). Her assumed ignorance leads Archer to examine the premises by which he lives. In particular, three dialectical exchanges help him distinguish "Taste" from "Truth."

The first dialogue – which is the most complicated one, and demands more analysis than the other two – occurs shortly after Archer sees Ellen at Mrs. Mingott's house. Although he and May have gone there to tell the older woman about their engagement, Archer finds himself unexpectedly ruminating over the roles accorded to the sexes. His reflection results in an argument for women's freedom. Impulsively, silently, he defends Ellen's nonconformity:

> Why shouldn't she be conspicuous if she chooses? Why should she slink about as if it were she who had disgraced herself? . . . I'm sick of the hypocrisy that would bury alive a woman of her age if her husband prefers to live with harlots. . . . Women ought to be free – as free as we are. (41–42)

Ellen's marital dilemma prompts Archer to review the complex double standard upon which his relationship to May and all women is based. Later, alone in his study, he realizes that "the case of the Countess Olenska had stirred up old settled convictions and set them drifting dangerously through his mind. His own exclamation: 'Women should be free – as free as we are,' struck to the root of a problem that it was agreed in his world to regard as non-existent" (43–44).

Archer sees a truth to which he has previously been blind; he also understands the abstract value of his discovery. He begins to look at the double standard in a "purely hypothetical" way; that is, he begins to consider Ellen's case according to reason instead of convention. This new approach leads him to the rather dangerous questioning of his own situation. And when he reflects on his upcoming marriage to May, he is filled with trepidation: "What if, for some one of the subtler reasons that would tell with both of them, they should tire of each other, misunderstand or irritate each other?" Freedom through divorce is practically impossible in his society. With a "shiver of foreboding," Archer envisions a marriage like every other: "a dull association of material and social interests held together by ignorance on the one side and hypocrisy on the other" (44–45).

As he continues to absorb this dialectical lesson, Archer begins to extend his insights about marriage and divorce to the New York tribe as a whole. He sees that the van der Luyden's tribunal, which decides on Ellen's reception in New York, is based not on the quality of justice but the tradition of "family" (56–57). He also thinks of his own engagement as a ritual of "Primitive Man" in which "the savage bride is dragged with shrieks from her parents' tent." The single goal of Archer's genteel world is preservation of its artificial reality, a point Wharton reinforces with her portrayals of Julius Beaufort (who, as long as he appears financially solvent, is accepted as such) and Ellen Olenska (who, because she appears to have had an affair, is condemned). This artifice is vastly different from the truth toward which Archer's inquiries lead him in this first dialectical lesson. He draws the unsettling conclusion that "in reality they all lived in a kind of hieroglyphic world, where the real thing was never said or done or even thought, but only represented by a set of arbitrary signs" (45).

Plato's definition of "reality" is useful to understand the dual meanings Wharton gives to the term "real thing." Archer's feeling that the world he lives in is "hieroglyphic" or "unreal" evokes the allegory of the cave in the *Republic.* Imprisoned cave dwellers sit before a fire watching reflections on the walls and think that these images are the true ones. When released from the cave, they see things in their proper light and apprehend true forms, not just their shadows. The novel's link to Platonic theory is explicit in a memory Archer experiences at the Mingott's affluent home: "He thought of a story he had read, of some peasant children in Tuscany lighting a bunch of straw in a wayside cavern, and revealing old silent images in their painted tomb. . . ." (214, original ellipsis). Wharton suggests that old New York merely approximates or imitates reality, and Archer – to the extent that he adheres to its values – is an unenlightened "cave man" in both the philosophical and anthropological sense.

Archer becomes increasingly aware of two levels of reality: one, the concrete, artificial world of New York conventionality ("reality"); and the other, the higher perception of truth, which is free from the senses and illusion ("Reality"). Wharton capitalizes the word once in the novel, when Archer judges that the members of his society are all "old maid[s]" "when it comes to being so much as brushed by the wing-tip of Reality" (86). This reference to winged Reality alludes not only to the *Republic,* but to the *Phaedrus,* in which the winged Psyche, or soul, ascends toward truth. Sadly, it is an ascent that Archer does not make. When he reflects at the end of the novel that "most of the real things of his life had happened" in his library (344), he refers to the conventional facts of his life, not the higher levels of reality possible for those who free themselves from the cave.

The second dialectical lesson occurs when Archer and Ellen speak at the van der Luydens' party about the nature of love and beauty. Here Wharton designs a conversation that parallels the one between Socrates and Alcibiades at the banquet in the *Symposium.* In addition to playing a Socratic role in this scene, Ellen also personifies beauty itself. Old New York's opinion is that she has "lost her looks" (59), yet Archer is aware of her "mysterious authority of beauty, a sureness in the carriage of the head, the movement of the eyes, which, without being in the least theatrical, struck him as highly trained and full of a conscious power. At the same time she was simpler in manner than most of the ladies present" (61).

Ellen initiates the dialogue, asking Archer if he is very much in love with May. His unchecked response, "as much as a man can be," prompts Ellen to ask, "Do you think, then, there is a limit?" When Archer responds that he has not yet found it, Ellen "glow[s] with sympathy" for his romance with May (64–65). Again, Ellen's naiveté is the deliberate strategy of a knowing discussant engaging an unknowing one: Archer does not yet realize how desperately lacking in romance his attachment to May is. Ellen next asks whether May and Archer's marriage has been arranged. Archer scoffs that in America such a thing is never done, but, in fact, society has dictated the terms of this relationship as it does all others.

Archer's third exchange with Ellen also takes place over the subject of love, more specifically love that ends in divorce. Pressured by his family, Archer unwillingly agrees to handle Ellen's divorce case and experiences a critical conflict between the traditional values of New York and a higher order of truth. Ironically, his decision to side with the family and persuade Ellen to remain married prevents him from having what he desires most: a chance to love Ellen freely. In advising her against divorce, Archer chooses bondage over freedom. Unable to apply his previous platitudes about women's freedom to Ellen's case, he assumes that rumors about her having an affair are true. Dependent on family approval, he finds himself issuing "all the stock phrases" to defend the customs of his tribal culture: "the individual . . . is nearly always sacrificed to what is supposed to be the collective interest," he tells Ellen. Archer concludes he had "better keep on the surface, in the prudent old New York way" (112). A true teacher, Ellen puts her pupil in charge of his own learning. She subordinates personal interest to the larger issue of truth and waits as Archer unsteadily gropes his way toward it.

At this point, Wharton introduces a tension in Ellen's role as Hellenic lover and philosopher. Ellen decides to follow old New York's advice and not seek a divorce from her husband. She explains her decision by comparing the loneliness she will face if she remains married to the greater loneliness of living among hypocrites: "Does no one want to know the truth here, Mr. Archer? The real loneliness is living among all these kind people who only ask one to pretend!" (78). However, as Ellen pursues the reasonable – that is, the Platonic ideals of truth – she also relinquishes an opportunity to fulfill her own passionate needs. Wharton does not explore this problematic departure from Platonic theory; instead, book 1 of *The Age of Innocence* develops the extent of Archer's conventionality and the occasions for his enlightenment. Archer must choose between truth and hypocrisy, reality and illusion. He does recognize the falseness of life around him and the potential for a more honest, fulfilling existence, but personal weakness and social circumstance conspire to trap him in New York's narrow world. Although he longs to "tell [Ellen] . . . the truth" and "ask for the freedom he had once refused" (321), Archer fails to learn Ellen's lesson or break away. Book 2 develops the consequences of this failure.

Arrested Ascent

Wharton opens book 2 with Archer's wedding to May Welland, an occasion of deathlike unreality: "a long time had apparently passed since his heart had stopped beating" (185). In the first printing of the novel, Wharton did, in fact, confuse words of the wedding ceremony with those of the funeral ceremony, correcting the error in subsequent printings (Lamar 38). The wedding is social, not sacred: "How like a first night at the Opera!" (180), Archer muses as he looks out at the assembled guests. "The invisible deity of 'Good Form' "[5] – not of love – presides. Archer measures his distance from the world that used to be so important, assuming that somewhere else "real things" were happening to "real people":

> The things that had filled his days seemed now like a nursery parody of life. . . . Yet there was a time when Archer had had definite and rather aggressive opinions on all such problems, and when everything concerning the manners and customs of his little tribe had seemed to him fraught with world-wide significance. (182)

Although vision is a common metaphor in Western literature, it is specifically used in the *Symposium* and the *Republic* to express the qualities of the good, a transcendent reality that can be apprehended but never fully comprehended. Wharton similarly uses this metaphor to describe the extent of Archer's growth. Thus, Ellen's second conversation with Archer helps him "look at his native city objectively. Viewed thus, as through the wrong end of a telescope, it looked disconcertingly small and distant" (76–77). Ellen looms larger in Archer's adjusted vision, and May dwindles to a "faint white figure" (78). When Archer leaves Ellen, New York again becomes "vast and imminent" (80). Briefly, he holds out the hope of leading May to an enlightenment like his own: he would "take the bandage from this young woman's eyes, and bid her look forth on the world." But he quickly recalls another narrative that alludes to Plato's allegory of the cave and its metaphor of vision: the case of "the Kentucky cave-fish, which had ceased to develop eyes because they had no use for them." He realizes that such vision might not be possible: "What if, when he had bidden May Welland to open [her eyes], they could only look out blankly at blankness?" When

Archer suggests that "[we] strike out for ourselves," May "extinguish[es] the whole subject" by pronouncing any deviation from the norm "vulgar" (83–84).

May's blindness to the value of experience proves stronger than Archer's incipient vision of its worth. On the eve of Ellen's departure, Archer stares with "unseeing eyes" at May's guest list for the farewell dinner (332), and May, having succeeded in vanquishing her rival, gazes at Archer with "blue eyes wet with victory" (343). The dinner party confirms Archer's entrapment in a lower order of reality: "a deathly sense of the superiority of implication and analogy over direct action . . . closed in on him like the doors of the family vault" (335–36).

Over time, Archer becomes dulled to the distinction between Ellen's message of reason and truth, and May's instinctual dependence on tradition. He "revert[s] to all his old inherited ideas about marriage. . . . There was no use in trying to emancipate a wife who had not the dimmest notion that she was not free," and he sinks back into "old habits of mind" (195– 96). Ellen's importance as a teacher fades; she lingers in his memory as romantic longing.

The Platonic model of love contrasts with the conventionality of Ellen and Archer's forbidden romance, providing an alternative to a narrative of unfulfilled desire.[6] Archer's passion consumes him; when he goes to the Blenkers' house to see Ellen and mistakes another woman's parasol for Ellen's, for example, he shows that he is as much in love with love itself as he is with her.[7] The reader learns little about Ellen's feelings, but we are led to understand that although she loves him, Ellen also cares greatly about the rightness of their actions. She is characterized not by passion, but by "passionate honesty" (312) and desire for truth. This passionate honesty translates into a love of beauty and virtue, which in Plato's *Symposium* provides the only true happiness – but which in Wharton's text comes close to puritanical renunciation.

Wharton eschews a romantic ending for her characters, not only because of her well-developed sense of literary realism, but because she attempts to present a higher ideal toward which such love may be directed. Many scenes – the couple's first private conversation in Ellen's apartment, the vigil Archer keeps on the Newport dock, the intimate lunch and boat ride in Fall River, the confused meeting in May's carriage – burn with romantic intensity. But just as the Cupid weathervane at the Blenkers' estate is broken, so Eros is defeated. Ellen attempts to lead them both toward a love that transcends erotic passion – toward a life of truth, beauty, freedom, *and* love. Such a vision, however, denies the body and its desire.

The scene describing Ellen and Archer's afternoon in Boston and Fall

River makes the search for Platonic ideals clear. Archer feels a closeness to Ellen that goes beyond erotic desire: "They seemed to have reached the kind of deeper nearness that a touch may sunder" (237). During their lunch, Archer is "conscious of a curious indifference to her bodily presence" (242). The lovers vow to be together by remaining physically apart. By promising not to return to Europe so long as they honor this agreement, Ellen keeps the relationship in delicate balance and calls on Archer to go beyond the level of the senses to achieve a kind of Puritan Hellenism. Archer feels "a tranquillity of spirit" and on the way home from his visit with her, he has "the conviction . . . of having saved out of their meeting much more than he had sacrificed" (245).

The couple's pledge is the keystone of the entire novel. Refreshed and uplifted from this meeting, Archer next encounters M. Rivière, Ellen's personal secretary, a character who functions not only as her emissary but as her double. Rivière reaffirms for Archer the value of reason, not senses, telling him, "the air of ideas is the only air worth breathing." Rivière is a poor man, but he demonstrates by action as well as words that true poverty is not being "able to look life in the face: that's worth living in a garret for, isn't it?" (200). His words echo Ellen and Archer's agreement not to act on their attraction. As Ellen says to Archer: "I promise you: not as long as you hold out. Not as long as *we can look straight at each other like this*" (243, my emphasis). They look each other in the face and see each other truly, without hesitation or shame.

Months later, Ellen and Archer meet in May's carriage when Ellen returns from Washington because of Mrs. Mingott's illness. Desperately in love, Archer throws reason to the wind and issues his most romantic plea: "I want – I want somehow to get away with you into a world where words like that – categories like that – won't exist. Where we shall be simply two human beings who love each other, who are the whole of life to each other; and nothing else on earth will matter." Ellen's rejoinder, experienced, wise, and a touch cynical, is "Oh my dear – where is that country? Have you ever been there?" (290). She alludes, not to the Platonic freedom awaiting released cave dwellers, but to social exile. Archer, in a fit of despair, groans, "Ah, I'm beyond that," to which Ellen again responds as guide and teacher: "No, you're not! You've never been beyond. And *I* have, and I know what it looks like there" (291, original emphasis).

The central image in this scene is the Gorgon, with its effect on (spiritual) sight. Again echoing their pledge, Ellen tells Archer that looking at the Gorgon has dried her tears and opened her eyes. Archer, too "pained" to hear Ellen's truth, leaves her, only to encounter May, a reminder of all that he has given up: "Never . . . would she surprise him by an unexpected mood, by a new idea, a weakness, a cruelty or an emotion. . . . She was simply ripening into a copy of her mother, and . . . trying to turn him into a Mr. Welland." May contrasts with Rivière, whom Archer had met after reaching his previous Platonic agreement with Ellen. Whereas then he had felt refreshed, now he feels hopeless and defeated: "I *am* dead – I've been dead for months and months" (295, original emphasis).

Ellen encourages Archer to look "not at visions, but at realities." But Archer, too wrapped up in his passion, maintains that "the only reality to me is this" (289). If they act on their attraction, Ellen will become his mistress, no different from any woman involved with a married man. "Don't let us be like all the others!" she pleads, but Archer tells her, "I don't profess to be different from my kind" (311–12). When Ellen reluctantly agrees to see Archer again, the relationship is debased, with Archer feeling as if "he had been speaking not to the woman he loved but to another, a woman he was indebted to for pleasures already wearied of" (308–9). He thinks that he sees "love visible" and "inner radiance" in Ellen's eyes; in fact, the two look now at each other "almost like enemies" (313).[8]

Ellen and Archer's affair is doomed both because of the strength of tribal traditions and because of Ellen's insistence on Platonic rather than romantic ideals. However, Ellen's renunciation of passion seems more Puritan than Platonic. She departs from Platonism in not seeing that the fulfillment of desire is compatible with higher ideals. The failure is Wharton's as much as Ellen's, reflecting the author's long-standing Calvinist belief in sexual guilt and payment for pleasure. The loss is Archer's as well.[9] When May announces a coming child, Ellen slips quietly back to Europe, beyond old New York's pettiness; and Archer dutifully resigns himself to the role of husband, father, and " 'good citizen' " (346). By the end of his life, he has "lost the habit of travel" (350), a metaphor Wharton borrows from Plato to represent the soul's journey.

Admittedly, there is good in the well-regulated life Archer has chosen. There has even been affection for May – he "honestly mourned" her death. But Archer also knows that he has missed "the flower of life" (347). He has contented himself with fragments rather than the whole. His "artistic and intellectual life" has gone on "outside the domestic circle," and May reigns as "the tutelary divinity of all his old traditions and reverences" (196); but Ellen, who still represents Aphrodite in the classical pantheon, remains central to his true development:

> He had built up within himself a kind of sanctuary in which she throned among his secret thoughts and longings. Little by little it

became the scene of his real life, of his only rational activities. . . .
Outside it, in the scene of his actual life, he moved with a growing
sense of unreality and insufficiency, blundering against familiar preju-
dices and traditional points of view as an absent-minded man goes on
bumping into the furniture of his own room. (262)

Archer lives between two orders of reality, "float[ing] somewhere between
chandelier and ceiling" (335), just as he did at Ellen's farewell dinner.
Although he is still starved for a higher level of meaning, the rich atmosphere that Ellen offers is too "dense" and "stimulating for his lungs" (358).
Archer attributes his loss to luck rather than effort and makes a truce with
life by expecting less from it. Ellen's memory, for example, becomes a
"thing so unattainable and improbable that to have repined would have
been like despairing because one had not drawn the first prize in a lottery"
(347). He lives an honorable life, but in a contained, limited way. He
becomes an expert in civic and charitable matters and even follows a call
for political service – but he is not elected to a second term: his life-long
attachment to the narrow interests of his genteel world has ill-prepared him
for greater public involvement, especially in a rapidly changing, twentieth-
century culture.

Wharton ends the novel without reconciling the opposing demands of
desire and duty. Ellen leads Archer away from conventional romance and
toward a higher level of truth, but she also represents a certain denial of the
flesh, which in Plato's philosophy exists simultaneously with the spirit.
Wharton situates Archer's conflict as a three-way tension between the real
(the actual or conventional), the romantic, and the ideal. Initially Archer is
fixed in the concrete world of old New York. He discovers romantic love
and, with it, the opportunity to take romance to a higher level of love and
truth. One of Archer's painful lessons – indeed, the lesson of Plato's
Symposium – is that romantic passion must give way to the rationality
required to ascend to a higher love. In the *Symposium,* Alcibiades' disor-
derly and disruptive speech proclaims his compelling passion for Socrates;
its parallel is Archer's desire for Ellen. But the *Symposium* also includes
Socrates' speech about the life of practical reason; its parallel is Ellen's
ethical and spiritual teachings. As Martha Nussbaum points out, both kinds
of love are valid, but they pose "two kinds of value, two kinds of knowledge; and we see that we must choose" (167). Ellen, who has looked reality
in the face – who has seen the Gorgon – understands the choice. Archer,
fluctuating between reason and passion, and between reason and tradition,
barely discerns the dimensions of the choice and is ill-prepared to make it.
He remains not a philosopher, but a "dilettante" and discontented gentle-

man – a passive observer to whom, like Henry James's John Marcher, "nothing on earth was to have happened" (17: 125).

In the novel's final chapter, Archer has one more opportunity to give his life meaning of the first order. After twenty-five years of silence and separation, he finds himself in Europe near Ellen Olenska's home. During this time, Ellen has lived independently in Europe; Archer assumes that her life is filled with art, music, and conversation, as it was in New York years ago. Initially, he imagines that he will see her that afternoon, and he wanders in ecstatic anticipation through museums, "from gallery to gallery through the dazzle of afternoon light . . . filling his soul with the long echoes of beauty." He has been starved for this beauty and light; now, in Ellen's proximity, he may have it again. When he briefly considers their romance, he realizes the importance of its philosophical rather than passionate aspects: "For such summer dreams it was too late; but surely not for a quiet harvest of friendship, of comradeship, in the blessed hush of her nearness" (357). This transformation of romance into friendship faintly echoes the Platonic pledge that Ellen and Archer made to each other twenty-five years earlier. Ellen still represents the Platonic ideal. The square where she lives emits a "central splendor," and her house is bathed in a "golden light [that] became for him the pervading illumination in which she lived" (358). Archer shares vicariously in this illumination while he contemplates visiting Ellen, but as the light – and his opportunity – fade, he remains on the park bench. He gazes upward at Ellen's window and settles on his own reality: " 'It's more real to me here than if I went up,' he suddenly heard himself say; and the fear lest that last shadow of reality should lose its edge kept him rooted to his seat as the minutes succeeded each other" (361).

Ultimately, Archer is, as he says, "old-fashioned" (360) – that is, he is fashioned by old conventions. In Platonic terms, he grasps true reality, but his wings fail to carry him to the soul's upper regions. The *Phaedrus* describes a hierarchy of bodily incarnations that reflects the levels of the soul's ascent. Ellen, who fits Plato's description as a seeker of wisdom, beauty, and truth, is at the first, or highest, level. However, since she forgoes passion (we can only speculate whether she has lovers in Europe), the novel's vision of the Platonic ideal, with its Puritan-like emphasis on restraint and denial, admits more spirit than flesh. And Archer, who dabbles in politics, resembles the "law-abiding monarch" or "statesman" that Plato explains as having achieved only the second or third level of reality (31). In terms of the cave parable, he apprehends true reality, but he remains in the cave – in the shadow of reality – rather than venturing into brightness. Archer watches Ellen's window until it becomes dark; and when he sees the light go on within and the shutters pulled – "as if it had been the signal he waited for" (361) – he relinquishes his last chance for winged ascent, turns into the darkness, and walks away.

Ellen Olenska is Edith Wharton's most fully realized heroine. Her escape from an effete society that offers security in exchange for freedom and imagination constitutes a triumph. Ellen's development parallels Wharton's own successful struggle to free herself from stifling New York values and to forge a literary life in Europe, her closest approximation of much sought-after ideals. But Wharton's treatment of Ellen's passionate nature raises questions about the role of Eros, both within the novel and within Wharton. Culture and art represent stages of the seeker of love's progression from social and romantic values to the supreme good. Yet Wharton, with her Puritan sensibility, still suggests that women must renounce sensual love in order to reign as philosopher-queens. Like Ellen, she had lost a lover, and she shows through Ellen's journey how it is possible to go beyond love's body to love itself; but *The Age of Innocence* also shows that Wharton could not completely integrate female passion and spirituality.

6

Catholicism: Fulfillment or Concession?

I don't believe in God but I do believe in His saints – and then?
Edith Wharton, commonplace book, qtd. in Lewis

Religious thought is certainly a great power. The greatest of all. It embraces everything.
Edith Wharton, qtd. in Elisina Tyler, *Diary*

Later [Edith Wharton and I] talked a little of religion. The Roman Catholic Church ranks highest, as a great social force for order, and for its finest ritual, its great traditions, its human understanding. We said that it is really not difficult to believe.
Elisina Tyler, *Diary*

IF Wharton flirted with agnosticism in midlife, she came to faith in her later years, expressing a confidence in heaven and its ruling deity. Such belief is clear from her correspondence. About the death of her friend Lily Norton's aunt, Wharton wrote in 1926, "I hope she is now in some happy world talking over Montaigne with a group of sympathizers, or, better still, talking to the Great Man himself" (Letters, 12 June). In 1934, she again commented to Lily: "The thing that moved me most in your letter was the inscription on the war-graves: 'Known to God.' It was an inspiration" (Letters, 19 October). Increasingly, this faith became aligned with Catholicism, constituting – to borrow the title of her 1934 short story – Wharton's personal case of "Roman fever."

More Than an Observer

Although Edith Wharton never converted to Catholicism, it is clear that she identified with the Church of Rome and made it, more than any other, her faith at the end of her life. Wharton's first biographer, Percy Lubbock, quotes friends who thought she was on the verge of conversion (232–39); R. W. B. Lewis concurs that the church was a powerful influence in her last decades (509–12). Although Wharton's Catholicism may seem an isolated development, it resulted from previously cultivated sensibilities and a gradually evolving system of belief. Even in childhood, Rome stood out in Wharton's memory; she recalls one day that was "particularly vivid, when in the million-tapered blaze of St. Peter's, the Pope floated ethereally above a long train of ecclesiastics seen through an incense haze so golden that it seemed to pour from the blinding luminary behind the High Altar" (*Backward* 30–31). Over the years, Wharton collected a number of books on Catholic doctrine. She read the lives of the saints and the history of the church, and she developed close associations with Catholic clergy, particularly with the curé at St. Brice and Abbé Mugnier, whom she had known since 1908 (Lewis 510–11). Wharton's godson, William Royall Tyler, "convinced" that Wharton was "a devout Christian," writes that she "felt strongly drawn toward the Church of Rome" ("Memories" 104). He remembers that when he was sixteen or seventeen years old, Wharton read to him from the writings of the French Catholic prelate Jacques Bossuet (1627–1704); two months before she died, in June 1937, she gave him her own well-read copy of Bossuet's sermons (Interview, 12 April). She requested the hymn, "O Paradise, O Paradise," for her funeral service and chose the Latin inscription, *Ave Crux Spes Unica* (Hail cross our one hope), to grace her headstone.

As she grew older, Wharton's relationship to Catholicism shifted from that of tourist to participant; originally, she visited cathedrals because of their artistic, architectural, and historical interests but later she followed church teachings and doctrine as well. During her first trip to Rome in 1903, for example, she spent time examining villas, compiling material for articles and her book *Italian Villas and Their Gardens* (1904), and conferring with a Roman editor who had expressed interest in publishing *The Valley of Decision* (1902), her two-volume historical novel of social, political, and religious unrest in eighteenth-century Italy (Lewis 116). By the time she visited Rome in 1932, her involvement with Catholicism had undergone "a perceptible change," as Lewis notes. With her friend Nicky Mariano, she visited St. Peter's Cathedral, the chapels of the San Sebastiano catacombs, and the Borgia rooms in the Vatican. She also attended Pontifical

High Mass in San Paolo Fuore le Mure and Requiem Mass at Santa Maria sopra Minerva. Six months later, when she returned to Rome, she increased her attendance at mass – taking interest not only in the spectacle of the church, as she had in the past, but also in its teachings (Lewis 509).

By 1933, Wharton was planning her social activities around the church calendar, complaining in a letter to Lily Norton that a change of plans would interfere with the celebration of the Virgin: "All right, but I almost advise Wednesday for lunch, much as I shd like to see you on Tuesday – for the latter is the 'Assumption,' & I'm afraid in the afternoon that day I can't send the car, though in the morning I shall be delighted to" (Letters, 10 August). Wharton also participated in the Catholic life of the town of St. Brice, and, according to her neighbor Jacques Fosse, opened her gardens each August to the procession in honor of the Virgin (Interview). France and Italy, countries that Wharton preferred over Protestant England, were steeped in Catholic culture. Indeed, since Wharton's expatriation to France and interest in Catholicism developed simultaneously, one might speculate that life in Europe inspired her greater involvement with the Church of Rome.

Catholicism's allure was no mystery. First, Catholicism and aestheticism were mutually reinforcing. As Jackson Lears notes, both shared "a cult of taste" – an emphasis on luxury, collection, decoration, and drama – and a consumer ethos appropriate to developing corporate capitalism. They also shared psychological and religious origins. Aesthetes, whether Christian or agnostic – who sought freedom from bourgeois Victorianism – detached relics such as the chalice and crucifix from their traditional meanings to create a substitute religion of taste (Lears 184). Wharton's aestheticism and Catholicism thus became inextricably intertwined; like art, the church offered spiritual reassurance, a sense of being grounded in history, and an opportunity to transcend the mundane.

Second, the Catholic Church represented an authority lacking in Protestantism, which had seen its reliance on the Bible increasingly undermined by science, archaeological research, and textual studies. While the Catholic Church was not immune to these historical and anthropological advances, its hierarchical structure and its offer of assurance to believers willing to pledge their faith drew many weary spiritual followers. Since the early nineteenth century, Catholic writers had attacked Protestantism as fragmented, privately interested, and relativistic (Reynolds 146); in its place, Catholicism promised unification and conclusiveness.

Many Protestants, however, trained in hostility toward the worship of graven images, saw Catholicism as a barbarous pageantry designed to keep the senses captive, or as an easy way out of spiritual crisis. Margaret

Deland's main character in *Sidney* (1890), for example, rejects various religious solutions, including Roman Catholicism, which offers "the comfort of making somebody else your conscience" (qtd. in Welter 129). Henry Adams illustrates the Protestant dilemma in his 1884 novel *Esther,* in which the heroine wonders whether the profound effect of a high Episcopal service – with its captivating sermon and colorful displays that "rivalled the flowers of a prize show" – is truly spiritual, or merely dramatic (1–2). Esther falls in love with the minister of a beautifully appointed church, but aesthetics ultimately cannot convert her love into the faith necessary for a clerical marriage. Edith Wharton addresses the same issue in "A Venetian Night's Entertainment" (1903), a tale reminiscent of Hawthorne's "My Kinsman, Major Molineux," in which an eighteenth-century New England lad is led astray by politics, revelry, and romantic intrigue in Venice. The inexperienced youth is easily seduced by papal pageantry, so unlike his own austere practices. The Catholic benediction – "a beautiful sight" (*Stories* 1: 478) – contrasts sharply with the "axioms in his hornbook [that] had brought home to him his heavy responsibilities as a Christian and a sinner" (1: 476). Just before real danger strikes, the young man is saved from marauding Venetians by his stern New England minister, and all is well.

As Wharton's story about Catholicism's allure suggests, despite their disapproval of religious display – a disapproval Wharton only partially shared – Protestants could not help but feel the appeal of Gothic art and architecture, and they gradually allowed more music, ritual, and decoration into their services. William Dean Howells, in *A Hazard of New Fortunes,* captures the lure as well as the danger of aestheticism. When the March family enters Grace Church, they come not to pray but "to gratify an aesthetic sense, to renew the faded pleasure of travel. . . . It was a purely Pagan impulse" (59). The shift from Calvinist to Catholic sensibilities was a significant one. Even though the habit of introspection lingered as a weight on the spirit, by the end of the nineteenth century Calvinism "had dissolved into an Emersonian haze" (Lears 197). High churches, in particular, became more tolerant of wealth, worldliness, and priestly authority, as Wharton's frequent, tongue-in-cheek fictional accounts of clerical laxity and self-indulgence suggest. With its regular sacraments and protocols of confession, repentance, and absolution, Catholicism provided much-needed relief from moral burdens.

Catholicism also offered Wharton an alternative to the smugness and hypocrisy that arose from the unhealthy symbiosis of upper-class society and the Anglican Church. She satirizes this high-church culture in a novella written rather late in her career. Wharton's most sympathetic treatment of Catholicism, "New Year's Day" (1924) calls into question the religious sincerity of both individual and society, but it reserves the strongest criticism for society. Lizzie Hazeldean, "a woman who had never spoken . . . of religious matters," surprises the narrator by calling for a priest when she falls seriously ill. Catholicism provides "the solace which she needed. . . . At last she could confess her sin" and "be absolved of it." But how sincere is Lizzie's faith? Wharton hints that this worldly woman, used to "cards and suppers and chatter," sees religion merely as a "barrier" "against solitude" (549), and the priest as the last in a long line of "dull men" who visit her drawing room (548). Indeed, Lizzie appears to value the priest as much for his ability to rekindle memories of her late husband as for his spiritual guidance.

But if Lizzie's conversion is dubious, it is less objectionable than society's uncharitable judgments. Supported by a Protestant church that caters to the upper class, Lizzie's friends condemn her for having had an extramarital affair. The reader learns, however, that Lizzie sleeps with Henry Prest not because she loves or desires him, but because she needs his money to save her dying husband from financial worry. Lizzie's love for her husband constitutes a religion of its own; she speaks of him in language that is devoted and martyred: "He took me out of misery into blessedness. He put me up above them all. . . . I would have followed him into the desert – I would have gone barefoot to be with him. I would have starved, begged, done anything for him – *anything*" (533, original emphasis). Lizzie's selfless sacrifice – sentimental though it is – is unmatched in her society. Wharton further endorses Catholicism as a cure for the moral laxity of Episcopalianism with an anecdote about Lizzie's father, once a "sentimental overpopular Rector of a fashionable New York church." He was forced to resign after mishandling funds and enjoying "too great success as . . . director of female consciences" (519). The discredited man goes to Europe, converts to Catholicism, marries a Portuguese singer, and then finds "rest in the ancient fold" (549).

Catholicism's long and stable history attracted a host of American writers, beginning with Washington Irving, who longed to recover the European past. Fin-de-siècle Americans turned to Europe and the Church of Rome as an escape from increasingly rapid social change, commercialization, and a perceived dilution of values. Then, when World War I shook their confidence in the old order and heightened the need for moral foundations beyond social and temporal ones, Americans found authenticity in European structures and assurance in Roman Catholic practices. David Reynolds notes that Catholicism provided the consolation previously available through sentimentality (145). Lears observes that the fascination with Catholicism embodied a religious longing for transcendence that pervaded American society (178). Increasingly, with Protestant, Victorian notions of moral and spiritual progress under scrutiny, Old World Catholicism – with its tradition, mystery, and ceremony – reminded one that escape from the past was not only impossible but unnecessary. Emphasizing primal impulses and reinstating the supernatural, Catholicism released the worried worshiper from scientific rationalism *and* from the introspective brooding of Calvinism. Since both rationalism and Calvinism had plagued Wharton since adolescence, Catholicism was attractive, indeed.

Reservations

Those who knew Wharton well disagreed over what the Catholic faith meant to her and the extent to which her enthusiasm was born out of personal belief in doctrine or a more intellectual appreciation of the church's history, art, and ritual. Friends like Nicky Mariano and Bernard Berenson wondered, after observing the tranquillity Wharton found inside a cathedral, whether she "might find peace in the Roman Church." Gaillard Lapsley similarly felt that she had come to the point where rational systems no longer sufficed to explain "what life and reflections had taught her." Kenneth Clark was probably most correct when he paid Wharton the compliment that she, more than anyone he knew, understood equally the sentiment of both Catholicism and Protestantism. Wharton wrote in response to Clark that "it had always been her ambition to write a novel of which the centre should be the conflict of these two impulses" (qtd. in Lewis 510–11).

Wharton was deeply involved with the Catholic Church, but she did not convert or actively practice her faith. Remembering her at Pavillon Colombe, in St. Brice, her neighbor Jacques Fosse declares emphatically, "Elle ne practique pas" (She did not practice) (Interview). The Catholic Church grants followers assurance only in exchange for complete surrender to its teachings and practices. This, in the end, was something that Edith Wharton could not or would not do.

The fact that Wharton was divorced may have been an obstacle to conversion. Another problem was that her belief was held in check by rival impulses – in particular, by reason. The church achieves faith at the expense of reason or intelligence, as Vivaldi, the philosopher in Wharton's early novel *The Valley of Decision*, explains. Vivaldi's criticism of religious authority in the eighteenth century was also relevant in Wharton's time, when Victorians sought to reconcile scientific theories of evolution with traditional beliefs. Vivaldi describes how new developments threaten religious systems:

> The Church . . . has proved her astuteness in making faith the gift of grace and not the result of reason. By so doing she placed herself in a position which was well-nigh impregnable till the school of Newton substituted observation for intuition. . . . The ultimate claim of the Church rests on the hypothesis of an intuitive faculty in man. Disprove the existence of this faculty, and reason must remain the supreme test of truth. Against reason the fabric of theological doctrine cannot long hold out, and the Church's doctrinal authority once shaken, men will no longer fear to test by ordinary rules the practical results of her teaching. (*Valley* 1: 154–55)

Intellect, important for all Victorian writers, was especially valuable in helping a woman prove her worth in a male-dominated culture. Wharton could not easily relinquish reason, no matter how strong Catholicism's appeal.

Wharton also remained skeptical of Catholicism, as she did of any organized religion, because it fell short of the ideals to which she aspired. Imperfections ranged from personal foibles and abuses to institutional flaws; in the extreme, Wharton felt that the church itself became corrupt. In *The Valley of Decision,* for example, church authority becomes so aligned with society's standards of conduct that morality is reduced to social convention. Similarly, in contemporary New York, the church merely reflected the ruling class's whims or fears. Even if the church's integrity remained intact, individuals could abuse religion by their disregard of its doctrines and teachings. In the story "The Last Asset" (1904), for example, Mrs. Newell's social and financial future rests on her daughter Hermione's marriage to a French count, which in turn rests on Hermione's conversion to Catholicism. With brisk efficiency and no faith at all, Hermione converts and the marriage is accomplished. In *The Custom of the Country* (1913), Wharton vilifies Undine Spragg for her cavalier marriage to a French nobleman. Concerned only with money and status, Undine neither understands nor honors a Catholic marriage. As these narratives demonstrate, Wharton was skeptical of religious practice unless it was motivated by sincere belief.

A final reason for Wharton's reluctance to embrace the Catholic Church fully may have been her sensitivity to its treatment of women – although her strongest criticisms came early rather than late in her career. On the one hand, Catholicism provided the perfect venue for the celebration of women. Although both Protestantism and Catholicism reinforced women's social inferiority, Catholicism alone taught women's spiritual and moral superiority, primarily through the revered figure of the Virgin Mary. Mary – powerful and sacred – was sister to the feminine goddesses Demeter and Aphrodite, figures Wharton incorporated into her fiction. Like her contemporaries – especially Henry Adams, who worshiped the medieval Virgin – Wharton longed to surrender to this feminine source of power and protection.[1] Moreover, Mary, the paradigm of patient, motherly devotion, provided a model that had been greatly lacking in Wharton's personal life: Mary could become the loving mother Wharton never had. The figure of Mary also appealed because it combined maturity with asexuality; the Virgin was miraculously free of the problems of erotic relationship that had tormented Wharton. Finally, with sentimental ideology exhausted, Mary brought the feminine back in invigorated form. The Virgin's popularity among Americans stems from their complex relationship with the masculine and feminine images of the divine and, perhaps, from their overvaluation of the masculine godhead. As Julia Kristeva suggests in her poetic meditation on the Madonna, the fact that feminism flourishes in Protestant countries "is due to Protestantism's *lacking* some necessary element of the Maternal which in Catholicism has been elaborated with the utmost sophistication" ("Stabat" 139, original emphasis).

Unfortunately, however, faith in the Virgin meant a return to earlier, sentimental notions of female separateness, as well as an acceptance that the primary creative force issues from a male God. As Leonardo Boff puts it, although Mary leads one to God, she achieves her greatness by "walking a narrow path of suffering, humility, and anonymity" (10). The Madonna, then, is not the strong autonomous goddess of earlier times. Her power is strictly subordinated to male authority; her function restricted to unquestioning maternal nurturance; and her fate endless, passive suffering. When Wharton presents the Catholic Church father Augustine in *Hudson River Bracketed* (1929) and *The Gods Arrive* (1932) as a model for her hero, she also inadvertently enlists Augustine's disparaging view of women as God's secondary creation, inherently weak and in need of man's rule: God "did not even create the woman . . . but created her out of the man. . . . The mother as little creates her offspring, as she created herself. . . . [Satan made] his assault upon the weaker part of that human alliance. . . . In accordance with the natural order [man is] the head of the household" (*City,* bks. 12, 14, 19). And when Wharton alludes to the Virgin Mary in her depiction of Halo Tarrant, she also conveys Augustine's sense that women serve best by serving others rather than themselves.

Other fiction shows Wharton's awareness of women's vulnerability in the patriarchal Catholic Church. Her short story "The Confessional" (1901), set in New England but focusing on Catholicism and the mid-nineteenth-century Italian struggle with Austria for political independence, criticizes ecclesiastical authority. In this story a priest breaks his vows, allowing a husband to take his place in the confessional in order to determine whether his wife has taken an Austrian lover. The priest wrongly places politics and male solidarity above his duty to minister to all parishioners.

Wharton makes a similar point in "The Duchess at Prayer" (1900), a brilliant account of marital infidelity in eighteenth-century Italy that denounces not only wayward priests, but the church's complicity with men's domination of women. Neglected by a cold and aging duke, a young duchess secretly takes a lover, whom she meets in a crypt adjoining a chapel. To escape detection, she affects piety and devotion to the relics housed in the crypt. When a priest discovers the affair and tells her husband, the duke commissions a large statue of the duchess, which he places at the entrance of the crypt, entrapping the duchess's lover within. By watching the event, the priest becomes party to the murder. In both "The Confessional" and "The Duchess at Prayer," men of the cloth aid the schemes of jealous husbands, thus conspiring against women and forsaking their spiritual duties. In "The Confessional," in particular, women rank low in the church's hierarchy of values. They are dismissed as "minor matters": "on cardinal points . . . [the priest] was inflexible, but in minor matters he had that elasticity of judgment which enables the Catholic discipline to fit itself to every inequality of the human conscience" (Stories 1: 315).

The same mistrust of Catholicism's treatment of women is visible in "Bunner Sisters," a novella published in 1916 but written twenty-five years earlier, when Wharton was less enamored of papal practices. Wharton traces the tragic lives of two impoverished sisters, who drift apart when one, Evelina, leaves home to marry, returns in misery, and converts to Roman Catholicism. The story reflects the church's appeal to the immigrant and urban poor, who found themselves mostly ignored by well-to-do Protestant churches. But the unmarried sister, Ann Eliza, who has sacrificed her own hope of happiness for Evelina's, feels betrayed by this religious conversion. Experience has taught her that "she could no longer trust in the goodness of God, and that if he was not good he was not God, and there was only a black abyss above the roof" (421). The Catholic Church, male authority, and the injustices of marriage have all robbed her of her sister's affection. The rosary that Evelina wears becomes, to Ann Eliza, a "sacrilegious amulet," "the diabolical instrument of their estrangement" (427). When Evelina dies, the priest makes the funeral arrangements, and Ann Eliza, relegated to mere spectator, "beheld with stony indifference this last negation of her past" (433).

Wharton would not have been immune to popular Catholic notions of femininity, in both America and France. Catholic teachings about women during the nineteenth century emphasized the domestic ideology found in the culture as a whole. Priest-author Bernard O'Reilly's immensely popular

The Mirror of True Womanhood, for example – reprinted seventeen times between 1876 and 1893 – taught that woman was the more spiritual of the two sexes, home her God-appointed sphere, and sacrifice her vocation: "No woman animated by the Spirit of her Baptism . . . ever fancied that she had or could have any other sphere of duty or activity than that home which is her domain, her garden, her paradise, her world. . . . Practical and continual self-denial [is] the very soul of womanly virtue" (qtd. in Kennelly, "Ideals" 4). "Woman's Rights" and suffrage, in particular, had no place in this ideal womanhood. One notable Catholic priest, Isaac Hecker, argued that men and women are equally susceptible to the call of the Holy Spirit, with neither holding exclusive province over love or truth; but even he maintained that the vote was superfluous because the church already gave "full scope to women's capacities and powers" (qtd. in Kennelly, "Ideals" 6).[2]

The real solution to the "woman problem," these conservatives believed, was a return to traditional values. In the 1890s, Archbishop William Stang, reviving the seventeenth-century theology of Alphonsus Ligouri, reintroduced the concept of woman as temptress into American Catholic theology and reinforced the dichotomy between woman as nun and woman as sexual being (Kennelly, "Ideals" 13) – a bifurcation that Wharton reproduces years later in her own contrasting portrayals of Halo Tarrant and Floss Delaney in *Hudson River Bracketed* and *The Gods Arrive.* When women finally won the vote in 1920, the Catholic clergy did "a quick about-face" (Kennelly, "Ideals" 16), projecting the appearance of solidarity and support. Satisfied through surveys of Catholic women that suffrage had not significantly altered their loyalty to church teaching, priests and bishops now exhorted women to use their votes to head off threats to church and family by radicals, and to work actively to defeat measures such as the federal equal rights amendment. A bishops' letter in 1919 urged women to use their votes to purify and elevate politics; in 1922, the Conference of Catholic Women resolved to use the vote to defend "the principles sacred to Christian Civilization" (Kenneally 140). The Catholic hierarchy gradually supported expanded education for women, but the issue of women's sexual freedom was still far from its agenda.

Such was the Catholic atmosphere in America. In France, attitudes and conditions were even more conservative. France, in fact, served as the model for American middle-class Catholics. Advice books were translated from the French; daughters were sent to French boarding schools; Catholic journals advertised French articles; and prayers and daily devotions were recited in the French language (McDannell 57). Along with their fascination for French styles, customs, and language, aspiring Americans reaffirmed

French institutions such as the patriarchal household and the confinement of women to domestic and subordinate roles.

Wharton, who lived in France occasionally after 1903 and permanently after 1910, was immersed in Old World Catholicism and its conservativism. She lived the French life that bourgeois Catholic Americans emulated; in a sense, her participation in Roman Catholicism was but one sign of her expatriation. Ironically, Wharton rebelled against the aimless, leisured life-styles of New York and Newport in order to gain autonomy for herself as a woman, but she willingly accepted established Catholic traditions that prescribed feminine subordination.[3] Her late fiction reflects both commitment to women's development and loyalty to the Church of Rome; increasingly, however, her criticism of women enslaved by church ideology gave way to greater acceptance and even praise for the selfless service of maternal women. This tradition has its basis in Augustine's *Confessions,* to which Wharton refers in her novels *Hudson River Bracketed* and *The Gods Arrive.* It is exemplified by Monica, Augustine's mother, who inspired writers such as Francis de Sales – a copy of whose letters Wharton owned (Maggs)[4] – and Mme de Chantal. Indeed, Bougaud's 1866 *The Life of Saint Monica* was also enlisted at the turn of the century as a counterargument to the demands of the "New Woman." Wharton draws on Monica as well as Mary as models for her heroine Halo Tarrant.

Wharton's late period, then, is marked by ambivalence. Catholicism reinforced Wharton's deepening conservativism in general, although it remained in tension with her Protestantism. The rich atmosphere of the High Episcopal and Roman Catholic churches drew Wharton aesthetically as well as spiritually, offering solace in exchange for surrender, and permanence in the midst of social change. But the more intense, austere strains of Protestantism still spoke to Wharton's deepest beliefs about individual will and responsibility. Ultimately, although both faiths drew her, neither could fully satisfy the complexity of her longings. Nor could either branch of Christianity answer her call for respectful, positive roles for women. When Wharton, lamenting the social chaos of the twentieth century, embraced the patriarchal order and stability of the Catholic Church, she necessarily incorporated its conservativism regarding women's roles. Perhaps it was in part for this reason that she set her last novel, *The Buccaneers* (1938), not in France or Italy, but in Protestant England, where her adventurous young heroines are less hampered by Catholic traditions. This unfinished novel is generally cited as evidence that in her final years Wharton envisioned a positive and feminist future for her female characters.[5] However, her last completed novels, *Hudson River Bracketed* and *The Gods Arrive,* suggest a more complicated outlook.

These two novels trace the development of a young midwesterner, Vance Weston, who gains after many false starts and misadventures the necessary insight to "become a man" (*Gods* 411). In them, Wharton reveals her conservativism about what it means to become a woman. She not only assigns the role of writer to her male protagonist, Vance, rather than to her female protagonist, Halo Tarrant – who is his peer in intelligence and literary talent – but she relegates Halo to the sacrificial roles of mother, muse, and, in the final scene of *The Gods Arrive*, Madonna.

Wharton frequently portrayed male rather than female artists, contradicting her own experience as an extraordinarily successful writer of fiction. Mary Suzanne Schriber speculates "that the younger Edith Wharton was not secure enough" to create a female artist as protagonist, and that the older Wharton "purposely did not assign her own gender to an artist, choosing instead to satirize the state of the arts as governed by men" (*Gender* 179). *Hudson River Bracketed* and *The Gods Arrive* conform to this pattern with their male protagonist, but it is not entirely clear that the novels are intended as satire. Wharton does satirize the vanity, rootlessness, and chaos of twentieth-century American life, and she presents Vance as a naive and shallow interpreter of Western literary and religious traditions. But she seems to take his literary quest seriously, and she appears equally sincere in her depiction of Halo Tarrant. Halo serves as an inspiration for Vance and embodies many of the values – respect for the past, patience, aesthetic judgment – that he lacks.[6] Wharton reinforces traditional gender roles in these novels by drawing upon the autobiography of Augustine, the Christian Neoplatonist and Catholic theologian, as a subtext. Becoming a man – and a woman – means following patriarchal gender arrangements.

Augustinian Allusion in *Hudson River Bracketed* and The Gods Arrive

Hudson River Bracketed and *The Gods Arrive* are modeled thematically and structurally on Augustine's *Confessions*. In depicting a young man with a fervent desire to "invent[ ] a new religion" (*Hudson* 3) who comes to know himself, his art, and his God, Wharton presents a type of Augustine himself. Vance Weston begins, as does Augustine, as a weak and dissolute spiritual wanderer entranced with the powers of rhetoric, distracted by lust, and unable to reach his full potential as writer or husband. Like Augustine, he struggles to free himself from sensuality and physical obsession, eventually renouncing his mistress. And like Augustine, Vance receives help from a strong woman, Halo, who, following the example of Augustine's mother Monica, keeps faith when the errant seeker is distracted by the glamours of rhetoric and worldliness. With this maternal guidance,

Vance, like Augustine, undergoes spiritual cleansing and awakening and attempts to realize his proper relation to self, God, and vocation. The Augustinian subtext establishes these two novels, then, as spiritual as well as literary quests and makes it clear that Vance is their primary focus, with Halo as his supportive counterpart.

By modeling her hero after the figure of Augustine, Wharton not only associates him with a founding father of the Catholic Church, but links her interests in classical philosophy with two branches of Christianity: Catholicism and Calvinism. Since Wharton's readings in religion, philosophy, and religious history were extensive, we can assume that these connections are conscious ones. Augustine came to his belief in God through the Neoplatonist teachings of Plotinus; his religion of the New Testament is fused with the Platonic tradition. Augustine's writings also provided early justification for the tenets of Calvin, Luther, and the Jansenists. His emphasis on sin, grace, free will, divine sovereignty, and predestination – as well as his intensely personal relationship with God – makes him the most Calvinist of all Catholic philosophers. In selecting Augustine, then, Wharton aligns herself with the entire Catholic tradition, draws upon the Calvinist sensibility that marks earlier texts such as *Ethan Frome,* and connects Christianity to the Platonic elements that appear in novels such as *The Age of Innocence. Hudson River Bracketed* and *The Gods Arrive* are thus integrating or culminating texts in a religious sense, but with respect to women, they are reductive and regressive.

Wharton's last completed novels, while important to a study of her religion and spirituality, are not outstanding fiction. Essentially two volumes of the same work – Wharton planned the sequel to *Hudson River Bracketed* while it was still being serialized (Lewis 490) – the novels are overly long, with tedious conversations and descriptions. They also suffer from a failure to focus on one theme or subject matter, a problem that occurs in earlier fiction such as *The Fruit of the Tree.*[7] Ostensibly about the growth of the artist, the novels at times become social critique, detailing the commercialism in society, religion, and literature.

Hudson River Bracketed opens with Vance Weston, a suburban midwesterner and aspiring writer, setting out for New York and a literary future. During a stay with distant relatives along the Hudson River, Vance visits a venerable old home, the Willows, which has been inherited by an energetic, intelligent young woman named Halo Spear. Here he discovers for the first time the value of tradition, culture, and literature. Both the Willows and Halo become a source of spiritual inspiration for Vance, contrasting with the chaotic, self-serving, social and literary world with which he first becomes involved.

Wharton uses the occasion of Vance Weston's personal quest to criticize modern liberalism as well as her protagonist's naiveté. Sensing a lack of spiritual ideals in his life, Vance decides to devote a total of one week to the invention of a new religion, squeezing it in among his other activities. He has no sense of the past or its foundations: "all the religions he had heard of had been in existence ever since he could remember; that is, at least sixteen years." Following relatives', neighbors', and friends' advice "not to get into a rut," Vance seeks a new and rootless faith that will correspond with the rootlessness of every other aspect of society. Even ministers in Vance's developing suburb encourage an easy connection between religion and progress, "emphasiz[ing] religion as the greatest known Short Cut to Success." With no models to guide him, Vance cannot "dissociate stability from stagnation" (*Hudson* 3, 5) and misguidedly begins his search – in a way that parallels Augustine's beginning with the Manichaeans – among the "heretics" in New York society.

Wharton devotes many rambling pages to satiric chronicles of Manhattan publishers' cocktail parties, where authors are defrauded and patronized, or jaunts through Europe's fashionable resorts and cities, where the latest literary fads are indulged. Through Vance's aimless adventures – paralleled in her own loose style – Wharton shows how easily one is distracted from the main spiritual or creative goal. Vance is misled by flattery and eagerly accepts others' praise, only to realize later that publishers, critics, and even artists have lost all sense of value. Clearly the voice of the author speaks here. Vance, like Wharton, finally rejects the new experimental and psychological forms of fictions, convinced "that the surface of life was rich enough to feed the creator's imagination" (*Gods* 112). Halo similarly prefers old-fashioned realism, asking Vance, "Why not try . . . the exact opposite of what all the other on-the-spot editors are straining to provide? Something quiet, logical, Jane-Austen-y" (*Hudson* 235).

The modern business of publishing cheapens both the process and product of literary endeavor and destroys all-important continuity and tradition in literature. Vance's editors at "The Hour" prod him to submit unconsidered work: "Why, that's just what we're after . . . a fellow's first reactions, *before* he's ready. We want to wipe out the past and get a fresh eye on things" (*Hudson* 270, original emphasis). One author, Octavius, is revered by the smart set for having his masterpiece still uncomposed in his head. Vance knows that he himself is praised "for the wrong reasons" (*Gods* 286), yet he has difficulty resisting society's seductions. He is the product of middle-class, individualist values – as his name, which derives from his hometown "Advance," implies. Ultimately, however, Vance's progression is from the "West" "on" to the East, opposite the general pattern of

American migration. His journey toward maturity involves immersing himself in traditions and literature of the "Past" – in the deep roots of Christianity and Catholicism, not the twentieth-century religious fads that take quasi-Platonic theories as their models. Wharton herself followed the path that she charts for Vance, writing to Sara Norton some years earlier: "I am steeping myself in the nineteenth century, which is such a blessed refuge from the turmoil and mediocrity of today – like taking sanctuary in a mighty temple" (qtd. in Lewis 424).

Although Vance is easily distracted from serious religious pursuits, he increasingly focuses on his writing, and his literary aspirations begin to take on the qualities of a spiritual quest. His "soul . . . like a desert," he is at first nourished by the power of language, relishing the *"feel"* of words (*Hudson* 20, 175, original emphasis); this phase loosely parallels Augustine's period with the Manichaeans and his fascination with an argument's rhetorical dazzle rather than the reason or justification for it. Vance repeatedly uses religious language to describe his innermost feelings before his "conversion" is effected. In periods of especially great literary productivity, for example, he feels "possessed by a brooding spirit of understanding, some mystic reassurance," and refers to himself and his vocation as "blessed" (*Gods* 183). He believes that he is in touch with a kind of undifferentiated godliness, an experience complicated by the fact that, as an artist, he strives to be a self-contained, self-sufficient entity.

Popular creeds encourage Vance to function as his own god, to yield to daydreams, and to identify with the artists and writers of the earlier decadent period. Cursing the weakness of his own passionate nature, for example, he asks, "Would he ever achieve the true artist's faculty of self-isolation? 'Not until I learn to care less about everything' " is his answer (*Gods* 277). Wharton's satire is unmistakable here; in truth, Vance needs to care *more* about everything and, at the same time, to see his own will in the larger framework of God's. Hindered by ego, he is filled with romantic dreams about poetry and religion and their ability to carry him toward some transcendent "god." His search is confused by a notion that he can "find out how to release that god, fly him up like a kite into the Infinite, way beyond creeds and formulas," and thus put himself, not his god, in charge (*Hudson* 18). He finds support for this self-serving thinking in New York society in general and in his grandmother in particular.

A woman with a large heart and eclectic creed, "who had always cared about [religion] more than about anything else" (*Hudson* 5), Grandma Scrimser is one of Wharton's more memorable characters, a curious blend of Christian fundamentalist and transcendentalist. Wharton criticizes her simple – and simplistic – faith. "Love is everywhere!" she tells Vance, and "heaven is wherever we love Nature and our fellow-beings enough" (*Hudson* 20). Reflecting on Grandma Scrimser's conception of God, Vance muses:

> Perhaps what she called "God" was the same as what he called "The Mothers" – that mysterious Sea of Being of which the dark reaches swayed and rumoured in his soul . . . perhaps one symbol was as good as another to figure the imperceptible point where the fleeting human consciousness touches Infinity . . . (*Hudson* 449, original ellipses)[8]

But romantic and transcendental ideals, based on Platonic notions of self-sufficiency or matriarchal visions, are not enough. Augustine teaches, as Vance eventually learns, that one symbol is not as good as another, unless it is monotheistic and male. The tradition that privileges the individual over all others is thrown into question by Wharton's ironic treatment of Grandma Scrimser's Neoplatonic philosophy. Although praising Catholic ritual, Mrs. Scrimser conflates the realms of divine and human achievement, merging two distinct Augustinian concepts, "City of God" and "City of Man":

> [God] was in men's souls; He was always creating, but also He was always being created. The quaint old idea of the Mass, of the priest turning bread into God . . . had something in it after all, if you looked at it as the symbol of the wonderful fact that man is always creating God; that wherever a great thought is born, or a noble act performed, there God is created. . . . Talk of the equality of man with man! Why, we'd got way past that. The new Revelation wasn't going to rest till it had taught the equality of man with God. (*Hudson* 455)

Vance's own newly formed religion quickly disintegrates once he realizes that it consists of little more than "a sort of vague pantheism, and went back in its main lines to the dawn of metaphysics" (*Hudson* 238). He wisely refuses to accept his grandmother's message, even when she follows a "call" and begins a Christian lecture tour, for which she is hailed as a "prophetess of a new faith" by an undiscriminating populace that wishes to purchase salvation for the price of an admission ticket (*Hudson* 469, 451). If Vance is spiritually misguided, Wharton suggests, the masses are more so. Mrs. Scrimser's work is easily corrupted by ignorant people looking for a quick solution to life's moral and spiritual problems: "the fraud was there, it was only farther back, in the national tolerance of ignorance, the sentimental plausibility, the rush for immediate results, the get-rich-quick system applied to the spiritual life" (*Hudson* 520). Moreover, Mrs. Scrimser is a poor model as well as teacher because her life and marriage lack integration with her principles. She has no earthly use for her own beauty and is uncomfortable with matters of the flesh. Her husband's secret rendezvous with Floss Delaney – the same woman who tempts Vance – suggests the unhealthy disassociation of body and spirit in her marriage. Only near death, when she rejects sunny Emersonianism for Calvinist truth, does Mrs. Scrimser offer Vance something of value: "Maybe we haven't made enough of pain. . . . Don't be afraid of it" (*Gods* 402).

At the end of *The Gods Arrive,* Vance reads the Christian message in Augustine's *Confessions* and begins to understand its requirement of submission, but at earlier points in his spiritual journey, his own ego – expressed often through his fiction and poetry – stands in the way. In depicting Vance's attempts to free himself spiritually through his creative endeavors, Wharton engages in a dialectic between Platonic and Christian thought, one similar to Augustine's in the *Confessions.*

Augustine, after turning from the Manichaeans, was drawn to the spiritual monism of the Neoplatonists. According to Neoplatonic theory, available chiefly through Plotinus, one can reach the Good by returning to oneself, by embarking on an inner struggle to ascend from the physical to the divine plane. However, this struggle for self-sufficiency conflicts with the Christian doctrine of necessary submission to God's will. Augustine eventually rejected the Platonic model for the Christian one; Vance, influenced by material and physical pleasures, cannot make this transition. In the "after-war welter," for example, he attempts to become his own source of inner illumination, "a steady light somewhere inside" (*Hudson* 392). In contrast, Augustinian doctrine teaches that God's light is superior to humans' inner light. The critic George Frenside encourages Vance to think of the greatest of his works as a function of his own greatness: "The artist has got to feed his offspring out of his own tissue" (*Hudson* 394). These words ironically echo those of Augustine that Vance will later read, words reminding him that the ultimate sustenance is God himself, not man: "Become a man and thou shalt feed on Me" (*Gods* 411).

Vance's spiritual quest is also facilitated by his discovery of the value of history. When he arrives in the East, he is full of glamorous expectations of a "superabundance of all the things he had been taught to admire" (*Hudson* 42). The relatives with whom he boards, however, live outside of New York in a sleepy town along the Hudson River. The town of Paul's Landing is lost in the past, but Wharton makes it clear with her descriptions of sagging, aged buildings that time alone does not determine value. Mrs. Tracy's house is "neglected and dingy," and Mrs. Tracy herself is "disheartened," her original beauty and vigor now only a "phantom prettiness . . . seen through a veil . . . of failure" (*Hudson* 39, 40). Vance is initially disappointed to find that Paul's Landing has missed "the whole period of industrial development which [he] had been taught to regard as humanity's supreme achievement" (*Hudson* 43). His expectations are more than met, however, with his discovery of the Willows, the nineteenth-century house that has passed through the family from generation to generation. This house, sacred because of the traditional values that it embodies, is Vance's first true "church."

The Willows, a dominant symbol of inspiration in *Hudson River Bracketed,* is important because of its age – "an old house!" Vance exclaims because he has never seen one before (*Hudson* 57) – and because of its aristocratic culture. Preserved in its original condition since its owner Miss Lorburn passed away, the house offers Vance a treasury of great books. "Why wasn't I ever told about the Past before?" Vance wonders as he enters the Willows. He realizes that "this was what his soul had been alight for, this was what the word Poetry meant, the word which always made wings rustle in him when he read it" (*Hudson* 62, 63). Miss Lorburn, like Mrs. Scrimser, becomes a kindred spirit; even her "books have souls" (*Hudson* 119). As Vance contemplates an aged wistaria that runs across the front of an arcaded veranda, he notes that he "had never seen so prodigal a flowering, or a plant so crippled and ancient." The house, with "its age, its mystery, its reserve, laid a weight on his heart." He remembers awakening in the night and "hearing the bell of the Roman Catholic church slowly and solemnly toll the hour." The toll "spoke to his wakefulness with a shock of mystery." The mystery and inspiration of both house and church are conflated as Vance feels "in the age and the emptiness of [the house] something of the church bell's haunting sonority – as if it kept in its mute walls a voice as secret and compelling" (*Hudson* 58–59).

Halo's Light

Hudson River Bracketed and *The Gods Arrive* focus on Vance's romantic as well as literary and spiritual development. They trace the uneven relationship between him and Halo Spear, including their initial attraction, their separate marriages to unsuitable partners, the strain of Halo's divorce, and their efforts to hold on to their own fragile happiness. Despite the relationship's flaws – which Wharton traces to the "old problem" between the sexes, "that never, even in their moments of closest union, would they really understand each other" (*Gods* 121) – it has a quality of endurance and feeling, and seems to be one that Wharton intends the reader to view positively.

As one would expect from novels with such a patriarchal foundation, *Hudson River Bracketed* and *The Gods Arrive* are conservative, even reaction-

ac//, so far as domestic arrangements are concerned. Wharton depicts Vance as a *self*-conscious artist firmly positioned in the classical role of paterfamilias. She *also* presents his relationship with three different women, each exemplifying *aspects* of womanhood but none complete in herself.

Laura Lou is the *helpless* female who withers without a man's protection. Naively faithful and *sentimental*, she suffers from Vance's neglect and finally dies from tuberculosis. Floss Delaney, the aggressive vamp who prostitutes herself for money – *which* she calls "her god" (*Gods* 228) – is the temptress Vance must flee. And *Halo* Tarrant, a woman of strength, initiative, and intelligence, eschews a *vocation* of her own to devote herself to Vance and his career. Her sexless, nurturing *qualities* eclipse her other features, as she, too, depends upon Vance for *identity*.

Floss and Halo represent two types of womanhood *in* Augustine's writing: the whore who dwells in the "City of Man"; and the *wife* and mother who may enter the "City of God." Laura Lou seems to be *Wharton's* contribution to this scheme, a version of the sentimental, sacrificial *female* who appears in earlier novels such as *Sanctuary* (1903) and *The House of Mirth* (1905). Vance never thinks of Laura Lou as a person in her own right; she is "a translucent vessel" or object, a "tropical shell with the sun shining through it" (*Hudson* 239, 206). On the day of their marriage, "he had already decided that part of his duty as a husband was to be older and stronger than she was, and to know more than she did about everything" (*Hudson* 243–44). Of Floss he concludes, "There's no novelty in finding out again what she is – I knew it well enough before. . . . The residue of it all was a sick disgust. . . . She seemed to distil a poison such as no other woman secreted" (*Gods* 238). Halo's roles are more complex and problematic.

Vance does all of his best writing at or near the Willows, with the loving guidance of Halo Spear. Halo serves as Vance's literary critic and conscience. Recognizing the "authentic note" of the true artist (*Hudson* 221), she challenges him by offering a standard by which he assesses the honesty and quality of his writing. As heir to the Willows, Halo also presides over what is valuable in past traditions. Cultivated and wise, she transcends the pettiness and narrow-mindedness of her impoverished, aristocratic family. Whereas her parents love the family home for its status and the money its sale will bring, Halo loves it for itself. She is particularly sensitive to nature, art, and the effect of environment on the human psyche. She is also the most responsible member of her family; in some respects she is the true mother of both her brother and parents, covering for her brother's habitual lies and marrying Lewis Tarrant in order to repay his loan and ensure her parents' financial security. Wharton invests her with a strong sense of obligation, a commitment to honesty derived from "Puritanism" (*Gods* 3), and a tendency toward self-sacrifice that links her to other Puritan daughters such as Lily Bart (*The House of Mirth*) and Nona Manford (*Twilight Sleep*).

Halo also plays the role of Vance's teacher and lover, as does Ellen Olenska for Newland Archer in *The Age of Innocence*. All of her roles, except that of lover – which Wharton does not develop – are idealized and supportive. She is a Madonna (Vance compares her head to a statue of the Virgin), a mythic goddess, a Muse, and, at the end of *The Gods Arrive,* a soon-to-be mother and wife. Vance romantically thinks of her as "goddess-like and remote, mistress of the keys of knowledge and experience," the "mysterious vehicle of all the new sensations pouring into his soul – as if she had been the element harmonizing the scene, or a being born of the sunrise and the forest" (*Hudson* 96, 101). Like Augustine's mother Monica, Halo guides Vance toward fulfillment of his potential. She also serves as his confessor:

> He had told her everything . . . his distresses and anxieties, the misery of his marriage, the material cares that made work so difficult, his secret resentment of what had appeared to him her hardness and indifference when they had parted at the Willows. . . . He had sought her out as the one confidant of his literary projects, had imagined that pride and loyalty forbade any personal confession. But once his reserve had broken down there rushed through the breach all the accumulated distress of the long months since he had seen her. (*Hudson* 410–11)

Halo's ability to listen but ask no personal questions – to understand Vance's failures as well as his successes – helps her establish a sacred communion with him that Vance himself describes in religious terms as "the peace that passeth understanding" (*Gods* 190).

In depicting a strong, resourceful, modern woman as the chief source of inspiration and comfort for her male protagonist, Wharton no doubt intends to pay homage to womanhood. However, she still faces an age-old choice between female autonomy and service to others. Wharton describes Halo, like Ellen Olenska, in Platonic terms as a Psyche figure, with the ability to lift Vance's soul without losing her own: she "stood poised in the dusk of the porch as if her outcry had given her wings"; "it was as if, at her touch, wings had grown from him" (*Hudson* 90, 105). She thus implies that Halo is spiritually enlightened and self-aware. But whereas Ellen is associated with autonomous goddess figures, Wharton firmly places Halo within the Judeo-Christian tradition, in which woman is seen as weak and secondary to man.

Halo's real name is Héloïse, an allusion to the twelfth-century story of Héloïse and Abelard. Like the Héloïse of the famous letters, Halo not only possesses great intelligence, passion, and strength, she provides her lover with ideas for his writing. According to the letters, Héloïse and Abelard were secretly married, despite Héloïse's protest that such a marriage was unnecessary and unethical and that legal bonds were inferior to those freely given. This philosophical commitment to being a mistress instead of a wife in order that her partner might more fully pursue his philosophical contemplations is paralleled in Halo's decision not to tell Vance of her divorce or press him for marriage: "The only thing I care for is his freedom. I want him to feel free as air," she tells George Frenside (Gods 212, original emphasis). At this point, however, Wharton departs from the twelfth-century Héloïse. Calling her character not Héloïse but Halo, a name that connotes angelic obedience as well as refracted light, she inscribes her within conservative Christian doctrine and counteracts her more free-thinking qualities.

Halo's character is replete with contradictions, although some critics interpret her domestic subordination positively. Ammons describes her as "tranquil and grave, full bodied with the promise of new life, arms raised in strength to the heavens" (194); Wershoven reads her reunion with Vance as "an emblem of Halo's rediscovered strength and maturity." Wershoven also notes that Halo — "a blend of both convention and nonconformity" — is an independent woman who can prefer to raise her child alone in a home that she owns and at the same time serve as a model of Christian womanly decorum (Female 143). This dual portrait of Halo in a sense describes Edith Wharton herself, reflecting what Lewis calls her "conflict . . . between the nun and the wild woodland woman" (510). It also recalls previous fiction, in which Wharton splits her women into opposites: Zeena-Mattie, Anna-Sophy, May-Ellen. She attempts a synthesis in Hudson River Bracketed and The Gods Arrive, but the result is far from satisfactory.

As Halo sacrifices her reputation, her social position, and eventually her happiness to remain loyal to Vance, she does, in fact, experience the loss of self that such service entails. "I must just adapt myself; I must learn to keep step," she tells herself; "she would prove to him that her only happiness was in knowing that he was happy" (Gods 28, 58). She tries to convince herself that no "happiness could equal that of a woman permitted to serve the genius while she adored the man" (Gods 29). But when Vance neglects her and ceases to confide in her, Halo feels herself "sinking into the character of the blindly admiring wife." She is determined to "hold her breath and wait" for his attentions to return (*Gods* 40), even though she knows that as a woman she is "fated to disappointment" (*Hudson* 231).

Christian teachings caution against the sin of hubris; but for a woman, whose life may already be an endless chronicle of caring and sacrifice for others, giving up ego comes perilously close to giving up self altogether.[9] Vance, on the other hand, retains his sense of self: "he could never give up the right to live his inner life in his own way . . . though it troubled him to hurt her" (*Gods* 108). Throughout the novel, their relationship is portrayed as one between impulsive child and forgiving, patient mother. Vance's final supplication at Halo's skirts at the end of *The Gods Arrive,* and Halo's prayerful posture and exclamation, "But then I shall have two children to take care of instead of one!" (*Gods* 432), underscores their dangerously unbalanced union.

Becoming a Man; Remaining a Woman

One of Vance's responses to social pressures and chaos is to dissociate himself from others and find solace in nature. The sea, the mountains, and even a simple apple branch at the cottage that he rents outside of New York City have the power to renew his creative energies. His grandmother's death precipitates his decision to give up his lust for Floss Delaney and face the conditions of his life. This moral crisis differs from previous ones in that Vance now feels a responsibility for and commitment to self-scrutiny, "a boundless need to deal with himself, cut a way through the jungle of his conflicting purposes, work out some sort of plan from the dark muddle of things. . . . He wanted first of all to measure himself with his pain, to wrestle alone with the dark angel and see how he came out of that conflict" (*Gods* 404). He chooses a remote winter retreat to resolve this inner crisis. When he discovers a copy of Augustine's *Confessions* among his books (provided by another supportive female, his admiring sister Mae), the "Gods arrive" for Vance, and he feels "his whole life summed up." A particular passage speaks to Vance's struggles for self-control and acceptance of God's will:

> I said, "Give me chastity and self-control – *but not just yet . . .*" I was shaken with a gust of indignation because I could not enter into Thy Will, yet all my bones were crying out that this was the way, and no ship is needed for that way, nor chariot, no, nor feet; for it is not as far from me as from the house to the spot where we are seated. . . .

And Thou didst beat back my weak sight, dazzling me with Thy splendour, and I perceived that I was far from Thee, in the land of unlikeness, and I heard Thy voice crying to me: "I am the Food of the full-grown. Become a man and thou shalt feed on Me." (*Gods* 410–11, original emphasis and ellipses).

Vance rereads Augustine's *Confessions* night after night, absorbing their message of faith and submission. Eventually he undergoes a serious illness, a physical manifestation of his spiritual crisis. He is nursed back to health by Aaron Brail, a recluse in the northern woods who once aspired to the ministry. In this crude monastic setting, Vance recovers his health and learns Brail's story. Brail is a clumsy, inarticulate man reminiscent of Ethan Frome. He has dealt with his own measure of pain – mortification at being unable to pass the seminary's entrance examination, rejection by a woman who is improbably a circus lion tamer – by shutting down his feelings and isolating himself from society. Blinded by his experience, as his name suggests, he has given up on life. Vance, on the other hand, ostensibly learns to transform his pain into creative work.

Vance's experience in the wooded retreat recalls the religious asceticism of the Middle Ages and Wharton's treatment of saints' lives in stories such as "The Hermit and the Wild Woman" (1906). The modern reader must view Vance's spiritual conversion with some skepticism, however; Brail is more pathetic than inspirational, and Vance himself liberally interprets Augustine's message. Wharton's tone is both satiric and serious as she attempts to portray a protagonist who can combine romantic, artistic independence and creativity with the Christian mandate to subordinate one's own will to God's. She attempts to hold these two philosophies in tension, but with mixed results.

Wharton's emphasis on the importance of creative work to Vance's development departs from Augustine. A moralist, Augustine has low regard for art because it threatens man's direct relationship with God and keeps him from proper piety and right action. As Robert O'Connell explains:

Augustine remains profoundly suspicious of the distracting power of poetry, myth, theater, even of the sweet-sounding melodies of the Ambrosian psalms. Such delights, he is astute enough to detect, make terminal claims upon the soul's attention and esteem. They would lull the soul into forgetting that its journey must go further, always further still. (116)

For Wharton, however, art was a crucial part of civilization and of life itself. Like T. S. Eliot, she believed in the close connection between literature and faith. As Charles Berryman points out, these states have "the same origin, and it is the task of the poet to find the pattern of words to give form to his continuing experience of the divine" (190). Wharton would thus seem to be sympathetic toward the modern latitude with which Vance interprets Augustine: "I read something up there in the woods about God . . . or experience . . . it's the same thing . . . being the food of the full-grown" (*Gods* 431, original ellipses). However, the vagueness of "read something" and the conclusion that "God" and "experience" are "the same thing" call Vance's intelligence and faith into question. Vance revises the Christian message for his own purpose, and he makes Augustine's words so general that they will fit any meaning he assigns to them. In the end, he cannot be said to have successfully reconciled self and art with the Augustinian God.

Wharton's tone at the end of *The Gods Arrive* remains uncertain. The reader is encouraged to believe that Vance has begun to resist the self-indulgent, romantic escapes he has pursued throughout his life. He is "determined not to abandon himself to such dreams" (*Gods* 417) but to be ruled by realities. Seen in terms of the Christian emphasis on the necessity of memory in order to make adequate confession, Vance's return to the Willows is a sign of his acceptance of faith. In the Platonic view, memory constantly ties the soul back to the body, hindering its ascent to the Good and threatening to enslave it in habit; but in the Christian view, memory is the heart of identity. In the early days of their relationship, both Vance and Halo believed that they could outrun memory and the past. Traveling with Halo, for example, Vance considered memory an enemy to happiness: "he pictured a man suddenly falling over the ship's side, and seized and torn to pieces by the pack of his memories . . . and thought: 'For a little while longer we shall outrace them' " (*Gods* 19). His final decision to return to Halo and the Willows seals the bonds of tradition, memory, faith, and art. It is unclear, however, that Vance will go on to be a great – or even a good – writer. His newly invented religion remains a weak amalgam of traditional doctrine and contemporary whim – a pastiche rather than a coherent philosophy.

Wharton's attitude toward Halo is more problematic. Her sacrifice recalls that of Lily Bart in *The House of Mirth:* how much has she accomplished? Equally troubling, Wharton leaves little room for female desire, safely desexualizing Halo in her final pose as embracing wife and mother and freezing both Halo and Vance in a religious allegory. Wharton attempts to modernize Augustinian concepts to accommodate Vance's creative impulses, but she does not revise Augustine's script for her female protagonist. Halo, unlike Vance, never achieves the stature of artist. Instead, Wharton follows traditional Christian, and specifically Catholic, doctrine by channeling her creative energies into supportive, maternal roles. No matter how exalted Halo is in these roles, she fails as a heroine in her own right.

Wharton's decision to portray an intelligent, able woman who is also submissive suggests her ambivalence toward women's power and – at the end of her life – a fear of change as much as a desire for it. Further, because Wharton demonstrates in these novels that she sees creativity as deriving from an essentially "mysterious and unknowable" source (Vita-Finzi 49) rather than exclusively from the self, she invites questions about the gender of divine inspiration. In *Hudson River Bracketed* and *The Gods Arrive,* the feminine, romantic archetype of the "Mothers" is rivaled by a more exacting, masculine deity. In the Christian narrative that serves as Wharton's subtext, creativity issues from an exclusively male God. This God appoints man as his agent, but woman and her creative aspirations remain secondary and inferior.

Hudson River Bracketed and *The Gods Arrive* are, finally, confused. If we read them as satires of the male literary establishment, as Schriber has suggested (*Gender* 179), then we must also read Wharton's depictions of Vance's spiritual conversion as satirical, despite evidence that Vance – like Wharton herself – finds true comfort in the Catholic Church. If, on the other hand, we read these novels as sincere, we must conclude that as a female artist, Wharton still suffered anxiety about her own literary powers and source of literary creativity. Whatever tone we assume is Wharton's intended one, gender, Catholicism, and literary talent form an uneasy alliance in *Hudson River Bracketed* and *The Gods Arrive,* threatening to heighten the very conflicts they ostensibly resolve. In these rather didactic novels, then, Wharton's Old World Catholicism reflects Old World notions of gender relations, and her celebrated transatlantic flight to Europe and freedom must be viewed with the restrictions that this faith imposed.

Coda

W HO, then, is Edith Wharton? What motivated her religious, spiritual, and philosophical quest? And what answers did she find? Despite her ability to portray social customs with faultless detail, critics are mistaken when they conclude, as does early commentator E. K. Brown, that her work is *"indépendante du divin"* (324, original emphasis). Nor is it true that her fiction exhibits no cosmic philosphy (Russell 432) or moral center (Dixon 211). It is the case that Wharton's religious sensibilities developed as a result of widely different influences – including genteel religion that often subordinated strenuous faith to sociability and comfort; a love of life's pleasures that competed with codes of truth telling and punishment for happiness; and a desire to strengthen woman's vulnerable position within the structures of patriarchy.

Edith Wharton was born an Episcopalian; she inherited a Calvinist sensibility; and she flirted with transcendental philosophies. She arrived finally at the door of Catholicism, but neither it nor Protestantism – whether homespun or genteel – could fully answer her spiritual needs. All religions fell short of the philosophical ideals to which she aspired – and none incorporated the qualities of the feminine to the extent that she would have liked. Wharton was a member of the group that Jackson Lears calls "tourists of the supernatural" (174), whose agnosticism and hard-edged positivism prevented her surrender to historical nostalgia or simple belief, yet whose spiritual longings sustained the search for immutable values. Wharton thus remains an outsider to both the retrospective world of faith and the modern world of reason. She belongs to the tradition of disillusioned romantics who want to believe in God strongly enough that they find his absence intolerable, and who strive, even though they fail, to create a harmony of individual spirit, society, and the divine.

While in no way discounting Wharton's realism, I suggest that her work extends the tradition of what Leslie Fiedler calls "tragic humanism," a literature "in which the rich paradoxes and tensions of Calvinism are not simplified in the interests of simple-minded orthodoxy or sentimental liberalism." This philosophy maintains

> that the world of appearance is at once real and a mask through which we can dimly perceive more ultimate forces at work; that Nature is inscrutable, perhaps basically hostile to man, but certainly in some sense alien; that in man and Nature alike, there is a "diabolical" element, a "mystery of iniquity"; that it is impossible to know fully either God or ourselves, and that our only protection from destruction and self-deceit is the pressure and presence of others; that to be alone is, therefore, to be lost; that evil is real, and that the thinking man breaks his heart trying to solve its compatibility with the existence of a good God or his own glimmering perceptions of goodness. (432)

Wharton's fiction not only fulfills, but exceeds, these criteria: in her tragedies of human nature, characters are denied even the solace of others. Struggling in a commercialized, Darwinian world stripped of God and estranged from nature, they find no social or private havens from the onslaughts of life. In novels from *The House of Mirth* to *The Age of Innocence,* community is as alienating as nature or God.

It may be fairer to describe Wharton's fiction, with its plots about failed quests and unachievable ideals, as moral rather than social realism, with elements of the tragic overshadowing the comic. Terms like "soul," "sanctity," "fate," "gods," and "abyss," which appear frequently in her work, evoke classical and Christian tragedy as well as a modernist despair.[1] Moreover, Wharton's effort to find a harmonizing principle by which to unite the accepting soul with the discerning intellect constitutes a romantic tendency common to other American realists, as Eric Sundquist points out. Materialism and conventionality – and the misapplied or outmoded philosophical and religious systems that support them – become in Wharton's fiction "threats to ideal space" (Sundquist 10) to which her characters long to escape.

Wharton also keeps company with early twentieth-century modernists such as Eliot, Hemingway, Faulkner, and Warren, whose fiction exhibits, as Cleanth Brooks has observed, a "residual" Christianity (129). Her Puritan strain in particular, at odds with genteel New York culture, places her squarely in this American tradition. Chard Powers Smith, for example, suggests that the young iconoclasts of the twenties were really the last, or next to last, wave of Puritanism, despite their use of the term as the ultimate abuse (451–59). Perry Miller compares these writers with the transcendentalists: both speak for the spirit rather than materiality, and both belong to a series of revolts against "American Philistinism" (*Transcendentalists* 8). Similarly, in a description of American writers he calls "dissenters," Henry May links Wharton to a hardheaded realism born of Calvinism, which, although unpopular in an age of expansion, still expressed concern over the relationship between the size of one's pocketbook and the state of one's soul. Dissenters in any period, he continues, are rooted in a Protestant past and share characteristics with seventeenth-century New England intellectuals and their heirs: "a habit of agonized self-doubt, a deep suspicion of material appearances, a positive hatred of blandness and complacency, and above all, a most intense and even painful seriousness about oneself, one's country, and its mission." May includes Edwards, Hawthorne, James, and Faulkner as well as Wharton in this group (62–63).[2]

If Wharton found herself, by constitution and gender, shut out of the mystery and benevolence of faith, she found some consolation in the experience of failure itself. In much of her fiction, she depicts individuals futilely struggling to fulfill personal desires while meeting arbitrary social expectations. The moral dimensions of their struggles have roots in Christian and classical thought. Ethan Frome barely comprehends the meaning of his Calvinist suffering, and suffers all the more. Lily Bart has fleeting glimpses of herself in relation to a moral code that her materialistic society abandons, and although she settles her material and spiritual accounts before dying, her selfless acts save no one. Anna Leath follows the moral and social conventions of patriarchal society only to feel their betrayal; even then, however, she cannot embrace change. Charity Royall also sees her hopes for romance fade and must accept the reality of compromise rather than the dream of transcendence. Like Charity, Newland Archer sets out on a path toward spiritual independence, but circumstances and conventions block the way. Vance Weston discovers a new religion, unaware of how much this fresh beginning retraces older patriarchal patterns.

It is usually not possible to speak of happiness in Wharton's fiction, a fact that leads critics to note that reality, not romance, characterizes her work. As Blake Nevius observes, the "clearest message" in Wharton's later works is that "the pain of life must be accepted" (*Wharton* 218). It is true that in Wharton's world, society often has the force of moral law, and characters' limited imaginations and lack of will imprison them. Yet, despite the grimness of her world, Wharton does propose transcendent values toward which each individual can reach. She locates these ideals rather than relative values in systems of thought and belief that are central to Western culture – from goddess worship to Platonism, Catholicism, and Calvanism. If we do not recognize the religious or philosophical context of her characters' pain, we read Wharton's fiction as merely deterministic.

Wharton has been faulted for her lack of a unified cosmic vision. The point is that she never pretended to have such a vision: from her early days in Mlle Michelet's dancing class, to her last days at St. Brice, she experimented with different philosophies and religions. An intelligent woman, Wharton was not easily won over by a religion that required faith without reason; she was equally unable, however, to live with a purely mechanistic view of the universe. As a result, in Wharton's fiction, one simultaneously encounters aspiration, ambivalence, and resignation. Her characters achieve no single, completely satisfying synthesis or moral or religious outlook. For Wharton, there was never a solution to the "mind–body" split or to the conflicts between personal and social obligation. There were only paths to explore.

Notes

Introduction

1. Throughout this book, I use the terms moral, philosophical, religious, and spiritual to describe Edith Wharton's quest for meaning. Although the terms are interchangeable to the extent that they refer to nonmateriality, I use them in distinctive ways. "Moral" concerns the judgment or principles of right and wrong in relation to human character and behavior, as determined both by external standards and by one's inner sense or conscience. "Philosophical" refers to systems of thought, value, or meaning as well as to the processes of inquiry into such systems. In keeping with Wharton's interests, I focus to a greater extent on aesthetics and metaphysics and to lesser extent on logic, ethics, and epistemology. By "religious," I mean faith in a superhuman power or powers and adherence to the traditions, teachings, and practices associated with that faith. I also take religious to mean an attitude of reverence or devotion that faith inspires. "Spiritual," the broadest of the terms, refers to the sacred and to matters of the soul and its vital energy and nurturance.

2. See Gilbert and Gubar, who, although they focus on social rather than spiritual issues, find in Wharton's fiction "the most searching – and searing – feminist analysis of the construction of 'femininity' produced by any novelist in this century" (128).

3. See, for example, E. K. Brown, who argues that religion appears in Wharton's writing only as part of the social scene (323–24). See also Tuttleton and Milne, other early and influential proponents of Wharton as novelist of manners; and Lindberg, who recently claims that the novel of manners is Wharton's "inevitable mode," although he admits that society is "problematic" in her fiction (4–5).

4. See Lindberg, who finds two levels of plot – "one overt and public, the other buried, private, and usually fragmentary" – in Wharton's fiction. This buried fable, which "plays over and over against the stories she actually is telling,"

213

places the protagonist at odds with himself as well as society and "moves [him] toward the release of full psychological and moral insight" (44–45).

5. Humphries observes that American writers, despite their obsession with morality, are disinclined to use the maxim and fable forms (vii). Wharton's use of allegories, fables, and parables suggests otherwise.

6. Proofs of *The House of Mirth* arrived from the publisher with the text from Ecclesiastes 7.4 reprinted. Wharton, afraid of being thought a heavy moralist, drew "an inexorable blue line through the text" (*Letters* 94).

7. For example, Margaret Deland, an Episcopalian, promoted sentimentality as well as New Thought and spiritualism in some of her thirty-seven books; Augusta Evans Wilson, a Southern Methodist, opposed female suffrage but argued the superiority of women in novels such as *Beulah* and *St. Elmo;* and Elizabeth Stuart Phelps developed a softened form of Calvinism that she called "Christlove" in *The Gates Ajar, Beyond the Gates,* and *The Gates Between.*

8. From the beginning, Wharton had difficulty striking an appropriately sentimental tone. Her most sentimental stories are early ones, for example, "Friends" (1900), a Freeman-like story about a New England schoolteacher's diminished opportunities; and "April Showers" (1900), an autobiographical tale about a young sentimental fiction writer who lacks a publisher but receives compensatory sympathy from her father, who once also aspired to the pen. Wharton responded to her publisher's criticism of an early version of "Friends": "I see perfectly that the contrast is too violent between her 'schwärmerei' [rapture] in pink satin & the ensuing squalor" (*Letters* 32). See also my analysis of "A Bottle of Perrier" (first published in 1926, with the title "A Bottle of Evian"), in which I argue that Wharton transforms Freeman's tale of mothering in "The Wind in the Rose-bush" into a critique of class and power (273–74).

9. Other critics note Wharton's tendency to penetrate social surfaces, although they do not pursue this observation. For example, Monroe writes that Wharton was "deeply concerned with moral consciousness, without subscribing to any system of dogma or well-defined ethical code" (119), and Kazin credits her with talking "the language of the soul at a time when the best energies in American prose" were focused on capitalism (79). Those aware of Wharton's Puritanism include Burdett, who calls her "a literary Pilgrim Father, with a lusty brood of native-bred descendants latent in her books" (168); Hays, who writes that Ethan Frome's "rigid, code-bound New England Puritanism" dictates where he sits during the fateful sled run (n.p.); and Wilson, who comments, "there is a Puritan in Edith Wharton, and this Puritan is always insisting that we must face the unpleasant and the ugly" (23). None of these critics develops these observations or relates the Puritanism in Wharton's fiction to her overall religious or philosophical views. An exception is Tyree, whose dissertation study discusses Wharton's "deep strain of puritanism" (10) in *The Custom of the Country, The Age of Innocence,* and *Twilight Sleep.*

10. For critiques of women's roles in Judeo-Christian traditions, see Carr; Clark

and Richardson; Daly, *Church* and *Beyond;* Ruether, *Liberation, New,* and *Religion.*

11. Sir Arthur Evans, for example, an important archaeologist influenced by matriarchal theory, excavated the Palace of Knossos on Crete; classicist Jane Ellen Harrison, in her 1903 *Prolegomena to the Study of Greek Religion,* used such excavations as the basis for reinstating the Great Mother. In some circles, Athens was seen as a culture built on the suppression of female culture (Ruether and Keller 9).

12. See Donovan, who reads Wharton's personal and artistic development in terms of the Demeter–Persephone myth (43–83); Waid, who claims that Persephone is Wharton's "figure for the woman writer" (3); and my essay with Sweeney, which argues that the myth in Wharton's story "Pomegranate Seed" serves as an indeterminate, ambiguous paradigm for relationships among the characters in the story (190–95). Also see Sherman, who maintains that the Persephone myth in general represents more a "regression" than an "integration," denying women's needs for full individuation and development (19–20).

13. Ammons similarly finds in Wharton's late fiction an attempt to synthesize "her new endorsement of motherhood with her lifelong belief in woman's right to self-determination." She notes Wharton's evocation of literary, religious, and mythic figures, especially the Mothers, found in Goethe's *Faust,* to provide divine feminine principles for the modern world (189).

14. See Fryer, who writes that Wharton's "gardens were to be perfect fusions of art and nature: wild nature in the garden is trained, pruned, and structured" to achieve classical harmony (174).

15. The tone of resignation in *Summer* relates to what Lindberg describes as a Stoic style in Wharton's fiction. He cites epigrams such as "Genius is of small use to a woman who does not know how to do her hair" (*Touchstone* 55) and "He had a mental palate which would never learn to distinguish between railway tea and nectar" (*The House of Mirth* 20) as examples of calm acceptance of the unavoidable, brought about when "the best ideas are at odds with a corrupting society" (148–49).

16. Wharton was well acquainted with these figures and owned works by all of them (Maggs). She knew Wilde personally. She read Arnold aloud with Henry James (Lewis 140) and Charles Eliot Norton (*Letters* 186), and quoted him in letters to Fullerton (*Letters* 149, 281). In "Life and I" she pays tribute to Ruskin, whom she discovered as a girl reading in her father's library: "His wonderful cloudy pages gave me back the image of the beautiful Europe I had lost, & woke in me the habit of precise visual observation. The ethical & aesthetical *fatras* [items of useless knowledge] were easily enough got rid of later, & as an interpretor of visual impression he did me incomparable service" (1084). In *A Backward Glance,* she writes that she and her father followed "step by step Ruskin's arbitrary itineraries" on their trip to Italy (87). She mentions reading Pater's *Plato and Platonism* while "in the mood for the Hellenic" and refers to his *Marius the Epicurean* (*Letters* 100, 148).

17. See Waid, who notes the influence of Butler's *Lives of the Saints* in Wharton's 1902 poem "Margaret of Cortona." She observes a pattern of erotic communion, violence, pain, and female sacrifice in this and other poems in *Artemis to Actaeon* (54–60).

18. The term "wild woman" also had currency in the women's rights movement of the 1890s. Wharton may have written her story as a sympathetic commentary on this struggle. Mrs. Lynn Linton wrote a series of articles for *Nineteenth Century* castigating "Wild Women" for "warring as they do against the best traditions, the holiest functions, and the sweetest qualities of their sex" (qtd. in Gilbert and Gubar xiii).

19. As Wolff notes, the neoclassical emphasis in portraiture at the time was predicated on "deception": New York society propagated "the pleasing illusion that the *idealized* renderings [of women] . . . were in fact *realistic* representations" (*Feast* 113, original emphases).

20. "Mrs. Wharton was never able to dissociate good breeding from the other desirable badges of distinction – character, sensibility, a high degree of cultural awareness, and even good looks" (Nevius, *Wharton* 106).

21. On Wharton's disapproval of homosexuality, see Lewis 443. Also see my analysis of homoeroticism and class in Wharton's "A Bottle of Perrier."

22. "What a jolly book!" Wharton declared about Santayana's 1916 *Egotism in German Philosophy*. She had equally high praise for his 1920 *Character and Opinion in the United States*: "I'm having a private gloat . . . over Santayana's new book. I'd read the James & the Royce before . . . but the other chaps are new to me. 'The Moral Background' is precious – & oh, what a tone, what standards!" (*Letters* 386, 433–34).

23. "I think she would do it well, judging from her books," Wharton wrote to Sara Norton in 1903. Lewis thinks that Wharton "deplored" Paget's subject – "Art and Life" (118) – but her letter suggests that she deplored the trivial treatment of such topics, not the topic itself or her friend's ability to handle it. Paget, Wharton continued in the letter to Norton, did not want to " 'lecture to fashionable women in bonnets' . . . for which I respect her," but to have audiences at select colleges like Bryn Mawr and Harvard (*Letters* 81). For more on Wharton's friendship with and regard for Paget, see *Backward* 102, 130–34, 141.

24. See, for example, Ammons 6; Goodman, *Women* 88; Lewis 75; McDowell 87; and Waid 19.

25. The opinions of Jacques Fosse (Interview), who was Wharton's young neighbor at St. Brice, and of her doctor, M. Artin (Interview), who cared for her during her final illness.

26. Henry Drummond was a Scottish Evangelical whose *Lowell Lectures on the Ascent of Man* (1894) transformed the threat of Darwin's *The Descent of Man* into a hopeful alternative. Also a scientist, Drummond saw continuity extending from the physical world to the spiritual. Wharton's view was less optimistic and more complex. In her story "Souls Belated," she implies that

Lydia's lover Gannett is foolish and hypocritical because he talks with the hotel chaplain "by the hour about . . . Professor Drummond" (*Stories* 1: 122).

1. Priestess of Reason

1. According to the nineteenth-century view, women's talents were not only different from men's, but were static, neither requiring nor warranting development: "Man has skills and talents, but woman's gifts, like her knowledge, come from a deeper source and do not respond to training or practice since they are the product of genius. Man reasons and is just; woman loves and is merciful" (Welter 78).

2. See *The Decoration of Houses* (1897), *Italian Villas and Their Gardens* (1904), and *Italian Backgrounds* (1905).

3. Wharton documents the intellectual desert of her home, claiming, "I never exchanged a word with a really intelligent human being until I was over twenty" ("Life" 1082–83). I find this and other evidence compelling, but see Winner, who argues that Wharton exaggerated the extent of her family's and social class's anti-intellectualism (3).

4. Wharton's library was eventually offered for sale by Maggs Brothers. A list of its contents confirms Clark's observation. Thomas Hayes, former executive director of Edith Wharton Restoration, cautions that the list is incomplete, in that only first volumes are cited although Wharton may have owned others. I am grateful to him for information regarding the library.

5. Wharton mentions Alfred Wallace's *Darwin and Darwinism* (she probably meant *Darwinism: An Exposition of the Theory of Natural Selection,* published in 1889); Charles Darwin's *The Origin of Species;* Aldous Huxley; Herbert Spencer; George Romanes; Ernst Haeckel; Edward Westermarck; and "all the various popular exponents of the great evolutionary movement" (*Backward* 94).

6. See, for example, full-length studies by Donovan; Erlich; Goodman, *Women;* Schriber; Waid; and Wolff, *Feast.* Not all recent scholarship by women is sympathetic or feminist. Ozick, for example, criticizes Wharton for being too self-consciously formal and intellectual (50–52).

7. Wilson echoes Kazin, who declares Wharton's career "the tenuous product of so many personal maladjustments" (77).

8. Wharton similarly describes Mrs. Ballinger in her story "Xingu" (1911): "her mind was an hotel where facts came and went like transient lodgers, without leaving their address behind, and frequently without paying for their board" (*Stories* 2: 214). By the time Wharton published this story, however, she was confident enough to associate these traits with a fatuous society woman who could not be mistaken for the author herself.

9. Wharton commented on Kuno Fischer's treatment of Schopenauer in his multivolume history of philosophy (*Geschichte der neuern Philosophie*): "it is a perfect delight – so lucid & direct in style – almost as good prose as Schopenhauer's." Several years later she wrote to Bernard Berenson that Wagner's *Life*

"wd have been immortal" "if he'd written like Nietzsche or Schopenhauer" (*Letters* 102, 240).

10. As Lewis notes, Wharton's review of Eliot's biography is "drawn from the depths of Edith Wharton's self-definition and self-appraisal" (109). Wharton argues that Eliot was "a conservative in ethics. She felt no call to found a new school of morals. A deep reverence for family ties, for the sanctities of tradition, the claims of slowly acquired convictions and slowly formed precedents, is revealed in every page of her books" (250). Lewis writes that Wharton follows Eliot in having no interest in founding a new school of ethics (109), yet Wharton's fiction is replete with heroines who do challenge the status quo – from Lydia Tillotson in "Souls Belated," who wants "to found a new system of ethics" (*Stories* 1: 110) to Lily Bart in *The House of Mirth*, who cannot "understand the laws of a universe which was so ready to leave her out of its calculations" (26), to independently minded heroines such as Fulvia in *The Valley of Decision*, who bravely suffers restrictions on social and moral freedom.

11. Wharton most likely read the revised 1872 edition, which is essentially the same as the original edition of 1857, as the revision's preface indicates.

12. Lyde argues that Coppée plays a major role in Wharton's fiction. When dealing with moral issues, Wharton adheres to principles of logic, reducing the most complex moral and physical problems to "the three terms of a syllogism": "the individual, society, and the resulting action – revolt or submission" (33). While this analysis has merit, it ties Wharton's beliefs and thoughts too tightly to convention and neglects her search for a more transcendent philosophy or belief that could free the individual from society's regulation.

13. As Lyde notes, since there is no book by that title, Wharton probably meant *The Metaphysics of Sir William Hamilton*, a text used at the college where Wharton's brothers studied (28n.).

14. Taine (1828–93), a historian, literary critic, and philosopher, embraced science, drawing from it a cold rationalism that countered excessive emotionalism and spiritualist philosophy. He helped to provide a theoretical base for literary naturalism. Wharton responded enthusiastically, especially at an early stage of her intellectual development, to his positivism and ambitious desire to solve metaphysical problems through the scientific method.

15. See McDowell 52; Nevius, *Wharton*; Price, "Lily"; and especially Lyde for discussions of Wharton's naturalism.

16. Here I disagree with Lyde, who maintains that in conflicts between the individual and society, Wharton believed, with Spencer, that "ethics can only be relative" (44).

17. Fiske's *Outlines of Cosmic Philosophy* (1874) was one of the earliest books seeking to unite evolution with Christianity. Wharton was obviously interested in such a reconciliation – she owned two of Fiske's books, his two-volume *The Discovery of America* (1892) and *Excursions of an Evolutionist* (1884) (Maggs).

18. This attitude is also evident in another story, "The Last Asset" (1904), in which a man has only one use to his estranged, social-climbing wife: he can secure their daughter's marriage to a French count by agreeing to appear as part of the wedding party. He adopts an idea of Schopenhauer – whom Wharton read in 1902 (*Letters* 56) – claiming, "there are lots of ways of being miserable, but there's only one way of being comfortable, and that is to stop running round after happiness. If you make up your mind not to be happy there's no reason why you shouldn't have a fairly good time" (*Stories* 1: 591).

19. Norton provided Wharton with valuable help while she researched her eighteenth-century novel, *The Valley of Decision,* and he remained an important friend and intellectual guide. In 1926, Wharton looked back on Norton's mentorship in a letter to his daughter Lily: "It touched me very much to find that he believed in me all those long years ago, & when I think what it would have meant to know it *then,* when all my dreams were still in my head, & I never hoped to be able to express them, I am saddened by the endless waste of sympathy and opportunity" (Letters, 4 March, original emphasis).

20. Cowley distinguishes Edith Wharton, Robert Herrick, and Ernest Hemingway from other naturalists because their characters "possessed some degree of moral freedom" (146). Plante also notes that Wharton's affirmation of individual responsibility separates her from the naturalists (19). Straumann calls Wharton a determinist but not a naturalist because of her upper-class subject matter (45). Pizer takes a different approach, arguing that a novel such as *The Age of Innocence* is naturalistic because Archer must accept external contraints on what he believed was personal freedom (139).

21. For Wharton, the creation of art itself was a kind of metaphysical mystery. In *A Backward Glance,* she writes that "the *soul* of the novel . . . is (or should be) the writer's own soul" (115, original emphasis), and she muses over "exactly what happens at that 'fine point of the soul' where the creative act, like the mystic's union with the Unknowable, really seems to take place" (121).

2. Spiritual Homelessness

1. See, in particular, Nevius's book on Wharton and naturalism; Michaels's chapter on *The House of Mirth;* and discussions by Bell 239; McIlvaine; Price, "Lily"; Robinson; and Schriber, "Darwin."

2. Wharton's original titles for the novel emphasized gender and Darwinism: *A Moment's Ornament* suggests that Lily is unfit for anything but decoration; *The Year of the Rose* may allude, as McIlvaine suggests, to J. D. Rockefeller's notorious statement that "the American Beauty rose can be produced in the splendor and fragrance which bring cheer to its beholder only by sacrificing the early buds which grow up around it. This is not an evil tendency in business. It is merely the working out of a law of nature and a law of God" (184). Wharton's final title, drawn from the Bible, makes the novel a spiritual

as well as social critique. See Dahl, who reads the novel as a literal "gloss" on Ecclesiastes, in my opinion misreading Selden's "wiser standards" as "an unspoken rebuke" of Lily's vanity (573–74). As I demonstrate, Selden is thoroughly entrenched in the values of "the house of mirth"; if anyone possesses wisdom, it is Lily.

3. Here I differ from Nevius, who writes that Lily is "as completely and typically the product of her heredity, environment, and the historical moment which found American materialism . . . as the protagonist of any recognized naturalistic novel" (*Wharton* 57). I am more in accord with Montgomery, who sees Lily as the molded beauty who "has paid for her refinement by losing the ability to adapt" (896), and Ammons, who argues that Lily is destroyed because she refuses to marry but is ill-equipped for any other role (30–32). However, unlike them, I suggest that Lily's very uselessness commends her for a more important role than wife or laborer.

4. Critics differ on Lily's moral strength. In her introduction to the novel, Wolff writes that "Lily's nature yearns for something better, but her strength is too weak, too incompletely formed perhaps, to invent some more authentic and meaningful form of existence" (xxiii–xxiv). Lyde praises the novel's honest approach to "a struggle . . . between the world and the spirit" (139); Dixon similarly argues that Wharton's subject is "morality," although she finds no moral center in Lily Bart (217). McDowell points out that Wharton "emphasizes not only the power that a materialistic culture exerts upon Lily, but her increasing insight, assurance, and sympathy for others" (49). Lawson argues that Lily's demise results not only from "naturalistic determinism" but from her "blunders," which are the "outward signs of a deeper personal development," which includes compassion, moral scruples, and honesty (33). Dimock also notes Lily's moral and "heroic" refusal to participate in society's exchange system (788).

5. Wharton typically denied authorial influence, especially from American writers. She wrote in 1908 to her publisher William Brownell, about his forthcoming essay on Hawthorne, that she was "counting the minutes till I see the egregious Nathaniel expire without shedding of blood," and she "especially enjoyed" Brownell's "bringing out his lack of poetry and his lukewarmness" (qtd. in Lewis 237).

6. Lily's momentary stasis at Grand Central resembles Charlotte Ashby's hesitation at her front door in Wharton's story "Pomegranate Seed" (1931). In both narratives, a woman pauses on a figurative or literal threshold, unsure whether to seize an opportunity that also constitutes a social transgression. For Charlotte Ashby, the chance for "independent interpretation and expression" involves appropriating the masculine power of reading and writing (Singley and Sweeney 177); for Lily Bart, it means daring to marry for love rather than money.

7. In contrast, the train is a socially sanctioned mode of transportation that grants women license and protection so long as they follow society's rules. On the

train to Bellomont, Lily is free to use whatever means necessary to entice Gryce to marry her.

8. As Brownstein explains: "What the female protagonist of a traditional novel seeks – what the plot moves her toward – is an achieved, finished identity, realized in conclusive union with herself-as-heroine. Her marriage or death at the end of the narrative signifies this union" (xxi).

9. Mayers argues that in the female literary tradition, the external process of sewing reflects inner experience (675–76), in which case, Lily's acts of sewing provide a spiritual rootedness and connection to life. The fact that she is fired for failing to master the skill of sewing, then, represents the cultural dominance of material rather than spiritual values.

10. Other nonbiblical associations for Lily include a decorative flower in the Art Nouveau style; Henry James's story about another society flower, Daisy Miller; and the childhood nickname "Lily," given to Edith Wharton by her Newport friends, the Rutherfords (Wolff, *Feast* 109–10; Lewis 155).

11. A. Kaplan astutely notes that when Selden fails to act on Lily's behalf with the reporter Dabham, he "loses his objective status and participates in the same game of publicity and spectatorship that everyone else takes part in" (97).

12. Michaels argues that Lily is a lover of risk (229), noting that at the turn of the century, the uncertainty of gambling satisfied the cultural need for certainty. Although he discusses risk in terms of a speculative economy, his observation that, according to psychologist Clemens J. France, the passion for gambling is linked to a passion for scientific, philosophical, and religious certainty, is relevant to my argument: Lily is the only character willing to take the ultimate risk – her life for the unknown afterlife.

13. Selden's famous declaration that Lily is "so evidently the victim of the civilization which had produced her, that the links of her bracelet seemed like manacles chaining her to her fate" (10) also links him to Darwinism.

14. See Bauer, who similarly reads Lily's decision to burn the letters as an act of "resistance" in which Lily creates a work of art, takes on authority, and momentarily escapes society's power (97–98).

15. See Price, who notes the novel's "tragic dimension" and argues that "it is Lily who, by refusing to exploit an edge, transcends the level of her tormenters" ("Lily" 243).

16. Wharton writes that as a child she was "exasperated by the laxities of the great Louisa [Alcott]." She later criticized readers and reviewers "who had for years sought the reflection of local life in the rose-and-lavender pages of their favourite authoresses – and had forgotten to look into Hawthorne's" (*Backward* 51, 294).

17. As Karcher points out, despite their relative power, all the women in *The House of Mirth* depend on a man for their identity, financial well-being, or both (231–41).

18. Nineteenth-century sentimental fiction abounds with selfish men and re-forming women. As Kelley notes, there was a dark side of the redemptive

vision: "Man is not always redeemed . . . and there are not always happy endings. . . . To such a man, money and social position are far more important than his intimates. . . . Death [in this case] was its own final drama of the unrealized familial Eden" (443, 445). Wharton exploits this "dark side" of sentimentality by showing the futility of Lily's sacrifice.

19. See Showalter, who similarly argues that Wharton's revision of the sentimental tradition is deliberate: the novel "adapt[s] the characteristic plot of mid-nineteenth-century 'woman's fiction' and renders it ironic by situating it in the post-matriarchal city of sexual commerce" (137).

20. Lily resembles another Jamesian character, Isabel Archer, who by agreeing to marry Gilbert Osmond, feels "that she was not only taking, she was giving" (4: 82). Both women's actions are detrimental to personal happiness and reflect, as James suggests, a Puritan-like "appetite for renunciation" (4: 392).

21. In keeping with this helping role, another of Carry Fisher's many causes has been "an energetic advocacy of Christian Science" (74), a faith in spiritual healing and the divine goodness underlying scientific reality.

22. See Spacks, who notes that Wharton "demands more of the reader" than simple acceptance of "Selden's illusions" or Lily's "idealization of him" (178–79).

3. Calvinist Tortures

1. Here I borrow Greven's terms – "genteel," "moderate," and "evangelical" – to describe the range of American religious temperaments (12–14). His classifications refer to the colonial period, but they also help to explain nineteenth-century American religious life.

2. Although Wharton was displeased by the church architecture, she warmed to the "singularly beautiful voice" of the Reverend Dr. Washburn ("Little" 362). Lewis also recounts that she was so moved by the "majestic cadences" of the King James Bible read at Sunday evening services that "she unconsciously pulled off, one by one, the long white hairs from the camel's-hair coat of Emelyn Washburn sitting next to her" (33).

3. Sarum Rule, or Use, was a local modification of the Roman rite in use at the cathedral church of Salisbury. In the years preceding the Reformation, the output of Sarum books was enormous; their rediscovery and reediting in the nineteenth century led to the revival of Sarum customs and ornaments in many English churches.

4. According to Carpenter (28–29), George Eliot was strongly attracted to the study of prophecy and possessed detailed knowledge of the "continuous historical" school of interpretation; Cumming's writings were but one part of a large body of religious literature that influenced her writing.

5. For a study of orphans in Wharton's fiction, see Gimbel. Themes of inadequate mothering appear throughout Wharton's fiction. Her 1903 novel *Sanctuary* is an account of exaggerated, heroic mothering, perhaps to compensate for the

deprivation Wharton felt with her own mother. In later novels, especially *The House of Mirth, Ethan Frome, The Reef, Summer,* and *Twilight Sleep,* daughters suffer maternal neglect or abandonment.

6. Erlich suggests another context for Wharton's difficulty with atonement, arguing that she sacrificed her sexuality to atone for an "oedipal rivalry with her mother" (125). Erlich's psychosexual interpretation complements my religious one: the mother remains a persecutor and atonement produces no release.

7. *The Valley of Decision* is drawn from Joel 3.14; *The House of Mirth* from Ecclesiastes 7.4; *The Fruit of the Tree* from Genesis 3.3; and "That Good May Come" from Romans 3.8.

8. The cadence of Old Testament stories sparked Wharton's imagination. She loved to hear Reverend Washburn read from scripture: "It is to Dr. Washburn that I owe the discovery of the matchless beauty of English seventeenth-century prose; and the organ-roll of Isaiah, Job, and above all, of the lament of David over the dead Absolom, always come back to me in the accents of that voice" ("Little" 362). Wharton transforms this memory into fiction in an unfinished manuscript, "Literature," also a source for *Hudson River Bracketed* and *The Gods Arrive.* In the published novels, Vance Weston finds that the Bible's "haunting words and cadences were the richest of his mental possession" (*Hudson* 19). See also Vita-Finzi's discussion of "Literature," 91–94.

9. I thank Scott Marshall, deputy director of Edith Wharton Restoration, Lenox, Massachusetts, for drawing my attention to these elements of decor.

10. See Eggenschwiler, who also describes *Ethan Frome* as a complex allegory. For him, however, Ethan's tragedy is "strictly classical" (245) rather than Calvinist.

11. As Lewis, notes, *Ethan Frome* "portrays her personal situation . . . carried to a far extreme, transplanted to a remote rural scene" (309).

12. Wolff dates *Ethan Frome*'s genesis to 1906 or 1907 (*Feast* 161); Lewis says 1907 (296). MacCallan reprints the French draft.

13. See Ammons, who reads the novel in terms of Wharton's dissatisfaction with women's social roles (61–77); Hovey, who discusses its literary realism; and Bernard and Eggenschwiler, who analyze romantic elements such as symbolism and allegory.

14. See Blackall, who, citing Wharton's evocation of Brontë – there exist "as savage tragedies in our remoter valleys as on her Yorkshire moors" (*Backward* 294) – claims *Ethan Frome*'s aesthetic debt to Brontë ("Imaginative").

15. On similarities between Poe and Wharton, see Dwight and my coauthored essay with Sweeney. Poe's "A Predicament," with its protagonist named Zenobia, may have influenced *Ethan Frome.*

16. Writing to Sara Norton in June 1902, Wharton declared that "Lenox has had its usual tonic effect on me, & I feel like a new edition" (*Letters* 66). Years later, she commented to Bernard Berenson: "You see I'm essentially a country person, & pine in towns in summer" (*Letters* 304). Such fair-weather preferences lead Hamblen to accuse Wharton of "going slumming" when she writes of New England, a region and way of life she knows nothing about (240). For

a more balanced view of Wharton's New England portrayals, see Leach. See also Rose, who argues that Wharton felt in the New England barrenness "the full extent of the negation, the sense of void which . . . has been seen as fundamental to experience in America" (424).

17. When Sara Norton declined the offer in order to play hostess to visitors she did not like, Wharton commented sarcastically to another friend, Gaillard Lapsley: "What fun it must be to be a Bostonian! It's the only surviving habitat of the Moral Imperative" (*Letters* 496). In *A Backward Glance,* she characterizes Bostonians as "a community of wealthy and sedentary people seemingly too lacking in intellectual curiosity to have any desire to see the world" (61–62).

18. See Rusch, who argues that Edwards's *Freedom of the Will* influenced *Ethan Frome*. Edwards would have appealed to Wharton because, like her, he combined emotion with reason and sought to satisfy logical, scientific standards as well as religious impulses.

19. On the Manichaean vision in realism and modernism, see Schneider; on Hawthorne and Manichaeanism, see Chase (74–79) and Winters (157–75). Coale's view is particularly relevant to *Ethan Frome:* "Hawthorne looked out upon a dark, imprisoning world. He also looked to a soul imprisoned and isolated. The world oppressed the self, which in turn oppressed the soul, the inner spirit. The ultimate horror, however, was the perception of the inner soul and an outer world both of which were dark and impenetrable. . . . What remains is the sense that the dark soul and the dark world can obliterate each other" (4–5). Wharton may have learned about Manichaeanism from Augustine, whose *Confessions* she quotes in her novel *The Gods Arrive.*

20. The causes of alienation in *Ethan Frome* and "Ethan Brand" are actually opposite. Whereas "a sense of loss, anxiety, and dislocation" in "Ethan Brand" derives from Hawthorne's fear of the encroaching machine age (Marx 120), Ethan Frome suffers from *lack* of culture and innovation, not excess. Wharton was enthusiastic about modern technology; she motored incessantly in late model automobiles, was the first to install a hydraulic lift in a private residence, and complained about her elite society's "blind dread of innovation" (*Backward* 22).

21. Manichaeanism holds to a strict dualism affecting spirit and matter, in which good and evil are opposite principles that have become mixed in the world through the action of the evil principle. Unlike Calvinism, which it greatly resembles, Manichaeanism divides the universe into three, not two, destinies: paradise, hell, and a mixture that means going back to the world for a period of time before hope was possible. Wharton may have had this third possibility in mind when she devised the punishing ending for Mattie and Ethan.

22. Just why the Varnums and Hales prosper and the Fromes suffer is a question Wharton raises but does not answer, but Ruth Varnum Hale may be an ironic allusion to John Hale, who took part in the Salem witch trials and later recanted. Ruth is more humane toward Ethan's "trial" than were the judges at the actual witch trials, but New England in each case remains austere and

forbidding. Wharton ascribes Starkfield's harshness to New England generally; see, for example, her depiction of Hillbridge in *The Touchstone,* an upstate New York or New England town, "where misfortune was still regarded as a visitation designed to put people in their proper place and make them feel the superiority of their neighbors" (52).

23. Murad accounts for the intensity of *Ethan Frome* by suggesting that another man, in addition to Fullerton, created marital tension. She hypothesizes that Wharton was frustrated over Walter Berry's failure to commit to a relationship with her (97). I suggest that the force of *Ethan Frome* derives not from the number of conflicts in Wharton's life at this time, but from their intensity. To trigger such guilt, one man – Fullerton – was enough.

24. Hays also reads the accident in terms of Calvinism, but he emphasizes Ethan's sense of duty to others. Ethan, "close-mouthed, stalwart, and puritanical," has so thoroughly internalized New England codes that he insists on sitting first in the sled, an arrangement he believes will allow him to die but spare Mattie (n.p.).

25. Critics have noted that Wharton's narrative technique invites reader participation. See Blackall, who explains how Wharton's ellipses "entice the reader to enter into imaginative collaboration" ("Edith" 145); A. Smith, for whom absence in Wharton's ghost fiction constitutes mysterious presence; my essay with Sweeney, which interprets the ghostly presence of absence in the story "Pomegranate Seed"; and Ammons, who argues that in *Ethan Frome* the long ellipsis before the narrator's account establishes that the story "belongs to a community of people (ourselves now included)" (62).

26. That science was "worthy of all reverence" seemed obvious to any but "the most perverted intellect," Herbert Spencer declared. Charles S. Peirce went so far as to call the ethos of science essentially religious (qtd. in Turner 250).

27. Wharton implicitly identifies herself with the narrator in her preface: "only the narrator of the tale has scope enough to see it all, to resolve it back into simplicity, and to put it in its rightful place among his larger categories" (vii). As Brennan notes, the narrator "is actually a writer in disguise with the technical skill of a professional novelist and the sensibility of a poet" (348). Both are sophisticated observers capable of seeing and shaping experience. Wolff also discusses this doubling, reading the novel as a dream vision in which the narrator, as Ethan's double, plunges into the repressed parts of his psyche. The narrator emerges from his "private nightmare" stronger and more whole; the doubling of author and narrator thus serves to validate the young writer (*Feast* 183–84).

28. See Benstock's treatment of Wharton as both a modernist forerunner and outsider in Paris (61–65).

4. Fragile Freedoms

1. Wharton is recognizable in all three main characters, as in *Ethan Frome.* Like Anna, after years in a loveless marriage, she experienced midlife passion, only

to be neglected by her lover. Like Sophy Viner, she unleashed natural feeling and vitality when she began seeing Fullerton. And like George Darrow, who regrets his involvement with Sophy, Wharton eventually looked back with distaste on her affair.

2. The theme of betrayal was important to Wharton at this time. In 1912, the year *The Reef* appeared, she also published "Afterward," a ghost story about the consequences of marital lies. A businessman fails to tell his wife about swindling a partner and mysteriously disappears, presumably claimed by the wronged partner's ghost.

3. This theme – of slavish conformity to social convention – was also important to Wharton during this period. See, for example, "The Long Run," published in 1912, the same year as *The Reef.*

4. See Donovan, who similarly argues that the ideology of the novel "assures that the patriarchal cultural imperative, exchange of women, will continue unchallenged." However, Donovan associates Sophy with Artemis rather than Sophia and claims that the novel's plot is "a patriarchal inversion of the ancient Daphne myth" (70).

5. Nevius claims that Sophy emerges as the more sympathetic character because "the dice are loaded against [her]" (*Wharton* 138); Lawson (59–60) and Walton (70) praise her integrity and ability to survive a hostile environment; Earnest argues that she is "perhaps the finest one in the novel," "a superior person when compared to her rival fiancée" (246, 248); and Wershoven declares her "the big 'winner' " (*Female* 104). In contrast, Gargano praises Anna for upholding "the humane order" rather than following, as Sophy does, codes of "personal indulgence" and "easy accommodations" (47); Maynard similarly argues that Anna "surpasses Sophy . . . in 'passion,' in devotion, and in the capacity to 'see things as they are' " (289). Gooder, pursuing an argument compatible with mine, sees Anna as a questioner and truth seeker, but argues that "she can never, even when the truths are plain . . . understand the realities" (51).

6. I am grateful to Edith Wharton's godson, William Royall Tyler, for showing me Wharton's personal copy of the Apocrypha, which she gave to him before her death.

7. Wharton also considers the problem of damaging truth in *The Mother's Recompense* (1925), which describes a romantic triangle involving a mother, her lover, and her daughter. In this novel, Kate Clephane returns from Europe after twenty-five years to discover that a recent lover is engaged to her daughter. Kate's minister advises her that telling the daughter would only cause "sterile pain" (266); rather than disclose the truth, Kate returns to Europe.

8. Wharton often associates love letters with betrayal. See, for example, *The Touchstone* (1900), in which a man sells a woman's love letters for profit; *The House of Mirth* (1905), in which Lily Bart decides not to betray Bertha and Lawrence by selling their love letters; "The Letters" (1910), in which a woman

learns after discovering unopened love letters that her husband married her for money, not love; and "Pomegranate Seed" (1931), in which letters from a dead first wife lure a man from his new bride.

9. On the significance of ellipses, absences, and blanks in Wharton's fiction, see Blackall ("Edith" 148–53); A. Smith (149–59), and my essay with Sweeney (188–97).

10. See Gooder (48) and Maynard (287–88), who take Sophy's declaration of love at face value, although they reach opposite conclusions about her character. In contrast, I argue that Sophy's love for Darrow is not supported by the plot. Were she in love with him after the affair, she would not have so easily engaged herself to Owen; nor would Anna's endorsement of the marriage have rung true or the end of Owen's and Sophy's relationship have the tragic implications that it does. Wharton gives no indication that Sophy hesitates or is unsure about marrying Owen *until* Darrow arrives and imposes his egotistic order on the household.

11. Children serve as moral touchstones in *The Reef*. Effie disrupts the couple, first by requiring a governess – who turns out to be Sophy – and later by seating herself between Anna and Darrow in the motor car to keep their conversation from becoming personal. Another child, a neighbor, is hurt and similarly interrupts Anna and Darrow's evening walk.

12. See, for example, Auchincloss: the final chapter "is jarringly out of tune" (*Edith* 23); Lawson: "no connection binds the body of the novel with the somewhat unexpected epilogue" (59); Nevius: "it is one of the most regrettable passages in Edith Wharton's fiction" (*Wharton* 140); and Wolff: the novel is "never resolved into a coherently focused image" (*Feast* 219).

13. Unlike Nevius (*Wharton* 140) and Auchincloss (*Edith* 23), I do not read this scene as Wharton's condemnation of Sophy through her sister. Rather, I read it as Walton does, as "a scathing comment on Anna. . . . One is made finally to realize . . . the distinction of Sophy's character [and] integrity that Anna, with all her refinement, cannot achieve" (70). Wershoven similarly contrasts "Anna's naiveté and horror of such a setting with Sophy's ability to transcend it" (*Female* 107).

14. Susan Goodman also notes Whitman's granting of sexual license but believes that Wharton ignored Whitman's promiscuity while appreciating his originality and universality ("Sketch" 5). I argue Wharton includes deviant sexual behavior in *Summer,* in her depiction of Lawyer Royall and the Mountain people.

15. Wharton relates *Summer*'s inception to her World War I efforts: "I began to write a short novel, "Summer," as remote as possible in setting and subject from the scene about me; and the work made my other tasks seem lighter. The tale was written at a high pitch of creative joy, but amid a thousand interruptions, and while the rest of my being was steeped in the tragic realities of the war; yet I do not remember ever visualizing with more intensity the inner scene, or the creatures peopling it" (*Backward* 356).

16. Wolff finds ordered, mature passion in the marriage of Lawyer and Charity Royall (*Feast* 292–93); but Ammons calls their incestuous union an "unhealthy" ending of Charity's passionate life (140), and Erlich terms it Charity's "final defeat" (126). Nevius calls *Summer* a "chronicle . . . of pinched, defeated lives" that concludes with a "pathetic compromise with fate" (*Wharton* 168); McDowell also reads the novel fatalistically, with Charity losing her freedom and resigning herself to a "life of emotional barrenness" as Royall's wife (69).

17. Although Wolff interprets these lines as indicating Wharton's emotional and psychological "need to retreat," I argue for their spiritual significance. Wharton was weary of organized religion, false worship, and materialism, and longed for a system in which people were simply accepted, not judged. In 1898, she also quoted Whitman's poem "Life" in its entirety in her commonplace book, focusing on his use of battle as metaphor for the endless searchings of the soul:

> Ever the discouraged, resolute, struggling soul of man;
> (Have former armies fail'd? then we send fresh armies – and fresh again;)
> Ever the grappled mystery of all earth's ages old or new;
> Ever the eager eyes, hurrahs, the welcome-clapping hands, the loud applause;
> Ever the soul dissatisfied, curious, unconvinced at last;
> Struggling to-day the same – battling the same.
>
> (qtd. in Wolff, *Feast* 90)

18. As James Miller notes, Whitman "rejects society's deluded conventions and declares for natural or Adam's law" (50). See, for example, the free play of the mind and emotions of the Adamic lover in "Spontaneous Me," the lover consorting with "Nature's darlings" in the face of a hostile or disapproving society in "Native Moments" (4), or the "defiance of the world" in "One Hour to Madness and Joy" (7).

19. See Erlich's treatment of father–daughter incest, especially her discussion of Charity's "joyless union" with Royall (126–31).

20. For a similar view, see Wershoven, who notes that *Summer* "is both Charity and Lawyer Royall's story, a dual conflict and, more importantly, a dual growth achieved through 'looking life in the face' " ("Divided" 6).

21. Wharton also quotes this line in her notes for the Whitman essay, praising the power of Whitman's language: "Of some of his adjectives it might be said: Who touches this touches a man."

22. Charity's earlier decision not to go to school also unites her with Royall and foreshadows their marriage. She loudly objects when Miss Hatchard observes that she is too young to understand the possible sexual implications of staying with Royall, "Oh, no, I ain't" (26). When Royall gives her the Crimson Rambler, their union is sealed.

23. Wolff argues that *Summer* "is a hymn to generativity and marriage. . . . Pregnancy is not the inevitable 'punishment' for sexual indulgence; it is an opportunity to participate in the social and Natural continuum that informs our lives

with meaning" (*Feast* 293). Again we may think of Whitman's "Song of Myself," in which motherhood is the most holy and natural of states: "And I say there is nothing greater than the mother of men" (*Leaves*, line 427).

24. See, for example, "Song of Myself," especially section 15; "Song of the Open Road"; "Song of Prudence"; "To a Common Prostitute"; "To Think of Time"; "The City Dead-House"; and "You Felons on Trial in Courts."

5. Platonic Idealism

1. Tuttleton writes that *The Age of Innocence* "lovingly records the manners of the world of Edith Wharton's youth" (129). For Lewis, it is an "act of reconciliation" in which Wharton "sought to come back to herself" (425); Wolff similarly calls it a "coming to terms with one's past" (*Feast* 313). Nevius argues that Wharton's "indictment" of old New York "outweighs the defense. . . . But underlying her protest was . . . nostalgia" (*Wharton* 177). For similar views of the novel as elegiac or nostalgic, see Auchincloss, *Edith* 29; Beach 294–95; Lindberg 100; McDowell 92; and Robinson 4. Conflicting views include those of Van Doren, who believes that Wharton "had come to question" New York's authority (278), and Wilson, who writes that, despite "the poetic mist of distance," "the old impulse of protest makes itself felt as the main motive" (26).

2. For discussions of anthropology's role in *The Age of Innocence*, see Ammons (143–56) and Fryer (129–42), who differ on the source of power in this tribal society; Fryer claims a matriarchy and Ammons a patriarchy.

3. Monroe notes that Wharton "gives to conventions almost the force of moral laws" (115), but I argue that she distinguishes between customs and morals here and in her other fiction.

4. For a corroborating view, see Saunders's discussion of May's feigned innocence (35–36).

5. Although the Platonic world beyond the cave is one of pure form, I interpret "Good Form" here to mean mere convention – taste, not truth.

6. Wharton avoids ending Ellen's romance in marriage, thereby giving her a freedom other protagonists lack. For example, in an early story, "The Lamp of Psyche" (1895), Delia remains married even after she realizes that marriage falls short of her ideals. In "Souls Belated" (1899), Lydia Tillotson marries her lover but loses romance. Wharton did experiment with the ending of *The Age of Innocence*, abandoning an early outline in which Ellen marries Archer and regrets the decision; when she realizes "that for the next 30 or 40 years they are going to live in Madison Ave in winter & on the Hudson in the Spring & autumn, with a few weeks of Europe or Newport every summer, her whole soul recoils" (qtd. in Price, "Composition" 24).

7. Banta similarly argues that Archer's love for Ellen "is actually desire": it is easier for him to love an idealized notion than the woman herself (448–49).

8. A. Stein also points out the moral "shabbiness" of Archer's would-be romance with Ellen, but he makes this point not to praise Ellen but to argue old New York's worth (271).

9. See Tyree, who writes that Archer, "engaged in a struggle for his soul, ultimately achieves victory in a quintessentially Puritan mode – the ability to live in this world but not of it" (8).

6. Catholicism: Fulfillment or Concession?

1. Other nineteenth-century American writers who pay tribute to the Madonna in their fiction include Alcott (*Little Women*), Hawthorne (*The Marble Faun*), and James (*The Bostonians*). Harold Frederic, Wharton's contemporary, employs the motif ironically in *The Damnation of Theron Ware:* Celia Thaxter serves as a false Madonna for a distraught Protestant minister.

2. A notable exception to this ideology was John Lancaster Spalding, bishop of Peoria, Illinois, who championed equal rights for women. Two other supporters of women's rights who signed a suffrage statement issued in 1902 by the National American Woman Suffrage Association were Bernard McQuaid, bishop of Rochester, New York, and John Ireland, bishop and later archbishop of St. Paul, Minnesota (Kennelly, "Ideals" 9, 12). In 1900, however, only six Catholic clergymen were on the NAWSA list; and as late as 1915, suffrage organizers targeted Catholic women as an important group from whom they needed to win support (Kenneally 127).

3. Wharton seems unaware of these conflicting attitudes. For example, in *French Ways and Their Meaning* (1919), she argues that French women are more mature than their American counterparts and their relations with men more "balanced," "close and constant and interesting" (113, 102). She does not discuss women's place in specifically Catholic traditions.

4. Maggs cites an 1866 edition, which I cannot locate. There are, however, two 1865 editions that Wharton may have owned.

5. Wolff argues, for example, that the girls in *The Buccaneers* "have fundamental quality. One can rest easy, knowing that they are the guardians of the future" (*Feast* 403).

6. See Walton, who similarly argues that "one cannot take the hero as seriously as he is offered," although Vance's "freshness and innocent energy" earn the reader's sympathy. Halo's more emancipated behavior "seems . . . conventional. One is indeed often in considerable doubt about Edith Wharton's attitude to her character" (166, 169).

7. This blurred focus is apparent in the novels' asymmetrical titles. "Hudson River Bracketed" is taken from a book on landscape gardening by A. J. Downing and refers to a particular style of architecture. "The Gods Arrive" is borrowed from Emerson's poem "Give All to Love." Emerson's lines, "When half gods go / The gods arrive," suggest the novels' more philosophical and religious concerns.

8. Here and elsewhere in *Hudson River Bracketed* and *The Gods Arrive,* Wharton alludes to the Mothers in part two of Goethe's *Faust.* On the Mothers' primal and goddesslike power, see Ammons, who argues that the spiritual power in the novels stems from mythic and pagan goddesses rather than from traditional

Christianity (188–96). However, at the end of *The Gods Arrive*, Vance's contact is not with pagan myth but with *The Confessions*. Similarly, Halo's final posture, arms raised "in the ancient attitude of prayer" (*Gods* 432), evokes the Virgin Mary and Christian piety as much as ancient worship.

9. See Carr, who notes that Christian concepts of sin and grace are problematic because the traits associated with sin – pride, self-assertion, and rebellion – apply more to men than to women (8). Some feminist theologians have tried to make such concepts more gender-inclusive. Farley, for example, redefines Christian love as "equal regard and equality of opportunity"; self-sacrifice and ser-vanthood as "active receptivity" rather than submissiveness; and justice as that which serves the individual *and* the common good (634–44).

Coda

1. J. H. Miller notes that modernist writers responded to the loss of an objective God with metaphors of emptiness and darkness (13).
2. Rusch echoes May: comparing *Ethan Frome* with Jonathan Edwards's *Freedom of the Will*, he argues that Ethan is a "prisoner of moral . . . not natural necessity" (244).

Works Cited

By Edith Wharton

The Age of Innocence. 1920. Introd. R. W. B. Lewis. New York: Scribner's, 1970.
A Backward Glance. New York: Scribner's, 1933.
"Beatrice Palmato." *Edith Wharton: A Biography*. By R. W. B. Lewis. New York: Harper, 1986. 547–48.
The Buccaneers. New York: Appleton-Century, 1938.
"Bunner Sisters." *Xingu and Other Stories*. New York: Scribner's, 1916. 307–436.
"Chartres." *Scribner's Magazine* 14 (September 1893): 287.
The Children. New York: Appleton, 1928.
The Collected Short Stories of Edith Wharton. Ed. R. W. B. Lewis. 2 vols. New York: Scribner's, 1968.
Commonplace Book, 1896–1911. Private collection of William Royall Tyler.
"The Criticism of Fiction." *The Living Age* 282 (25 July 1914): 204–11.
The Custom of the Country. 1913. Introd. Marilyn French. New York: Berkley, 1981.
The Decoration of Houses. New York: Scribner's, 1897.
Edith Wharton: Novellas and Other Writings. Ed. Cynthia Griffin Wolff. New York: Library of America, 1990.
Ethan Frome. 1911. New York: Scribner's, 1970.
"Fiction and Criticism." Edith Wharton Collection. Beinecke Rare Book and Manuscript Library, Yale University, New Haven, CT.
"The First Year [All Souls' Day]." *Twelve Poems*. London: Medici Society, 1926. 47–51.
French Ways and Their Meaning. New York: Appleton, 1919.
The Fruit of the Tree. New York: Scribner's, 1907.
"A Further Glance." Edith Wharton Collection. Beinecke Rare Book and Manuscript Library, Yale University, New Haven, CT.
Ghosts. New York: Appleton-Century, 1937.

The Glimpses of the Moon. New York: Appleton, 1922.

The Gods Arrive. New York: Appleton, 1932.

The House of Mirth. New York: Scribner's, 1905.

Hudson River Bracketed. New York: Appleton, 1929.

In Morocco. New York: Scribner's, 1920.

Italian Backgrounds. New York: Scribner's, 1905.

Italian Villas and Their Gardens. New York: Century, 1904.

The Letters of Edith Wharton. Ed. R. W. B. Lewis and Nancy Lewis. New York: Scribner's, 1988.

Letters to Lily Norton and Sara Norton. Edith Wharton Papers. Houghton Library, Harvard University, Cambridge, MA.

"Life and I." *Edith Wharton: Novellas and Other Writings.* Ed. Cynthia Griffin Wolff. New York: Library of America, 1990. 1069–96.

"Literature." Edith Wharton Collection. Beinecke Rare Book and Manuscript Library, Yale University, New Haven, CT.

"A Little Girl's New York." *Harper's Magazine* 176 (March 1938): 356–64.

"Margaret of Cortona." *Artemis to Actaeon and Other Verse.* New York: Scribner's, 1909. 24–31.

The Mother's Recompense. New York: Appleton, 1925.

A Motor-Flight through France. London: Macmillan, 1908.

New Year's Day (The 'Seventies). 1924. *Edith Wharton: Novellas and Other Writings.* Ed. Cynthia Griffin Wolff. New York: Library of America, 1990. 489–549.

"Permanent Values in Fiction." *Saturday Review of Literature* 10 (7 April 1934): 603–4.

"Pomegranate Seed" [verse]. *Scribner's* 51 (March 1912): 284–91.

"A Reconsideration of Proust." *Saturday Review of Literature* 11 (27 October 1934): 233–34.

The Reef. New York: Appleton, 1912.

Rev. of *George Eliot,* by Leslie Stephen. *The Bookman* 15 (May 1902): 247–51.

Sanctuary. New York: Scribner's, 1903.

"Sketch of an Essay on Walt Whitman." Edith Wharton Collection. Beinecke Rare Book and Manuscript Library, Yale University, New Haven, CT.

A Son at the Front. New York: Scribner's, 1923.

The Spark (The 'Sixties). 1924. *Edith Wharton: Novellas and Other Writings.* Ed. Cynthia Griffin Wolff. New York: Library of America, 1990. 445–88.

Summer. New York: Appleton, 1917.

"Terminus." *Edith Wharton: A Biography.* By R. W. B. Lewis. New York: Harper, 1986. 259–60.

The Touchstone. 1900. New York: HarperCollins, 1991.

Twilight Sleep. New York: Appleton, 1927.

The Valley of Decision. New York: Scribner's, 1902. 2 vols.

"The Vice of Reading." *North American Review* 177 (1903): 513–21.

The Writing of Fiction. New York: Scribner's, 1925.

Xingu and Other Stories. New York: Scribner's, 1916.

Other Works

Adam, Adela M. *Plato: Moral and Political Ideals.* Cambridge: Cambridge UP, 1913.

Adams, Henry. *The Education of Henry Adams: An Autobiography.* Boston: Houghton, 1918.

Esther. 1884. New York: Scholars' Facsimiles, 1938.

Alcott, Louisa May. *Little Women: or, Meg, Jo, Beth, and Amy.* Boston: Roberts, 1869.

Ammons, Elizabeth. *Edith Wharton's Argument with America.* Athens: U of Georgia P, 1980.

The Apocrypha. Authorised Version. Oxford: Oxford UP, n.d.

Arnold, Matthew. *Culture and Anarchy.* 1869. Ed. J. Dover Wilson. Landmarks in the History of Education Ser. Cambridge: Cambridge UP, 1935.

Artin, M. Personal interview. 1 July 1991.

Auchincloss, Louis. *Edith Wharton.* University of Minnesota Pamplets on American Writers 12. Minneapolis: U of Minnesota P, 1961.

Edith Wharton: A Woman in Her Time. New York: Viking, 1971.

Introduction. *The Reef.* New York: Collier-Macmillan, 1965.

Augustine, Aurelius. *The City of God: Works of Aurelius Augustine.* Trans. and ed. Marcus Dods. Edinburgh: Clark, 1871. 2 vols.

Confessions. Trans. R. S. Pine-Coffin. Middlesex: Penguin, 1984.

Bachofen, Johann Jakob. *Mother Right.* 1861. *Myth, Religion, and Mother Right: Selected Writings of J. J. Bachofen.* Ed. Joseph Campbell. Trans. Ralph Manheim. Bollingen Ser. 84. Princeton: Princeton UP, 1967.

Banta, Martha. *Imaging American Women: Idea and Ideals in Cultural History.* New York: Columbia UP, 1987.

Bauer, Dale M. *Feminist Dialogics: A Theory of Failed Community.* Albany: State U of New York P, 1988.

Baym, Nina. "Passion and Authority in *The Scarlet Letter.*" *New England Quarterly* 43 (1970): 209–30.

Bazin, Nancy Topping. "The Destruction of Lily Bart: Capitalism, Christianity, and Male Chauvinism." *Denver Quarterly* 17 (1983): 97–108.

Beach, Joseph Warren. *The Twentieth Century Novel: Studies in Technique.* New York: Century, 1932.

Beaty, Robin. " 'Lilies That Fester': Sentimentality in *The House of Mirth.*" *College Literature* 16 (1987): 263–75.

Beer, Gillian. *Darwin's Plots: Evolutionary Narrative in Darwin, George Eliot and Nineteenth-Century Fiction.* Boston: Routledge, 1983.

Bell, Millicent. *Edith Wharton and Henry James: The Story of Their Friendship.* New York: Braziller, 1965.

Bender, Thomas. *New York Intellect: A History of Intellectual Life in New York City from 1750 to the Beginnings of Our Time.* New York: Knopf, 1987.

Bendixen, Alfred, and Annette Zilversmit, eds. *Edith Wharton: New Critical Essays.* New York: Garland, 1992.

Benstock, Shari. *Women of the Left Bank: Paris, 1900–1940*. Austin: U of Texas P, 1986.

Bercovitch, Sacvan. *The Puritan Origins of the American Self*. New Haven: Yale UP, 1975.

Berkove, Lawrence. " 'After Holbein': Edith Wharton's Parable of Judgment." Edith Wharton at the Mount Conference. Lenox, Massachusetts. June 1987.

Bernard, Kenneth. "Imagery and Symbolism in *Ethan Frome*." *College English* 23 (1961): 178–84.

Berryman, Charles. *From Wilderness to Wasteland: The Trial of the Puritan God in the American Imagination*. Port Washington, NY: Kennikat, 1979.

Blackall, Jean. "Edith Wharton's Art of Ellipsis." *Journal of Narrative Technique* 17 (1987): 145–62.

"Imaginative Encounter: Edith Wharton and Emily Brontë." *Edith Wharton Review* 9 (Spring 1992): 9–11, 27.

Bluestone, Natalie Harris. *Women and the Ideal Society: Plato's Republic and Modern Myths of Gender*. Amherst: U of Massachusetts P, 1987.

Boff, Leonardo. *The Maternal Face of God: The Feminine and Its Religious Expressions*. San Francisco: Harper, 1987.

Book of Common Prayer. Oxford: Oxford UP, n.d.

Bougaud, Emile. *The Life of Saint Monica*. 1866. Trans. Mrs. Edward Hazeland. London: Art, 1900.

Brennan, Joseph X. "*Ethan Frome:* Structure and Metaphor." *Modern Fiction Studies* 7 (1961–62): 347–56.

Briffault, Robert. *The Mothers: A Study of the Origins of Sentiments and Institutions*. New York: Macmillan, 1927.

Brock, H. I. "Edith Wharton." Review of *The Reef*. *New York Times Book Review* 24 November 1912: 685.

Brooks, Cleanth. *The Hidden God: Studies in Hemingway, Faulkner, Yeats, Eliot, and Warren*. New Haven: Yale UP, 1963.

Brown, E. K. *Edith Wharton: Étude Critique*. Paris: Librairie Droz, 1935.

Brown, Raymond E., trans. and ed. *The Gospel according to John*. Garden City, NY: Doubleday, 1964. Vol. 29A of *The Anchor Bible*. 44 vols.

Brownstein, Rachel. *Becoming a Heroine: Reading about Women in Novels*. New York: Viking, 1982.

Études critiques sur l'histoire de la littérature française. 1880–1907. Paris: Hachette, 1925.

Honoré de Balzac. Paris: Calmann-Levy, 1906.

Burdett, Osbert. "Edith Wharton." *Contemporary American Authors*. Ed. J. C. Squire. Introd. Henry Seidel Canby. New York: Holt, 1928. 151–76.

Butcher, Samuel Henry. *Some Aspects of Greek Genius*. New York: Macmillan, 1891.

Butler, Alban. *Lives of the Saints*. Ed. Herbert J. Thurston and Donald Attwater. New York: Kennedy, 1969. 4 vols.

Cady, Susan, Marian Ronan, and Hal Taussig. *Sophia: The Future of Feminist Spirituality.* New York: Harper, 1986.

Carpenter, Mary. *George Eliot and the Landscape of Time: Narrative Form and Protestant Apocalyptic History.* Chapel Hill: U of North Carolina P, 1986.

Carr, Anne E. *Transforming Grace: Christian Tradition and Women's Experience.* New York: Harper, 1988.

Cather, Willa. "The Novel Démeublé." 1922. *Great Short Works of Willa Cather.* Ed. Robert K. Miller. New York: Harper, 1989. 325–30.

Chadwick, Owen. *The Secularization of the European Mind in the Nineteenth Century.* Cambridge: Cambridge UP, 1975.

Chase, Richard. *The American Novel and Its Tradition.* New York: Doubleday, 1957.

Chopin, Kate. *The Awakening.* 1899. Ed. Margaret Culley. Critical ed. New York: Norton, 1976.

Christ, Carol P. *Diving Deep and Surfacing: Women Writers on Spiritual Quest.* Boston: Beacon, 1980.

Christ, Carol P., and Judith Plaskow, eds. *Womanspirit Rising: A Feminist Reader in Religion.* New York: Harper, 1979.

Clark, Elizabeth A., and Herbert Richardson, eds. *Women and Religion: A Feminist Sourcebook of Christian Thought.* New York: Harper, 1977.

Coale, Samuel Chase. *In Hawthorne's Shadow: American Romance from Melville to Mailer.* Lexington: UP of Kentucky, 1985.

Coppée, Henry. 1857. *Elements of Logic: Designed as a Manual of Instruction.* Rev. ed. Philadelphia: Butler, 1872.

Cowley, Malcolm. "Natural History of American Naturalism." *A Many-Windowed House: Collected Essays on American Writers and American Writing.* Ed. Henry Dan Piper. Carbondale: Southern Illinois UP, 1970. 116–52.

Dahl, Curtis. "Edith Wharton's *The House of Mirth:* Sermon on a Text." *Modern Fiction Studies* 21 (1975): 572–76.

Daly, Mary. *Beyond God the Father: Toward a Philosophy of Women's Liberation.* Boston: Beacon, 1973.

———. *The Church and the Second Sex.* New York: Harper, 1968.

———. *Gyn/Ecology: The Metaethics of Radical Feminism.* Boston: Beacon, 1978.

Darwin, Charles. *The Descent of Man.* 1871. New York: Hurst, n.d. 2 vols.

———. *On the Origin of Species.* 1859. Ed. Paul H. Barrett and R. B. Freeman. New York: New York UP, 1987. Vol. 15 of *The Works of Charles Darwin.* 29 vols. 1987.

Deland, Margaret. "At the Stuffed-Animal House." *Dr. Lavendar's People.* New York: Grosset, 1903. 313–70.

———. *John Ward, Preacher.* New York: Regent, 1888.

———. *Sidney.* Boston: Houghton, 1890.

De Voto, Bernard. Introduction. *Ethan Frome.* New York: Scribner's, 1938. v–xviii. Rpt. in Nevius, *Wharton's* Ethan Frome 91–95.

Dickinson, Emily. *The Complete Poems*. Ed. Thomas H. Johnson. Boston: Little, 1960.

Dickinson, Goldsworthy Lowes. *The Greek View of Life*. New York: McClure, 1906.

Dimock, Wai-chee. "Debasing Exchange: Edith Wharton's *The House of Mirth*" *PMLA* 100 (1985): 783–92.

Dixon, Roslyn. "Reflecting Vision in *The House of Mirth*." *Twentieth Century Literature* 33 (Summer 1987): 211–22.

Donovan, Josephine. *After the Fall: The Demeter–Persephone Myth in Wharton, Cather, and Glasgow*. University Park: Pennsylvania State UP, 1989.

Douglas, Ann. *The Feminization of American Culture*. New York: Avon, 1977.

Downing, A. J. *A Treatise on the Theory and Practice of Landscape Gardening, Adapted to North America*. 1842. 2nd ed. New York: Wiley, 1844.

Drummond, Henry. *The Lowell Lectures on the Ascent of Man*. New York: Burt, 1894.

Dwight, Eleanor. "Edith Wharton and 'The Cask of Amontillado.' " *Poe and Our Times: Influences and Affinities*. Ed. Benjamin Franklin Fisher IV. Baltimore: Edgar Allan Poe Society, 1986. 49–57.

Earnest, Ernest. *Expatriates and Patriots: American Artists, Scholars and Writers in Europe*. Durham: Duke UP, 1968.

Edel, Leon. *Henry James: A Life*. New York: Harper, 1985.

Edwards, Jonathan. 1754. *Freedom of the Will*. Ed. Paul Ramsey. New Haven: Yale UP, 1957.

Eggenschwiler, David. "The Ordered Disorder of *Ethan Frome*." *Studies in the Novel* 9 (1977): 237–46.

Eliot, George. "Evangelical Teaching: Dr. Cumming." *Westminster Review* 64 (1855): 436–62. Rpt. in *Essays of George Eliot*. Ed. Thomas Pinney. New York: Columbia UP, 1963. 158–89.

Eliot, T. S. "*Ulysses*, Order, and Myth." *Selected Prose of T. S. Eliot*. Ed. and introd. Frank Kermode. New York: Harcourt, 1975. 175–78.

Emerson, Ralph Waldo. *The Complete Works of Ralph Waldo Emerson*. Centenary Edition. Boston: Houghton, 1903–30. 12 vols.

Engelsman, Joan Chamberlain. *The Feminine Dimension of the Divine*. Philadelphia: Westminster, 1979.

Erlich, Gloria C. *The Sexual Education of Edith Wharton*. Berkeley: U of California P, 1992.

Farley, Margaret A. "New Patterns of Relationship: Beginnings of a Moral Revolution." *Theological Studies* 36 (1975): 627–46.

Faulkner, William. 1930. *As I Lay Dying*. New York: Random, 1957.

Fetterley, Judith. *The Resisting Reader: A Feminist Approach to American Fiction*. Bloomington: Indiana UP, 1978.

——. "The Temptation to Be a Beautiful Object: Double Standard and Double Bind in *The House of Mirth*." *Studies in American Fiction* 5 (1977): 199–211.

Fiedler, Leslie A. *Love and Death in the American Novel.* Rev. ed. New York: Stein, 1975.

Fiorenza, Elisabeth Schüssler. *In Memory of Her: A Feminist Theological Reconstruction of Christian Origins.* New York: Crossroad, 1983.

Fischer, Kuno. *Geschichte der neuern philosophie.* Heidelberg: Winter, 1897–1904. 10 vols.

Fishburn, Janet Forsythe. *The Fatherhood of God and the Victorian Family: The Social Gospel in America.* Philadelphia: Fortress, 1981.

Fiske, John. *The Discovery of America.* Boston: Houghton, 1892.

——. *Excursions of an Evolutionist.* Boston: Houghton, 1884.

——. *Outlines of Cosmic Philosophy.* 2 vols. Boston: Houghton, 1874.

Fosse, Jacques. Personal interview. 1 July 1991.

Foucault, Michel. *Discipline and Punish: The Birth of the Prison.* 1975. New York: Vintage-Random, 1979.

Francis de Sales, Saint. *Lettres addressés à des gens du monde.* Nouvelle ed. Pref. Silvestre de Sacy. Paris: n.p., 1865.

Francis de Sales, Jane de Chantal: Letters of Spiritual Direction. Trans. Peronne Marie Thibert. Introd. Wendy M. Wright and Joseph F. Power. New York: Paulist, 1988.

Frederic, Harold. 1896. *The Damnation of Theron Ware.* Cambridge: Harvard UP, 1960.

Freedman, Jonathan. "An Aestheticism of Our Own: American Writers and the Aesthetic Movement." *Metropolitan Museum of Art* 385–99.

Freeman, Mary Wilkins. *Pembroke.* New York: Harper, 1896.

Freud, Sigmund. *Civilization and Its Discontents.* London: Hogarth, 1961. Vol. 21 of *The Standard Edition of the Complete Psychological Works of Sigmund Freud.* Trans. James Strachey with Anna Freud. 24 vols. 1961–74.

Friedrich, Paul. *The Meaning of Aphrodite.* Chicago: U of Chicago P, 1978.

Frost, Robert. "The Oven Bird." *Mountain Interval.* New York: Holt, 1916. 35.

Frye, Northrup. *Anatomy of Criticism: Four Essays.* Princeton: Princeton UP, 1957.

Fryer, Judith. *Felicitous Space: The Imaginative Structures of Edith Wharton and Willa Cather.* Chapel Hill: U of North Carolina P, 1986.

Fuller, S. Margaret. *Woman in the Nineteenth Century.* 1845. Introd. Madeleine B. Stern. Columbia: U of South Carolina P, 1980.

Gage, Matilda Joslyn. *Woman, Church and State: A Historical Account of the Status of Women through the Christian Ages, with Reminiscences of the Matriarch.* 1893. Watertown, MA: Persephone, 1980.

Gargano, James W. "Edith Wharton's *The Reef:* The Genteel Woman's Quest for Knowledge." *Novel: A Forum on Fiction* 10 (Fall 1976): 40–48.

Gilbert, Sandra M., and Susan Gubar. *Sexchanges.* New Haven: Yale UP, 1988. Vol. 2 of *No Man's Land: The Place of the Woman Writer in the Twentieth Century.* 2 vols. to date. 1988–.

Gilman, Charlotte Perkins. *His Religion and Hers: A Study of the Faith of Our Fathers and the Work of Our Mothers.* 1923. Westport, CT: Hyperion, 1976.

Gimbel, Wendy. *Edith Wharton: Orphancy and Survival.* Landmark Dissertations in Women's Studies Ser. Ed. Annette Baxter. New York: Praeger, 1984.

Girard, René. *Violence and the Sacred.* 1972. Trans. Patrick Gregory. Baltimore: Johns Hopkins UP, 1977.

Goethe, Wolfgang von. *Faust: A Tragedy.* 1808, 1832. Trans. Bayard Taylor. Boston: Osgood, 1871. 2 vols.

Goldenberg, Naomi R. *Changing of the Gods: Feminism and the End of Traditional Religions.* Boston: Beacon, 1979.

Gooder, Jean. "Unlocking Edith Wharton: An Introduction to *The Reef.*" *Cambridge Quarterly* 15 (1986): 33–52.

Goodman, Debra Joy. "The Scapegoat Motif in the Novels of Edith Wharton." Diss. U of New Hampshire, 1976.

Goodman, Susan. "Edith Wharton's 'Sketch of an Essay on Walt Whitman.' " *Walt Whitman Quarterly Review* 10 (1992): 3–9.

——. *Edith Wharton's Women: Friends and Rivals.* Hanover, NH: UP of New England, 1990.

Greenwald, Elissa. *Realism and the Romance: Nathaniel Hawthorne, Henry James, and American Fiction.* Ann Arbor: UMI Research P, 1989.

Greven, Philip. *The Protestant Temperament: Patterns of Child-Rearing, Religious Experience, and the Self in Early America.* Chicago: U of Chicago P, 1977.

Haeckel, Ernst. *The Riddle of the Universe at the Close of the Nineteenth Century.* 1899. New York: Harper, 1900.

Hamblen, Abigail Ann. "Edith Wharton in New England." *New England Quarterly* 38 (1965): 239–44.

Hamilton, William. *The Metaphysics of Sir William Hamilton.* Ed. Francis Bowen. Boston: Allyn, 1861.

Harrison, Jane Ellen. *Prolegomena to the Study of Greek Religion.* 1903. 3rd ed. Cambridge: Cambridge UP, 1922.

Hartwick, Harry. *The Foreground of American Fiction.* New York: American, 1934.

Hawthorne, Nathaniel. *The Centenary Edition of the Works of Nathaniel Hawthorne.* Ed. William Charvat et al. 20 vols. to date. Columbus: Ohio UP, 1962–88.

Hays, Peter L. "First and Last in *Ethan Frome.*" *NMAL: Notes on Modern American Literature* 1 (1977): Item 15.

Heilbrun, Carolyn G. *Writing a Woman's Life.* New York: Norton, 1988.

Herrick, Robert. "Mrs. Wharton's World." *New Republic* 2 (13 February 1915): 40–42.

Higginson, Thomas Wentworth. "The Greek Goddesses." *Atlantic Monthly* 24 (July 1869): 97–108.

Hofstadter, Richard. *Social Darwinism in American Thought.* 1944. Rev. ed. Boston: Beacon, 1955.

Hovey, R. B. "*Ethan Frome:* A Controversy about Modernizing It." *American Literary Realism* 19 (1986): 4–20.

Howe, Irving, ed. Introduction. *Edith Wharton: A Collection of Critical Essays.* Englewood Cliffs, NJ: Prentice-Hall, 1962. 1–18.

Howells, William Dean. *A Hazard of New Fortunes*. 1890. New York: Harper, 1911.
The Rise of Silas Lapham. 1885. Ed. Don L. Cook. Critical ed. New York: Norton, 1980.
Humphries, Jefferson. *The Puritan and the Cynic: Moralists and Theorists in French and American Letters*. New York: Oxford UP, 1987.
Huxley, Thomas. *Collected Essays*. 9 vols. New York: Appleton, 1893–94.
Irving, Washington. 1820. *The Sketch-Book of Geoffrey Crayon, Gent. Washington Irving: History, Tales and Sketches, 1819–20*. Ed. James W. Tuttleton. New York: Library of America, 1983.
James, Henry. *The American Scene*. New York: Harper, 1907.
The Novels and Tales of Henry James. New York ed. 26 vols. New York: Scribner's, 1909.
James, William. *The Works of William James*. Gen. ed. Frederick H. Burkhardt. Cambridge: Harvard UP, 1975–. 17 vols.
Jehlen, Myra. "Archimedes and the Paradox of Feminist Criticism." *Signs: Journal of Women in Culture and Society* 6 (1981): 575–601.
Jewett, Sarah Orne. *A Country Doctor*. Boston: Houghton, 1884.
"A White Heron." Vol. 2 of *The Best Stories of Sarah Orne Jewett*. Pref. Willa Cather. Boston: Houghton, 1925. 1–21. 2 vols.
Kaplan, Amy. *The Social Construction of American Realism*. Chicago: U of Chicago P, 1988.
Kaplan, Fred. *Sacred Tears: Sentimentality in Victorian Literature*. Princeton: Princeton UP, 1987.
Karcher, Carolyn. "Male Vision and Female Revision in James's *The Wings of the Dove* and Wharton's *The House of Mirth*." *Women's Studies* 10 (1984): 227–44.
Kazin, Alfred. *On Native Grounds: An Interpretation of Modern American Prose Literature*. New York: Reynal, 1942.
Kelley, Mary. "The Sentimentalists: Promise and Betrayal in the Home." *Signs: Journal of Women in Culture and Society* 4 (1979): 434–46.
Kenneally, James. "A Question of Equality." Kennelly 125–51.
Kennelly, Karen. "Ideals of American Catholic Womanhood." Kennelly 1–16.
, ed. *American Catholic Women: A Historical Exploration*. New York: Macmillan, 1989.
Killoran, Helen. "Pascal, Brontë, and 'Kerfol': The Horrors of a Foolish Quartet." *Edith Wharton Review* 10 (Spring 1993): 12–17.
Kristeva, Julia. "The Ethics of Linguistics." *Desire in Language: A Semiotic Approach to Literature and Art*. Ed. Leon S. Roudiez. Trans. Thomas Gora et al. New York: Columbia UP, 1980. 23–35.
"Stabat Mater." Trans. Arthur Goldhammer. *Poetics Today* 6 (1985): 133–52.
Laffey, Alice L. *An Introduction to the Old Testament: A Feminist Perspective*. Philadelphia: Fortress, 1988.
Lamar, Lillie B. "Edith Wharton and the Book of Common Prayer." *American Notes and Queries* 7 (1968): 38–39.

Lawrence, D. H. "Whitman." *Studies in Classic American Literature.* New York: Thomas Selzer, 1923. 241–64.

Lawson, Richard H. *Edith Wharton.* New York: Ungar, 1977.

Leach, Nancy R. "New England in the Stories of Edith Wharton." *New England Quarterly* 30 (1957): 90–98.

Lears, Jackson. *No Place of Grace: Antimodernism and the Transformation of American Culture, 1880–1920.* New York: Pantheon, 1981.

Le Doeuff, Michèle. "Women and Philosophy." *French Feminist Thought: A Reader.* Ed. Toril Moi. New York: Basil Blackwell, 1987. 181–209.

Lee, Vernon (Violet Paget). *The Beautiful: An Introduction to Psychological Aesthetics.* Cambridge: Cambridge UP, 1913.

——. *Studies of the Eighteenth Century in Italy.* 1880. New ed. London: Unwin, 1887.

Levine, George. *Darwin and the Novelists: Patterns of Science in Victorian Fiction.* Cambridge: Harvard UP, 1988.

Lewis, R. W. B. *Edith Wharton: A Biography.* New York: Harper, 1986.

Lidoff, Joan. "Another Sleeping Beauty: Narcissism in *The House of Mirth.*" *American Quarterly* 32 (1980): 519–39. Rpt. in *American Realism: New Essays.* Ed. Eric J. Sundquist. Baltimore: Johns Hopkins UP, 1982. 238–58.

Lindberg, Gary H. *Edith Wharton and the Novel of Manners.* Charlottesville: UP of Virginia, 1975.

Lubbock, Percy. *Portrait of Edith Wharton.* New York: Appleton-Century-Crofts, 1947.

Lyde, Marilyn. *Edith Wharton: Convention and Morality in the Work of a Novelist.* Norman: U of Oklahoma P, 1959.

MacCallan, W. D. "The French Draft of *Ethan Frome.*" *Yale University Library Gazette* 27 (July 1952): 38–47.

McDannell, Colleen. "Catholic Domesticity, 1860–1960." Kennelly 48–80.

McDowell, Margaret B. *Edith Wharton.* Twayne United States Authors Ser. 265. Boston: G. K. Hall, 1976.

McIlvaine, Robert. "Edith Wharton's American Beauty Rose." *Journal of American Studies* 7 (1973): 183–85.

Maggs Brothers. "The Library of Edith Wharton." Edith Wharton Collection. Beinecke Rare Book and Manuscript Library, Yale University, New Haven, CT.

Mahaffy, John Pentland. *Greek Life and Thought: From the Age of Alexander to the Roman Conquest.* New York: Macmillan, 1887.

Marx, Leo. *The Machine in the Garden: Technology and the Pastoral Ideal in America.* New York: Oxford UP, 1964.

May, Henry Farnham. *Ideas, Faiths, and Feelings: Essays on American Intellectual and Religious History, 1952–1982.* New York: Oxford UP, 1983.

Mayers, Ozzie J. "The Power of the Pin: Sewing as an Act of Rootedness in American Literature." *College English* 50 (1988): 664–80.

Maynard, Moira. "Moral Integrity in *The Reef:* Justice to Anna Leath." *College Literature* 14 (1987): 285–95.

Melville, Herman. *The Writings of Herman Melville*. Gen. eds. Harrison Hayford et al. Evanston: Northwestern UP; Chicago: Newberry Library. 15 vols. to date. 1968–.

Metropolitan Museum of Art. *In Pursuit of Beauty: Americans and the Aesthetic Movement*. New York: Metropolitan Museum of Art, 1987.

Michaels, Walter Benn. *The Gold Standard and the Logic of Naturalism: American Literature at the Turn of the Century*. Berkeley: U of California P, 1987.

Mill, John Stuart. *Utilitarianism*. 1863. Ed. George Sher. Indianapolis: Hackett, 1979.

Miller, J. Hillis. *Disappearance of God: Five Nineteenth-Century Writers*. Cambridge: Harvard UP, 1963.

Miller, James E., Jr. *A Critical Guide to* Leaves of Grass. Chicago: U of Chicago P, 1957.

Miller, Perry. *The New England Mind: The Seventeenth Century*. New York: Macmillan, 1939.

———, ed. *The Transcendentalists*. Cambridge: Harvard UP, 1950.

Miller, Perry, and Thomas H. Johnson, eds. Introduction. *The Puritans*. Rev. ed. Vol. 1. New York: Harper, 1963. 1–79. 2 vols.

Milne, Gordon. *The Sense of Society: A History of the American Novel of Manners*. Rutherford, NJ: Fairleigh Dickinson UP, 1977.

Monroe, N. Elizabeth. *The Novel and Society: A Critical Study of the Modern Novel*. Chapel Hill: U of North Carolina P, 1941.

Montgomery, Judith H. "The American Galatea." *College English* 32 (1971): 890–99.

Moore, G. E. *Principia Ethica*. 1903. Great Books in Philosophy. Buffalo: Prometheus, 1988.

Morgan, Edmund. *The Puritan Family*. Rev. ed. New York: Harper, 1966.

Murad, Orlene. "Edith Wharton and *Ethan Frome*." *Modern Language Studies* 13 (1983): 90–103.

Murray, Gilbert. *Four Stages of Greek Religion*. New York: Columbia UP, 1912.

Myers, Allen C., ed. "Lily." *The Eerdman's Bible Dictionary*. Grand Rapids: Eerdmans, 1987. 657–58.

Nevius, Blake. *Edith Wharton: A Study of Her Fiction*. Berkeley: U of California P, 1953.

———, ed. *Edith Wharton's* Ethan Frome: The Story with Sources and Commentary. New York: Scribner's, 1968.

Nietzsche, Friedrich. *Beyond Good and Evil*. Trans. Helen Zimmern. Vol. 12; *The Twilight of the Idols* and *The Antichrist*. Trans. A. M. Ludovici. Vol. 16 of *The Complete Works of Friedrich Nietzsche*. Ed. Oscar Levy. New York: Russell, 1964. 18 vols.

Nussbaum, Martha. "The Speech of Alcibiades: A Reading of Plato's *Symposium*." *Philosophy and Literature* 3 (1979): 131–72.

Ochshorn, Judith. *The Female Experience and the Nature of the Divine*. Bloomington: Indiana UP, 1981.

O'Connell, Robert J. *Art and the Christian Intelligence in St. Augustine.* Cambridge: Harvard UP, 1978.

O'Reilly, Bernard. *The Mirror of True Womanhood: A Book of Instruction for Women in the World.* New York: Collier, 1878.

Ovid. *Metamorphoses.* Trans. A. D. Melville. Introd. E. J. Kenney. New York: Oxford UP, 1987.

Ozick, Cynthia. "Justice (Again) to Edith Wharton." *Commentary* 6 (October 1976): 48–57.

Pagels, Elaine H. "What Became of God the Mother? Conflicting Images of God in Early Christianity." Christ and Plaskow 107–19.

Parrington, Vernon L. "Our Literary Aristocrat." Howe 151–54.

Pascal, Blaise. *Pensées.* 1844. Trans. A. J. Krailsheimer. New York: Viking, 1966.

Pater, Walter. *Marius the Epicurean: His Sensations and Ideas.* London: Macmillan, 1927.

Plato and Platonism. 1893. London: Macmillan, 1910.

Pickrel, Paul. "*Vanity Fair* in America: *The House of Mirth* and *Gone with the Wind.*" *American Literature* 59 (1987): 37–57.

Pizer, Donald. "American Naturalism and Its 'Perfected' State: *The Age of Innocence* and *An American Tragedy.*" Bendixen and Zilversmit 127–42.

Plante, Patricia R. "Edith Wharton: A Prophet without Due Honor." *Midwest Review* (1962): 16–22.

Plato. *Phaedrus.* Trans. and introd. W. C. Helmbold and W. G. Rabinowitz. Indianapolis: Bobbs-Merrill, 1956.

The Republic of Plato. Trans. Francis Macdonald Cornford. New York: Oxford UP, 1945.

Select Dialogues of Plato: A New and Literal Version, Chiefly from the Text of Stallbaum. Trans. Henry Clay. New York: Harper, 1875. 5 vols.

The Symposium. Trans. W. Hamilton. Baltimore: Penguin, 1951.

Poe, Edgar Allan. "A Predicament." *The Collected Works of Edgar Allan Poe.* Ed. Thomas Ollive Mabbott. Vol. 2. Cambridge: Harvard UP, 1978. 347–62. 3 vols. 1969–78.

Pound, Ezra. *Make It New: Essays.* London: Faber, 1934.

Powers, Lyall H., ed. *Henry James and Edith Wharton: Letters, 1900–1915.* New York: Scribner's, 1990.

Price, Alan. "The Composition of Edith Wharton's *The Age of Innocence.*" *Yale University Library Gazette* 55 (July 1980): 22–30.

"Lily Bart and Carrie Meeber: Cultural Sisters." *American Literary Realism: 1870–1910* 13 (1980): 238–45.

Ransom, John Crowe. "Characters and Character: A Note on Fiction." *American Review* 6 (1936): 271–88.

Renan, Ernest. *The Life of Jesus.* 1863. New York: Modern Library, 1955.

Reynolds, David S. *Faith in Fiction: The Emergence of Religious Literature in America.* Cambridge: Harvard UP, 1981.

Robertson, Frederick W. *Sermons on Christian Doctrine*. London: Everyman's, n.d.

Robinson, James A. "Psychological Determinism in *The Age of Innocence*." *Markham Review* 5 (1975): 1–5.

Romanes, George J. *Animal Intelligence*. London: Trench, 1882.

Rose, Alan Henry. " 'Such Depths of Sad Initiation': Edith Wharton and New England." *New England Quarterly* 50 (1977): 423–39.

Rubin, Gayle. "The Traffic in Women: Notes on the 'Political Economy' of Sex." *Toward an Anthropology of Women*. Ed. Rayna R. Reiter. New York: Monthly Review, 1975. 157–210.

Ruether, Rosemary Radford. *Liberation Theology: Human Hope Confronts Christian History and American Power*. New York: Paulist, 1972.

———. *New Woman/New Earth: Sexist Ideologies and Human Liberation*. New York: Seabury, 1975.

———, ed. *Religion and Sexism: Images of Women in the Jewish and Christian Traditions*. New York: Simon, 1974.

Ruether, Rosemary Radford, and Rosemary Skinner Keller, eds. *Women and Religion in America, 1900–1968: A Documentary History*. Vol. 3. New York: Harper, 1986. 3 vols.

Rusch, Frederik L. "Reality and the Puritan Mind: Jonathan Edwards and *Ethan Frome*." *Journal of Evolutionary Psychology* 4 (1983): 238–47.

Ruskin, John. "Fairy Stories"; "Mornings in Florence." *The Works of John Ruskin*. Ed. E. T. Cook and Alexander Wedderburn. Vols. 19; 23. London: George Allen, 1905; 1906. 233–39; 285–457. 39 vols. 1903–12.

Russell, Frances Theresa. "Melodramatic Mrs. Wharton." *Sewanee Review* 40 (1932): 425–37.

St. Armand, Barton Levi. "Heavenly Rewards of Merit: Recontextualizing Emily Dickinson's 'Checks.' " *After a Hundred Years: The Emily Dickinson Society of Japan*. N.p.: Apollon-sha, 1988. 215–24.

Samuels, Ernest. *Bernard Berenson: The Making of a Connoisseur*. Cambridge: Harvard UP, 1979.

Santayana, George. "The Genteel Tradition in American Philosophy." *The Winds of Doctrine: Studies in Contemporary Doctrine*. 1912. New York: Scribner's, 1926. 186–215.

———. "Materialism and Idealism in American Life." *Character and Opinion in the United States*. 1920. New York: Scribner's, 1924. 165–91.

———. "The Poetry of Christian Dogma." *Interpretations of Poetry and Religion*. 1900. Ed. William G. Holzberger and Herman J. Saatkamp, Jr. Cambridge: Massachusetts Institute of Technology P, 1989. 51–72.

———. *The Sense of Beauty*. 1896. Ed. William G. Holzberger and Herman J. Saatkamp, Jr. Cambridge: Massachusetts Institute of Technology P, 1988.

Saunders, Judith P. "Becoming the Mask: Edith Wharton's Ingenues." *Massachusetts Studies in English* 8 (1982): 33–39.

Schneider, Daniel J. *Symbolism: The Manichean Vision: A Study in the Art of James, Conrad, Woolf, and Stevens*. Lincoln: U of Nebraska P, 1975.

Schriber, Mary Suzanne. "Darwin, Wharton and 'The Descent of Man': Blueprints of American Society." *Studies in Short Fiction* 17 (1980): 31–38.

Gender and the Writer's Imagination: From Cooper to Wharton. Lexington: UP of Kentucky, 1987.

Sergeant, Elizabeth Shepley. "Idealized New England." *New Republic* 3 (8 May 1915): 20–21. Rpt. in Nevius, *Wharton's* Ethan Frome 83–85.

Sherman, Sarah Way. *Sarah Orne Jewett: An American Persephone.* Hanover, NH: UP of New England, 1989.

Showalter, Elaine. "The Death of the Lady (Novelist): Wharton's *House of Mirth.*" *Representations* 9 (1985): 133–49.

Shurr, William H. *Rappaccini's Children: American Writers in a Calvinist World.* Lexington: UP of Kentucky, 1981.

Singley, Carol J. "Gothic Borrowings and Innovations in Edith Wharton's 'A Bottle of Perrier.' " Bendixen and Zilversmit 271–90.

Singley, Carol J., and Susan Elizabeth Sweeney. "Forbidden Reading and Ghostly Writing: Anxious Power in Wharton's 'Pomegranate Seed.' " *Women's Studies* 20 (1991): 177–203. Rpt. in Singley and Sweeney, *Anxious* 197–217.

, eds. *Anxious Power: Reading, Writing, and Ambivalence in Narrative by Women.* Albany: State U of New York P, 1993.

Smith, Allan Gardner. "Edith Wharton and the Ghost Story." *Gender and Literary Voice.* Ed. Janet Todd. Women and Literature New Ser. 1. New York: Holmes, 1980. 149–59.

Smith, Chard Powers. *Yankees and God.* New York: Hermitage, 1954.

Spacks, Patricia. *Gossip.* Chicago: U of Chicago P, 1985.

Spencer, Herbert. *The Principles of Ethics.* 2 vols. New York: Appleton, 1892–93.

Principles of Psychology. 1879. New York: Appleton, 1919.

Spiller, Robert E., et al., eds. *Literary History of the United States.* Vol. 2. New York: Macmillan, 1948. 2 vols.

Stanton, Elizabeth Cady. *The Woman's Bible.* 1895–98. American Women: Images and Realities. New York: Arno, 1972. 2 vols.

Stein, Allen F. *After the Vows Were Spoken: Marriage in American Literary Realism.* Columbus: Ohio State UP, 1984.

Stein, Roger B. "Artifact as Ideology: The Aesthetic Movement in Its American Cultural Context." Metropolitan Museum of Art 23–51.

Stowe, Harriet Beecher. *The Pearl of Orr's Island: A Story of the Coast of Maine.* Boston: Ticknor and Fields, 1862.

Uncle Tom's Cabin; or, Life among the Lowly. 1852. Columbus, OH: Merrill, 1969.

Straumann, Heinrich. *American Literature in the Twentieth Century.* 1951. 3rd. ed. rev. New York: Harper, 1965.

Sundquist, Eric, ed. Introduction. *American Realism: New Essays.* Baltimore: Johns Hopkins UP, 1982. 3–24.

Thackeray, William Makepeace. *Vanity Fair.* 1848. New York: Modern Library, 1933.

Thickstun, Margaret Olofson. *Fictions of the Feminine: Puritan Doctrine and the Representation of Women.* Ithaca: Cornell UP, 1988.

Tichi, Cecelia. *Shifting Gears: Technology, Literature, Culture in Modernist America.* Chapel Hill: U of North Carolina P, 1987.

Tintner, Adeline. "Two Novels of 'The Relatively Poor': *New Grub Street* and *The House of Mirth. NMAL: Notes on Modern American Literature* 6 (1982): Item 12.

Tompkins, Jane. *Sensational Designs: The Cultural Work of American Fiction, 1790–1860.* New York: Oxford UP, 1985.

Traubel, Horace. *With Walt Whitman in Camden.* Vol. 3. New York: Kennerley, 1914. 7 vols. to date. 1906–.

Trible, Phyllis. "Women in the Old Testament." *The Interpreter's Dictionary of the Bible.* Supplementary vol. Ed. Keith Crim. Nashville: Abingdon, 1976. 963–66.

Trilling, Lionel. "Manners, Morals, and the Novel." *The Liberal Imagination: Essays on Literature and Society.* 1950. Garden City, NY: Doubleday, 1957. 199–215. "The Morality of Inertia." Howe 137–46.

Turner, James. *Without God, Without Creed: The Origins of Unbelief in America.* Baltimore: Johns Hopkins UP, 1985.

Tuttleton, James W. *The Novel of Manners in America.* Chapel Hill: U of North Carolina P, 1972.

Tyler, Elisina. *Saint Brice Diary* 1937. Possession of William Royall Tyler.

Tyler, William Royall. Letter to author. 7 July 1990.
   Personal interview. 12 April 1990.
   Personal interview. 25 April 1990.
   Personal interview. 29 October 1990.
   "Personal Memories of Edith Wharton." *Massachusetts Historical Society Proceedings* 85 (1973): 91–104.

Tyree, Wade. "Puritan in the Drawing-Room: The Puritan Aspects of Edith Wharton and Her Novels." Diss. Princeton U, 1979.

Tyson, Lois. "Beyond Morality: Lily Bart, Lawrence Selden and the Aesthetic Commodity in *The House of Mirth." Edith Wharton Review* 9 (Fall 1992): 3–10.

Van Doren, Carl. *The American Novel, 1789–1939.* 1940. Rev. ed. New York: Macmillan, 1946.

Van Doren, Carl, and Mark Van Doren. *American and British Literature since 1890.* New York: Century, 1925.

Veblen, Thorstein. *The Theory of the Leisure Class.* 1899. Introd. Robert Lekachman. New York: Penguin, 1981.

Vita-Finzi, Penelope. *Edith Wharton and the Art of Fiction.* London: Pinter, 1990.

Waid, Candace. *Edith Wharton: Letters from the Underworld.* Chapel Hill: U of North Carolina P, 1991.

Wagner, Richard. *My Life.* 1870. Trans. Andrew Gray. Ed. Mary Whittal. Cambridge: Cambridge UP, 1983.

Wallace, Alfred. *Darwinism: An Exposition of the Theory of Natural Selection, with Some of Its Applications*. London: Macmillan, 1901.

Walton, Geoffrey. *Edith Wharton: A Critical Interpretation*. Rutherford, NJ: Fairleigh Dickinson UP, 1970.

Warren, Sidney. *American Freethought: 1860–1914*. New York: Columbia UP, 1943.

Weber, Max. *The Protestant Ethic and the Spirit of Capitalism*. 1904–5. Trans. Talcott Parsons. New York: Scribner's, 1958.

Welter, Barbara. *Dimity Convictions: The American Woman of the Nineteenth Century*. Athens: Ohio UP, 1976.

Wershoven, Carol. "The Divided Conflict of Edith Wharton's *Summer*." *Colby Library Quarterly* 21 (1985): 5–10.

———. *The Female Intruder in the Novels of Edith Wharton*. Rutherford, NJ: Fairleigh Dickinson UP, 1982.

Westbrook, Perry D. *Free Will and Determinism in American Literature*. Rutherford, NJ: Fairleigh Dickinson UP, 1979.

Westermarck, Edward Alexander. *The Origin and Development of the Moral Ideas*. London: Macmillan, 1906–8. 2 vols.

Whitman, Walt. *Leaves of Grass: Comprehensive Reader's Edition*. Ed. Harold W. Blodgett and Sculley Bradley. New York: New York UP, 1965. *The Collected Writings of Walt Whitman*. Gen. eds. Gay Wilson Allen and Sculley Bradley. 6 vols.

White, Barbara A. *Edith Wharton: A Study of the Short Fiction*. Twayne's Studies in Short Fiction Ser. 30. New York: Twayne, 1991.

Wilde, Alan. *Horizons of Assent: Modernism, Postmodernism, and the Ironic Imagination*. Philadelphia: U of Pennsylvania P, 1987.

Wilson, Edmund. "Justice to Edith Wharton." Howe 19–31.

Winner, Viola Hopkins. "The Paris Circle of Edith Wharton and Henry Adams." *Edith Wharton Review* 9 (Spring 1992): 2–4, 16.

Winters, Yvor. "Maule's Curse: Seven Studies in the History of American Obscurantism." *In Defense of Reason*. Denver: U of Denver P, 1937. 151–357.

Winthrop, John. "A Modell of Christian Charity." *The Winthrop Papers*. Ed. Stewart Mitchell. Vol. 2. Boston: Massachusetts Historical Society, 1931. 282–95. 6 vols. 1929–92.

Wolff, Cynthia Griffin. *A Feast of Words: The Triumph of Edith Wharton*. New York: Oxford UP, 1977.

———. Introduction. *The House of Mirth*. New York: Penguin, 1985. vii–xxvi.

Index

Bible (*cont.*)
  Genesis, 42, 223 n7
  Isaiah, 3, 104
  Joel, 2, 223 n7
  John, 131, 133
  Matthew, 2, 71, 77–8
  Philippians, 85
  Proverbs, 87–8, 130–1, 145
  Romans, 2, 94, 223 n7
  Song of Songs, 2, 69, 77–83, 86–7, 104
  Wisdom of Solomon, 130
  see also Wharton, Edith: biblical allusion;
    Wisdom literature
Bigelow, William Sturgis, 22
Blackall, Jean, 223 n14, 225 n25, 227 n9
Bluestone, Natalie Harris, 168–9
Boff, Leonardo, 191
Book of Common Prayer, 95, 96
Bosanquet, Bernard, 168
Bossuet, Jacques, 65, 185
Bougaud, Emile, 194
Bourget, Paul, 45, 50
Brennan, Joseph X., 225 n27
Briffault, Robert, 15
Brock, H. I., 127
Brontë, Charlotte, 109
Brooks, Cleanth, 210
Brown, E. K., 209, 213 n3
Brown, Raymond E., 133
Brownell, William, 19, 113, 220 n5
Brownstein, Rachel, 221 n8
Brunetière, Ferdinand, 65
Bunyan, John, 73
Burdett, Osbert, 214 n9
Burlingame, Edward, 46
Butcher, Samuel Henry, 168
Butler, Samuel, 59

Cady, Susan, 130–1, 132
Calvin, John, 196
Calvinism
  as aesthetic, 89, 108, 165
  community in, 116
  Darwinism, compared with, 12, 103,
    108, 117, 122–3, 150–1
  doctrine of, 11, 39, 61, 95–6, 107–13,
    115–27
  and Episcopalianism, 8, 21, 95
  female roles in, 39, 62–3, 95, 111–13
  fierce God in, 11, 99–105, 108,
    121

introspection in, 20, 100–1, 187–9
and modernism, 107–8, 117–18
payment for pleasure, 11, 103–6, 120–6
secularized, 62–3, 117, 148, 165–6, 187–
  8
and sentimentality, 8–9
see also Manichaeanism
capitalism, 2, 9, 21, 92–3, 153–4
  see also materialism
Carpenter, Mary, 98
Carr, Anne E., 13, 231 n9
Cather, Willa, 36, 125
Catholicism, 184–208
  and aestheticism, 35–7, 185–7, 194
  and class, 35, 191–2
  and corruption, 190–2
  and divorce, 3, 189
  female roles in, 24–5, 96, 190–4
  Protestantism, compared with, 16, 36–7,
    186–91
  and sentimentality, 188–9, 190–2
  spiritual solace of, 37, 186–9, 194
  stability and authority of, 36, 186–9,
    194–201
Chadwick, Owen, 24,
Chanler, Margaret, x, 51, 163
Chantal, Mme Jane de, 194
Chase, Richard, 109, 224 n19
Chopin, Kate, 86
Christ, Carol P., 15, 86, 127
Christianity (*see also* specific creeds)
  and anthropology, xii, 7, 166–7, 186
  body–spirit split, 12, 17–18, 25, 39, 125,
    151
  in comparative light, xii, 4, 7, 15, 22, 39,
    186
  female roles in, 8, 12–17, 24–5, 37–9,
    79–88, 94–7, 129–33, 145–7, 151,
    161–2, 170, 190–4, 201–5, 207–8
  Platonic idealism, compared with, 35–6,
    126, 169–70, 200, 207
  sacrifice and redemption, 8–11, 69–73,
    80–7, 104–7
  secularized, 7, 9–10, 21, 35, 61–3, 70,
    77, 86
  see also Atonement, religion, science–reli-
    gion debate, sentimentality
Church of England
  see Episcopalianism
Clark, Elizabeth A., 214 n10
Clark, Kenneth, 44, 189

Weber, Max, 93, 117
Welter, Barbara, 8, 42, 187
Wershoven, Carol, 130, 146, 204, 227 n13,
   228 n20
Westbrook, Perry D., 95
Westermarck, Edward, 15, 168, 217 n5
Wharton, Edith
   aesthetic and moral principles, 26–8, 30–
      4, 98–9, 163–4, 185–7, 194, 206
   aesthetic sensibility, 5–6, 21–9, 72–3, 81,
      86, 98–101
   affair with Fullerton, 12, 17–19, 51–2,
      103, 107–8, 118–20, 125, 128, 146,
      147, 149, 152
   agnosticism, 25, 30, 57, 60–3, 184, 209
   allegory and fable, use of, 4–5, 28, 34,
      69, 73–8, 85–8, 107, 115–18, 175,
      177–8, 182–3, 207
   as American author, ix–xii, 6–11, 22–3,
      36–7, 68–9, 109–15, 125–6, 190–1,
      209–12, 214 n5
   "anxious power," 46
   and Apocrypha, 9, 132–3, 145–7
   and Atonement, 11–12, 17, 103–4
   Augustinian allusion, 3, 4, 38, 191, 194–
      202, 205–6, 224 n19
   "Awakeners," 53–7
   biblical allusion (see also Bible), 2–3, 6,
      13, 28, 49, 69–71, 74, 77–83, 85–8,
      94, 104, 130–3, 145–7, 223 n7
   and Brontë, 109
   Calvinist interests and leanings, xi, xii,
      3, 7–8, 11–12, 19–20, 35, 38–9, 61–
      6, 89–91, 93, 94–107, 187–9, 209–
      12
      The Age of Innocence, 166, 180–3
      Ethan Frome, 89, 107–26, 163, 196
      Hudson River Bracketed and The Gods
         Arrive, 196, 199–200
      Summer, 148, 150–1, 161–2
   Catholic interests and leanings, xi, xii, 3,
      34–8, 65–6, 184–208, 212
   childhood reading, 23, 26, 43–4, 74, 96,
      97, 104, 107, 168
   and Christianity, see Wharton, Edith: spe-
      cific creeds, religious faith, religious
      practice
   classicism, xi, 2, 4, 14–17, 25, 36, 39,
      104, 117, 168–81, 210–11
   convention and morality, xi, 2, 11, 13–
      14, 21, 28–9, 36–7, 55–6, 63–4, 98–

      105, 129–30, 134–47, 163–7, 171–
      83, 210–11
   critical reception of, x, 7, 45–6, 50–1,
      The Age of Innocence, 165
      Ethan Frome, 109, 125
      The Reef, 129–30
   and Darwinism, xii, 2, 8–10, 11–12, 18,
      20, 27, 41–2, 49, 50–4, 56–61, 64–
      73, 77, 79–81, 84–5, 89, 103, 108,
      117, 122–3, 150–1, 158, 161, 210–
      12
   Emily Dickinson, compared with, 27, 51,
      73
   dissatisfaction with women's roles, 4–5,
      8, 12–17, 25, 37–9, 62–3, 76–7,
      129–33, 145–7, 151, 161–2, 166–
      71, 190–4, 209
      see also Christianity, female roles
   divorce, 3, 189
   education, 41–5
   Jonathan Edwards, compared with, 109,
      112, 121, 211
   and George Eliot, 6, 54, 65, 98
   T. S. Eliot, compared with, xi, 36, 115,
      117, 125, 206–7, 210
   Emerson, regard for, 17, 19–20, 23, 147–
      8, 150–1
   Episcopalianism, xii, 8, 35, 38, 103, 194,
      209
   ethics, 2, 6, 13–14, 21, 38–40, 59–64,
      137–8
   and Europe, 22–3, 73, 98, 146, 186, 208
      see also Wharton, Edith: France
   fairy tale, use of, 23–4
      Ethan Frome, 117–18
      The Reef, 138–40
   father, 43–4, 47, 91
   female doubles, 130, 132, 144–6, 172–3,
      193, 202–5
   female friends and mentors, xi, 17–18,
      25, 33, 36–7, 44, 51, 110–11, 149,
      163, 164, 168, 184, 185, 186, 189
   and female literary tradition, 8–11, 43–4,
      46–7, 54, 73, 77, 98, 125
   feminism of, 1, 12–17, 25, 29–30, 37–9,
      192–4, 209
      The Age of Innocence, 164
      Ethan Frome, 111, 125
      Hudson River Bracketed and The Gods
         Arrive, 207–8
      The Reef, 129–34, 145–7

CAMBRIDGE STUDIES IN AMERICAN
LITERATURE AND CULTURE